The Public Relations Handbook

The Public Relations Handbook is a comprehensive and detailed introduction to the theories and practices of the public relations industry. It traces the history and development of public relations, explores ethical issues which affect the industry, examines its relationship with politics, lobbying organisations and journalism, assesses its professionalism and regulation and advises on training and entry into the profession.

The Public Relations Handbook combines theoretical and organisational frameworks for studying public relations with examples of how the industry works in practice. It draws on a range of promotional strategies and campaigns from businesses and consumer groups including Railtrack, Voice of the Listener and Viewer, Marks & Spencer, the Metropolitan Police, the Prince's Trust, Daewoo Cars and the NSPCC.

The Public Relations Handbook includes:

- interviews with PR practitioners about their working practices
- case studies, examples, press releases and illustrations from a range of campaigns from multinational corporations, local government and charities
- specialist chapters on financial public relations, business ethics, online promotion and the challenges of new technology
- over twenty illustrations from recent PR campaigns.

Alison Theaker currently lives in Newton, Massachusetts, where she is Scholar in Residence in the School of Communication, Emerson College, Boston, USA. She was Head of Education and Training at the Institute of Public Relations and was formerly Principal Lecturer and Course Leader in Public Relations at Leeds Business School. She is a Fellow of the Institute of Public Relations and co-author of *Effective Media Relations*.

Media Practice

Edited by James Curran, Goldsmiths College, University of London

The *Media Practice* handbooks are comprehensive resource books for students of media and journalism, and for anyone planning a career as a media professional. Each handbook combines a clear introduction to understanding how the media work with practical information about the structure, processes and skills involved in working in today's media industries, providing not only a guide on 'how to do it' but also a critical reflection on contemporary media practice.

The Newspapers Handbook 3rd edition

Richard Keeble

The Radio Handbook 2nd edition

Carole Fleming

The Advertising Handbook 2nd edition

Sean Brierley

The Television Handbook 2nd edition

Patricia Holland

The Photography Handbook 2nd edition

Terence Wright

The Magazines Handbook

Jenny McKay

The Public Relations Handbook

Alison Theaker

The Public Relations Handbook

Alison Theaker

London and New York

First published 2001
by Routledge
11 New Fetter Lane, London EC4P 4EE

Simultaneously published in the USA and Canada
by Routledge
29 West 35th Street, New York, NY 10001

Reprinted 2002

Routledge is an imprint of the Taylor & Francis Group

Typeset in Times by
Florence Production Ltd, Stoodleigh, Devon
Printed and bound in Great Britain by
St Edmundsbury Press, Bury St Edmunds, Suffolk

British Library Cataloguing in Publication Data
A catalogue record for this book is available from the British Library

Library of Congress Cataloguing in Publication Data
Theaker, Alison.
 The public relations handbook/Alison Theaker.
 p. cm. – (Media practice)
 Includes bibliographical references and index.
 1. Corporations–Public relations. I. Title. II. Series.

HD59 .T474 2001
659.2–dc21 00-065306

ISBN 0-415-21333-9 (hbk)
ISBN 0-415-21334-7 (pbk)

Contents

...

Part III Stakeholder public relations 119

Part IV Shaping the future 239

Notes on contributors

Jo Chipchase runs Can-U-Hack-It Ltd – a Brighton-based new media company that provides internet, editorial and publicity services to a diverse range of clients. Jo has worked on both sides of the fence – in PR and journalism – and specialised in internet coverage. She also co-runs the UKPress online discussion forum for journalists and PR people <www.ukpress.org>.

Johanna Fawkes is Course Leader for BA Public Relations at Leeds Metropolitan University (LMU), where she teachers mass communications and social psychology. She has also led the Institute of Public Relations Diploma at LMU. Jo began teaching in 1990, at the London College of Printing, after fifteen years as practitioner, mostly in local government and trade union public relations. After completing an MA in Creative Writing at Lancaster University in 1994, she helped develop, deliver and eventually lead the BA in Public Relations at the University of Central Lancashire until 1998.

Anne Gregory is Head of the School of Business Strategy at Leeds Metropolitan University. Her main area of interest is public relations as a management function. She headed up the University's Public Relations Studies Group until 1994.

Before moving into academic life nine years ago, Anne was a full-time public relations practitioner and held senior appointments both in-house and in consultancy. Anne continues with consultancy work and is also a non-executive director of Bradford Community Health Trust with special responsibility for communication issues. She is author of *Planning and Managing Public Relations Campaigns*, editor of the Institute of Public Relations/Kogan Page series 'Public Relations in Practice' and managing editor of the *Journal of Communication Management*.

Keeley Middleton has worked in financial services and financial PR for 6 years, having begun her career in the beauty industry. In switching career paths she gained a degree from Leeds Metropolitan University in PR and Spanish. Now a director and partner of Millham Communications Ltd, a financial PR consultancy with offices in Leeds and London, Keeley concentrates on northern-based PLCs.

Ian Somerville (Ph.D., The Queen's University of Belfast, 1994) is a lecturer in the Department of Media and Communication Studies at Queen Margaret University

viii **Notes on contributors**

College, Edinburgh. His research interests include political public relations and the discourses utilised by organisations which produce and provide 'new media' services.

Emma Wood MA is a lecturer in Corporate Communication and Course Leader of the Institute of Public Relations' postgraduate Diploma at Queen Margaret University College, Edinburgh. Before joining academia she worked in public relations, latterly as assistant director of CBI Scotland where she was responsible for the CBI's public relations north of the border.

Preface

..

When starting to write this book, my main aim was to provide a textbook which drew on the UK experience of public relations, having been frustrated during many years of teaching the subject that the majority of textbooks originated from and used case studies from the United States environment.

In addition, I wanted to bring together the theoretical and organisational framework of public relations with examples of how it worked in practice. However, this is not a 'how to' book. There are already plenty of excellent books written by experienced PR practitioners which set out the nuts and bolts of writing press releases, producing internal publications and managing campaigns.

The first part describes the context of public relations. Johanna Fawkes sets out the history and development of PR and its role in society. Ian Somerville discusses the relationship between PR and politics that has led to the charge of spin doctoring being laid against the profession. Anne Gregory sets out the management role of PR and its relationship with other functions. Finally, the development of PR as a profession, its entry standards and ethics are described.

The second part looks at strategic PR. Emma Wood discusses corporate communication, image and identity. Public affairs and issues management are defined, together with the implications of the rise of pressure groups. Ian Somerville sets the practice of corporate social responsibility against the framework of ethical theories.

The third part looks at stakeholder PR – addressing specific areas of the economy. Keeley Middleton gives an introduction to financial PR, whilst Jo Chipchase looks at PR in the IT sector and the implications of technical developments for the PR practitioner. Also examined are media relations, internal communications, community relations, cause-related marketing and PR in the public sector, for consumer goods and in the business-to-business area.

Finally, some crystal ball gazing in Part IV examines changing media and how that may affect PR practice. The debate about the use of research and evaluation techniques is set out. The concluding chapter looks at future challenges for the profession.

Topical case studies are used throughout the book to illustrate current practice.

I trust that the book fulfils its original objectives as well as providing an informative and accessible account of public relations in the UK today.

Alison Theaker,
December 2000

Part I

The context of
public relations

1 What is public relations?

Johanna Fawkes

Most students – and, indeed, practitioners – are familiar with the problem of trying to explain what they are studying or how they are earning their living:

'Public relations? Is that working with people? You know, like an air hostess, shop assistant?'
 'No, more problem solving, really. And working with the media.'
 'Oh yes, all those parties.'
 'Well . . .'

Somewhere along the line words like 'spin doctors' are likely to crop up, replacing the more traditional 'gin-and-tonic' shorthand for PR. And, of course, everyone has heard of Max Clifford. But, how to explain that he doesn't call himself a PR practitioner but a publicist – especially if the distinction isn't all that clear to the speaker?

This chapter aims to cover the issues of definition and distinction of PR from related activities, but a word of warning. These will not solve the dilemma of trying to 'explain' public relations in a phrase. The fact remains that it is a complex and hybrid subject; it draws on theories and practices from many different fields, such as management, media, communication and psychology. These links will be explored more fully in this book. Readers are more likely to have an understanding of the subject and an ability to evolve their own definitions when they have reached the end of the book, rather than the end of this chapter.

In 1976, Rex Harlow scoured through 472 definitions of public relations to come up with the following paragraph:

> Public relations is a distinctive management function which helps establish and main-tain mutual lines of communication, understanding, acceptance and co-operation between an organisation and its publics; involves the management of problems or issues; helps management to keep informed on and responsive to public opinion; defines and emphasises the responsibility of management to serve the public interest; helps management keep abreast of and effectively utilise change, serving as an early warning system to help anticipate trends; and uses research and ethical communi-cation techniques as its principal tools.
>
> (Harlow, quoted in Wilcox *et al.* 1992: 7)

Although this is useful – it contains many key concepts – and saves us ploughing through hundreds of definitions, it describes what PR does rather than what it is. Since then, of course, there have been many more attempts to capture its essence.

The 1978 World Assembly of Public Relations Associations in Mexico agreed that:

> Public relations is the art and social science of analysing trends, predicting their consequences, counselling organisation leaders and implementing planned programmes of action which will serve both the organisation's and the public interest.
>
> (Wilcox *et al*. 1992: 6)

The words 'art' and 'social science' are helpful in explaining the continuing tension between understanding PR as a measurable, science-based application of communication tools, and the affection of many practitioners for the looser, more creative, aspects of the work. In the USA the social science elements dominate the understanding of PR, as is reflected in their education and texts about the subject. In the UK, PR is largely – though not exclusively – considered a management function and is taught in business schools. In both countries it is sometimes found in schools of journalism.

The Institute of Public Relations (IPR) is the UK's leading professional body for public relations practitioners and was established in 1948 (see Chapter 5). The definition framed by the IPR in 1987 is still useful:

> Public Relations is the planned and sustained effort to establish and maintain goodwill and understanding between an organisation and its publics.

There are several key words worth noting here: 'planned' and 'sustained' suggest these relationships are not automatic or effortless. Indeed, they have to be 'established' and 'maintained'. Public relations work exists in time – it is not a series of unrelated events. Also note that the aim is not popularity or approval, but goodwill and understanding. Many think that PR is just about promoting an organisation, whereas most PR work involves ensuring publics have an accurate view of the organisation, even if they don't like what it does. The Inland Revenue doesn't expect to be loved for its activities, but it might hope to be respected, or at least understood.

The definition also raises that strange word 'publics', which will be discussed more fully elsewhere. It is important, however, to stress that public relations is not about dealing with 'the public' as people often think. In PR we say there is no such thing as the public – there are instead many different groups of people – not just consumers, but suppliers, employees, trustees, members, local and national trade and political bodies, local residents, among many others. One of the key concepts of PR is the idea that these groups – or publics – have different information needs and exert different demands on organisations. Understanding these differences is a vital skill of PR.

Philip Kitchen (1997: 27) summarises the definitions as suggesting that public relations:

1 is a management function . . .
2 covers a broad range of activities and purposes in practice . . .
3 is regarded as two-way or interactive . . .
4 suggests that publics facing companies are not singular (i.e. consumers) but plural
 . . .
5 suggests that relationships are long term rather than short term.

It can be seen that none of the above descriptions involves parties, gin and tonic or spinning. However, public relations continues to have a serious PR problem. It has failed to communicate its core activity successfully to the wider public. As a result, many professionals have considered changing the name to avoid the associations. Job ads now seek specialists in Corporate Communications, or Image Management where once they would have looked for PR people. Sometimes the jobs have changed; often it's just the labels. Burson–Marsteller, one of the oldest and most respected PR consultancies, recently changed its title from public relations agency to 'perception management'.

The IPR addressed these concerns by extending its definition to:

> Public Relations practice is the discipline concerned with the reputation of organisations (or products, services or individuals) with the aim of earning understanding and support.

This is sometimes simplified further to:

> Public relations is about reputation – the result of what you do, what you say and what others say about you.

This is probably the most satisfying of the current definitions: it is simple and doesn't attempt to catalogue all the tasks involved in managing reputation. It may even help students and practitioners explain what on earth it is they do.

Distinctions

Sometimes, of course, it's easier to explain what you don't do. The following sections look at areas often confused with PR. As with definitions, the lines are not always clear. To repeat, PR draws on expertise and experience from many fields, it overlaps with other disciplines; it tends to integrate rather than exclude – this is its strength as a practice, but a weakness when it comes to descriptions and definitions.

Marketing

This is the field most commonly confused with PR – not unreasonably since marketing refers to PR in its texts and practice as part of the marketing mix. To marketing practitioners and academics, public relations is one of the 4 Ps – product, place, price and promotion – which make up a successful marketing campaign. This is not incorrect – public relations can play an essential role in creating successful products – if the other elements are right, of course. It can help create awareness of the product – especially new technological developments, where consumers need to understand what a gizmo is before they can distinguish between brands of gizmo. Once, campaigns had to explain what a fridge did, more recently the 'market' needed educating about the virtues of DVD and WAP technology.

Publicity is also essential to launch a new product or service, which is where marketing PR excels. While the marketing team may create special offers and sales promotions, the publicity people will be seeking media coverage and arranging launch events. Together, they can create worldwide successes, from the latest Star Wars film to Prozac.

So what's the difference?
The Institute of Marketing defines marketing as:

> The management process responsible for identifying, anticipating and satisfying consumer requirements profitably.

The two central words here are 'consumer' and 'profit'. Understanding the consumer and producing products or services that will satisfy consumer needs to the profit of the supplier is the traditional arena of marketing. Kitchen (1997: 28) explains,

> Public relations and marketing are two major management functions within an organisation, but how they are organised depends upon managerial perceptions, organisational culture, and historical precedent.

Organisations dealing in fast-moving consumer goods (fmcg) are more likely than not to have a large marketing department containing a PR function. Those who depend on good intelligence about the political environment as well as consumer tastes, especially not-for-profit organisations, will have a larger PR or public affairs function. However, recent developments in marketing, such as relationship marketing and cause-related marketing, are similar to elements of public relations, and are blurring the distinctions somewhat.

In public relations texts (and this is no exception), marketing is described as primarily concerned with sales and sales-related functions. In marketing texts, public relations is rarely considered to be more than publicity. The argument concerning which is the wider discipline can be found in textbooks, university staff rooms, student debates and companies themselves. (See also Chapters 15 and 17 in this book.)

Advertising

The distinction between advertising and PR is more easily made: advertising involves paying a medium (TV, radio, newspaper or magazine, for example) for airtime or column inches in which to put across a promotional message. The content of an ad is always controlled by the advertiser, unlike the content of editorial pages or programmes, which are controlled by journalists. Public relations practitioners try to persuade journalists to cover their products and services on the grounds of newsworthiness. An ad doesn't have to satisfy any news value – it just has to be legal and paid for.

The Institute of Practitioners in Advertising defines advertising as follows,

> Advertising presents the most persuasive possible selling message to the right prospects for the product or service at the lowest possible cost.

Here, the phrase 'selling message' distinguishes the two disciplines – PR aims not to increase sales, but to increase understanding. Sometimes, of course, understanding a product or service improves sales, but PR does not claim a direct causal link.

However, there are grey areas: *corporate advertising* is where an organisation purchases space in a paper, magazine or broadcast programme to put across a general message about itself, not its products. This message might extol its efforts to be green or socially responsible, or it might put the management view in an industrial dispute or takeover. The content of the message is likely to be PR-driven, related to the corporate strategic aims of the organisation rather than product support.

Table 1.1 Characteristics of four models of public relations

Characteristic	Model			
	Press agentry/ publicity	*Public information*	*Two-way asymmetric*	*Two-way symmetric*
Purpose	Propaganda	Dissemination of information	Scientific persuasion	Mutual understanding
Nature of communication	One-way: complete truth not essential	One-say; truth important	Two-way; imbalanced effects	Two-way; balanced effects
Communication model	Source → Rec.	Source → Rec.	Source → Rec. ↙ Feedback	Group → Group ↙
Nature of research	Little; 'counting house'	Little; readability, readership	Formative; evaluative of attitudes	Formative; evaluative of understanding
Leading historical figures	P.T. Barnum	Ivy Lee	Edward L. Bernays	Bernays, educators, professional leaders
Where practised today	Sports, theatre, product promotion	Government, non-profit associations, business	Competitive business; agencies	Regulated business; agencies
Estimated percentage of organisations practising today	15	50	20	15

Source: Grunig and Hunt 1984: 22. Reproduced by permission of Harcourt Inc.

Another grey area is the *advertorial*, where the space is bought, just like an ad, but is filled with text and images very similar to the surrounding editorial. This is increasingly common in magazines and, although the word 'advertorial' is usually clear at the top of the page, it's in small print and the casual reader may well believe they are reading another article about, say, skincare products. As a result they may believe the text reflects the impartial view of the magazine rather than the more interested view of an advertiser. Harrison (1995: 5) comments,

> The strength of advertorials over advertisements is that their style and format give greater credibility to the products they are advertising, by explaining them in apparently objective terms through a third party, the journalist. But what does that do to the credibility of the journalist or the publication in which the advertorial appears? If there is no intention to mislead the reader into confusing the advertising message with a news or feature report, why not just use an advertisement?

PR history

Knowing where, when and how something started is also often helpful in working out what it is. The following section briefly looks at the ways PR has been used in the past and how it has changed during the past century. Given the difficulty of defining public relations, it is not surprising that its history is full of confusion. Should we start with flags and Roman coins as early examples of corporate identity, or go back as far as cave paintings? What about the leaflets that circulated in the late eighteenth and early nineteenth century, such as Tom Paine's *Rights of Man*? The rise in literacy and printing presses in the nineteenth century led to many reforming campaigns concerning health, suffrage and education conducted by pamphlet and newspapers articles. Are these examples of early pressure group PR?

Grunig and Hunt's four models

James Grunig and Todd Hunt (1984) suggested a useful way of looking at PR history, by using four categories of communication relationship with publics, placed in a historical context (see Table 1.1). Grunig and Hunt used examples from US history. The following discussion includes some UK illustrations also.

Press agentry/publicity model
This is probably the kind of activity that most people associate with public relations. A press agent or publicist aims to secure coverage for a client, and truth is not an absolute requirement. This type of PR is most common in showbusiness – celebrity PR – where individuals are promoted through media coverage. Grunig and Hunt point out that 'practitioners in these organisations concern themselves most with getting attention in the media for their clients' (1984: 25). Understanding is not necessary for this kind of PR, which is likely to measure success in column inches or airtime.

Past examples. Grunig and Hunt's example of this kind of PR is the American circus owner P.T. Barnum, who in the 1850s obtained massive coverage for his 'Greatest Show on Earth'. He coined the term 'there's no such thing as bad publicity' and used stunts such as the 'marriage' of circus stars Tom Thumb and Jenny Lind to gain massive media coverage. The theorist Daniel Boorstin called events like these 'pseudo events' – activities created solely for publicity purposes. However, he added:

Contrary to popular belief, Barnum's great discovery was not how easy it is to deceive the public, but rather, how much the public enjoyed being deceived.

(Boorstin, quoted in Harrison 1995: 15)

Current examples. Barnum's obvious successor today is publicist Max Clifford, who has an astonishing reputation for securing front page coverage for his clients, though he also claims that much of his work is spent keeping them out of the papers. Both activities would be typical of press agentry, which is not always over-concerned with the factual accuracy of information provided. One of Clifford's most memorable coups must be the *Sun's* front page headline 'Freddie Starr ate my hamster', which would certainly be covered by the Boorstin quote above.

A more recent example might be the much publicised 'romance' between Chris Evans and Geri Halliwell, both clients of leading PR practitioner Matthew Freud. Many people felt the relationship had more to do with her forthcoming single than true love, but few seemed to mind. Celebrity PR has increasingly influenced the news content of daily newspapers, as well as providing the material for a proliferation of magazines like *Hello!* and *OK!*

Public information model

This kind of communication provides information to people – where accuracy is now important, indeed essential. This model does not seek to persuade the audience or change attitudes. Its role is similar to that of an in-house journalist (Grunig and Hunt 1984), releasing relevant information to those who need it. This practitioner may not know much about the audience, and tends to rely on one-way communication, from sender to receiver.

Past examples. Grunig and Hunt cite the work of Ivy Leadbetter Lee at the turn of the twentieth century. He was a business journalist who tried to obtain information about the highly secretive US industrial conglomerations that dominated the economy of the time. Lee felt that business secrecy was a poor policy and in 1904 he set up an agency, declaring his principles to the press:

> This is not a secret press bureau. All our work is done in the open. We aim to supply news. This is not an advertising agency; if you think any of our matter properly ought to go to your business office, do not use it. Our matter is accurate. Further details on any subject treated will be supplied promptly, and any editor will be assisted most cheerfully in verifying directly any statement of fact. Upon enquiry, full information will be given to any editor concerning those on whose behalf the article is sent out.
>
> (quoted in Grunig and Hunt 1984: 33)

An early illustration of his principle in practice was his advice to a rail company to tell the truth about an accident instead of concealing it. The company's reputation for fairness increased and the value of public information was established. Lee's own reputation was destroyed in the 1930s when he tried to advise Nazi Germany on how to improve German–American relations.

Other examples. Public information functions were established in the UK from the nineteenth century. One of the earliest appointments in the field was the British Treasury spokesman appointed in 1809. The Post Office and local government also played

pioneering roles in supplying regular and reliable information to the public, as their role and responsibilities expanded to reflect the social change through the late nineteenth century and early twentieth century (L'Etang 1998). Practitioners from local government also played a leading part in defining public relations, through articles in the 1920s and 1930s and, later, by setting up the Institute of Public Relations in 1948 (L'Etang 1998)

Current examples. Local and central government continue to practise public information communication. Press releases giving details of committee decisions, budget allocation, or movement of personnel are typical public information activities. In recent years, the shift from public to private sector utilities has placed a similar emphasis on the need to explain pricing policies to customers. Many large organisations have improved their 'transparency' – the availability of information to the public. Much of this has been improved – or driven – by improved technology via the internet.

Two-way asymmetric PR

This model introduces the idea of feedback or two way communication. However, it is asymmetric or imbalanced because the intended change is in the audience's attitudes or behaviour rather than in the organisation's practices. It is also described as persuasive communication and can be demonstrated in health campaigns, for example.

Persuasive communication relies on an understanding of the attitudes and behaviour of the targeted publics, so planning and research are important to this kind of public relations.

Past examples. Persuasive communication was developed by pioneers like Edward L. Bernays, who came to prominence in the US Creel Committee, established to build support for the First World War. Bernays described the power of their wartime propaganda:

> Intellectual and emotional bombardment aroused Americans to a pitch of enthusiasm. The bombardment came at people from all sides – advertisements, news, volunteer speakers, posters, schools, theatres; millions of homes displayed service flags. The war aims and ideals were continually projected to the eyes and ears of the populace.
>
> (quoted in Harrison 1995: 19)

Bernays developed these ideas after the war, starting the first PR education course at New York University in 1922, and writing the first book on the subject, *Crystallising Public Opinion*, in 1923. Bernays' understanding of the psychology of persuasive communication may well have been influenced by his uncle Sigmund Freud and certainly drew on contemporary developments in social sciences. In any event, Bernays was the first PR academic and his influence continued throughout his long life (he died in 1995).

Other examples. In Britain, PR was developing along similar lines. L'Etang (1998) describes the work of Sir Stephen Tallents, who helped create the Empire Marketing Board in 1924 to promote trade in Empire products. He spent over £1 million on campaigns involving posters, films and exhibitions. Tallents wrote *The Projection of England* (1932) which was influential in 'persuading British policy makers of the benefit of a cultural propaganda policy and formed the blueprint of the British Council (1934)' (L'Etang 1998). Tallents went on to help found the Institute of Public Relations in 1948.

Tallents, like many contemporary public relations practitioners in the UK and USA, learned his communication skills in propaganda efforts in the two world wars. The line between persuasion and propaganda was not seen as a problem, as the quote above illustrates.

Current examples. Today propaganda is seen as undesirable and persuasion as suspicious – which partially accounts for the general distrust of public relations. Grunig argues that the asymmetrical model may be unethical as it is 'a way of getting what an organisation wants without changing its behaviour or without compromising' (1992: 39). But other academics, such as Miller (1989), describe public relations and persuasion as almost synonymous, because they both use symbols (texts or images) to attempt to control the environment. Miller states that if the persuadees are engaged in the symbolism they may persuade themselves to accept the message. L'Etang points out that the 'concept of free will is important in separating persuasion from its negative connotations of manipulation, coercion, "brainwashing" and propaganda' (L'Etang 1996c: 113).

Examples of positive persuasive communication might include public health campaigns, such as reducing smoking or encouraging safer driving habits. These campaigns depend on theories of social psychology and much audience research. It is easy to argue that while the organisation – in this case the government – clearly benefits from reduced health care costs and fewer motoring fatalities, the person changing his or her habits (the persuadee) also clearly benefits from a longer, healthier life.

Another timeless example is political campaigning at elections, where each candidate seeks to influence their constituents. However, the recent discussion of political 'spin' raises the possibility that tactics used legitimately in elections are now being used in government, instead of the more traditional public information approach. Perhaps it is not the practice that is new – Joseph Doane was appointed by the government as a 'Reporter to the Press' on behalf of George III to 'manage' press coverage of the monarch's madness (Boston 1996). But in recent years the media has paid more attention to the process by which political information reaches the public – very useful material for the student of public relations.

Persuasion is not, of course, confined to the public sector and two-way asymmetric public relations is probably the most widely used type of PR. Most businesses – indeed most public relations – today try to persuade key publics that their goods or services are reliable, safe, value for money and so on. Advertising is perhaps the most extreme version of this approach and some theorists (such as Noam Chomsky) say persuasion often slides into propaganda, because the benefits are largely enjoyed by the advertiser, not the consumer.

Two-way symmetric PR

This model is sometimes described as the 'ideal' of public relations. It describes a level of equality of communication not often found in real life, where each party is willing to alter their behaviour to accommodate the needs of the other.

While the other models are characterised by monologue-type communication, the symmetric model involves ideas of dialogue. It could lead an organisation's management to exchange views with other groups, possibly leading to both management and publics being influenced and adjusting their attitudes and behaviours. Communication in this model is fully reciprocal and power relationships are balanced. The terms 'sender' and 'receiver' are not applicable in such a communication process, where the goal is mutual understanding (Windahl *et al.* 1992).

In both two-way models the public relations practitioner can act as a negotiator between the interests of the organisation and the interests of the particular public – what Grunig (1992: 9) calls 'boundary-spanning'. L'Etang (1996b) has found a number of similarities between public relations and diplomacy, which illustrates this point. She contrasts the role of diplomat (two-way symmetry) with that of advocate (two-way asymmetry). It is the diplomacy role which aims to facilitate the 'mutual understanding' described above and contained in the definition of public relations provided by the IPR. Grunig and other theorists suggest that this model is the most ethical, because it creates an equality of exchange. Others, like L'Etang, point out that the public relations practitioner is never disinterested – there is always an employer or client – and, as organisations rarely act against their own interests, the communication is still asymmetrical (L'Etang 1996c).

Past examples. Grunig suggests that there are few examples of two-way symmetry in practice and that most of this approach is theoretical, as taught in universities rather than practised in the workplace. However, perhaps as a result of this trend in education, practice is changing.

Current examples. PR practitioners aim increasingly to be part of the decision-making process. The rise in strategic PR reflects the rise in awareness of the need to understand publics and anticipate and defuse potential problems. These days PR often involves persuading the organisation to change its practice in the face of public pressure. Recently, supermarkets' response to public opposition to genetically modified foods (see the Marks & Spencer case study in Chapter 10) illustrates how an astute PR awareness of public concern can create opportunities for organisations willing to change their behaviour. The growth in focus groups and market research to ascertain public opinion on a wide range of political as well as consumer issues could illustrate growth in two-way symmetric PR. New Labour has enthusiastically sought to use a range of market research techniques to influence policy making. However, genuine two-way symmetry can occur only where both parties have equal power to influence the other – and it is worth remembering that this is the rarest form of PR.

It is important to note that these models do not reflect the 'real' world. They are not placed in chronological order and they do not exist in isolation. Grunig and Grunig (1989) point out that more than one model is usually used in organisations and 'organisations may use different models as strategies for dealing with different publics or different public relations problems'.

As this chapter has shown, there are many arguments against the ideas put forward by Grunig and Hunt's four models, but, as the chapter has also shown, they do help us to understand different kinds of public relations in theory and in practice.

2 Public relations and communications

..

Johanna Fawkes

T he previous chapter demonstrates that history is full of professional communi-
cators – whether on behalf of kings or circuses. The four models suggest different
approaches to communication – one-way and two-way – that reflect the relation-
ship between the communicating parties. This chapter looks at different ways of
describing the communication process, introduces some ideas about the psychology of
communication and examines the role of the media in communicating to and between
organisations and individuals in society.

What is communication?
..

It is impossible not to communicate – you don't need words, grammar or syntax.
Humans communicate before and after they can use language by using sounds and
gestures. Babies yell at different frequencies depending on whether they are hungry,
frustrated or have a full nappy. Usually their carer can tell the difference. Later, on
holidays, people point and smile and nod at strangers and, usually, find the beach, bank
or souvenir shop.

All you need to communicate is someone else. 'It takes two to speak', said Thoreau,
'one to speak and another to hear.'

Communication seems so simple until we begin to examine it. Then all sorts of terms
and concepts creep into the conversation. Even the definitions add to the confusion:
Windahl and Signitzer (1992) point out that there are two main traditions in defining
communication – the one-way transmission model and the two-way exchange concept.
They quote Theodorsen and Theodorsen (1992: 6) who define communication as 'the
transmission of information, ideas, attitudes, or emotion from one person or group to
another (or others) primarily through symbols'. The Shannon–Weaver model of commu-
nication illustrates this approach (see p. 16). In contrast, Rogers and Kincaid define
communication as 'a process in which the participants create and share information
with one another in order to reach a mutual understanding' (Windahl and Signitzer
1992: 6). This is quite close to Grunig's two-way symmetric model examined in the
last chapter. Before looking at more models it's worth clarifying a few terms.

Levels of communication

Berger (1995) identifies four levels of communication: intrapersonal (thoughts); inter-personal (conversations); small group communication (like a lecture) and mass commu-nication. He points out that 'talking to oneself' uses the neurological/chemical apparatus of the brain as the channel of communication; talking to another or others uses the airwaves to carry the verbal message, as well as non-verbal communication, like body language, facial expression and so on. Mass media communication uses print, broad-cast or phone wires to communicate with a wide range of geographically scattered people.

Core concepts of communication

Burgoon *et al.* (1994) suggest that *intent* is a key concept – where both source and receiver know that communication is occurring. This excludes all the accidents of over-hearing or instances where the television is on, but the room is empty.

Meaning is also crucial: without a shared understanding of the meaning of words and symbols, communication is at best limited, at worst impossible. Imagine driving in a country where a red traffic light meant 'go'. The discussion on semiotics (pp. 19f.) and Chapter 7 on corporate identity help explain these issues.

Anther issue is *noise*, which is interference between elements in a communication, and can mean technical interference (like static on the line), semantic interference (where the meaning is unclear) and psychological interference (where the receiver is unable to understand the message because of their own state of mind or personality). Shannon and Weaver's model looks at noise.

Feedback is also an important concept. It is what makes the difference between one-way communication, where the sender has no knowledge – or possibly interest – in the receiver's response, and two-way communication, where the receiver can comment or even alter events by responding to a message. Berlo (1960), writing about feedback, said, 'How can anyone know that a communication has taken place unless there is a response from the receiver?'

Finally we must consider the concept of *mediation* – the means by which the commu-nication is transmitted, whether in person, by language or gesture, or via another medium, print or broadcast.

Unmediated communication means any two-way contact that does not pass through a channel or medium. This can be one-to-one (a conversation), one-to-many (a speech), or even many-to-one (a protest). It's worth pointing out that even direct communica-tion between individuals contains a number of variables such as: voice, body language, proximity and facial expression.

Mediated communication adds a channel – a means of transmitting the message. This could still be one-to-one, like a telephone conversation. Or it could be one-to-many, like a radio broadcast. The kind of channel used and its technical efficiency will affect the message (see the section on 'noise' on p. 16), for example talking on your mobile as you enter a railway tunnel will reduce the efficacy of the message. The internet and the World Wide Web provide a wholly new possibility – many-to-many communica-tion using newsgroups to talk to newsgroups.

Fiske (1990) distinguishes between presentational and representational media. The presentational media are those which are not mediated, such as voice, body language and facial expressions. They require the presence of both the communicator and the

receiver to create *acts* of communication. Representational media may include these elements but the communicator does not need to be actually present. This would include television interviews for example, but could also include paintings, photographs, books, even gardens and buildings – anything, in fact, that makes a statement or 'text' but does not require its creator to be present for a 'reading' to be taken. Fiske calls these *works* of communication. He also examines the 'mechanical' media of television, radio and telephone and points out the extra technical requirements of these media. Other theorists would describe technical issues as relating to channels not media, but they are often used to mean the same thing.

The media most relevant to public relations are the *mass media* – newspapers and magazines, radio and television and, increasingly, the internet (but see p. 18). These media allow communicators to reach at low cost (compared to contacting them individually) large numbers of people who have already chosen to purchase or consume that paper or magazine or programme. The audience may be vast, like the readership of a national newspaper, or quite small, like a magazine's subscribers.

To reach these audiences via the mass media involves having your message selected for inclusion by journalists according to formal or informal ideas of what they think the reader or viewer wants, sometimes called news values. The journalist takes on a 'gatekeeper' role, deciding what does and does not get forwarded to the medium's users. Of course, advertisers can reach the same audiences without going through this 'gate', but they lose credibility or third-party endorsement in the process.

Most public relations communication is mediated, though it is worth remembering that public relations also uses direct media, such as exhibitions, leaflets or corporate videos, where the content is wholly controlled by the sender. Interestingly, the internet allows both kinds of communication. Some sites are run by media organisations where inclusion is controlled by journalists, such as the *Guardian*'s newsunlimited sites or BBC Online. But websites, chatrooms and newsgroups allow direct communication with interested parties – and, of course, between them.

The communication models discussed below help explain these developments.

A brief history of communication models

Aristotle (384–322 BC) is often cited as the first authority on communication. His works on rhetoric – the art of influencing others through the spoken word – developed with the growth of democracy in Ancient Greece and are still highly influential. Many political speeches depend on the techniques he advocated, such as the use of repetition in Tony Blair's 'education, education, education' speech. Aristotle believed communication consisted of three elements:

- *ethos* – the nature or qualities of the communicator
- *logos* – the nature, structure and content of the message
- *pathos* – the nature, feelings and thoughts of the receiver or audience.

More recently, in 1948, political scientist Harold Laswell created a formula to describe the communication process:

- who says
- what

- to whom
- with what
- effect?

This has been very influential, and reflects interest at that time in the power of propaganda. But it assumes that communication will always have an effect and suggests that communication is always persuasive. In this model, the communicator or sender decides what and how to communicate and the receiver just waits to be affected – an approach that is now considered very limited (McQuail and Windahl 1993).

Claude Shannon, a mathematician, created a representation of Laswell's formula as a linear, mathematical equation in 1949. He and his partner Warren Weaver worked for Bell Telephones and their interest was driven by the technical requirements of a medium. They introduced the crucial concept of interference in communication, which they called 'noise'. Interference might occur in the handset of the speaker or receiver, or in the lines connecting them. As a result the message could be distorted and misunderstood. The same principle could be translated to different media, for example radio static, poor TV reception, small print, blurred photographs. Noise was later expanded to include daydreaming, physical discomfort or other kinds of distraction. It was an important reminder that communication sent is not always – if ever – the same as communication received.

A simple communication model will include a source or sender who selects information (encodes) to create a message that will be transmitted by a channel to a receiver who selects a meaning from the message (decodes) and responds with action or no action (feedback). Harrison's adaptation of the Shannon and Weaver model demonstrates this clearly (Figure 2.1). This model has some useful elements for public relations, particularly regarding the role of feedback. When two people are in conversation, the speaker is free to adjust his or her tone, speed, language, emphasis and so on, according to questions, nods, smiles and other responses from the listener. Indeed, if something is not understood, it can quickly be made clear. The source and receiver are in a constant feedback and adjustment loop. This feedback element is crucial to effective public relations – we need to know if the message was received, how it was understood and what actions or changes in attitude or behaviour have followed receipt of the message. Feedback is what tells the practitioner that his or her sense of humour or wit has backfired or, more simply, that the language is too complex for a particular audience.

However, this still presents two problems. First, it is linear: feedback is not the same thing as equal participation in the communication, and second, it is hard to place the mass media comfortably in this model. The Osgood–Schramm model (Figure 2.2) suggests a more equal model of communication while the Westley–Mclean model describes the role of the mass media in communication.

Osgood and Schramm were central to the development of the second approach suggested by Rogers and Kincaid, which was discussed earlier in the chapter when we looked at contrasting concepts of communication. In 1954, they created a circular model, which showed that the receiver as well as the sender is engaged in a continuous and active act of communication. Each party has to interpret the message and shape a response before sending it out or back. Schramm added,

> In fact it is misleading to think of the communication process as starting somewhere and ending somewhere. It is really endless. We are really switchboard centres handling and rerouting the great endless current of information.
>
> (quoted in McQuail and Windahl 1993: 20)

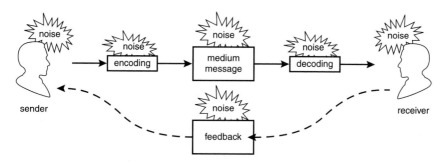

Figure 2.1 Harrison's adaptation of Shannon and Weaver's model

Source: Harrison 1995: 30, Figure 3.1. Used by permission of Thompson Learning

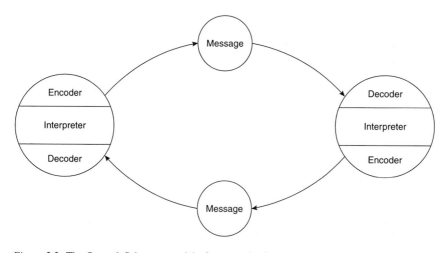

Figure 2.2 The Osgood–Schramm model of communication

Source: McQuail and Windahl 1993: 19, Figure 2.2.3. Used by permission of Longman

This more equal communication relationship was continued in the work of McLeod and Chaffee whose co-orientation models (1973) influenced much of Grunig's thinking on two-way communication.

The second problem with the linear models, which also applies to Osgood and Schramms, is that they do not include a mass media role. Feedback in mass media communications is quite different from personal or group communications. There may be letters to the editor, of course, but often the effect of a communication is very hard to measure. By far the most useful model from this period is the Westley–McLean model of 1957 (Figure 2.3) because it is the first to address the role of the mass media in communication.

Westley and McLean introduce the role of the gatekeeper or channel (C) into the communication flow between (A) which is similar to a source and (B) which is similar to a receiver. However, they elaborate these roles so that (A) becomes the advocate, the 'purposive role', and (B), the individual or group public, is deemed to have a 'behavioural role'. This model also shows events in the environment (X) and the response of

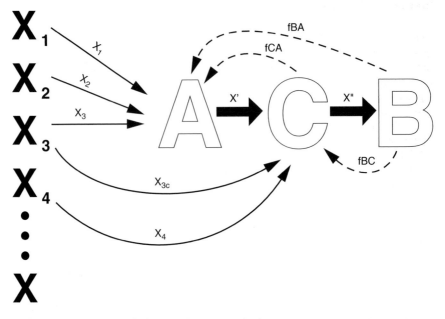

Figure 2.3 The Westley–McLean model of communication

Source: Windahl *et al*. 1992: 121, Figure 11.1. Reprinted by permission of Sage Publications Ltd

all the players to those events. It is the first to describe the role of the public relations professional so clearly. (A) has to gather relevant information from the internal and external environment and create an appropriate message (X') to pass through the channel (C) or gatekeeper who may alter it (X") before it can reach the public (individual or group) over whose behaviour (B) influence is sought. The model reminds the PR that the journalist or gatekeeper has access to more information (X_{3c}) than their press releases. The model also describes the complexity of feedback in mass media communication with feedback loops running between the PR and the journalist, the PR and the public and the public and the journalist, though the feedback via mass media is delayed.

It is worth noting that the internet is reducing the gatekeeper role of the journalist, as organisations can post whatever materials they choose on their own website, and create direct links with their key audiences. Likewise, the behaviour group (B) is no longer dependent on the mass media for information and can access the events in the environment directly. (B) can also contact other members of the audience and exchange communication without contact with (A) or (C).

The Westley–McLean model has proved a valuable starting point for examining the process of communication, but the emphasis is still on how the sender constructs the message. There are other theorists who see the process and the actions of the sender as quite irrelevant. They emphasise the role of the audience or receiver in constructing meaning.

Communication as meaning

Semiotics is a vast field of study originating in the study of language using theories of signs and symbols that have been adopted and adapted by other communication academics, such as reception theorists. Semiotics cannot be fully explored here, but it is worth pointing out a few elements from this approach which are relevant to students of public relations. The first is that such theorists are not interested in sources, or where messages come from – only in how meaning is created in the mind of the receiver. It argues that audiences 'decode' images and words according to their own personal, cultural or social terms of reference to obtain their own meaning of a message.

All communication is constructed of signs, made of words and gestures. While gestures for food or sleep might be universal, the words are not. Semiotics breaks signs into the thing itself (for example what you eat), the sign for it (the letters F-O-O-D, which are, of course, inedible) and the meaning you associate with that sign (food means different things to the starving and the bulimic reader) (Fiske 1990). It investigates the gaps between what is intended – or encoded – by the source, and what is understood – or decoded – by the receiver. Meanings can be described as:

1 *Denotative* – what the word means in the dictionary sense, for example 'chair: a piece of furniture for sitting on.

2 *Connotative* – the images or associations created in the mind of the receiver, for example 'school' can evoke the happiest days of your life, or an eternity of terror and boredom.

3 *Ambiguous* – where the same word means different things in a given language, for example 'bear' can be a noun describing a woolly beast or a verb meaning to carry. Puns and poems depend on ambiguity for their effect.

4 *Polysemic* – where readers/viewers can derive different meanings from the same set of information – pictures or text. This builds on the different connotations people bring to a message, but reflects the wider social context of a message, not just the subjective response. For example, an image of a woman in a swimming costume may represent different meanings to people of different cultures or different political and ideological views.

Semiotics is good for public relations practitioners because it makes us think about how people use the information – text, image, sound, colour – to construct their own versions of our message.

Public relations practitioners need to be aware of the varying reactions people can have to the same word or image. Failure to do so can lead to misunderstanding or even offence.

Uses and gratifications approach

Another approach to communications which is useful for understanding public relations is Blumler and Katz' uses and gratifications approach. This suggests that people are active seekers of information who choose to read or watch particularly magazines or programmes because they expect that medium to supply them with a particular need. McQuail *et al.* (1972) identify these needs as falling into four main categories

1 *Diversion* – escape from routine or personal problems.
2 *Personal relationships* – such as companionship.
3 *Personal identity* – which might include a fanzine or other entertainment aimed at their age group.
4 *Surveillance* – which means finding out about the world.

The public relations practitioner needs to understand the different ways in which people use each medium – and to remember that people haven't bought a magazine or turned on the TV just to hear the message the PR wants to put across.

The psychology of communication

This chapter has looked at the role of the sender as outlined in the Westley–McLean model, the meaning of the message as explained by semiotics, and the motivations of the receiver through the uses and gratifications approach. The German scholar Maletzke provides an overview of the whole communication process, combining all these elements (Figure 2.4).

There are many useful points for public relations practitioners in this model, such as the role played in communication by the communicator's personality, the social context, the working environment and other pressures. Likewise, the receiver is placed in a social context, subject to his or her own environmental pressures. It makes the processes of encoding and decoding quite detailed and explicit. Maletzke suggests that the medium is surrounded by a series of pressures or constraints. From the communicator's perspective there are choices to be made – how to shape the message and prepare it for the journalist, for example. The medium itself has constraints – material prepared for broadcast is different from material prepared for press. The fact that the communication is public also brings restraints. These can all affect the selection and structuring of content and might also cover awareness of such elements as the legal aspects of the medium and relevant news values.

The receiver is also placed in their own context – their 'reading' will be affected by their self-image, personality, social environment and membership of the media audience. Each medium has its own characteristics that affect the way the receiver experiences the content, from the feel of a newspaper to shared viewing at a cinema. Different attitudes to the internet illustrate this point: there are those who logged on years ago, enthusiastically navigating their way through cyberspace, while others hesitate, scared of the mouse.

Mass media effects

One of the longest running disputes in communication and media theory is the question of how much the media influence their audiences and how persuasive communication can be. Some academics study the psychology of individuals to understand different responses to messages such as advertisements or health campaigns. Other academics study the connections between violence on television and violence in society. There are those who argue that the media have a powerful role to play in shaping public opinion, and others who say it is actually very hard to persuade others, especially via the mass media. This section cannot cover all of these debates but looks at some of the issues most relevant to the student of public relations.

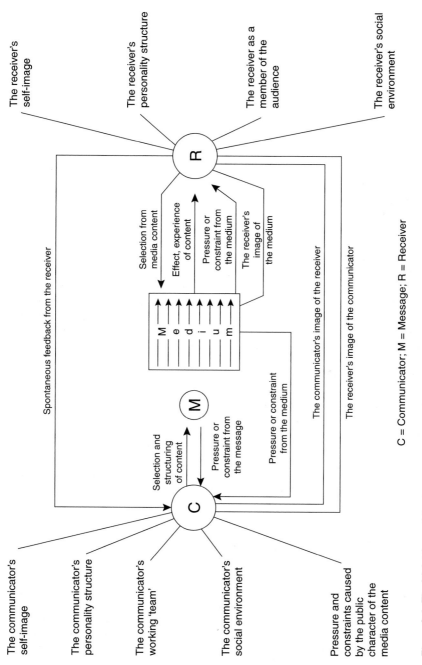

The communicator's
self-image

The communicator's
personality structure

The communicator's
working 'team'

The communicator's
social environment

Pressure and
constraints caused
by the public
character of the
media content

Selection and
structuring
of content

Pressure or constraint from
the message

Pressure or constraint
from the medium

The communicator's image of the receiver

The receiver's image of the communicator

Spontaneous feedback from the receiver

Selection from
media content

Effect, experience
of content

Pressure or
constraint from
the medium

The receiver's
image of
the medium

The receiver's
self-image

The receiver's
personality structure

The receiver as a
member of the
audience

The receiver's social
environment

C = Communicator; M = Message; R = Receiver

Figure 2.4 The Maletzke model *Source:* Windahl *et al.* 1992: 126, Figure 11.2. Reprinted by permission of Sage Publications Ltd

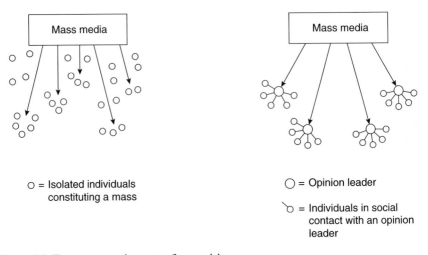

Early mass communication model

Two-step flow model

○ = Isolated individuals
 constituting a mass

○ = Opinion leader

᠐ = Individuals in social
 contact with an opinion
 leader

Figure 2.5 The one-step and two-step flow models

Source: McQuail and Windahl 1993: 62, Figure 3.2.1. Used by permission of Longman

Early theories of media effects evolved between the two world wars and were heavily influenced by the Nazi use of new media such as cinema as propaganda. The Frankfurt School of academics who fled Nazi Germany in the early 1930s carried overwhelming fears that mass media would generate mass effects and that whoever controlled the media would control their society. Their view is sometimes described as the 'hypodermic model', suggesting that audiences are passive and react in a uniform manner to a media message. But US social scientists (especially the Yale School) after the Second World War – also concerned about the power of propaganda – conducted extensive research into voter behaviour which suggested that people are actually more likely to be influenced by their friends and neighbours or other 'opinion formers' than the papers they read. This was called the 'two-step flow' theory and was developed by Katz and Lazerfield (1955 (Figure 2.5)).

This idea dominated discussion of the media and communication effects and stimulated more research into the psychology of individuals and how people respond to messages. Questions of attitude formation and change, beliefs, values and opinions were investigated as part of the research into persuasive communication. However, in the 1970s some academics (including the Birmingham School) returned to the ideas of the Frankfurt School and re-examined them. They looked at the effect of the media on society and on class and found that the media tended to support the interests of capitalism (and its owners, of course). Researchers found negative media images of working people, women, ethnic minorities and others with less power in society. At this time ideas such as 'agenda-setting' were developed, where journalists select what is important to publish according to their implicit or explicit views of society. Unlike the Frankfurt School or the Yale School, this group looked at effects on society as a whole, rather than on individuals. Their more subtle description of effects has gained continuing currency, while questions of effect on individuals – such as those exposed to violence – is still unclear.

The influence of semiotics gave rise to the reception theory of media effects, where meaning is 'constructed' in the reader or viewer. Stuart Hall (1980), a leading member of the Birmingham School, proposed that the media create 'preferred readings' which suggest how reality should be seen. Others have looked at the way the media, especially television, 'constructs reality' through its use of images. The media can also exert influence on society by suggesting what is 'normal' behaviour and what is not. They can set the agenda for discussion and can exclude certain topics. Current theories suggest that the media do have a profound influence but it is not a simple case of cause and effect. However, many public relations practitioners still behave as if the stimulus–response/message–effect links are unchallenged (Windahl et al. 1992). These communicators have not moved on from the linear model and tend to be engaged in publicity or other one-way communications. It is after all hard to explain that your campaign may not work because the theories about the effects of communication are unclear. Better to suggest that as long as people receive the message, they're bound to fall in with it. However, as health campaigners have found over the decades, the reality is very different.

Professional communicators need to be aware of the potential for good and harm contained in their messages – an example is the current debate about the effect of the use of very thin models on the rate of eating disorders in young girls. Clearly, those who argue for control of images are not saying that one fashion spread can make a healthy girl ill, but they are saying that through general representations of 'desirable' women, girls and young women receive an impression of an 'ideal' body weight that is actually distorted.

The concepts and theories explored in this chapter suggest ways of looking at communication and at the mass media. Many 'how to' PR books suggest communication is easy; the reality is that it is complicated and involves not only the personalities of the sender and the receiver, the particular requirements of each medium, the public nature of the messages, but also the power to influence, directly or indirectly, society as a whole. Public relations can be a powerful agent – handle it with care.

3 Public relations, politics and the media

Ian Somerville

I t seems that almost every week public relations is pilloried for its role in contaminating and corrupting the political process in Britain. Spin doctoring, negative campaigning and the pernicious influence of lobbyists are all highlighted as examples of how public relations tactics have degraded the political process. There are frequent calls to return to a type of political activity where such tactics had no place. Headlines in the press tend to follow a similar theme in this regard; 'Prescott bins the spin for real policies' (the *Independent*)[1] is typical. This presumption, frequently asserted by the media and politicians, of the tainting effect of public relations on British political culture, should be questioned. Indeed, it could be argued, the media, politicians and public relations specialists are increasingly bound together in a relationship that the media and politicians find more beneficial than they care to admit.

A discussion of the role of public relations within the political sphere naturally falls into two sections, the use of public relations practices by government and the use of public relations practices by non-governmental actors, or lobbyists, in the political process. This chapter will assess the role of political public relations in Western democracies with a particular focus on governmental bodies within the United Kingdom. A later chapter in this book (Chapter 8) will discuss lobbying. The first three sections of this chapter will assess the increasing importance of public relations specialists in government communications in Britain and will focus particularly on several forms of media management and information management techniques employed by government public relations practitioners. The role of the media will also be assessed in regard to this aspect of the political process in Britain. The penultimate section in the chapter will discuss recent attempts to develop a 'Grunigian' model of government public relations and the final section will examine the case of the new devolved Scottish Parliament and whether or not the communication processes surrounding this institution offer an alternative to the existing political culture in Britain.

Government public relations in democratic societies

Whilst the government's 'management' of the media on a day-to-day basis is the focus of this chapter, it is self-evident that governments must win elections to take or maintain power. So, while this chapter will not discuss electioneering in detail, it is worth

noting that it is in relation to election contests that the changing nature of communicative activity surrounding democratic politics is sometimes thrown into sharpest relief. Several recent studies of political communication during election campaigns have highlighted very similar themes *vis-à-vis* the role of public relations and political advertising.

> For Boris Yeltsin's referendum campaign, Saatchi and Saatchi were invited by . . . Yeltsin's pollsters, to accompany Gallup Poll and Matrix Public Relations on a research study among Russian voters. We were then asked to present recommendations to help Yeltsin.
>
> (Hilton 1993, quoted in Negrine 1996: 146)

> The victory of Ernest 'the bull' Pérez Balladares in the Panamanian presidential elections . . . marks the second time in a fortnight that Saatchi and Saatchi has won an election in central America.
>
> (Gunson 1994, quoted in Negrine 1996: 146)

It is not just in the West that public relations is credited with a central role in the capturing and maintaining of political power. From political cultures as different as Russia and Central America it appears that it is not ideas or personalities which win elections but Anglo-American advertising and public relations companies. Saatchi and Saatchi is, in a British context, most famous for its political advertising campaigns on behalf of Margaret Thatcher's Conservative government but it is important to remember that the company was also significantly involved in the related area of public relations.

Whilst the role of public relations in election campaigns is not central to the present discussion, it should be recognised that the development of the role of the public relations specialist in elections is part of a wider trend. This is reflected in the expansion of the role of public relations specialists in the day-to-day relationship between the media and the government. British politicians, and especially the government, are, in many ways, at the heart of the news machine and the television news, in particular, feeds us a constant daily diet of stories about Westminster, Whitehall and the devolved parliaments. Knight and Curtis (1987: 49) note that 'News prioritises the state and its agents, treating even minor state activities as inherently newsworthy, viewing agents of the state as "reliable" sources and as interesting speakers and portraying the visible aspects of relations among states.' Why is there this willingness by news organisations, particularly television news broadcasts, to devote so much time to political news stories? To a great extent the answer to this question lies in the success of 'political public relations' (McNair 1994) and more specifically to the success recent British governments have had in *media management* and *information management*.[2] The two processes are, of course, intimately related but for the purposes of the ensuing discussion they will be discussed as separate activities.

Media management

The relationship between politicians and the media, and more importantly between the government and the media, will obviously involve a struggle between what are theoretically two different sets of interests. The journalist is supposed to be attempting to seek out and present the facts while the politician will want to ensure that a news story reflects the 'message' that he or she wishes to convey. There is nothing particularly

new in the attempt of the political elites to try and control media representations, as is revealed in various accounts of the development and growth of political public relations from the early years of the twentieth century onwards (Pearson 1992; McNair 1994). However this discussion will focus on the role of public relations in the 1980s and 1990s in Britain, a period which witnessed a rapid transformation in the role and status of public relations within the political process. This expansion of public relations activity has unsuprisingly been accompanied by an increasing reliance upon media management strategies. Some commentators (Franklin 1994; McNair 1994) have pointed to the rise of the 'soundbite' and the 'pseudo-event' as clear attempts by politicians to control media representations of them and their policies.

Soundbites and pseudo-events

We noted earlier that the 'news machine', and particularly the television news, spends an enormous portion of its time focusing on the political sphere, and journalists, with tight deadlines, like most people find it hard to resist if their news gathering task is made easier for them. Cockerell *et al.* (1984: 11) note that, in reference to the workings of the British Parliament, 'Very few journalists have had the incentive to dig deeper, to mine the bedrock of power rather than merely scour its topsoil.' It is the television journalist's 'job' to pick out the key details or important points of any political event or speech. If that task is made easier, if the speech contains memorable phrases (soundbites) which summarise the main points, then there is a good chance that these portions of the speech will be selected and broadcast on the few minutes allotted to the 'story' on the news bulletins. Tony Blair's phrase 'tough on crime, tough on the causes of crime' from a speech made when he was Shadow Home Secretary has entered the national consciousness. It is indeed a memorable phrase but it is important to remember that being 'tough' and talking about being 'tough' was a carefully constructed aspect of the Blair style. Fairclough (2000: 8) argues that 'Blair's "toughness" has been self-consciously built into his communicative style as a matter of policy and strategy.'

McNair (1994) points out that most political speeches, which increasingly tend to be loaded with soundbites, occur within the context of the 'pseudo-event', by which he means the staged rally or the strictly controlled party conference. Obviously this kind of political pseudo-event has a long history from Caesar entering Rome after another famous military victory to the Nuremberg rallies in 1930s Germany. Nevertheless the impression of a united and adoring audience exulting in the great and powerful leader is memorable and again creates an easy, if rather shallow, 'story' for the few allotted minutes on the television news agenda.

In Britain in the 1980s, the Conservative Party, which was in government throughout the decade, increasingly offered this image of a united party behind a strong leader, Margaret Thatcher. Speeches by Thatcher and the Tory hierarchy at their party conferences were largely successful in supplying the television news organisations with 'easily-reportable "bits" of political information' (McNair 1994: 120) which tended to set the news agenda in the politician's favour. By contrast, during much of the 1980s the Labour Party was presented in the media as being in a state of, at best, disarray, at worst, total disintegration. After its election defeat in 1979, Labour, as one would expect, went through a period of internal 'ideological' conflict and, at times, damaging splits occurred (several leading members of the party left and formed the Social Democratic Party). Bitter internal conflicts tended to be fought out at the party conferences and the Labour Party leadership found it difficult to impose control over events. Media organisations looking for a representative few minutes for the news bulletins tended to reflect

this bitter infighting and there was little concerted attempt by the Labour Party leadership to influence, let alone manage, the news agenda. The contrast with the Tory Party, during the 1980s, was stark. The Tories were united, Labour were divided; the Tories had a strong leader, Labour had a series of weak and ineffectual leaders; the Tories were in control of events, Labour were at the mercy of them; and so on. The party conference allowed the leadership of the Tory Party to successfully manage media representations of them for a significant period of time. Behind the scenes the party elite was far from united behind the powerful leader, but it was *behind* the scenes where the personal and ideological disagreement, and the subsequent bloodletting, occurred. Ministers were frequently sacked for being disloyal, that is, disagreeing with Margaret Thatcher, and it is clear that bitterness and rancour existed within the Tory Party as it had within the Labour Party. Yet the fact that the media seemed to be caught by surprise by the eventual internal *coup d'état* which ousted Thatcher as party leader, and British Prime Minister, only reveals how successfully the media had been 'managed' for much of her rule.

By the early 1990s the Labour Party led by Neil Kinnock, and under the guidance of political public relations specialists like Peter Mandelson, was attempting to emulate the success of the Tory Party in managing the media and setting news agendas. There were significant failures in their attempts to stage manage media opportunities (McNair 1994) but on the whole the Labour Party's media managers learned from their mistakes and for most of the decade, including the general election success of 1997, Labour was very successful at managing the media.

Spin doctoring

In most accounts of recent Labour success in media management the role of 'media spin' and, in particular, Tony Blair's formidable 'spin doctor' Alastair Campbell are highlighted. Several authors (Jones 1999; Fairclough 2000) have discussed the media management surrounding the government's welfare 'reforms' as a case study which illustrates 'New Labour's management of news and "media spin"' (Fairclough 2000: 129). Labour opted to launch a 'welfare roadshow' in a bid to attempt to control the news agenda, with Tony Blair going 'on the road' to put his case for welfare reform to the people of Britain. Blair's first speech was in Dudley, and the day before this speech Alastair Campbell gave private briefings to the media in which he emphasised, with lots of facts and figures, the costs to the nation of benefit fraud. The next day – the official launch of the welfare roadshow – two national newspapers, *The Times* and the *Mirror*, carried articles 'written' by Tony Blair which were virtually indistinguishable from the briefing Campbell had given the day before. That evening, in Dudley, Blair's speech again reinforced the message, with virtually the same language, that he was determined to do something about benefit fraud. Fairclough (2000: 130) notes that:

> The risk of unpredictable and uncontrollable media uptake of the speech is minimised by trailing the speech in a way which presents it in the way the Government wants it to be seen – which puts a particular 'spin' on it.

This was, of course, only the beginning of the welfare reform process which proceeded through a 'consultation' stage[3] and eventually to a Bill presented to the Westminster Parliament. Fairclough (2000: 129) argues that the whole process, from initial campaign, through the consultative stage, to the presentation of the Bill to Parliament, was 'largely managed through managerial and promotional means rather than democratically through

dialogue'. 'Part of the art of "spin"', according to Fairclough (2000: 131), 'is calcu-
lating what additional emphases and foregrounding newspapers . . . will predictably add,
which may be an effective way for the Government to convey implicitly messages it
may not wish to convey explicitly'. In the case of the welfare reform legislation, issues
surrounding benefit fraud were only a small part of the Bill but there was a constant
stream of messages about how Tony Blair would 'get tough' on benefit fraud. This
allowed politically conservative newspapers like the *Daily Mail* to use headlines
such as 'Welfare: The Crackdown'. Fairclough (2000: 131) suggests that the *Daily Mail*
report 'effects certain transformations which significantly and (from a press officer's
perspective) predictably convey a "tougher" message than Blair's', but the key point
is that this 'message' will reassure the *Daily Mail*'s largely Tory readership.

Using 'spin' to convey certain kinds of messages and to produce certain kinds of
'readings' of important documents or events is increasingly a media management tech-
nique used by the current Labour government. Insofar as it often tends to be bound up
with private briefings by spin doctors like Alastair Campbell it can also be viewed as
an important aspect in the government's management of information.

Information management

All democratically elected governments must communicate with their electorates. After
all, in most theories of democratic government there is an assumption that the govern-
ment is the servant of the people, elected to carry out its will. Just because govern-
ments have this duty to provide information to the general public does not mean, of
course, that they will not attempt to control and manipulate the amount of, and kinds
of, information they disseminate. Information management in regard to government
simply means the processes and procedures by which governmental agencies dissemi-
nate the information they want us to receive.

The public relations state?

It is an inescapable fact that throughout the 1980s and 1990s there have been massive
increases in resources devoted to the aspect of government administration responsible
for information management. For example, 'Whitehall and Downing Street now employ
1,200 press officers with a combined budget estimated to approach two hundred million
pounds' (Budge *et al*. 1998: 315).

Many commentators note how careful management of information turns it into a very
valuable resource. Cockerall *et al*. (1984: 9) suggest that what government 'chooses to
tell us through its public relations machine is one thing; the information in use by
participants in the country's real government is another'. Negrine (1996: 10) notes the
'increasing use of carefully crafted communication strategies by governments to ensure
that . . . the information they seek to impart to their citizens has an appropriate "spin"
on it'. Obviously this increased use of public relations specialists by the government
may merely reflect a more general 'promotional culture' in Britain (Miller 1998).
However, some observers have expressed disquiet at the increasing use of information
management techniques by the government. Deacon and Golding (1994: 7) have noted
with concern the rise of the 'public relations state' and Schlesinger (1990: 82) notes
that there are important questions

> about the nature of information management in a society by a variety of groups in
> conditions of unequal power and therefore unequal access to systems of information

production and distribution and these questions are particularly acute in regard to government because 'the apparatuses of the state . . . enjoy privileged access to the media'.

There are various ways in which governments manage information in order to privilege their own views on an issue. Leaks of important information, or even important documents, are one way in which the government or powerful interest groups within the state may attempt to control the media agenda,[4] but perhaps the key weapon in the government's information management armoury is the 'Lobby' system.

The Lobby

The Lobby – so called because journalists used to assemble in the Member's Lobby of the House of Commons – has been described as 'the Prime Minister's most useful tool for the political management of the news' (Cockerell *et al.* 1984: 33).

This system is a very important resource that British governments use – and it could be argued abuse – for keeping control of information flows to the media and hence to the general public. It is also clear, despite claims to the contrary by those who have utilised it,[5] that it is a unique system within Western democracies. This does not mean that other governments do not attempt to manage information – of course they do – but it is normal practice to appoint a party political spokesperson who openly represents the government position and is attributable. Not so in Britain; the Government Press Officer is actually a member of the Civil Service, and thus officially politically neutral, and, uniquely, deals with the media through a kind of secretive 'ritualistic process' (Franklin 1994: 87). Cockerell *et al.* (1984: 42) argue that the Lobby system 'mirrors the secrecy that surrounds so much of the government in Whitehall and allows the government of the day to present its own unchallenged versions of reality'.

All of the national newspapers and television and radio broadcasters are represented in the Lobby where they are usually briefed by the Prime Minister's Press Secretary. Cockerell *et al.* (1984: 33) note that 'what the Press Secretary says at these briefings is what the Prime Minister wants the press, radio and television to report'. Franklin (1994: 86) argues that a key change occurred in the Lobby system in the post-war period which involved the '*codification* of a set of rules enforcing the non-attribution of news sources while simultaneously obliging journalists to rely on a single source, usually the Prime Minister's Press Secretary'. In effect the Lobby became a government press conference which could dispense unattributable information. Franklin points out that when a Government Press Secretary gives a briefing there is a strong likelihood that it will appear as a news item, 'replete with the political spin he places on it' (1994: 86). Clearly the Lobby works well for the media, in the sense that it is relatively easy to obtain a news 'story' in time for the evening news or the morning editions. It also works well for the government of the day by providing a system of information management which allows it to control and structure the media's political news agendas. However, Hennessy condemns the practice as not working in the interests of anyone else. He argues that 'any system of mass non-attributable briefings is a restrictive practice rigged for the benefit and convenience of the givers and receivers of information and against the interests of the consumer – the reader, the listener, the viewer and the voter' (quoted in Franklin 1994: 91).

Political public relations and the media: interdependence or dependency?

Franklin (1994: 3) notes that representatives of the media like to present the media as constituting the *fourth estate* 'which subjects all aspects of political life to close scrutiny and is consequently a key mechanism for securing the accountability of politicians to the general public'. He points out, however, that these 'watchdogs' are viewed by those critical of British political culture as little more than 'lapdogs'. He notes that 'Marxists identify the media as central agencies in the construction of a social and political consensus, encouraging the acquiescence of the public, by distributing and reinforcing the values and beliefs of the dominant social and political group within society' (1994: 3). Whilst it could be argued that the media are not necessarily dominated by politicians in any direct or conspiratorial way, the way in which the British political sphere is constructed and maintained by both the media and the politicians somewhat undermines any suggestion that the media constitute the fourth estate.

Nevertheless it is sometimes claimed that there is a mutual interdependence of politicians and the media. Bernard Ingham, Margaret Thatcher's former Press Secretary, suggested that the relationship is 'essentially cannibalistic. They feed off each other but no one knows who is next on the menu' (Ingham, quoted in Franklin 1994: 14). Ingham's metaphor may seem outlandish but it is clear that the relationship between the media and politicians is in some senses a symbiotic one. Politicians in general, and government public relations specialists in particular, obviously rely on the media to communicate with the general public. But it must be said that broadcasters and journalists understand that without a degree of co-operation from politicians, political journalism would be difficult, if not impossible.

However, other commentators would argue that with the advent of 'media managers' in Western democracies like Britain the politician–media relationship has been pushed beyond the 'state of mutual interdependence to one of *media dependence* on, and deference to, politicians' (McNair 1994: 115). Whether or not one agrees that the relationship is one of media dependency a cursory look at media ownership in the UK would indicate that the media are not independent of powerful economic and political interests in British society (Negrine 1994). It is also obvious that ultimately broadcasting and press 'freedoms' are at the mercy of the legislative process. In Britain, as noted above, this relationship is epitomised by the Westminster 'Lobby' which, while it involves some degree of mutual interdependence, tends ultimately to allow government media managers a great deal of control in structuring news agendas.

The situation in Britain obviously suits the government, but it does have a downside in that it leads to a level of mistrust and cynicism about the kind of information governments disseminate. There is an obvious tension between controlling the information flows for one's own benefit and structuring news agendas to such an extent that everything you say is treated as 'spin'. As we have seen, at the heart of this debate is the role of government public relations and it has been argued that governments and government public relations specialists in many Western democracies are practising a type of public relations which stifles 'open' government and leads to distrust amongst the electorate. It should be no surprise to students of public relations to find James Grunig arguing that in certain Western democracies, what he describes as 'asymmetrical' government communication activities need to be replaced by a symmetrical model.

Symmetrical government public relations

Grunig and Jaatinen (1999) argue that government public relations is different depending on which Western democracy you analyse. They suggest that governmental organisations in the USA are more likely to practise a 'public information model'[6] of public relations. The reason for this one-way information-based communication approach is because they have a *pluralistic* view of government. Other countries, such as Canada and Norway, practise strategic, two-way communication because the perspective underpinning governmental communication in these countries is *societal corporatist*. Unsurprisingly Grunig and Jaatinen (1999: 219) conclude that in order to adhere to the generic principles of 'excellent' public relations – that is, strategic, symmetrical public relations – a governmental agency needs 'to view its relationship with publics from a societal corporatist perspective rather than from a pluralist perspective'. But what precisely do these authors mean by 'pluralist' and 'societal corporatist' perspectives of government public relations?

Pluralism versus societal corporatism

Grunig and Jaatinen suggest that pluralist theorists understand the relationship between 'government agencies and publics as one of competition – a competition among interest groups for access to government funds and services' (1999: 223). The role of 'government agencies' is defined rather differently here than in most pluralist theories, which view the government as a kind of referee, in what the English philosopher John Stuart Mill called the 'free market place of ideas' (Moloney 1996: 23). Nevertheless the idea of competing interest groups is at the heart of pluralist theory and this is reflected in the above definition.

Grunig and Jaatinen make the point that a 'societal corporatist' system is distinct from a 'corporatist' system. They argue that a 'corporatist political system can be dangerous to democracy if either government agencies or publics dominate the other or collaborate to achieve their mutual interests at the expense of other groups in society' (1999: 224). However, in a societal corporatist system 'government agencies collaborate and bargain with publics they are supposed to serve or regulate to balance the interests of those publics and society at large through symmetrical communication' (ibid.). The types of relationships epitomised by societal corporatism 'embody collectivist collaboration rather than individualistic competition' (ibid.).

In regard to communication strategies Grunig and Jaatinen would argue that the pluralist, corporatist and societal corporatist perspectives all have significant effects on how governments and government agencies interact with their publics. They note:

> Government agencies in the pluralist sphere do not need to practise strategic public relations because they expect activist groups to come to them for services; and the agency has no need to identify them. In pure corporatism, the agency typically chooses to collaborate with the most powerful interest groups; and little strategic management is needed to identify them. In societal corporatism, however, the agency must engage in environmental scanning and other forms of strategic public relations to identify those groups with whom it has a responsibility to interact – in the interests of those groups, the government and society at large.
>
> (1999: 227)

It is clear that for Grunig and Jaatinen a theory of government public relations must not only be built upon the generic principles of 'excellence' in public relations but must also include the principles of societal corporatism.

Grunig and Jaatinen suggest that government communication policies in countries like Norway and Canada reflect these principles of societal corporatism, whereas countries likes the USA and the UK tend to operate from within a pluralist perspective. Whether or not one agrees with their conclusion that governmental communication requires an application of the 'excellence' principles within a framework of societal corporatism, it would be difficult to argue that the approach of the UK government to communicating with the general public reflects open, participative, symmetrical communication practice. However, in the UK in the late 1990s significant changes to the political landscape occurred with devolved parliaments and assemblies being established or re-established in Scotland, Wales and Northern Ireland. The final section of this chapter will focus on the new Scottish Parliament and discuss whether or not the constitutional changes have created an opportunity to change government communication practice.

Government public relations and Scottish devolution

Following elections in June 1999 political structures in the United Kingdom changed in the most significant way since the Act of Union in 1707. For first time since that date, Scotland elected a legislative parliament in its capital city, Edinburgh. This final section of the chapter will focus upon the particular case of the Scottish Parliament and the argument that the political culture it represents is a conscious attempt to replace the Westminster model with a more open, accountable and participative system.

In July 1997 the British government published its devolution White Paper, *Scotland's Parliament*. Shortly after this, on 11 September 1997, there was a two-question referendum in which Scotland's voters were asked to decide whether there should be a Scottish Parliament and whether this Parliament should have tax-varying powers. The 'Yes–Yes' campaign was backed by the three political parties in Scotland that had representation at Westminster, and the European Parliament, the pro-devolution Labour and Liberal Democrats and the pro-independence Scottish National Party. It was opposed by the Conservative Party, which had recently lost all its Scottish seats at Westminster, and the European Parliament. Of the Scottish electorate who voted (60.4 per cent of those eligible) 74.3 per cent supported the creation of a Scottish Parliament and 63.5 per cent agreed that the proposed Parliament should have tax-varying powers.

The Scottish Parliament has legislative control, in Scotland, over areas such as health, education, local government, economic development and transport, environment, agriculture, forestry and fishing, law and home affairs, sport and the arts, and will be able to vary upwards or downwards the basic rate of income tax applicable in Scotland by up to 3 pence in the pound, with proceeds adding to, or reducing, the Parliament's spending power. The devolved Parliament will not be responsible for legislation for such areas as constitutional matters, UK financial matters, foreign policy, defence, social security and broadcasting.[7]

At the first Scottish general election, on 6 May 1999, 129 Members of the Scottish Parliament (MSPs) were elected: 73 were elected by the first-past-the-post system in existing Westminster constituencies,[8] the remaining 56 members were elected from party lists via an additional member voting system with seven seats from each of the eight

European parliamentary constituencies. Labour was the largest party and has formed a coalition government with the Liberal Democrat Party who came fourth just behind the Conservative Party. The Scottish National Party who came second have taken up the role of opposition along with the Conservatives, the one Scottish Socialist Party MSP and the first Green Party candidate to be elected to a UK parliament.

Accompanying these political developments in Scotland there have been significant statements relating to how the whole mechanism of political communication is expected to operate in this new political culture. Donald Dewar, the Parliament's First Minister,[9] stated publicly in regard to political reporting: 'We are not likely to wish to recreate the lobby system' (quoted in Schlesinger 1998: 69). Before the setting up of the Scottish Parliament an All-Party Consultative Steering Group (CSG) chaired by Henry McLeish, the then Minister for Devolution in the Scottish Office, was charged with gathering views on how the Parliament would operate. The CSG Report, which outlined comprehensive proposals for the working of the new Parliament, was published on 15 January 1999. The CSG Report identified four key principles:

- the Scottish Parliament should embody and reflect the sharing of power between the people of Scotland, the legislators (the Members of the Scottish Parliament) and the Scottish Executive (the Scottish Ministers);
- the Scottish Executive should be accountable to the Scottish Parliament and the Parliament and Executive should be accountable to the people of Scotland;
- the Scottish Parliament should be accessible, open, responsive and develop procedures which make possible a participative approach to the development, consideration and scrutiny of policy and legislation;
- the Scottish Parliament in its operation and its appointments should recognise the need to promote equal opportunities for all.[10]

In the new Scottish political system it is not just the executive which has the power to initiate legislation. This is also a power vested in parliamentary committees which are made up of between 5 and 15 MSPs selected according to the balance of the various political parties and groupings in the Parliament. Meetings of the Parliament's committees are normally held in public and can take place anywhere in Scotland. One of the reasons given for using a committee system for much of the work of the Scottish Parliament is that it was felt that this would 'encourage significant public involvement in the Parliament's activities'.[11]

Conclusions

Grunig and Jaatinen (1999) would undoubtedly view the principles underpinning the new devolved political system in Scotland as a manifestation of a societal corporatist perspective and it is clear that it represents a departure from the existing British political culture. Phillip Schlesinger (1998: 71) remarked that 'the very prospect of Scotland's parliament is promoting the creation of an increasingly distinctive political culture, one that defines itself as *not*-Westminster'. Of course, it remains to be seen whether government agencies in a devolved Scotland will resist the temptation to exert the kind of control over information flows that is evident at Westminster and sustain the more symmetrical communication model outlined in the CSG Report. If they do so, the kind of system which has officially been embraced by the new Scottish Parliament, with its stated objectives of openness, accountability and participative democracy, may well

offer an exemplar for Westminster. What is clear is that the absence of a 'Lobby' style system of government communication is both a practical and a symbolic distancing of the Scottish political culture from that of Westminster.

Notes

1 For a discussion of this particular incident see Fairclough 2000: 1–3.
2 McNair (1994) helpfully provides a typology of political public relations activity which is useful in that it utilises terminology with which most students of public relations should be familiar. He notes that political public relations involves four specific types of activity: *media management* (which he regards as something akin to issues management), *image management, internal communications*, and *information management*. While recognising the conceptual and practical distinctions McNair draws, for the purposes of the present discussion I have subsumed the first three activities McNair refers to into the general category of media management.
3 British governments publish a 'Green Paper' before constructing a 'Bill' to set before Parliament. Interested parties respond to the Green Paper and are supposed to have a say in how legislation is framed. Fairclough (2000: 132–41) provides a useful discourse analysis of the text of the Green Paper on welfare reform.
4 For some interesting case studies of the British government's use of leaks in relation to issues surrounding British Coal, Northern Ireland and the sale of the Rover car group to British Aerospace, see Negrine 1996: 39–51.
5 Ingham suggests 'This [the Lobby] method of communication with journalists is universally practised in government and other circles the world over as a means of opening up the relationship [between government and media]' (quoted in McNair 1994: 135).
6 This model is, of course, one of the four included in Grunig and Grunig's (1992) famous typology. The others are press agentry, two-way asymmetrical and two-way symmetrical.
7 For a full list see <www.scottish.parliament.uk>.
8 The Westminster constituency of Orkney and Shetland was split into two constituencies.
9 I.e. Prime Minister.
10 This text is taken from a CSG Report which is available online at the Scottish Parliament website <www.scottish.parliament.uk>.
11 See <www.scottish.parliament.uk/welcoming_you>, p. 5.

4 Public relations and management

Anne Gregory

For many public relations professionals, a sign of having 'arrived' is obtaining a 'strategic' role signified by having a seat on the board and enjoying the respect and recognition of their peers. In reality, many public relations practitioners function at a 'tactical' level, implementing communications tasks defined by other people. However, there is growing evidence to suggest that public relations is an important and necessary tool for strategic management (Dozier *et al.* 1995) and that it has had a significant role in building the reputation of some of the world's most admired corporations (Skolnik 1994).

This chapter aims to do six things:

- describe public relations as a strategic activity taking the systems perspective as a basis for argument
- examine the different types of organisation and observe how organisation type affects public relations activity
- explain the roles of public relations practitioners
- suggest the forms of communication within organisations and the channels that can be used
- indicate the influences that set communication programme priorities
- describe the working linkages between public relations and other professional areas of organisations.

Systems theory and public relations

Any discussion of public relations and its role in organisations inevitably begs the question – 'what is an organisation?' Answering that question helps to reveal the pivotal nature of communication and therefore the strategic input that public relations can have.

Many public relations scholars (Cutlip *et al.* 2000; Grunig and Hunt 1984) refer to systems theory to explain the structure and operation of organisations and their interaction with the environment. In essence systems theory describes an organisation as a set of parts (or subsystems) which impact on each other and which together interact with the organisation's environment. Cutlip *et al.* (2000: 229) describe it thus:

A system is a set of interacting units which endures through time within an established boundary by responding and adjusting to change pressures from the environment to achieve and maintain goal states.

Systems theory provides a useful theoretical underpinning for thinking about the role of public relations because it stipulates that an organisation's well-being (or otherwise) is dependent on establishing and maintaining relationships both within itself and with its environment. It has to adjust and adapt as both it and its environment change.

Specifically, organisations are part of a *social* system which consists of individuals or groups of individuals (publics), such as employees, pensioners, suppliers, distributors and so on, who are all involved with it. The role of public relations is to develop and maintain relationships with these groups in order for the organisation to meet its goals.

Grunig and Hunt (1984) propose that organisations typically develop a formal communication function 'when the organisation or its publics behave in a way that has consequences upon the other'. If these consequences are adverse, then a public relations problem or issue is created. Grunig and Hunt's depiction of the role of the public relations department is shown in Figure 4.1. This relationship holds good for both internal and external publics.

When considering internal relationships, Grunig and Hunt describe the work of organisational theorists who have found that there are five similar subsystems in most organisations.

Production subsystems produce the products or services of the organisation. *Maintenance* subsystems work across the organisation, acting effectively as its glue, encouraging employees to work together. Human resources is a good example of such a subsystem. Other functions focus on the marketing and distribution of products and are called *disposal* subsystems. *Adaptive* subsystems help the organisation to adjust when the environment in which it operates changes; research and development and strategic planning departments are good examples. *Management* subsystems direct and control the other subsystems and manage conflicting demands between them. They also negotiate between the demands of the environment (for example requirement for low prices) and the survival needs of the organisation (profit). Typically the board of an organisation and/or a senior management grouping fulfil this role.

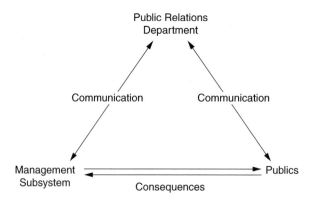

Figure 4.1 The public relations function in an organisation

Source: Grunig and Hunt 1984: 10. Used by permission of Harcourt Inc.

From a systems view, public relations professionals are seen as having a 'boundary-spanning' role. They straddle the edges of an organisation liaising both between its internal subsystems and between it and the external environment which contains its various publics. As Grunig and Hunt (1984: 9) put it, 'they have one foot in the organisation and one foot outside'. In this strategic role, public relations is usually seen to be part of the management subsystem.

Public relations professionals support other internal subsystems by helping them communicate within the organisation itself and by helping them in communicating with external audiences. They provide a counselling role, advising what and how to communicate and they can also provide an implementation role by undertaking the communication on behalf of the subsystems. For example, it will help the human resources department, part of the *maintenance* subsystem, with internal communication programmes or the marketing department, part of the *disposal* subsystem, with product promotion campaigns. (See also Chapter 11 for a discussion of systems theory relating to internal communications.)

Public relations in strategy making

The main role of the leader of an organisation and its senior managers (or board) is to provide vision and direction. Effective organisations have a sense of purpose. They know where they are going and they know how they are going to get there. The vision may be set by a strong individual with a particular driving-force, for example Bill Gates who wanted to put a PC on everyone's desk, or Anita Roddick who wanted to provide high-quality toiletries combined with an ethical stance. Alternatively the vision may be more broad-based and generic. For example, universities exist to provide higher education; their purpose is broadly the same – to undertake teaching, research and consultancy. However, even within that broad category there are those with different priorities; some are research driven, some want to serve a regional community, some specialise in certain subjects.

Whatever the type of organisation, successful ones have a strategy that determines long-term direction and the scope of the operation. It is not appropriate in this chapter to examine the different schools of strategy formulation, but suffice to say that strategy-making involves a great deal of information, analysis and decision-making. This decision-making and strategy selection is undertaken by the 'dominant coalition', that group within an organisation which has the power 'to make and enforce decisions about the direction of the organisation, its tasks, its objectives and its functions' (White and Dozier 1992: 93).

The contribution that public relations can make to the strategy-making process is twofold: first, helping to collect and interpret information from the social environment so that strategic decisions can be made, and second, the communication of the strategic vision. This second element will be discussed later in this chapter.

Information gathering

As boundary-spanners, public relations professionals are ideally placed to gather information from both the internal and the external environment. They do this in two ways. First, they are aware of the wider macro environment. Second, they are knowledgeable about the attitudes and behaviours of the various publics of the organisation who populate this broader environment because they are in regular dialogue with those publics.

Environmental scanning

How do public relations professionals undertake this intelligence gathering work? 'Environmental scanning' is the term used for gaining information about the macro environment. PR professionals use the same techniques as those available to strategic planners. They will undertake analyses of the environment using techniques such as PEST. This technique provides a framework that allows analysis of the environment by categorising it under various headings; a short example is given in Figure 4.2 (the capitalised first letter of each section spells out the acronym above).

Some strategists now regard PEST as no longer reflecting the complexity of the environment in which modern organisations operate. They recommend an expansion of the framework to encompass the *E*nvironment, that is, the physical or green environment, *I*nformation and the *L*egal or regulatory aspects. The acronym EPISTLE describes this analytical tool. The justification for including these additional elements is that the physical environment is judged to be one of the major concerns of the twenty-first century. Global warming, pressures to move from car-based transport, sustainability, waste disposal and so on are all key issues.

Access to and the ability to manage and use information is critical to organisations because information is power. The ubiquity and power of the internet radically alters the past position where certain kinds of information have been the protected domain of a privileged few. Furthermore the ability of outsiders to look into organisations (transparency) and the ability of insiders to transmit information outside the organisation (porosity) bring new challenges.

Organisations operate within an increasingly complex legal environment. In addition to growing amounts of national legislation, there are transnational regulations such as EU directives and international agreements such as GATT. There are also quasi-legal arrangements which often have a 'moral' dimension such as the agreements to reduce pollution or to alleviate third world indebtedness, all of which may impact on organisations.

Political	**Economic**
Trade legislation (including overseas trade agreements)	Interest rates
	Inflation
Change of government	
	Business cycles
Employment legislation	
	Employment levels
Emergence of new power blocks	
Social	**Technological**
Lifestyles	Internet
Consumer preferences	Rate of change
Social attitudes	Obsolescence
Disposable income	Investment in technology

Figure 4.2 An example of a PEST analysis

Some analysts also recommend that culture should have special consideration. As organisations become increasingly global they need to be aware of religious and social differences between and within the countries in which they operate. Organisational cultures differ too and values between suppliers, distributors and organisations or even different parts of the same organisation can be quite distinct. Companies within the same sector can have radically different cultures: Virgin's approach to airline travel is not that of British Airways.

The point of this kind of analysis is to identify the key drivers that will impact on the organisation. There are no standard responses; the drivers will be different depending on the country, sector and organisation. It is also vital to identify the inter-relationships between the key drivers. Economic trends may force political decisions and technology often affects lifestyles and social interactions. For example, the internet has transformed working, purchasing and leisure patterns.

Environmental scanning establishes the long-term drivers of change and their impact. These need localising to identify the effect that they will have on the organisation itself. Environmental analyses should not only be done in the here and now, but should also include forward projections so that organisations can plan a variety of futures which they will have to accommodate, try to change or adapt to.

Knowledge of publics

The second element of information gathering by public relations professionals is intelligence about the organisation's publics or stakeholders. Public relations planners are in a privileged position in that they interact with organisational publics frequently: their job is to manage and facilitate the communication between the organisation and its publics, sometimes in conjunction with colleagues from elsewhere in the organisation. Chapter 6 covers stakeholder theory in some detail, but here it is important to stress that the public relations professional will be alert to the relative power, influence, needs and expectations of stakeholders and the shifting dynamics both within and between stakeholder groups.

Furthermore, the public relations professional will be aware of the attitude towards or behaviour of the various stakeholders (or publics) in relation to the wider issues identified in the environment and towards the organisation itself. For example, the public relations professional working for a food retailer will be alert to the fact that genetic modification of food is a major issue. They will also be aware of the prevailing attitudes of the scientific community, suppliers, customers, shareholders and employees. They will be conscious that opinion is divided and that they will need to be alert to shifts in public opinion and buying habits.

Regular research and audits of the opinion of all their publics is a vital job for the public relations professional. A typical organisation interacts with an enormous number of publics. Esman (1972) has usefully categorised these into four types of organisational linkages, as illustrated by Grunig and Hunt (Figure 4.3).

Enabling linkages are those with organisations and groups that have the authority and resources to permit the organisation to exist. *Functional* linkages provide input into the organisation and consume its outputs. *Normative* linkages are those with peer organisations, and *diffused* linkages are with those who have no formalised relationship with the organisation, but have an interest in it.

This categorisation not only demonstrates the number of different publics that the professional communicator interacts with, but the range of interest of those publics.

Figure 4.3 Organisational linkages

Source: Grunig and Hunt 1984: 141. Used by permission of Harcourt Inc.

Information interpretation

White and Mazur (1995) suggest that because they have such extensive contacts with sources and information, public relations staff may be in a position to provide a central collation and interpretation function. Managing and interpreting information requires both research and analytical capabilities and is an indication of the skills set required of senior practitioners.

Where the environment is turbulent and creates uncertainty, those individuals who are capable of interpreting what is happening are invaluable in decision-making. Public relations practitioners are used to dealing with complex situations and of making sense of inter-linked issues involving a variety of publics. Thus they can make a valuable contribution to strategy-making by offering their skills of interpretation and counselling. Indeed a study by the European Centre for Public Affairs at Templeton College in Oxford (reported in White and Mazur 1995) found that the public affairs department had become very influential in decision-making in companies who had to survive in difficult environments.

Public relations practitioners are ideally placed to be able to access early sources of information and can interpret that information to identify emerging issues and those that may have a profound effect on an organisation. For example, media content analysis can identify matters of growing importance and help clarify the direction in which public

Figure 4.4 The organisation and its environment

Source: Thompson 1995: 14. Used by permission of Chapman and Hall

opinion is moving on a particular issue. Public affairs departments are often plugged into government thinking on prospective legislation or have access to think tanks who specialise in futures. Their boundary-spanning role helps public relations professionals maintain an independent perspective to decision-making. This independence is valuable to other managers who are often too tied into the 'organisational view' to act objectively or to understand the ramifications of their decisions and the impact they will have on stakeholders.

The role of public relations professionals in information gathering and interpretation can be mapped directly onto classical strategy models. These models describe the process of information gathering required when organisations are deciding which strategic approach to take. Thompson's model is shown in Figure 4.4.

Organisational types: a systems approach

Applying a systems theory perspective, organisations can be classified as falling into two main categories. The way that public relations is conducted is critically influenced by the type of organisation within which it is practised.

Systems can be categorised by the level and nature of interaction they have with their environments. At one extreme those systems that have impenetrable boundaries and have no or very little 'exchange' with their environment can be called 'closed' whereas those where the boundaries are permeable and there is a great deal of exchange can be called 'open'.

The parallel is that organisations can be seen to be relatively closed or relatively open – social systems can never be entirely closed or open. Thus, relatively closed organisations do not take much account of the environment, they do not adapt to changing circumstances and usually they eventually cease to exist. Relatively open organisations are very responsive to the environment. They are acutely aware of change, and adjust and adapt to either counteract or accommodate it. A key concept is that the organisation both affects and is affected by the environment in which it operates.

Relatively closed organisations react only when they must and usually to resist change. Open organisations, on the other hand, monitor their environment to gauge and anticipate change and decide on a course of action before they are driven to one by external events.

Applying this approach to public relations brings some interesting insights. Public relations activity is often referred to as being 'reactive' or 'proactive'.

'Closed systems' public relations

Reactive public relations is reflective of closed systems and is characterised as being of the 'corporate mail room' variety: measuring success by volume of output rather than by results. For example, media relations is judged on the number of releases produced and the level of press cuttings achieved, not on the appropriateness or effectiveness of the output. Activity is usually confined to publics which have an obvious contact with the organisation and the emphasis is on keeping publics informed of decisions that have already been made. Genuine feedback is rarely sought, only feedback on what techniques will make the transmission of information more effective.

Public relations practitioners are usually not part of the dominant coalition and have responsibility for communicating decisions in which they have had no part. 'They do not function in decision-making or even in advisory roles in relation to environmental concerns. Therefore they have little to say about what is said: they are mainly concerned with how things are said' (Bell and Bell, cited in Cutlip et al. 2000: 241).

This approach assumes '(1) that the purpose of public relations is limited to effecting changes in the environment and more mistakenly (2) that organisations have the power to change their environments, thereby eliminating the need to change themselves' (Cutlip et al. 2000: 240).

'Open systems' public relations

Proactive public relations is allied to open systems approaches and its role involves changing and influencing both the environment and the organisation as a result of changes in the environment. The emphasis here is on reciprocity – communication with publics takes the form of a genuine dialogue (the two-way systematical approach advocated by Grunig and Hunt and explained in Chapter 1) and the organisation is as likely to change as the target publics as a result of the communication exchange. This idea is illustrated in Figure 4.5.

The purpose of this approach is to have organisational goals that are mutually acceptable and supported by both the organisation and its publics. Where there is a difference in what these should be, change can be initiated before real issues or problems arise. This proactive stance is important for organisational decision-making and that is why public relations practitioners who operate in this fashion are often part of the dominant coalition.

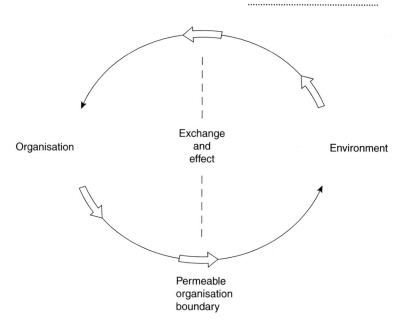

Figure 4.5 The exchange and effect relationship in open systems communication

Proactive public relations is characterised as involving a broad range of publics, not just the most obvious ones, being research-based, influential in bringing about attitudinal and behavioural change both inside and outside the organisation, essential in strategy-making and integral to the decision-making process. In other words, practitioners are principal decision-makers as opposed to just communicating results of decision-making.

It is worth making an aside here. The internet provides great opportunities for the public relations practitioner to undertake the research and monitoring required to fulfil this proactive role and this makes their position in the dominant coalition more secure. It is relatively simple to set up discussion groups to ascertain the opinion of key stakeholders and it is easy to obtain environmental information using the vast resources of the internet. However, more is possible. The internet can be used to build dialogue in a potent and dynamic way by providing a level of immediacy, reach and interactivity that has been impossible in the past. Issues management and agenda-setting is not only possible, but necessary in an environment where the publics themselves define and then seek to satisfy their information needs.

The roles of public relations practitioners

Within this strategic context it is appropriate to look at the specific roles of public relations practitioners. Work spearheaded by Glen Broom and David Dozier (summarised in Cutlip *et al.* 2000: 37–44) has identified two dominant public relations roles.

The communication technician

This often highly skilled individual carries out communication programmes and activities such as writing news releases, editing house-magazines and developing websites. They probably do not undertake research, except to decide which communication mechanism suits their prescribed purpose best; implementation is their focus. They will not be involved in organisational decision-making.

The communication manager

This person is in the dominant coalition, plans, manages and facilitates the communication programme, counsels management and makes policy decisions.

Communication managers in turn can find themselves in different roles.

The expert prescriber

They are seen as the authority on communication, and management relies on them to come up with solutions to problems. The expert prescriber researches and defines public relations problems, develops programmes and implements them, sometimes with the help of others.

There are dangers in this role: practitioners may become overconfident, perceiving themselves as in a position of great authority and with exclusive knowledge. The downside is that they may be solely accountable if things over which they have no or little control 'go wrong'.

For senior managers who are not directly involved in public relations there is an issue around abdicating responsibility for communication or overdependence on a particular individual.

In situations such as crises it is important for experts to guide and provide definitive advice, but in the longer term it is beneficial to diffuse public relations thinking, expertise and knowledge throughout organisations.

The communication facilitator

These individuals act as go-betweens: interpreting, mediating and keeping open two-way communication between an organisation and its public. They are often the official contact points in organisations, are trusted by stakeholders and the organisation alike and act in the mutual interest of all involved. Boundary-spanners in a very real sense, communication facilitators remove barriers and establish links between all interested parties. They work on the basis that mutual understanding facilitates good decision-making and provides shared benefits.

The problem-solving facilitator

These individuals work with others in the organisation to identify and solve problems. They are involved in strategic decisions from the beginning, helping to set objectives, defining communication needs and advising on implementation. Problem-solving facilitators are perceived to be skilled at helping others in analysis and solution finding and as such are invited into the decision-making coalition.

In reality, most public relations practitioners undertake a variety of these roles, often all at the same time. In general, junior practitioners tend to operate at the technician level while senior practitioners undertake the management roles. It may be tempting to denigrate the technician role, but the truth is that some technicians operate at a high level within organisations and have a great deal of influence, usually in a very specific

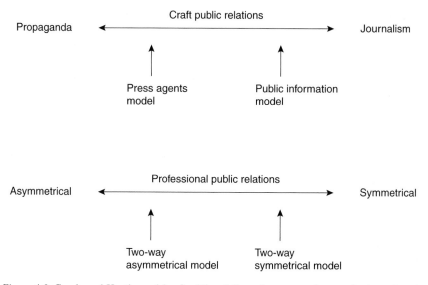

Figure 4.6 Grunig and Hunt's models of public relations shown as craft or profession oriented

Source: Grunig and Grunig 1992: 312. Used by permission of Lawrence Erlbaum Associates

area of expertise. For example, journalists who move into a public relations role can handle media relations at all levels in a highly skilled and effective way.

Reflecting on the actual roles that practitioners undertook led Grunig and Grunig (1992) to redraft the underpinning model of public relations practice developed by Grunig and Hunt as described in Chapter 1 of this book. Figure 4.6 illustrates this development. In this representation 'craft public relations' focuses on techniques or the technician role in which the effective use of communication techniques is seen as worthwhile in itself. 'Professional public relations', on the other hand, is seen to encompass a more strategic role where communication is used to resolve conflict and manage relationships with publics with the aim of achieving compliance (asymmetrical) or mutual problem solving (symmetrical) within a context where both organisations and publics are liable to change.

Communication in organisations

Van Riel (1995) identifies three forms of corporate communication:

- *Management communication* is essentially about obtaining co-operation and support; organisational managers need to obtain understanding and consent from internal stakeholders for organisational objectives to be achieved. Externally management communication is about communicating organisational vision to win the support of external stakeholders.
- *Marketing communication* is used to support the selling of goods or services. (This includes identifying customer needs.)
- *Organisational communication* is a general term that covers public relations, public affairs, investor relations, internal communication and corporate advertising. Most of these activities Van Riel states to be within the remit of public relations.

Varey and White (2000) narrow this down to two inter-related communication systems.

- *Internal systems* aim to enable the organisation to meet its goals by gathering and interpreting data on expectations, attitudes and conditions from the external environment via external communication channels.
- *External systems* aim to present information about the internal processes of the organisation to the external environment in an attempt to influence the behaviour of various publics.

Two questions therefore need to be asked: who are these 'publics'? and what are the communication channels? The Esman categorisation referred to earlier in this chapter answers the first question. The second question would require a list covering several pages and that would be inappropriate here. Many of the channels used are described later in this book, but some of the most commonly used in public relations are the media, conferences and exhibitions, direct literature, sponsorship, in-house journals, corporate identity programmes, special events, corporate advertising and the internet.

Bernstein (1984) has devised a wheel to illustrate the link between an organisation (the hub), its publics (the rim) and the channels (the spokes) it uses to communicate

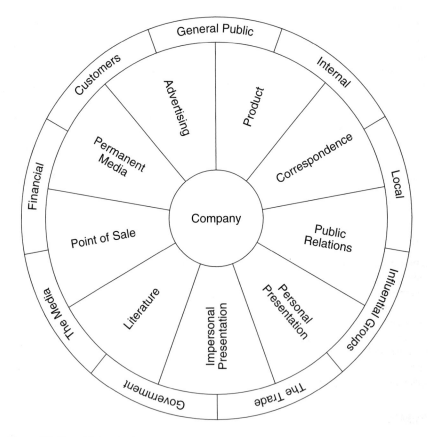

Figure 4.7 Bernstein's wheel

Source: Bernstein 1984: 118. Used by permission of Continuum Publishers

with these audiences (Figure 4.7). He suggests that each channel be borne in mind when an organisation considers communicating with its publics. His wheel shows that the communicator has $9 \times 9 = 81$ combinations of channel and audience – a formidable array of choices. Added to these are the intra-channel choices, for example the channel 'public relations' provides numerous tactical options. This model provides a clear demonstration of the scope and complexity of the public relations role.

Influences on public relations priorities in organisations

Public relations practice varies from organisation to organisation. There is no single blueprint for either the structure or the range of activities that should be undertaken, and priorities will differ in every organisation. There are a number of influences that will establish priorities for public relations programmes in an organisation and determine the way it is practised. Some of the most significant are given here.

Sector

Working in a well-established, stable sector will be more conducive to planned and sustained public relations programmes. New, fast growing and turbulent sectors such as the dot.com environment will require fast-moving, reactive as well as proactive programmes. Neither type of environment requires the public relations effort to be more or less strategic, but the speed of development and the in-built capability to change direction quickly will be more of a prerequisite in the latter.

Working in different sectors requires different emphases too. A manufacturer or retailer of fast-moving consumer goods could well require a heavier marketing communication focus whereas working for a trade or professional body may mean that membership communication or lobbying are the primary public relations activities.

Public relations for the public or not-for-profit sector, where public accountability is critical, generates one way of working whereas working in the private sector where shareholder accountability and profits are key generates a different set of priorities.

Size

Small organisations will have a small multi-skilled public relations department, indeed public relations may be subsumed into another department, typically marketing, or be a part of a single individual's job. It may even be outsourced to an individual or consultancy. The range of activities may well be restricted and undertaken by a public relations generalist. However, their input may have significant importance because the role of every individual is central to the operation of the whole organisation. Large organisations will have larger public relations departments. Within those departments the public relations remit will be broken down into task or functional areas with individual specialists taking on specific roles (see Chapter 1).

Publics

The range of public relations activities can be influenced significantly by the types of public involved. A number of factors need to be considered.

- Range, that is, the breadth of publics involved. Some organisations, for example niche manufacturers of space components, may have a limited range of publics. Others, for example the Department of Health, have an extended range of publics.
- Numbers and location. Some organisations have publics that form fairly discrete blocks, for example car dealers have groups of customers, suppliers and employees. Others, for example public relations consultants, will have a range of publics attached to each project. Some organisations have publics in a wide geographical area or several socio-economic bandings. Others focus on concentrated areas.
- Influence and power. There are publics which, although small, can gain a great deal of influence and power, for example pressure groups, especially if they enlist public support. Shell's reversal of its decision to sink the Brent Spar oil platform was forced by Greenpeace effectively galvanising public opinion.
- Connection with organisation. Employees are an example of a public intimately connected with an organisation. Other publics will have a more remote connection – again pressure groups are an example.

All these factors dictate the range and nature of the public relations programme that needs to be planned and implemented.

Development stage

Public relations activities are often dictated by the stage of development that the organisation has reached.

- Start-up. Usually organisations start small. The owners know suppliers, customers and employees. The public relations effort will often be one-to-one and the emphasis is often on growth, thus marketing communication will be a priority.
- Growth. More employees, customers and suppliers mean that one-to-one communication becomes difficult. At this stage a generalist public relations professional may be engaged to raise awareness of the company, its products and services. Internally, the formal communication programme may begin. Activities such as community relations and government and financial public relations are likely to be low priority if done at all.
- Maturity. Now the organisation is likely to be well established. The range of public relations activities will be expanding and could include financial public relations if a floatation is being considered. Employee communication is likely to be well developed, community relations will be a part of the agenda as the organisation takes on a corporate social responsibility agenda and developing and maintaining a cohesive corporate identity will be a priority. The in-house department of several staff, usually with specialisms, could well be complemented by engaging public relations consultancies to work in such areas as government affairs and investor relations.
- Decline. Open organisations usually avoid decline by adjusting their activities or moving into new areas. However, organisations do move into periods of temporary or permanent decline, for example through takeover, legislative change or bad management. Here public relations has a key role to play in identifying issues in the environment in order to avert crises. Ultimately, there is nothing public relations can do if a business is non-viable. However, it is possible to exit with dignity and with reputation intact, and public relations has a key role to play. Furthermore, if

an organisation has been unsuccessful in defending itself against a hostile takeover bid, the public relations teams in the acquired and acquiring company have a critical role in re-building the confidence and commitment of the acquired company's stakeholders and in building a new and successful corporate culture and identity.

Public relations and links to other functions

To complete this chapter on the role of public relations in organisations it is important to look briefly at links to other functions. There are three areas where there are clear links and overlaps and occasionally conflicts.

Public relations and marketing departments

It is the relationship between public relations and marketing that usually takes up most space and generates most heat. There have been extended and at times unprofitable debates about whether public relations is a part of marketing or marketing is a part of public relations: just three themes are identified for discussion here.

Terminology
To public relations people, public relations means managing the total communication of an organisation with all its publics. To most marketers public relations means publicity, that is, obtaining (usually) media coverage in support of products and services. To distinguish between public relations in its broad strategic sense and public relations as a part of the marketing communications mix, the latter has been called marketing public relations (MPR) (for example, Fill 1999).

Again, public relations professionals have tended to restrict the meaning of marketing to the notion of a profit-based exchange between an organisation and its customers. This is now an outmoded concept. Marketing has broadened its parameters to include relationships with internal customers (employees) and the broader external stakeholder community. As organisations become more open, more porous and often smaller, the justification for distinct functions is less and less clear. Furthermore, employees are usually required to be multi-skilled and flexible. Even so, different professional outlooks do maintain diverse perspectives which are of value to organisations.

The fact is that in modern organisations functions need to be integrated to be effective. A visitor to a website is not at all concerned if it is the marketing or the public relations department who has designed it and put together its content, as long as information needs are satisfied. What is obviously clear is that internally there needs to be a clear understanding of the roles of each discipline and where the responsibilities lie.

Encroachment
Public relations professionals fear 'encroachment' or the taking over of the discipline by non-specialists, especially marketers, but also management consultants. However, there is rejoicing when a public relations professional is made a chief executive or director of corporate communications (with marketing as a subservient partner). What is good for public relations is that as many people as possible from as many disciplines as possible are aware of the contribution that public relations can make in both strategic and tactical ways.

Status

For some public relations professionals it is important that public relations is seen to be a dominant and ascendant communication discipline. It is a sign that public relations has come of age that its unique contribution in stakeholder relations is recognised.

Some go further and say that the internet age requires the sophistication and knowledge of public relations professionals to handle the very complex world of internet communication, and the power plays between internet groups and their interaction with the organisation. It is true that the dialogue skills that public relations staff acquire with a range of stakeholder groups will be invaluable, but organisations also need to sell or obtain support for their products and services to survive. A good general reputation, often maintained through sustained public relations activity, will attract customers and users of services. Good service and products enhance reputation. Organisations need both marketing and public relations.

Public relations and human resources departments

There are potential areas for co-operation and conflict between these domains:

- Structural re-organisation. The human resources department has a clear role *vis à vis* contracts and liabilities in situations where there are mergers, lay-offs, acquisitions and re-organisation. The communication aspects of these matters, including how to communicate with employees and external stakeholders, would normally involve public relations expertise.
- Internal communication. Control of employee communication and the division between what is rightly communicated by human resources and public relations are areas of potential debate.
- Community relations. This might involve communication with employees who are located within the local community and also with potential employees, and again require careful assignment of responsibility for communication.

Again, as with marketing, it is important that each area recognises the expertise and contribution that they and their fellow professionals can make. It is also vital that, as with all good public relations, a frequent, honest dialogue is maintained with a willingness on both sides to give ground in order for the organisation's best interests to be served.

Public relations and legal departments

When organisations are under threat or handling crises there is often a tendency to turn to legal counsel. Legal concerns normally revolve around liability and risk and the natural instinct in the past has been to close down communication with the legendary 'no comment'. Lawyers are concerned that what is said may rebound on the organisation and often point out that there is no requirement to say anything.

However, there is an increasing recognition that corporate responsibility requires a more helpful response and that public interest should be served by providing information. 'No comment' implies something to hide, and will be seen as obstructive or insensitive by many stakeholders.

Public relations professionals are aware that expressions and demonstrable actions of sensitivity, concern and responsibility enhance reputation. They value openness and want to maintain dialogue. They are also acutely aware of the need to respond quickly to given situations – again the legal process usually takes time.

The recent trend has been for public relations professionals and legal advisors to work together in difficult situations. Product recalls and libel cases usually include both a public relations and a legal dimension and it is not uncommon for legal representatives and public relations professionals to speak on the same issue for an organisation. Again, the touchstone is a clear understanding of roles, and a recognition of the contribution of each specialist, cemented by regular and open dialogue.

Conclusions

This chapter has argued that there is a major strategic role for public relations in organisations. As expert boundary-spanners, public relations professionals can play a key role in the dominant coalition by gathering and interpreting information from the external and internal environments and presenting this as strategic intelligence. On the basis of this, organisations can adapt and change or initiate a dialogue so that the continued support of their key stakeholding publics can be assured.

It has also been demonstrated that public relations practitioners' roles vary according to the remit they are given in organisations. If restricted to the tactician role, they will never provide the full benefits that an organisation can derive from public relations, that is, intimate knowledge of key stakeholder attitudes and behaviour, issues management and a proactive stance towards a changing environment.

The range of channels of communication has been briefly discussed and public relations activity contextualised by the type of organisation within which it is situated. This has clearly demonstrated the variety of range and emphasis that public relations can have and has indicated the panoply of skills the expert practitioner requires.

Finally, the link between public relations and other disciplines has been commented on. The plea is for mutual understanding, recognition, respect and co-operation with fellow professionals for the benefit of the organisation. In short there is a call for genuine public relations within the management context.

5 Professionalism and regulation

··

The growth of social responsibility in public relations has led to a feeling amongst practitioners that they should be recognised as professionals, despite the origins of the industry in press agentry. Indeed, Cutlip *et al.* (1985: 17–19) suggest that 'Many credit public relations for heightened attention to social and public responsibilities amongst government administrators and business executives. They also point out the role that public relations plays in making organisations responsive to public interests'. They go on to suggest that the latter contributes to making the democratic process more effective. 'Social responsibility drives development of the body of knowledge underpinning public relations practice and continues the professionalisation of its practitioners.'

Professionalism

··

The *Concise Oxford Dictionary* definition of profession is 'a vocation or calling, especially one that involves some branch of advanced learning or science'. Some practitioners, who see themselves as creative rather than scientific, have resisted the general feeling that public relations is maturing into a profession. The growth of degrees at both undergraduate and masters level and the development of vocational qualifications have been greeted with suspicion rather than as evidence of professionalism (see Chapter 20).

Originally, the professions were law and medicine, and were practised by the sons of wealthy landowners after they had been to Oxford or Cambridge university. Private income was necessary as the professions offered little pay. Later, specialised knowledge became the basis for entry (Cutlip *et al.* 1985).

Elton (1993: 137) suggests the following prerequisites for a profession:

- an underlying discipline or cognitive base
- a body of practitioners
- a disciplinary organisation
- induction, training and licensing of members
- communication channels between members
- rewards and sanctions for members

- self-reflection, leading to improvement
- corporate evaluation and feedback
- a code of ethics and accountability to the profession
- corporate accountability to society
- quality assurance of the profession
- the ability to ensure high standards of remuneration.

Cutlip *et al.* (1985: 72) set out this list of related but differing conditions:

- specialised educational preparation to acquire knowledge and skills based on a body of theory developed through research
- provision of a unique and essential service that is recognised as such by the community
- an emphasis on public service and social responsibility
- autonomy and personal responsibility of members
- a self-governing association of colleagues to enforce codes of ethics and standards of performance.

The establishment of professional bodies in the UK, Europe and the USA have led to the introduction of codes of conduct, and calls for regulation of certain parts of the industry such as lobbyists. The Institute of Public Relations in the UK is over 50 years old, having been established in 1948 by a group of practitioners, with aims such as 'to provide a professional structure for the practice of public relations' and 'to enhance the ability and status of our members as professional practitioners'.

Grunig and Hunt (1984: 4) put forward the view that PR is a young profession, and only really started to approach that status in the 1980s:

The profession has its roots in press agentry and propaganda, activities that society generally holds in low esteem. Most of its practitioners have little training in the social sciences. Few have been trained in public relations ... We must admit that many people today who call themselves public relations practitioners still do not measure up to professional standards.

They continue,

True professionals possess a body of knowledge and have mastered communication techniques that are not known by the average citizen. They also have a set of values and a code of ethics that discourage the use of their knowledge and technical skills for antisocial purposes.

Kitchen (1997: 301) states 'It is now evident that public relations is an exiting contemporary managerial discipline with many skills, techniques and strategies to offer to business organisations in both a corporate and marketing communications domain.'

In this chapter we will examine some of the areas in which PR is addressing the question of professionalism.

Entry qualifications

One element of a claim to a professional status is an emphasis on well-qualified prac-
titioners. Years of training are necessary to become a doctor, lawyer or accountant,
followed by more years of on-the-job training.

Public relations education is more developed in the USA, where university-level
courses date from 1920, with early courses in publicity being offered at the University
of Illinois and Indiana University. The first PR course was offered in the journalism
department of the New York University School of Commerce, Accounts and Finance,
taught by Edward Bernays. Courses tended to be part of journalism qualifications, with
students able to specialise in PR through taking options. The 1981 Commission on
Public Relations Education recommended that the content of undergraduate and post-
graduate courses should include mass communications, PR theories, media relations
techniques, research methodology, case studies, work placements and PR management
(Cutlip *et al.* 1985). A further commission in 1987 added ethics, law and evaluation to
the list (IPRA 1990). This was updated by the work of the Public Relations Education
Commission set up by the Public Relations Society of America (PRSA) in 1999, which
looked at the knowledge and skills which should be included in undergraduate and
postgraduate courses. Business context, finance, communication theory and a supervised
work placement in practice were felt important at degree stage, with the emphasis
shifting to management science and research design at postgraduate level (Commission
of PR Education 1999).

The International Public Relations Association (IPRA) published guidelines for PR
education in 1990. They stated that

> public relations courses should be taught by individuals with a sound experience
> and understanding of both the academic and professional aspects of the field . . . We
> also strongly recommend [teachers] to continue to develop their professional experi-
> ence while they hold teaching appointments.
>
> (IPRA 1990)

The IPRA wheel of education is shown in Figure 5.1.

Some trades have achieved chartered status, such as the Chartered Institute of
Marketing. This necessitates having a majority of practitioners with a relevant voca-
tional qualification, as well as an emphasis on continuous professional development.

A number of years ago, the Institute of Public Relations (IPR) expressed its inten-
tion to achieve chartered status. It was felt that this would raise the status of the profes-
sion in general, as well as that of the Institute. The IPR moved towards tightening its
entry requirements. From 1992, if they had less than ten years experience in public
relations, all full members had to have a relevant vocational qualification.

The Public Relations Education Trust (PRET), a joint body set up by the IPR and
the Public Relations Consultants Association (PRCA), developed an education training
matrix, which set out the content felt necessary to give a good grounding for those in
the industry. Using this matrix as a base, the IPR approved six courses in 1989, including
vocational, undergraduate, postgraduate and masters programmes in the UK. The criteria
for approval have been revised and updated, and cover the content of the course, the
qualifications and experience of the teaching staff, links with industry, the inclusion of
some form of practical work experience and the employment record of those who
complete the course. Since then, the number of approved courses has risen to eighteen.
(A list of approved courses is available on the IPR website at <www.ipr.org.uk>.)

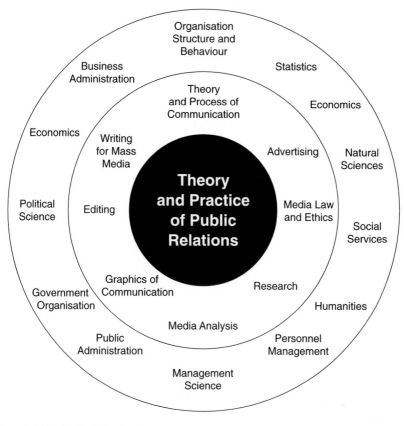

Organisation
Structure and
Behaviour

Business
Administration

Statistics

Theory
and Process of
Communication

Economics

Economics

Writing
for Mass
Media

Advertising

Natural
Sciences

**Theory
and Practice
of Public
Relations**

Political
Science

Editing

Media Law
and Ethics

Social
Services

Graphics of
Communication

Research

Government
Organisation

Humanities

Media Analysis

Public
Administration

Personnel
Management

Management
Science

Figure 5.1 IPRA wheel of education

On completion of one of these, there is still a requirement for up to four years' experience in PR before full membership is awarded. In 1998, the IPR also introduced its own qualification, the IPR Foundation Diploma and Diploma, which provides a part-time route to qualification for those who are already working in the profession and who are unable to return to full-time education. Mindful of the need to maintain standards in its delivery, these courses are only available at a few venues (again, details on the IPR website).

There are still many in the industry who do not have a relevant qualification, although with the numbers of graduate entrants rising, there are few who do not have any qualifications at all. Although it is still possible to enter the profession without a degree, the increasing numbers of graduates who are applying to work in PR mean that this route is becoming more difficult. The IPR's membership survey in 1998 showed that 36 per cent had a first degree and that 20 per cent had a further degree as well. IPR research carried out in 1999 found that 98 per cent of senior managers in the industry expected entrants to have a degree (IPR 1999). Few consultancies or in-house departments have a specifically designed graduate training scheme in public relations, but this may have to change as graduates begin to demand more thorough training. At the

moment, where training does occur it often tends to be *ad hoc*. The IPR and the PRCA took part in several debates on the questions of training, organised by the trade journal *PR Week* as part of its Best Practice campaign. This has led to a major initiative to improve the commitment to training within the industry. The IPR has also started to benchmark the provision of commercial training organisations with its Approved Training Provider kitemark.

Research and the body of knowledge

There has been a rather uneasy link between academic research, PR theory and practice in the UK, with many practitioners resistant to the idea that PR could be taught (see Chapter 20).

Cutlip *et al.* (1985: 467) suggest that 'Public relations education has advanced faster than the body of knowledge supporting the practice.' The US Commission on Public Relations Education reported

> Most public relations educators – not having attained PhD level – have not been required to do research . . . most are teaching skills courses that have little relationship to basic research. Public relations practitioners . . . have generally been too busy at their jobs to engage in basic research, not connected with specific public relations tasks.
>
> (IPRA 1990: 21)

There are signs that the body of knowledge in PR is growing, and that academics and practitioners are more willing to enter into a dialogue, but progress, as discussed in Chapter 20, is slow.

Training and professional development

Bines and Watson (1992) suggest three models of professional education. The first is apprenticeship or pre-technocratic, where professional education takes place mainly on the job, with some associated learning through day release at a relevant institution. The emphasis is on practical techniques. The technocratic model is more associated with professions, and consists of a systematic knowledge base founded on academic disciplines, the application of that base to practice, and supervised placements in practice. This most closely reflects the systems of IPR approved courses mentioned above. The third model, or post-technocratic, emphasises professional competence and bridges the gap between education and employment. There is still a debate on what constitutes competence, and difficulties in identifying the competences needed. The development of National Vocational Qualifications (NVQs) in PR had limited success. Although the qualifications were initially adopted, they were discontinued by the Qualifications and Curriculum Authority due to poor take-up.

To address the issue of lifelong learning, in April 2000 the IPR introduced Developing Excellence, a continuous professional development (CPD) scheme. This scheme, whilst initially voluntary, aims to encourage members to continue their development by undergoing vocational training, achieving subsequent academic qualifications, participating in the work of the IPR and contributing expertise to public relations students.

By ensuring that its members are properly qualified and engaged in current training, the IPR aims to ensure that they will be professional in their business conduct, and that

clients and employers will be able to use the standard of membership as an indicator that they are employing a competent practitioner.

A substantial amount of background research was done to inform the scheme, giving rise to four suggested levels of development:

Level 1 up to six years in PR (given that to gain membership of the IPR, several years of experience are necessary) or PR executive

Level 2 6–9 years in PR, or account manager or PR officer

Level 3 9–15 years in PR, or account director or head of department

Level 4 over 15 years in PR, or board member, managing director, chief executive

Particular skills are included at each level, from basic media training at level 1 to strategic issues management and board skills at level 4. All IPR workshops now carry an indication of their level, and the overall structure can be used by both individuals and companies when planning their training requirements. Courses of the Approved Training Providers are also linked to level and subject. The framework has been constantly updated, and contains an indication of the skills needed to ensure that PR practitioners can use new technology (see later discussions on the implications of new technology in Chapters 18, 19 and 20).

Crispin Manners, chair of the PRCA Professional Practices Committee, feels that the quality of people coming into PR is higher than ten years ago.

It is now a challenge to make sure that they stay. Five years ago, PRCA members were spending only ½% of their payroll on training, whereas management consultants recommend about 8 per cent. The criteria for the government's Investors in People (IP) emphasise developing employees. The PR sector has seen consistent growth. In 1999, there was 17% growth in the fee income of the top 50 consultancies, the year before that 10%. However, the industry has not been able to tool up fast enough to satisfy demand. This will need to change.[1]

Professional bodies and representation

The PRCA is the trade body for consultancies in the UK, and members are companies rather than individuals. It has strict criteria for membership, and is developing a Diploma in Consultancy Management. While the IPR has a Code of Conduct, the PRCA has a Professional Charter and Consultancy Management Standard which its members are obliged to follow. We will look at the content of these codes below. One problem with the raising of standards within PR is that these organisations do not represent all of those working in PR in the UK. The IPR has over 6,000 members, of which around 1,000 are students on the approved courses. The PRCA has 150 members, who represent around 6,500 staff, some of whom will also be individual IPR members. The size of the PR industry is subject to debate, with various figures being used. The size of the circulation of the trade publication *PR Week* is often used as a guide, and this is currently 17,500. Many people may work in a public relations capacity for an organisation, but may not be called a public relations practitioner. Some estimates of the numbers in PR are as high as 40,000, but around 20,000 would probably be more accurate. Despite the numbers game, it can be seen that the two associations account for a maximum of two-thirds of the industry. The requirements for qualification and professional and ethical behaviours can only apply to their own members. Likewise

with the requirements on members who engage in lobbying or investor relations activity – only those in membership can be held responsible.

Other influential professional bodies include the PRSA, which with 20,000 members is the largest association of individual practitioners in the world. It was founded in 1948 by the merger of the National Association of Public Relations Counsel and the American Council on Public Relations. In 1966, the PRSA merged with the American Public Relations Association to form a strong national association. The PRSA signed an agreement with the IPR in April 2000 which stated the intention of both bodies to co-operate in the fields of professional practice, training and education.

IPRA was founded in 1955 with only 15 members in five countries. Although still small by national association criteria, the organisation represents around 700 members in over 70 countries, although there has been talk of it merging with the IPR as the latter adopts a more global outlook.

Codes of practice

The IPR Code of Practice covers conduct relating to the practice of PR, how the practitioner deals with the media, the public, employers, clients and colleagues. The member is required to 'uphold the highest standards in the practice of public relations', and to bring neither the Institute nor the profession into disrepute. Professional activities must be conducted with 'proper regard to the public interest', and any conflict of interest must be declared. Members 'have a positive duty at all times to respect the truth and shall not disseminate false or misleading information knowingly or recklessly, and take proper care to check all information prior to its dissemination'. The latter clause is to counter public relations critics who regard it as 'spin', 'gloss', or lies.

There are several clauses which deal with the disclosing of interests. Interests of members who hold public office should be disclosed in the IPR Register of Interests and members should not undertake work which would have an improper influence on government or legislation. Discrimination on any grounds is unacceptable professional practice. Members are expected to keep confidences and not disclose them to other parties for financial advantage. Conditions to be taken into account when negotiating fees for work are set out. Members must also be aware of legislation relating to copyright and not plagiarise others' work or ideas, nor denigrate another member's expertise in order to gain work from a client or employer. Other recommended practice papers issued by the IPR cover public relations and the law; the role and parameters of PR practice; the use of embargoes, fees and methods of charging; and one of the major issues which the IPR has been campaigning against, the use of charges for inclusion of editorial in certain publications. The IPR undertook a major consultation on its Code in 2000, and the revised Code is published on its website.

The PRCA's Professional Charter covers similar ground, and indeed many of the clauses are identical. Of course, the Charter is written with the members in mind, and these are consultancies rather than individuals. Terms can be negotiated on the basis of the complexity of the issue and the difficulties associated with its completion; the specialised skills needed and the time to be spent; the amount of documentation needed; the place and circumstances where the work is to be carried out; and the value of the task to the client. Accuracy, openness about interests and regard to the public interest are also stressed. The PRCA also has specific codes which relate to investor relations, healthcare and parliamentary advice, which are in addition to the provisions of the Professional Charter. The specifics of these codes are concerned with the particular

environments and sensitivities that exist. There are recommendations for those in investor relations about dealing with price sensitive information. Healthcare professionals are directed to legislation and other relevant codes, and must ensure balanced and accurate information is given. Parliamentary lobbyists have an extensive code which relates to their conduct towards MPs and clients.

As Crispin Manners says

> There is an aspiration in the industry to become a profession. The quality of consultancy has improved over the past few years, but there is an increasing gulf between those who are keen to add value and to make that value tangible, and those who want to continue to trade on some black box mystique. The latter are dinosaurs.

In 1973, IPRA undertook a survey of its members in 46 counties, and found that of the 26 countries which replied, only 82 per cent had adopted a Code of Ethics and only 27 per cent had referred to ethics in their annual reports. In 38 per cent of the countries, PR had been criticised for unethical conduct (Lloyd 1973). 'Ethical codes can make unethical behaviour less likely ... but cannot make ethical people out of unethical ones', said John Budd (1994: 2).

Regulation of practice

Both associations have Professional Practice committees, to which complaints can be made if a breach of the codes of practice is discovered. However, as Director General of the IPR, Colin Farrington, says

> We are not equipped with police powers to investigate, and are reliant on complaints before we act. Whilst some might feel that as we are not a statutory body our disciplinary procedures are our own affair, the courts would expect us to act in a defensible way. If the disciplinary procedure resulted in a public reprimand or expulsion from the Institute, it would affect people's business and reputation.

Crispin Manners is keen that it is not just seen as a way to police bad behaviour, but also to promote and educate members and their employees to work within the Professional Charter. 'We try to fulfil the role of a private arbitrator, and if that doesn't work, to encourage the use of a public arbitration service.' Most of the problems which his committee has had to investigate have been cases resulting from poor systems of consultancy management, rather than problems of bad behaviour or ethics. To remedy this, the Consultancy Management Standard (CMS) was devised, and by the end of 2000, all PRCA members had to conform to it or be disqualified from membership. There are ten elements in the CMS, and member consultancies must score at least 50 per cent in each section to pass. The first element concerns the business plan, the next financial systems. Other sections cover audited accounts, the minimum annual fee income of £200,000, minimum levels of staffing, adherence to the Professional Charter, and campaign evaluation. Client satisfaction must be measured and service delivery monitored. A commitment to training and development is also included.

Some of the problem has lain with the question of what is and what is not acceptable in public relations. 'People are paid to be creative, and it's highly competitive. What is the difference between a PR stunt and a campaign? The rules have been established as we have gone along', says Colin Farrington. 'Although PR consultancies

may deal with people better than other kinds of organisation and are better creatively, they have not necessarily been noted as successful businesses and professional practitioners', says Crispin Manners.

> There is universal agreement that if anyone fell foul of the Charter, the Association will take action. Years ago the PRCA and the IPR were old boys' clubs, now that is long gone. We all live by the same laws of business management and can't afford to do something that would damage brand awareness. A lot of people have put a lot of work into developing the professional standards, and we are committed to upholding them.

Credibility of practitioners

'Honesty begins at home. It is synonymous with trust and trust is the lubricant that makes our practice function.' Despite this aspiration, John Budd (1994: 5) relates the example of Hill & Knowlton chief Robert Dilenschneider who in 1988 warned against

> twisting the facts 'a little'; unquestionably doing the unquestionable thing; ducking the truth, doing anything you knew 'in your bones' was wrong. Two years later [he] . . . advocates an array of highly questionable stratagems . . . publicly attack the competitor; steal his best people; insert Quislings into his ranks; and pre-empt his access to the media.

The conduct and regulation of lobbyists has been a key issue in raising questions about the ethical conduct of those engaged in public affairs. Back in 1956, Tim Traverse Healey warned that 'the further development of public relations depends on the confidence of the community in the integrity of our practitioners' (quoted in Budd 1994: 4). In the run up to the general election in 1997 a number of MPs lost their seats as a result of revelations in the media that some firms had allegedly been involved in paying them to raise questions in the House, whilst Ian Greer Associates, a long standing firm of lobbyists, was forced out of business. Subsequently, one of Labour's parliamentary aides, Derek Draper, was accused of boasting that he could secure access to Ministers for those who wanted to make their case. He was forced to resign. The various cases caused a media frenzy about 'spin doctors' and lobbyists, with calls for more regulation and slurs cast upon public relations practitioners of all kinds, not just those engaged in public affairs.

In October 1994, the then Prime Minister John Major set up the Committee on Standards in Public Life under Lord Nolan, to try and counter the poor reputation of some Conservative MPs that threatened, and indeed may have contributed to, the downfall of his government in the election in May 1997. The Committee's terms of reference were

> To examine current concerns about standards of conduct of holders of public office, including arrangements relating to financial and commercial activities, and make recommendations as to any changes in present arrangements which might be required to ensure the highest standards of propriety in public life.

The Nolan Committee published four reports from May 1995 to November 1997, covering the conduct of MPs, Ministers, quangos, civil servants, local government, NHS trusts and other public spending bodies. The first report recommended a ban on advocacy

by MPs on behalf of companies and organisations with which they had a paid relationship. It also suggested that MPs should be banned from making any links to political lobbying firms.

The Committee continued under the new Labour government with Lord Neill as chair, with an additional task given by Prime Minister Tony Blair to 'review issues in relation to the funding of political parties, and to make recommendations as to any changes in present arrangements'. A further report on this topic was published in October 1998. A review paper was then published, and further evidence was sought by May 1999.

Submissions were made to the Neill Committee by the IPR, PRCA and the Association of Professional Political Consultants (APPC). A statutory regulation of lobbyists which proposed that the disclosure of clients' identities would be required conflicted with Law Society rules. The three bodies stated that they had adopted supplementary and virtually identical codes to govern practice in this area. The APPC also made clear that its members are not permitted to have financial arrangements with members of parliament or peers. In evidence to the Neill Committee (19 July 1999), Michael Burrell said,

It is now widely accepted across the industry that it would be better if there were not such financial relationships, that there is no need for such financial relationships, that what they tend to do is embarrass the parties involved and that we can do our job without them.

International problems with recognition

The question of mutual recognition of qualifications across the European Community and globally is thorny and as yet unresolved. In some countries such as Switzerland, where only 17 people are qualified to join the Confédération Europenne de Relations Publiques (CERP) and so practise PR, there is stringent regulation of the PR industry. Colin Farrington is also wary of introducing conditions that might be construed as a barrier to trade across the EU: 'Also, if all qualifications are of equal standard, then it implies what is meant by public relations should be the same everywhere. There is some work going on in CERP to try and establish an agreement on that definition.'

Social accountability

The concerns of the public relations industry to be seen as an ethical profession are reflected in the work of the Trade and Industry Select Committee in the area of social accountability. This has given rise to the Ethical Trade Initiative, which has formulated guidelines for retailers, suppliers and manufacturers covering health and safety, workers' pay and conditions, child labour and the environment. Martin O'Neill, MP, speaking at a conference on social accountability in January 1999, described social accountability as the 'flavour of the month'. The concept of social accountability is becoming more widespread, and it is not only companies like the Body Shop and the Co-operative Bank that are setting up social auditing systems. A report was commissioned by BT at the beginning of 1997 to examine what roles companies could and should take in society, and whether undertaking these roles was good for business (Future Foundation 1998). (Related issues are discussed in Chapters 9 and 12 on

corporate social responsibility and community relations and corporate community involvement, respectively.)

In conclusion, PR possesses several of the prerequisites to be considered a profession, and the professional bodies show a clear desire to address the issues of entry, training and conduct of practitioners. They recognise that in order to achieve this, they must get the message across about ethical and professional working standards, to counter the historical beginnings of the industry in press agentry and publicity. Whether or not the IPR achieves chartered status, it has shown an increasing maturity in addressing the concerns of the industry as a whole, rather than concentrating simply on the concerns of its members. The problem, ironically in an industry which prides itself on the ability of its practitioners to communicate, is one of getting the message across to the relevant stakeholders in business and government.

Note

1 Unless otherwise stated, quotes are taken from interviews with the author.

Part II

Strategic public relations

6 Corporate communication

Emma Wood

Corporate communication is an instrument of management by means of
which all consciously used forms of internal and external communication
are harmonised as effectively and efficiently as possible, so as to create a
favourable basis for relationships with groups upon which the company is
dependent.

(van Riel 1995: 26)

V an Riel's definition of corporate communication is founded upon notions of
strategic management and relationship building; concepts explored in the previous
part of this book and exemplified in future chapters. The following case study
demonstrates the importance of a strategic approach to corporate communication and
illustrates what can happen if symmetrical or reciprocal relationships with key stake-
holders are not effectively managed.

The Bank of Scotland – a case study

The Bank of Scotland (BoS) is a leading UK clearing bank, headquartered in Edinburgh.
It employs around 21,000 people and has 325 high street branches (predominantly in
Scotland), issues a range of credit and charge cards (including cards to supporters of
nearly 500 affinity groups ranging from charities to universities) and is known for its
pioneering electronic and telephone home and office banking service.[1]

Its corporate statement clearly signifies a stakeholder approach to its business. It
specifies that the group aims:

- To meet its customers' needs by providing friendly, prompt, professional and imagina-
tive service
- To deliver a range of distinctive financial products and services throughout the United
Kingdom and internationally
- To train, develop, inform, encourage and respect staff so that they can perform an
effective and fulfilling role
- To maintain its reputation for integrity and stability

- To make a particular contribution to the cultural and economic prosperity in the local communities in which it operates.

(BoS website, July 2000)

In March 1999, the bank announced its intention to team up with US television evangelist Pat Robertson to set up a direct bank in the USA. The new bank would operate only through telephones and computers.

Robertson is well known in the USA as a religious broadcaster, entrepreneur and right wing politician who ran unsuccessfully for the US presidency in 1988. His Christian Broadcasting Network reaches 55 million viewers a year. As direct banking is less developed in the USA than in the UK, the combination of BoS expertise and Robertson's access to a vast network of potential customers seemed to guarantee a highly profitable business venture.

Soon after the announcement, the press published details about Robertson and his extreme right wing views. Robertson's attacks on homosexuals, feminists, Muslims, Hindus and other religious groups were reported, particularly in the Scottish media. Pressure groups were quick to publicly denounce Robertson, and the bank for being associated with him. Utilising the internet and other media, these groups co-ordinated attacks on the deal. They set up websites with links to the media and the bank to help the public to learn more about the issue and to register their condemnation. Direct action included calls for bank accounts to be closed and protesters handcuffing themselves to the bank's headquarters.

The bank remained adamant that it would not succumb to public or media pressure. Its PR strategy seemed to alternate between refusing to comment and blaming the media for distorting or exaggerating Robertson's views. Robertson's approach was similar; in addition he attempted to place legal restrictions on press reporting of his opinions. Far from diminishing interest or coverage of the issue this resulted in the media becoming more entrenched. Rather than being frightened off by threats of legal action, the media substantiated their attacks with evidence of Robertson's comments, using direct quotes from his TV shows, books and an open letter which claimed, 'The feminist agenda is not about equal rights for women. It is about a socialist anti-family political movement that encourages women to leave their husbands, kill their children, practice witchcraft, destroy capitalism and become lesbians' (*The Scotsman*, 24.4.99).

The bank was reported to believe that these views should not affect their potentially lucrative joint venture. Peter Burt, BoS chief executive, defended the deal by drawing a distinction between the intrinsic moral and ethical values of a commercial decision and the ethics of the individuals involved: 'An individual's personal religious views do not form the basis on which the bank makes its business and commercial judgement. And nor should it' (*The Scotsman*, 22.4.99). However, key opinion formers disagreed and major institutions began to publicly register their disapproval of the bank's association with Robertson.

The logical extension of this disapproval would be for these key institutions to disassociate themselves from the bank. Media coverage became dominated by reports of city councils, universities, trade unions, charities and churches threatening to close their accounts. Several high profile MSPs were happy to be named in condemning the deal and called for the Scottish Parliament's account to be removed from the bank if the deal went ahead (*The Scotsman*, 2.6.99).

The bank's defence of Robertson ceased in mid-May when he was reported as condemning Scotland as a 'dark land' overrun by homosexuals (*The Scotsman*, 2.6.99).

In early June the bank announced that it was abandoning its joint venture. A joint state-
ment said,

> Dr Pat Robertson and Peter Burt, following a meeting in Boston yesterday, agreed
> that the changed external circumstances made the proposed joint venture . . . unfeas-
> ible. In reaching this agreement Dr Robertson expressed regret that the media
> comments about him had made it impossible to proceed.
>
> *(The Scotsman, 7.6.99)*

The announcement was seen as terse by some, and interpreted as still blaming media
distortion for the failed venture rather than the bank fully condemning Robertson's
views. *The Scotsman* deemed it an 'apology that leaves a lot to be desired' (7.6.99),
the *Guardian*, 'a grudging, gritted-teeth apology' (19.6.99). Tim Hopkins of gay rights
campaigners Equality Network represented a number of views with his comments:

> People are still very angry with the bank and it will have its work cut out getting
> back their confidence. We would like to see the bank reaching out to minority groups
> to rebuild its reputation for equal opportunities, which before the Pat Robertson busi-
> ness was very good.
>
> *(The Scotsman, 7.6.99)*

It was only after a more full and personal apology was given to shareholders at the
annual general meeting, that public opinion was reported as mellowing towards the
bank. At the AGM, the bank's deputy-governor, Sir John Shaw, said:

> The board of the bank regrets any concern to customers, proprietors [shareholders]
> and staff caused by the events of the past few weeks. The bank failed to predict the
> strength of public reaction after announcing the deal with Dr Robertson. The last
> straw came when he described Scotland as an overly 'dark land'. We have a long-
> standing commitment to ethical values, tolerance, equal opportunities, and non-
> discrimination in all our dealings. Determination to uphold these principles as we
> develop our business world-wide will continue to characterise the Bank of Scotland.
>
> *(The Scotsman, 11.6.99)*

Analysis

This case study demonstrates several important aspects of corporate public relations
practice.

Reputation

> Better regarded companies build their reputations by developing practices that inte-
> grate economic and social considerations into their competitive strategies. They not
> only do things right – they do the right things. In doing so, they act like
> good citizens. They initiate policies that reflect their core values; that consider the
> joint welfare of investors, customers, and employees; that invoke concern for the
> development of local communities; and that ensure the quality and environmental
> soundness of their technologies, products and services.
>
> (Fombrun 1996: 8)

The aims outlined in the BoS's corporate statement reflect an understanding of this approach to reputation building. However, its actions (teaming up with Robertson and defending the deal by attempting to distinguish between the ethics of commercial decisions and the personal views of business partners) is not congruent with the core values its statement expresses. Its problems could be judged to have stemmed from its failure to 'integrate economic and social considerations'.

A consideration of the bank's withdrawal from the deal also provides a useful insight into this perspective of reputation building. The bank stood to make tens of millions of pounds' profit as a result of the Robertson deal, which would have resulted in the opening of millions of new accounts from American customers. At the time it withdrew from the venture, only 500 accounts had been closed by British customers (compared with more than 21,500 opened during the same period) (*Guardian*, 16.6.1999). Clearly the potential gains would vastly outweigh the losses. An analysis of the bank's early statements and subsequent apology seems to indicate that it did not abandon the deal because of ethical considerations. The motivation for the decision can be interpreted as stemming from concern that direct action from key stakeholders might escalate, irreparably damaging its British business (and profits). Clearly, the bank recognised its long-term reputation as being more valuable than the short-term profits it could have made as a result of going ahead with the venture.

The case not only illustrates how a reputation is earned (and damaged) but also its value and the relationship between a good reputation and profits. As Fombrun (1996: 81) explains,

> Corporate reputations have bottom line effects. A good reputation enhances profitability because it attracts customers to the company's products, investors to its securities, and employees to its jobs. In turn, esteem inflates the price at which a public company's securities trade. The economic value of a corporate reputation can therefore be gauged by the excess market value of its securities.

(See also the section on impact on share price, p. 72.)

Stakeholder approach

In his best-selling book *The State We're In*, Will Hutton argues for a democratic political economy that relates to the whole of British society. He criticises business for being short-termist and relentless in pursuit of some of the highest financial returns in the world: 'Companies are the fiefdoms of their Boards and sometimes of just their Chairmen; and companies are run as pure trading operations rather than productive organisations which invest, innovate and develop human capital' (Hutton 1996: 25).

In contrast to this view of companies being dominated only by the idea of improving returns for shareholders, the concept of stakeholding advocates a democratic approach to business which values relationships with a range of stakeholders.

The term stakeholder refers to groups or individuals who have an interest or stake in an entity such as an organisation, community or country. In corporate terms, a company's stakeholders typically include employees, suppliers, members of the local community and customers. Each of these groups can affect or are affected by the 'actions, decisions, policies, practices or goals of the organisation' (Freeman 1984, quoted in Grunig 1992: 126).

There is no firm consensus on the meaning of stakeholder theory.[2] It has been described variously as being based on Keynesian economics (Hutton 1996), communitari-

anism (rights matched by responsibilities) (Burkitt and Ashton 1996) and the Kantian notion of duty (as opposed to utilitarianism) (Etzioni 1988 in Burkitt and Ashton 1996; see also Chapter 9).

Burkitt and Ashton (1996: 10) describe New Labour's stakeholder economy as hinging on:

> the idea that many interest groups may be said to have a 'stake' in certain activities, not necessarily because they have a financial interest, but because they are affected by them. These stakes should be recognised by those whose actions may impinge upon them. Individuals should recognise that their behaviour can have repercussions upon society. They should act in a responsible way that does not damage others . . . Stakeholder firms must act with responsibility to their stakeholders.

In political terms, stakeholder theory is premised on the interelation of state, society and the economy as opposed to a 'free market' approach (where the market is not primarily concerned with notions of social responsibility and regulates itself through supply and demand rather than through state intervention). In the UK, the free market approach was advocated by Margaret Thatcher and the New Right, whereas stakeholder theory has been associated with New Labour's philosophy of social inclusion:

> It implies a third way that replaces both Old Labour's 'control' and the New Right's freemarketeering with 'voluntaristic morality'. It substitutes the 'realization of the individual through community' for the increasingly discredited New Right individualism and the Old Labour 'collective' that New Labour was keen to leave behind.
>
> (Burkitt and Ashton 1996: 8)

The concept of stakeholding is manifest in the Royal Society for the encouragement of Arts, Manufactures and Commerce (RSA) Inquiry into British business. The final report of this investigation, *Tomorrow's Company*, foregrounds the importance of developing reciprocal rather than adversarial relationships with – and between – employees, customers, suppliers, investors and the community in order to increase business performance and competitiveness.

The rationale for this approach is linked to the *death of deference* – employees, customers and communities increasingly expect individuals' needs and values to be respected. Other key concepts of the report include:

- *inclusive leadership* – the report calls for a shift from an emphasis on physical assets to realising the creative and learning potential of all people with whom the company interacts
- *sustainable development* – rather than looking for quick financial returns, companies should pursue development which can be sustained over time
- establishing a *'licence to operate'* – to be successful, organisations must maintain public confidence in the legitimacy of their operations and business conduct. 'Licence to operate' and competitiveness are closely linked.

Figure 6.1 identifies the external influences on a company's licence to operate, as set out in the RSA's *Tomorrow's Company* report, which states:

> A company which undermines its licence to operate by the wrong behaviour exposes itself to a range of sanctions. Whatever the issue – from animal rights to top

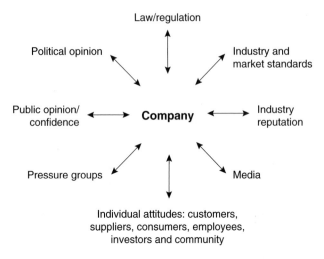

Figure 6.1 Various forces in the external environment combine to influence a company's
licence to operate

Source: RSA Inquiry 1995. Used by permission of the RSA

executives' pay – companies seen to be insenstitive to changing standards can find
themselves at the centre of public and media outcry.

(RSA 1995: 6)

The public and media outcry provoked by BoS's joint venture with Robertson certainly
bears this out. Indeed, the BoS could be deemed to have transgressed several of the
tenets of stakeholderism. Consequently, far from deferring to the bank's decision to go
ahead with the deal, a range of stakeholders publicly debated the bank's licence to
operate, and lack of public confidence in the moral legitimacy of the venture eventu-
ally resulted in its demise. Communities insisted on individuals' rights being respected,
and the bank conceded – preferring to find a new and less controversial partner than
Robertson, despite the millions of pounds which could have been quickly realised
through the proposed deal. The bank opted for sustainable development.

The RSA concept of inclusive management clearly resonates with Grunig and Hunt's
two-way symmetrical, ethical, model of public relations practice (see Chapter 2). Indeed,
just as Hutton argues for an end to short-termism in the financial community, Grunig
and Hunt's excellent model calls for public relations practitioners to take a long-term
view in managing organisational relationships with a range of stakeholders and publics.

Grunig and Repper distinguish between stakeholders and publics, arguing that
whereas many stakeholders are passive, publics are stakeholders who have become
aware or active in relation to an organisation: 'publics organise around issues and seek
out organisations that create those issues – to gain information, seek redress of griev-
ances, pressure the organisations, or ask governments to regulate them' (Grunig and
Repper 1992: 128).

'Excellent' practitioners, however, do not wait until publics are actively campaigning
before communicating with them. Effective public relations strategists are involved in
organisational decision making (see Chapter 4). Before decisions are made they would
draw a stakeholder map,[3] identifying their stakeholders, anticipating the ways in which

they may be affected by organisational decisions and how they would react to them. 'After thoroughly researching their stakeholders, public relations managers should rank or assign weights to them to indicate their impact on the organisation or the extent to which the organisation believes it should moderate its consequences on them' (Grunig and Repper 1992: 126).[4]

Grunig and Repper advocate a strategic approach to managing public relations based on research into stakeholder perceptions as illustrated in Figure 6.2. If the BoS used this type of strategic approach it is difficult to understand why it didn't either actively

1 *Stakeholder Stage*: An organisation has a relationship with stakeholders when the behaviour of the organisation or of a stakeholder has a consequence on the other. Public relations should do formative research to scan the environment and the behaviour of the organisations to identify these consequences. Ongoing communication with these stakeholders helps to build a stable, long-term relationship that manages conflict that may occur in the relationship.

2 *Public State*: Publics form when stakeholders recognise one or more of the consequences as a problem and organise to do something about it or them. Public relations should do research to segment and identify these publics. At this stage focus groups are particularly helpful. Communication to involve publics in the decision process of the organisation helps to manage conflict before communication campaigns become necessary.

3 *Issue Stage*: Publics organise and create 'issues' out of the problems they perceive. Public relations should anticipate these issues and manage the organisation's response to them. This is known as 'issues management'. The media play a major role in the creation and expansion of issues. In particular, media coverage of issues may produce publics other than activist ones – especially 'hot-issue' publics. At this stage, research should segment publics. Communication programmes should use the mass media as well as interpersonal communications with activists to try to resolve the issue through negotiation.

Public relations should plan communication programmes with different stakeholders or publics at each of the above three stages. In doing so it should follow steps 4–7.

4 Public relations should develop formal objectives such as communication, accuracy, understanding, agreement, and complementary behaviour for its communication programmes.

5 Public relations should plan formal programmes and campaigns to accomplish the objectives.

6 Public relations, especially the technicians, should implement the programmes and campaigns.

7 Public relations should evaluate the effectiveness of programmes in meeting their objectives and reducing the conflict produced by problems and issues that brought about the programmes.

Figure 6.2 The strategic management of public relations

Source: Grunig and Repper 1992: 124

manage its stakeholder relationships or 'moderate their consequences' on its stake-holders by deciding not to venture into a relationship with Robertson in the first place.

Stakeholder theory is used by public relations practitioners to inform a pragmatic, strategic approach to practice, but its implications are more far reaching. Stakeholding is 'intimately connected to societal values and power relations and interactive with them. Culture, polity and society are conceptualised as inextricably connected with the economy, each being highly interactive with each other' (Burkitt and Ashton 1996: 5). It remains to be seen how pervasive this philosophy is, but, as the BoS case illustrates, public relations practitioners ignore the values of stakeholding at their peril.

Impact on share price

Although it advocates a stakeholder approach to business, the RSA report does not disregard the shareholder. Indeed it argues that by adopting a stakeholder approach a company will be well managed and therefore able to deliver greater value to its share-holders. In contrast, 'organisations that continue to act as if shareholders are the only important group will colour the financial community's view of the quality of manage-ment and endanger the interests of the very group they seek to satisfy' (RSA 1995: 1). The effect of the Robertson venture on the BoS share price seems to bear this out. When the deal was first announced the share price rallied, but when public outcry emerged, it fluctuated – falling significantly following the publicity surrounding Robertson's 'dark land' comments.

Opinion formers

An analysis of the people and organisations that influenced the bank's decision is useful in identifying the range of opinion formers public relations practitioners should commu-nicate with. Council leaders, MSPs, church leaders, individual shareholders, the unions, pressure groups and civil rights leaders' views were all reported in the press.

New media

Email and the internet played an important role in the case. Not only did the internet enable pressure groups to mobilise public pressure; it also facilitated fast and effective access to information about the American preacher. For example, whilst Robertson complained about being misquoted, *The Scotsman* printed instructions for readers to download real-time video footage of the programme in which Robertson denounced Scotland as a 'dark land' (2.6.99).

Environmental scanning

At the AGM Sir John Shaw is reported as saying

> The bank was well aware that Mr Robertson was a controversial figure in the United States. We did not expect that the controversy he was associated with there would have transferred to here where he has no political constituency or business.

Critics could argue that in a global economy, geographical boundaries do not operate in the way Sir John had anticipated.

Effective public relations input at board level should have forewarned the bank that Robertson would be a controversial figure, particularly in the current business environ-

ment where discussions of ethical practice and social responsibility are prevalent on business and political agendas. The case serves as an effective argument that public relations expertise should be included in the strategic planning process and should be able to influence dominant coalition decision-making (see Chapter 4).

Crisis management

> If a company at the centre of a crisis is seen to be unresponsive, uncaring, inconsistent, confused, inept, reluctant or unable to provide reliable information, the damage inflicted on its reputation will be lasting – and measurable against the financial bottom line.
>
> (Regester and Larkin, in Kitchen 1997: 215)

'Tell it first, tell it fast' is one of the mantras of effective crisis management. However, both the bank and Robertson were often reported as being unresponsive, refusing to comment or blaming media distortion for their predicament. Eventually Robertson changed his PR approach and invited the press to America to visit his organisation and speak to him directly. However, media views were already entrenched.

The bank was also criticised for failing to apologise quickly enough to its customers for Robertson's offensive comments. As Dugdale Bradley, co-founder of Tomorrow's Company in Scotland, said: 'The bank did not come clean about it and apologise, like Perrier did in the Eighties. They have got in a muddle. But if people say "sorry, we made a mistake", people will be more forgiving' (*The Scotsman*, 12.6.99).

Commentators consider that a strong reputation helps companies survive crises with less financial loss. BoS's reputation was good before the Robertson debacle; it will be interesting to track how it weathers the storm and recovers its former position.

Best practice

Some of the approaches that the bank may use to rebuild its reputation are explored in the rest of this book.

A corporate reputation is an image developed over time. The next chapter examines whether corporate images can be managed, and subsequent chapters consider other aspects of corporate PR such as public affairs, issues management and corporate social responsibility. An effective communication strategy would also utilise the range of approaches for communicating with different stakeholder groups examined in Part III.

Notes

1 All figures published on the BoS website, July 2000 <www.bankofscotland.co>.
2 See Clarke (1997) for a useful analysis of different approaches to the concept of stakeholding.
3 For a comprehensive guide to stakeholder mapping see Johnson and Scholes (1999: 215–24).
4 Varey in Kitchen (1997: 89–110) provides a useful analysis of approaches to identifying, prioritising and communicating with stakeholders and publics.

7 Corporate identity

Emma Wood

M anaging corporate identity is about identifying the right image for an organ-
isation, and communicating it effectively. It is a vital aspect of motivating a
wide range of stakeholders (including voters, employees, shareholders and
consumers).

Nike is tough, aggressive and trendy. The Body Shop is socially responsible, it cares
about animals and the environment. Marks & Spencer is about conservative design,
good quality 'made in Britain' – or it used to be . . . At the time of writing, M&S can't
seem to decide what it stands for, and its fortunes are suffering as a result. Organisations
have personalities and the term 'corporate identity' refers to the combination of ways
in which this personality is expressed. As such, identity includes design aspects such
as logos, colour, typeface and house style but also embraces less tangible elements
such as behaviour, culture, values, mission, communication style and associations
(with personalities, charities, political parties or other organisations via donations or
sponsorship).

Red flag or red rose? Rule Britannia or cool Britannia? Getting the identity right is
strategically important. In a 1995 MORI poll, 166 senior people responsible for corpor-
ate identity in leading European companies rated the benefits of a strong corporate iden-
tity. Some of the results are shown in Table 7.1. Other benefits include helping
companies recover from crises and recruitment of top employees.

So, a strong corporate identity and positive corporate image are clearly beneficial.
But how easy are they to achieve? This chapter will explore the meaning of corporate
identity and image. It will then consider identity and image management and conclude
with a case study exploring an identity change programme.

Corporate identity v. corporate image

The terms 'corporate identity' and 'corporate image' are sometimes confused with each
other.[1] *Corporate identity* is what the organisation communicates (either intentionally or
unintentionally) via various cues, whereas its *image* is how its publics actually view it.
An image is a perception and exists only in the mind of the receiver. To formulate an
image, publics interpret an *identity* in a wider context with broader frames of reference.

For example, Nike's corporate identity is a carefully managed amalgam of associa-
tions (with fashionable sports personalities, major sporting events such as the Olympics

Table 7.1 Benefits of a strong corporate identity

	Percentage votes for each category by country		
	Great Britain	France	Germany
Public profile/recognition	53	23	68
Attracts customers/helps customer relations	30	10	3
Product/brand support	30	17	0
Visual presentation/unity	10	7	10
Financial advantages/ confidence among the financial community	20	23	6
Express culture/values	30	3	3
Staff motivation	10	3	23
Support for advertising/ communications	13	3	0

Source: adapted from Schmidt 1997: 42

as well as local and charitable events), clear design and mission. Many people exposed to these aspects of its identity may well formulate an image of Nike as a high quality and fashionable arbiter of good design. Others, aware of some negative media coverage of Nike's manufacturing policy in third world countries (interpreting the identity in a broader context), may form an image of Nike as exploitative and thus boycott its products.[2]

Clearly, then, organisations cannot *construct* a corporate image because they cannot control the context in which their communication is received, interpreted or understood. Nevertheless, a clear, well-managed corporate identity can go some way to effecting a strategically important image, and a neglected corporate identity may send out all the wrong messages. 'An organisation may commonly assume that it only communicates when it wants to, but unfortunately for many companies, a failure to control communications results in a confused image' (Ind 1990: 21).

But managing an identity well means embracing all aspects of what van Riel (1995) calls the corporate identity (CI) mix – symbolism, communication and behaviour. The Nike case illustrates this well. Despite well-managed *symbolism* and *communication*, perceptions of aspects of its *behaviour* (reported treatment of third world workers) has affected some publics' image of the company.

So, can corporate identity be effectively managed? And, if so, how?

Key concepts of corporate identity

Corporate identity management commonly involves:

- conducting research to determine senior management and a range of stakeholders'[3] views on an organisation's actual and desired image
- an audit of all elements of corporate identity to determine if they are congruent with the desired image
- formulating a plan to adjust the corporate identity if necessary.

It all seems simple enough. Clearly though, controlling identity is not simple or straight-forward. So, before considering the management process, it's important to consider a range of questions and issues.

Corporate strategy

One of the key issues of corporate identity management is its role in achieving overall organisational strategic objectives.[4] The aim of a corporate identity plan is to determine and communicate a corporate identity to meet these future strategic objectives. For example, the Labour Party's introduction of a new corporate identity in the 1990s (involving the introduction of a new logo, a red rose, and a new name, New Labour) was linked to its overall strategic plan to modernise the party to make it electable.

However, a number of thinkers in this area, most notably Grunig, would argue that the corporate identity management process should not just be designed to help implement a predetermined strategy. Instead, strategy should be formulated partly in response to stakeholders' needs and views. 'Excellent' organisations (Grunig 1992), practising a two-way symmetric[5] approach to communication management, should adapt their corporate strategies according to publics' opinions identified through research. Indeed, many would argue that the Labour Party's strategic objective to modernise was formulated in response to research conducted into publics' perceptions of the party's image.[6] Although few pundits deem the Labour Party 'excellent' for involving the public relations function in its strategic decision-making.

Symbolism

Using cultural codes and associated meanings, designers choose particular colours, shapes and typefaces to provoke particular emotional responses or to connote particular meanings. For example, a serif typeface such as Times New Roman used in broadsheets (the 'quality' press) has connotations of tradition, longevity and quality. A sans serif typeface, favoured by the tabloids, is often deemed to invoke modernity.

The controversy triggered by Labour's adoption of the red rose logo to replace the red flag illustrates the power of the symbol. The change in visuals was interpreted as symbolising a major ideological shift from hard left to centrist politics. A semiotic[7] analysis would infer that 'Labour abandoned the symbolism of the red flag (viewed by the leadership as a sign with negative connotations of bureaucratic, Soviet-style socialism) in favour of the red rose, a logo first successfully employed by the French socialists' (McNair 1994).

Olins (1999: 73) suggests that

> The problems in developing symbols are complex. In addition to avoiding negative connotations, technical, creative, fashion and cost requirements all have to be considered. Creating something which will encapsulate the idea behind the organisation, that won't go out of date, that is flexible and cheap in use, and that will evoke strong, positive emotional feelings in all those who come into contact with it, is actually a very difficult thing to do.

Of course, the significance of symbols within an organisation goes beyond aspects of design, such as the logo. It includes the existence (or absence) and distribution of status symbols such as executive washrooms, plush carpets and parking spaces. This aspect will be referred to later as part of a consideration of organisational culture.

Consistency

To ensure that a visual identity communicates the messages for which it was painstakingly designed, it must be applied consistently across all media. So 'house style' manuals are developed to control every aspect of application, from pantone number (representing exact colours) to typeface. Not all organisations want to represent themselves as a homogenised unit though. Some are decentralised and a corporate identity should signal this.

Olins (1999) specifies three categories to encapsulate different structures of identity:

1 *Monolithic* – where one name and visual identity are used throughout (e.g. IBM).

2 *Endorsed* – where an organisation has a group of activities or subsidiaries which it endorses with the same name and identity (e.g. Chanel).

3 *Branded* – where an organisation operates through a series of brands which may be unrelated (e.g. Procter & Gamble).

This seems relatively straightforward, but can, and should, other aspects of identity, such as communication and behaviour, be homogenised? Markwick and Fill (1997) argue that 'it is important to establish consistent and sustainable internal images among all employees in order that this consistency be projected as a positive cue to other stakeholder groups'. Clearly, organisations should involve a range of stakeholders in determining core philosophies and values and clearly communicate the agreed goals. But different stakeholder groups often have differing needs and expectations of single organisations, so expecting uniformity seems an unrealistic goal. This demonstrates the importance of defining what is meant by the term 'consistency'.

Van Riel (1995) overcomes the problematic notion of imposed uniformity with his concept of 'common starting points' (CSPs). CSPs are central values developed by communications staff from research into an organisation's desired corporate identity and image. Examples of CSPs include reliability, innovation, quality, profit-making and synergy (van Riel 1995). CSPs function as 'wavelengths' or 'parameters' to guide communication activity. The concept of CSPs fosters a notion of an organic process of developing and communicating organisational images rather than a top–down approach which limits staff to static, agreed perceptions. As Leitch and Motion (1999: 195) explain: 'An organisation may present multiple images to its various publics provided that these images are consistent, not with each other, but with the organisation's CSPs. The corporate identity task is to manage the multiplicity rather than to suppress it.'

Corporate culture

An organisation's behaviour reflects, or is reflected in, its culture (sometimes referred to as 'the way we do things around here'[8]). Changing organisational cultures to improve performance in our global economy is the subject of an entire industry of 'culture change' gurus. And a plethora of recipes for changing organisational cultures are currently on offer. Known as 'culture change programmes', Wilson (1992) explains that these often offer 'generalised templates' developed from analysis of a handful of 'successful' processes observed in particular companies (or sometimes productive national cultures such as in the Far East).

These approaches indicate that strong unified cultures can be created through strong leadership. The 'recipes' promise that cultures will become more effective by re-engineering particular aspects such as leadership styles or communication techniques.

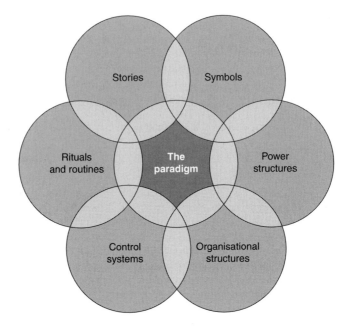

Figure 7.1 The cultural web

Source: Johnson and Scholes 1999. Used by permission of Prentice-Hall/Pearson

Space precludes a lengthy analysis of the concept of organisational culture and attempts to change it, but Wilson (1992) offers an interesting critical appraisal of many ideas and approaches.

Johnson and Scholes' (1999) cultural web is a useful tool for mapping and understanding organisational culture (Figure 7.1). The cultural web illustrates the complexity of organisational culture and, in practical terms, the areas that should be investigated as part of any attempt to audit culture as part of corporate identity. For example, Johnson and Scholes detail a whole range of appropriate research questions investigating areas such as the type of behaviour encouraged by particular routines; core beliefs reflected by stories; ways in which power is distributed in the organisation; and the status symbols favoured.

The model refers to an organisation's paradigm which can be explained as its 'taken for granted assumptions' (Johnson and Scholes 1999) or the link between structure and culture (Grundy 1993). It could also be argued as being a similar concept to corporate personality . . .

Corporate personality

Many approaches to corporate identity management are informed by the concept of corporate personality.

> Corporate personality is made up of the organisation's history, culture, values and beliefs (which drives its philosophy, mission and strategies) as realised through its staff, structures systems, its products and or services.
>
> (Gregory 1999: 1)

Bernstein (1989: 56) talks about stakeholders' experiences of an organisation building into a mosaic – 'the picture is that of an individual, a corporate portrait of a "Mr Cadbury" or a "Mr Shell" or "Ms Avon"'.

Olins (1978: 82) links the notion of corporate personality to an actual human personality: 'The carefully cultivated corporate identity becomes the substitute for the personality of the entrepreneur, just as the carefully planned marketing policy is the substitute for his intuitive feeling for what the market wants.' Markwick and Fill (1997) argue that the strategic management process, the way in which strategy is formulated, is a significant component of the corporate personality. Van Riel (1995: 34) explains that personality is displayed or revealed by corporate identity: 'unique corporate characteristics' are 'revealed in the company's products and buildings, in the nature and scale of its communication, and in its behaviour'.

Those that view an organisation as a collection of individuals may find the concept of a corporate personality difficult. In terms of trying to effect a particular corporate image, however, the notion of a corporate portrait (not an actual personality but a carefully constructed replica of a personality) is useful. In the same way that an actor would express human personalities through cues such as body language, tone of voice and choice of clothes, the public relations strategist highlights cues via 'behaviour, communication and symbolism' (van Riel 1995) to express a desired personality.

However, this notion becomes problematic if the projected personality does not reflect reality.

Reflecting reality?

Our preoccupation with, and reliance on, images has important implications for the study and practice of corporate communications. The image without any clear or certain relation to 'reality' is perhaps becoming the dominant form in both external and internal corporate public communications.

(Cheney 1992: 173)

The media revelled in ridiculing the BBC for spending reputed millions to adjust its logo from a slanting to an upright typeface. They gloried in maligning the Labour Party for replacing the red flag with a red rose. The source of the criticism was the perception that highly paid 'spin doctors' were concentrating on style as opposed to substance – trying to gloss over the problems both institutions were experiencing by creating an illusion of sleek professionalism. Whether this perception was fair or not will be debated elsewhere. The point here is that public relations practitioners must carefully consider the motives and ethics of their practice.

As Cheney points out

Contemporary public relations is fundamentally concerned with representing major organisations and institutions of our society with values, images, identities, issue positions and so forth. Thus, it is crucial that we probe the structure and meaning of that process of representation.

(Cheney 1992: 170)

In constructing carefully planned corporate identities, the practitioner must not lose sight of whose interests are served. The practitioner truly committed to the notion of a stakeholder society (which in this context emphasises employees' interests in particular) should strive to ensure that identity reflects, rather than conceals, reality. And

if an organisation's 'reality' is too undesirable to promote, a two-way symmetrical practitioner would set about counselling management to change the reality rather than designing a corporate identity plan to mask it.

Researching corporate personality

Identifying reality and a 'real' corporate personality can be problematic.

> To know the identity of a person is to be able to identify him or her – to distinguish him or her from others and to recognise him or her as a unique individual. Addresses, nationalities, ages and physical features are observable data, which are frequently used to identify an individual. Does this mean that one person really knows the identity of another person after having read his or her passport? Simple observation quickly becomes an insufficient method for understanding identity. Truly to know the identity of people, we must go much further. We must have long discussions with them, we must ask them about their tastes and convictions, and we must learn their histories.
>
> (Moingeon and Ramanantsoa 1997: 1)

To gain a real insight into a personality, it is also important to talk to a whole range of friends, family and acquaintances to assess their views and experiences. In the same way, when attempting to determine an accurate picture of the corporate personality, a range of stakeholders' views must be sought. Stakeholder analysis techniques (discussed in Chapter 6) should be used to identify the relevant stakeholders to be used in the research.

So how can we engineer 'long discussions' to learn more about an organisation's tastes, convictions and histories?

As with any research, triangulation[9] is essential to ensure validity. So a combination of research methodologies must be adopted, targeted at a range of stakeholders. These could include content analysis of corporate documents, surveys, focus groups, interviews and critical incident analysis.[10]

Researching actual and desired corporate image

Balmer's Affinity Audit (1996 in van Riel and Balmer 1997) is an innovative approach to revealing internal publics' views of organisations' 'dominant systems of values and beliefs' (Figure 7.2). Using a variety of methods of data collection, including semi-structured interviews, observation and an examination of organisational documentation, the Affinity Audit involves four stages:

1 Establish the corporate mission and strategy.
2 Reveal the dominant systems of values and beliefs within the organisation.
3 Evaluate such systems of values and beliefs against the corporate mission and strategy.
4 Nurture those values and beliefs that support the corporate mission and strategy.

The Affinity Audit provides a useful blueprint for approaching research into the corporate personality, 'a pre-requisite for an understanding of the organisation's identity'

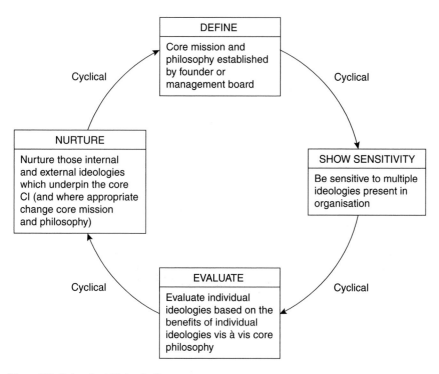

Figure 7.2 Balmer's Affinity Audit

Source: van Riel and Balmer, 1997. Used by permission of *The European Journal of Identity*

(van Riel and Balmer 1997). This type of research provides a valuable insight into internal publics' views on an organisation's mission and strategy. So, care must be taken to recognise Balmer's third and fourth stages as a two-way (symmetrical)[11] process rather than value engineering. Balmer specifies that core missions and philosophies may be changed where appropriate. As in 'excellent' (Grunig 1992) companies, dominant coalitions[12] may use corporate identity research as an opportunity to re-evaluate corporate strategies in light of public opinion, rather than using it to engineer the most persuasive messages to communicate predetermined, management led, values (an asymmetrical approach, Grunig and Hunt 1984).

Once internal perceptions have been mapped, further research must be conducted with external groups to determine their perceptions of actual and desired image.

When agreement has been reached on what image the organisation wishes to have, it can be compared to perceptions of its current or 'actual' image. Narrowing the gap between actual and desired image is the objective of a corporate identity programme. Each aspect of corporate identity must be audited to determine if it helps or hinders the formation of the desired image.

Auditing existing corporate identity

Van Riel's (1995) CI mix (communication, behaviour and symbolism) provides a useful guide to the aspects of identity to be audited.

Communication and behavioural audits

Behavioural audits, more commonly known as attitude surveys, measure job satisfaction, gather feedback on the effectiveness of internal policies and provide insight into the attitudes and behaviour of staff at all levels.

Communication audits survey the 'communication climate'[13] including communication style and structures as well as content.

Clearly communication and behaviour are 'inextricably linked'. Communication must be defined as more than merely communication techniques or styles of delivery. Organisations must not see the introduction of a team briefing system and some presentation training for managers as the panacea for all the problems identified through a communication audit or attitudes survey. As Grunig and Hunt (1984: 248) explain,

> Too often, management wants an easy way to gain the loyalty of employees and get more work out of them. And it's much easier to change the methods of communication than it is to change the organisational structure and role relationships – more realistic ways of affecting performance and satisfaction.

This raises broader issues relating to organisational structure and power. For example, if an organisation professes innovation as a core value, but has a highly bureaucratic structure involving layers of decision-making and centralised power, then innovation will not be fostered. A corporate identity analysis must address corporate 'behaviour' in its broadest sense and embrace all aspects of corporate culture discussed in the previous chapter, as well as structure and power. Johnson's culture web (p. 78) and Lewin's (1935) force field analysis[14] are useful for mapping a number of dimensions of corporate behaviour.

The visual or design audit

> The design audit is led by one of the designers on the corporate identity consultants' team. Its task is to study and document the way in which the different parts of the organisation present themselves in terms of the three traditional areas of design – factories, showrooms and so on; product, packaging and information material; vehicle liveries, signs, brochures, advertising, instruction manuals and every other form of graphics. What does it all look like? What message is it meant to convey?
>
> (Olins 1999: 162)

A visual audit is not superficial and should reveal more than where a new coat of paint is needed. Baker and Balmer (1997: 378) illustrate the value of the visual audit as a research tool and its contribution to strategy formulation at Strathclyde University, for example, where 'the visual audit revealed important characteristics of the University's identity i.e. the University was highly decentralised and had fragmented corporate communications'.

However, the design audit is only one aspect of the research into an organisation's corporate identity. 'The design audit is in a sense both complementary to, and an integral part of the communications audit, and both are inextricably involved with the behavioural audit' (Olins 1999: 162).

Corporate identity planning

The purpose in the process outlined above (researching the actual and desired image and identifying which aspects of corporate identity should be changed to connote appropriate meaning) is to use this information to formulate a corporate identity plan. Such a plan would often aim to manipulate the variables of corporate identity to ensure they suggest a coherent and desirable personality. But is it really possible to manipulate the appropriate variables (symbolism, communication and behaviour) effectively?

Corporate identity is such a complex concept, it is difficult to imagine that it is easily manipulated and controlled. However, consultants sometimes claim just this. Schmidt (1997), for example, promotes an approach to corporate identity management involving five dimensions: 'products and services, communications and design, corporate behaviour, market conditions and strategies and corporate culture'. He claims, 'our successful holistic approach made it possible to analyse, structure and control all relevant dimensions, including culture' (1997: 40).

Others hold conflicting views, Hatch and Schultz (1997) argue

> strategies and visions are created and interpreted through culturally-mediated language such as metaphor, stories and humour and demonstrated by material artefacts of culture such as products, buildings and physical arrangements. Corporate identity can, therefore, never be wholly managed.

Although perhaps not 'wholly managed', important inroads can be made into identifying and communicating a strategically important corporate identity. Provided readers retain a realistic mindset about what can really be effected, a number of useful multistep corporate identity management plans are available in the literature: Dowling (1994), Olins (1999), Bernstein (1989), van Riel (1995), Abratt (1989) and Ind (1997). Van Riel's contribution is among the most useful.

Van Riel's model (Figure 7.3) illustrates how comprehensive research (of the type investigated above) affects the corporate identity management plan. It should enable the following questions to be answered:

1 What is our current image?
2 In order to meet strategic objectives, what do we need our image to be?
3 What's the difference between 1 and 2?
4 What changes must be made to our corporate personality to narrow any gap between 1 and 2?

Van Riel's model suggests that the objectives of the corporate identity policy programme (CIPP) could be:

- to maintain an organisation's current position (research shows that 1 and 2 are the same), or
- to adjust its current position (1 and 2 are slightly dissonant), or
- to determine an entirely new position (1 and 2 are vastly dissonant).

A variety of tactics, centred around adjusting communication, behaviour and symbolism can then be employed.

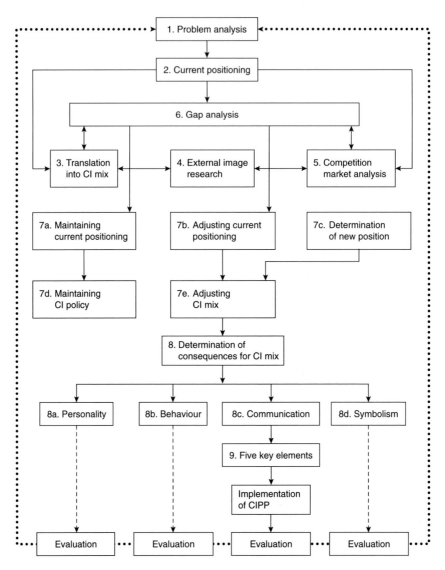

Figure 7.3 Adapted version of van Riel's model of corporate identity management

Source: adapted from van Riel 1995

In van Riel's original model, evaluation takes place at the end of the process and appears to be a final step. In this adapted version, feedback loops inserted between each type of evaluation and the beginning of the process (problem analysis) indicate the addition of a further step. This represents the process by which results from evaluation should be compared to the original 'problem analysis' (step 1 of van Riel's model) to ensure that the tactics employed have solved that original problem. The feedback loop also represents the cyclical nature of corporate identity management. It must not be seen as a one off procedure but as an ongoing strategic process. As with any strategy,

frequent evaluation should inform the planning process. Future evaluation of aspects of the CI mix could indicate new 'problems', which would initiate a new policy programme to help the organisation evolve and adapt to its environment.

However, as Ind (1997: 65) says:

> Whatever the validity of the model, organisations need to have the resources, structures, people and commitment to communication. Feedback loops are credible only if the organisation has the ability to listen to what it hears and the desire to act upon what it discovers.

An example of an organisation acting on feedback from extensive research into its corporate identity is given below. The QMUC case study illustrates many of the points made in the text, particularly in terms of illustrating the concept of corporate person-ality and how it is influenced. It shows the value of research and how organisations can react to research findings, and provides a valuable insight into a comprehensive corporate identity management programme involving key stakeholders.

Case study: Queen Margaret University College's corporate identity

Queen Margaret College (QMC) was founded in Edinburgh in 1875, a time when women were excluded from most universities. At the forefront of women's fight for access to higher education, it was originally a cookery school and then became known for health education. At that time, research was just beginning to demonstrate the link between poverty and ill health. The College worked to improve standards of health and living conditions and campaigned for the introduction of district nurses to care for women in their homes. Within a generation, infant mortality in Scotland was reduced by 50 per cent. QMC's contribution is still a source of pride, an important aspect of its culture often emphasised in speeches (which is interesting in relation to Johnson and Scholes' (1999) stories and myths).

In 2001, the much expanded Queen Margaret University College (QMUC) has four faculties: Arts, Business and Consumer Studies, Health Sciences, and Social Sciences and Health Care. Some 3,700 students from 50 countries worldwide study a wide range of subjects, from dietetics to drama, from radiography to retail business and, of course, corporate communication.

Despite these developments, QMUC's history still influences its corporate person-ality, as its mission statement makes clear:

> To serve society and enhance the quality of life through excellence and leadership in vocationally and professionally relevant education, research and consultancy, as an academic community which is outward looking and committed to innovation and life-long learning.

Strategic aims and objectives

In 1999, the Privy Council awarded QMC the title *University* College. The full 'univer-sity' title could not be conferred because QMC had less than 4,000 students. However, it aims to achieve the university title by 2003. As Professor Joan Stringer, QMUC Principal, explained

We believe we meet the requirement of 'university-ness' – the quality of our graduates, of our staff, our performances in Teaching Quality Assessment and other external indicators, demonstrate this. Although we are proud of our 'QM University College' title, our peers and our competitors are all universities and without full university title, we are operating at a disadvantage.

The 1999 addition of the word 'university' into QMC's title meant that its visual identity had to be updated. Rather than inserting the new word into the existing logo however, the Principal and senior management recognised the necessity of a more fundamental and wide-ranging corporate image audit to help the University College achieve its future strategic aims. As Marketing Manager Gregor McMeechan explains, 'We took an integrated and holistic approach and considered our identity in its fullest sense. Not just thinking about how we look, but about our culture, our values, and how we communicate an accurate image of who we are.'[15]

Corporate identity plan

QMUC's overarching strategic aim is to achieve full university status by 2003. The aim of the corporate identity programme was to ensure that QMUC's corporate identity consistently communicated QMUC's university level status ('university-ness') to all of its stakeholders.

The plan was also informed by a number of organisational objectives outlined in the University College's strategic plan. Primarily:

- To extend and develop the profile and reputation of the University College, locally, regionally, nationally and internationally.
- To continue to review organisational systems and structures to secure improvements in corporate policy formation and implementation, operational efficiency, flexibility and responsiveness to change and opportunity.

(QMUC Strategic Plan 1999–2000)[16]

The corporate identity plan also underpins objectives highlighted in the strategic plan relating to high graduate employment rates, international student recruitment and the development of strategic links.

Publics

QMUC's main publics include:

- employees at all levels within QMUC
- undergraduates, the majority of whom are British. QMUC is also a popular destination for European (particularly Norwegian) and international students
- potential students – QMUC is looking to widen access in terms of mature students, part time students, ethnic minorities, male students and distance learners
- education sector – schools, further education colleges, other universities
- post-graduate and research students
- continuing professional development (CPD) candidates and sponsors
- employers and potential hosts for placement students

- funding authorities and awarders of research grants
- collaborative research partners – particularly 'ancient' universities
- commercial consultancy clients
- professional associations and institutes
- politicians – local, MSPs, MPs and MEPs
- media
- local community.

Research

Several qualitative and quantitative research methods were employed to identify a range of stakeholders' views on QMUC's current and desired image:

- content analysis of documents ranging from prospectuses and strategic plans to media coverage and the internet
- surveys and questionnaires
- corporate personality mapping exercise with senior management
- semi-structured interviews
- focus groups
- visual audit.

Purposive sampling was used to ensure sufficient disclosure from a range of key stakeholder groups. These included the following:

Internal publics

- Academic staff (course leaders, admissions tutors, lecturers involved in seeking research funding and/or commercial consultancy, heads of research institutes or commercial centres).
- Administrative staff from areas such as business development, commercial services, marketing, student services, students' union.
- Governors

External publics

- Prospective undergraduate and post-graduate students.
- Professional and industrial contacts such as research sponsors and partners, placement hosts, members of advisory panels, commercial consultancy clients and the funding council.

Research questions

The problem with focusing a discussion on corporate identity is that most people associate corporate identity with design, which is often judged according to personal taste with everyone having views on what they like or dislike. The facilitator's major task in the focus groups was to explain the concept of corporate image and the role of corporate identity and keep the discussion focused on QMUC's corporate identity in relation to its strategic objectives. When staff considered a desired image for the University

College, for example, conversations were steered towards what needed to be achieved over the next ten years and how a particular corporate positioning could contribute to success, rather than becoming stuck on favourite colours and preferred typeface!

That said, asking for views on the existing logo and the image it communicated served as a useful icebreaker. Having expounded often dearly held opinions, participants could then be led through the group processes[17] up the conceptual ladder to a stage when valid and interesting views were proffered.

The research mapped participants' views on current and desired corporate image in relation to other universities and against expectations of what a university should be like.

Key findings

A number of attributes were identified. Some were commonly well regarded by participants whilst different publics held distinctive views about some important aspects. A summary follows.

Attributes valued by all constituents

- The name 'Queen Margaret' with its connotations of credibility, authority and prestige often associated with the old established universities.
- QMUC's Edinburgh location (although an over-emphasis on Scottishness should not imply parochialism and obscure QMUC's international status).
- The use of the crest in QMUC's visual identity, with its connotations of longevity, tradition, quality and learning.

Attributes valued by staff and professional contacts

- Quality teaching, research and consultancy and distinctiveness of character. Perceptions of quality include issues such as the high grading obtained in the independent quality assessment exercise, high level of individual attention given to students and the high graduate employment rate (the highest in Scotland).
- The relatively small size of the University College is an important aspect of staff perceptions of a friendly, caring and supportive nature.
- QMUC's strong research culture and history of academic achievement make staff feel more aligned with 'old' universities than with the 'new' university sector.
- The 'applied' nature of QMUC's academic expertise and strong vocational links with a range of professions.
- Caring and community values linked to concepts such as 'serving society', 'enhancing quality of life' (particularly for health faculties) and 'life-long learning' were also highlighted.

Problematic areas identified by staff

- Confusion regarding a clear strategy to manage increasingly conflicting demands (such as the need to earn income to offset government cuts, meet research targets, manage increased competition whilst still meeting student needs).
- Poor internal communication.
- The perception that QMUC's strategy to purchase a new campus had resulted in lack of investment in existing facilities and buildings.

Attributes valued by students and prospective students

- 'Specific attributes chosen as being particularly motivational showed students are looking for: quality and up to date teaching provision to make the most of their abilities, relevant knowledge and skills, a degree that is well regarded by employers, high level of individual attention and support, a pleasant environment and exciting social life.'

Conflicting perspectives

- Staff deemed concepts of 'serving society' and 'life-long learning' as important attributes of the corporate personality, whereas students rejected this image. Students were motivated by elements that would benefit them as individuals rather than notions of universities being about enhancing public quality of life. (This is particularly interesting in relation to the discussion of consistency above.)

Recommendations

Having considered the range of views expressed, researchers System Three[18] made the following recommendations:

- 'The desired identity for QMUC is one that effectively communicates: the key areas of activity, product quality in terms of established and independent endorsement (heritage, Quality Assessment ratings, graduate employment rate), a caring and supportive environment, as well as excitement and dynamism.'
- 'The desired tone of QMUC both on behalf of staff and students is a stamp of established quality and prestige, as well as modern relevance, advancement and innovation.'
- 'The high number of pressures placed on the University College necessitates a clear strategy for prioritising demands on staff and establishing a logical way forward guided by meaningful and non-conflicting objectives.'

Implementation of the new corporate identity

Symbolism

From the sea of research findings, the designers distilled the following desired perceptions to inform the new visual identity:

- heritage and established quality
- Queen Margaret title
- innovation
- modern relevance of courses
- quality of teaching
- individuality of the organisation
- Edinburgh location
- friendly, supportive approach.

The single most important message was identified as 'established quality'.

So, how can design communicate these attributes? Figure 7.4 shows the old and new logos for QMUC. Lauren Rennet, Creative Director of Graphicpartners, explains the design concept:

Queen Margaret University College
EDINBURGH established 1875

Figure 7.4a Queen Margaret University College, old logo
Used with permission

Queen Margaret University College
EDINBURGH

Figure 7.4b Queen Margaret University College, new logo
Used with permission

The concept of a crest was retained to communicate QMUC's heritage but was simplified and up-dated to reflect the current and future offer of the University College, not that of its early years when the original crest was drawn.

With this in mind the symbols within the crest were adjusted to more distinctively represent the University College. The main focus, Queen Margaret's crown, provides a memorable symbol of power, leadership and excellence.

Vibrant royal blue, futuristic silver and timeless typography complete this modern, streamlined crest without losing the valuable sense of established quality.

Staff have unique access to a corporate identity manual available solely online. The new visual identity will be consistently used across applications ranging from letter-heads to vehicle livery, uniforms to websites. Figure 7.5 illustrates the application of the new identity at QMUC's Corstophine campus.

The corporate identity mix

Van Riel (1995) highlights the importance of all aspects of the CI mix. Symbolism has clearly been affected by the QMUC corporate identity plan. But what about the other important aspects, behaviour and communication?

Research conducted among QMUC staff indicated a need for improved communication and leadership in prioritising and balancing demands on lecturers. A number of initiatives have been launched in response.

An improved career development and appraisal scheme provides a structure for staff to agree individual objectives within a framework which clearly links to organisational aims and objectives. Staff are involved in determining their own criteria for success.

Dorothy Wright, Director of Human Resources, is planning more far reaching cultural developments:

Figure 7.5 Queen Margaret University College, Corstophine campus signage
Used with permission

> The strategic plan specifies flexibility, commercial awareness, quality, innovation and creativity as key attributes of the culture we need to foster in order to achieve our corporate aims and objectives. My job is to look at the way we need to behave in order to deliver in these areas.

Her first task is to run a facilitated session with senior management, using tools such as force field analysis, to identify changes that need to be made. Then, a full attitudes survey has been commissioned to determine staff views.

Part of the attitudes survey will audit communication, and resources are available to implement more effective two-way communication systems. However, more profound behavioural changes are planned echoing Grunig and Hunt's (1984) sentiment that instead of merely altering communication tactics, 'changing the organisational structure and role relationships' are more realistic ways of affecting performance and satisfaction.

These changes include a major management development programme. As Wright explains,

> Our research will identify the management style needed to help QMUC develop and achieve future success. We will then design a training programme to help effect this approach. I anticipate that it will involve developing coaching skills associated with empowering staff and a communication style aimed at giving and receiving feedback.

Notes

1 Gregory (1999) provides a useful summary of current thinking:

> The two concepts of identity and image have suffered from a lack of clarity stemming partly from confusion between and conflation of the terms. Broadly speaking, corporate identity was originally seen as the visual symbols an organisation used such as logos, house style and other representations associated with design . . . For some practitioners, that view still persists . . . However, more recently the concept of corporate identity has been broadened to include linkages between corporate strategy and communication . . . In Margulies' (1997) terms 'identity means the sum of all the ways a company chooses to identify itself to all its publics.

2 Nike has launched a number of initiatives to overcome this image which can be explored via its website.

3 The term stakeholder refers to groups of publics (typically employees, suppliers, shareholders, customers and the local community) who have a significant effect on, or are affected by, an organisation. For a more detailed consideration of the concept, see Chapters 4 and 6.

4 For an explanation of corporate strategy and the strategic role of public relations, see Chapter 4.

5 For explanations of Grunig's (1984) symmetric and asymmetric models, see pp. 10–12.

6 For further discussion, refer to Franklin (1994) and McNair (1994).

7 The semiotic approach is outlined in Chapter 2.

8 'The way we do things around here' originated at management consultancy McKinsey & Company.

9 Triangulation refers to the combining of at least three research methodologies. Cross-referencing of findings will improve validity.

10 Van Riel (1995) provides a comprehensive summary of approaches.

11 See Chapter 1 for an explanation of Grunig's models.

12 The term 'dominant coalition' refers to 'the group of senior managers who control an organisation' (Grunig 1992). For further discussion of public relations' role in dominant coalition decision-making see Chapter 4.

13 See Hargie and Tourish (2000) for an in-depth guide to communication audits.

14 Grundy (1993) provides a useful guide to using force field analysis.

15 Unless otherwise stated, quotes are taken from interviews with the author.

16 QMUC's strategic plan is available online at <www.qmuc.ac.uk/stplan.html>.

17 Social scientists often refer to groups moving through several stages (forming, storming, norming) before they 'perform' and contribute more truthful and useful opinions. For further information refer to Vernelle (1994: 28–9).

18 Research was conducted by a number of consultants, including research company System Three and the author.

8 Public affairs and issues management

..

Public issues management became one of the key phrases in public relations circles in 1975 (Grunig and Hunt 1984). One definition of public issues management is that it makes it possible for organisations to

> shape government policy on issues which affect them, rather than just to adapt to policy changes. The interactive corporation tries to get a reasonably accurate agenda of public issues that it should be concerned with ... and develops constructive approaches to these issues.
>
> (Buchholz, quoted in Grunig and Hunt 1984: 296)

Defining issues management

..

Issues management is a long-term strategic management practice. Significant changes or issues which may affect the organisation are identified, and long-term strategic decisions are taken which may involve changes in policy and practice. An oft-quoted example of this is the growing importance of the environmental lobby. Ten years ago, most companies did not feel it important to state whether their products were environmentally friendly, dolphin friendly, produced without being tested on animals, or contained genetically modified ingredients.

Issues management is 'the process of identifying issues, analysing those issues, setting priorities, selecting programme strategy options, implementing a programme of action and evaluating effectiveness'. It is also managing 'corporate response to changes in operational environments' (Cutlip et al. 1985: 15).

Organisations try to identify and change issues before they become influential on government policy and legislation. Issues management is therefore preventative. One example issues management consultant Simon Bryceson uses to illustrate an issues management approach concerns Unilever, which through its subsidiary companies such as Birds Eye Walls, Gorton's and Findus is the largest buyer of fish in the world. In early 1996, Unilever was warned of a proposed campaign by Greenpeace which would highlight decreasing global fish stocks. Greenpeace was planning to target the company and criticise its fish buying practices, which Greenpeace felt were contributing to the problem. In order to avert this attack, Unilever established a partnership with the World

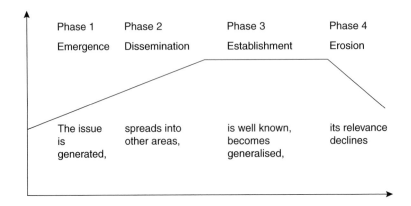

Figure 8.1 The issues life cycle

Reproduced with permission from Femers, Klewes and Lintemeier (2000)

Wide Fund for Nature, the largest environmental campaigning group in the UK. The two organisations formed the Marine Stewardship Council (MSC) to determine the sustainability of every fishery in the world and issue certification of those that were judged to meet strict criteria. Unilever then committed itself from the year 2000 onwards to source all its fish from MSC certificated fisheries only. Instead of a negative attack, the strategy resulted in a headline in *The Financial Times*, 'Unilever in fight to save global fisheries'. By taking the initiative, the company became associated with the solution rather than the problem, building its authority on global fisheries policy as well as protecting its brand and future business (see <www.bryceson.com>).

Femers, Klewes and Lintemeier (2000) suggest a structure for the life cycle of issues (see Figure 8.1). In the emergence phase, the issue is generated and defined, crystallising into 'a specific interpretation of social reality'. This version of events is then picked up by credible individuals or groups in the dissemination phase. Specialist media may play an important role in this process, finding the issue and publishing reports, which spreads it into a wider arena. The example quoted by Femers *et al.* is that of a problem with the Intel Pentium chip, which was picked up in a chatroom by a journalist. The problem with the chip eventually cost Intel several million dollars. In the third, establishment, phase, popular media deal with the issue and it becomes known to a large part of society. Finally, public interest declines and the issue drops off the media agenda. Erosion may also be caused by legislation which addresses the issue.

The rise of pressure groups

Throughout the liberal democratic world there has been a decline in confidence in the power of the nation state to regulate multinational corporations. Accompanying this has been a substantial rise in support for pressure groups that target those multinational corporations in order to highlight their polices on ... a range of quasi-ethical issues.

(Chris Rose, Campaign Director, Greenpeace
UK speech, December 1995)

The rise of pressure groups is a result of disaffection with mainstream politics and this has changed the nature of participation in the political process. Some groups are now no longer content to vote every five years and the growth of the road protest and animal rights movements has shown that diverse groups can come together for a common cause, sometimes adopting semi-terrorist tactics to gain their objectives. Simon Bryceson questions whether 'the culture of some environmental organisations has mutated into one that is incapable of hearing constructive criticism'. He also warns against the rise of anti-scientism. 'Emotion has a place in public policy debate but if it becomes a substitute for rational consideration, we are in very deep trouble indeed.' He concludes, 'The end does not justify the means, even where the end is the saving of the world!' <www.bryceson.com>.

A recent development has been the targeting of individual shareholders. John Vidal (2000) reported that shareholders in Huntingdon Life Sciences, which tests on animals for the pharmaceutical industry and has been the focus of much pressure group activity, had been sent a letter by the British Union for the Abolition of Vivisection Reform Group (AVRG) that warned them to sell their shares or face having their homes picketed. One individual who refused had been the victim of a peaceful demonstration outside his house. Companies are having to become more aware not only of their own policies, but of those of other companies that they may invest in.

'Modern day pressure groups have become a major political force in their own right', says Peter Hamilton, Managing Director of The Communication Group (TCG). Surveying more than 250 of the largest companies in Europe, TCG found that businesses were fearful of the power of pressure groups but complacent about how to handle them. Groups frequently outflanked businesses, and used global communications much more widely and swiftly than most companies. They also fired up public opinion, and influenced legislation, being seen as generally more effective at PR. Few companies had corporate strategies in place to deal with the problem, and tended to rely on media publicity to get their message across rather than taking a strategic approach to the issues raised by pressure groups (Hamilton 1997).

Shifts in the global situation

As companies expand onto the global scene, issues have to be tackled with increased lateral vision. Michael Murphy (1999) notes the importance of cultural identity. Whilst huge trading blocs such as the European Union have been established, and trends towards deregulation in the marketplace are apparent, there has also been a growth in nationalism. This has manifested itself in the UK in devolution to the national assemblies in Wales and Scotland. 'In Asia, the cultural patchwork is still more intricate . . . despite nearly half a century of autocratic centralised rule, China is still a complex nation of many different cultures and dialects.' Murphy feels that it is imperative that companies be sensitive to local market conditions: 'Any major issue . . . is likely to have international ramifications.'

This issue is further complicated by the increased speed of information flows due to new technology (see Chapter 18). Greater access to information allows people to make more informed choices. According to Murphy, '80 per cent of US journalists now go to the web as their first source of information.' With an information-rich society, especially in the developed capitalist countries, actions in one part of the globe can impact on a company elsewhere.

Defining lobbying

One of the techniques used most commonly in carrying out issues management campaigns is lobbying. Lobbying involves 'direct attempts to influence legislative and regulatory decisions in government' and public affairs is the 'specialised public relations effort designed to build and maintain community and governmental relations' (Cutlip *et al.* 1985: 14). Not surprisingly, because they have overlapping definitions, the two terms are often used interchangeably, although it can be argued that public affairs has a wider remit. Charles Miller at Citigate Public Affairs feels that there is difficulty in defining both public affairs and lobbying, and feels that the latter is '*any* attempt to influence the decisions of the institutions of government'.[1]

Organisations have increasingly used lobbying techniques to present their case to government and groups of stakeholders. Lobbying can be either defensive, designed to abolish or amend an existing law, or offensive, aimed at pushing the authorities to create a law. An example of offensive lobbying was the successful Snowdrop Campaign by parents of children killed at Dunblane, which quickly forced a change in the regulations on private hand guns. The key to lobbying is to understand the legislative process, and how that of the UK and the different national assemblies operate within the European Community. Increasingly, competition on an international scale means that it is necessary to take wide-ranging cultural and legislative practices into account. For example, Shell found that its decision to dispose of Brent Spar in the North Sea provoked a reaction from pressure groups across Europe. In the end, despite the rationality of its argument, a well-orchestrated campaign caused the company to change its policy.

Moloney (1997) comments on those who have put forward the case that lobbying is a guarantor of pluralism. He points out that not all groups in a liberal market are equal in power, influence and therefore access. He also noted that groups are not equal in wealth and while some can hire public relations consultants, others cannot.

Common lobbying mistakes

In order to be successful, the lobbyist needs to be aware of issues in advance. According to the lobbyist Charles Miller, 'Every hour spent on research and monitoring is worth ten on lobbying' (cited in Roche 1998: 22). The later a campaign begins, the fewer choices are open. Miller (Roche 1998: 23) names four common lobbying mistakes:

1 Contacts are no use unless you have a sound case.

2 No amount of entertaining can substitute for a well-researched case.

3 Think Government, not Parliament. It is also important to talk to MPs' advisors. Think system, and take account of the network of institutions.

4 Do not act unless you know how Government will react to your case.

Organisations who want to undertake lobbying have a choice of methods. They may take on an in-house specialist, as is most likely in large organisations that need to be constantly aware of issues and legislation. A specialist consultancy firm may be employed on a project basis, where help is needed on specific or *ad hoc* projects. Consultants may be used to supplement the knowledge and expertise of an in-house department. Miller feels that the bulk of professional lobbyists do the majority of their

work on the political side, but that issues may not have much to do with parliamentary decisions.

Organisations used to retain MPs or peers to provide them with advice and information, or to open doors and act as spokespeople. However, there have been calls for regulation of this process (see Chapter 5). The Neill Commission in 1999 recommended that independent lobbyists should be more regulated, although it did not go as far as the professional bodies, the IPR, the PRCA and the Association of Party Political Consultants (APPC), advocated. MPs and peers have to register their interests, so it can be seen whether their stance on particular legislation might have been influenced by lobbyists or organisations. The IPR and the PRCA have introduced supplements to their Codes of Practice relating to members who are lobbyists, largely reiterating the Code of the APPC. The problem remains that many lobbyists are not members of any of these professional associations and so cannot be governed by any of their rules.

There is also the question of what constitutes lobbying. Bryceson still carries out lobbying work on a pro bono basis for certain special interest groups he supports. Where does lobbying start – is it only when someone is paid to do it that regulation comes into play?

Lobbying since 1997

The general election in May 1997 brought a Labour government into power with a huge majority. This changed the way that lobbyists worked and shifted emphasis onto government advisors. Parliament was also noticeably younger and contained more women and ethnic MPs. Relationships had to be formed between lobbyists and these new MPs.

Research carried out amongst MPs in 1998 found that the following factors were felt to be important for successful lobbying (Roche 1998: 44):

1 Access to decision makers
2 Background research
3 Good timing
4 Communication skills
5 Knowledge of government procedure
6 Public interest
7 Support of opinion leaders
8 Effective targeting
9 Favourable media coverage
10 Knowledge of government structure.

Although favourable media coverage appears only ninth in this list, much of the lobbyist's effort is directed to making sure that their case is covered in the media appropriate to the MPs and civil servants who they want to influence.

Public perception of an issue will increase proportionately to the amount of attention given to that issue by the media. By simply paying attention to an issue and neglecting others, the media will affect public opinion. The public agenda then influences the political agenda, as politicians seek to respond to what voters want to ensure their own re-election. As politicians are elected by constituencies, often the local and

regional media are more important for individual MPs than the national media and
skilful lobbyists will seek to relate their causes to the particular local concerns of the
politicians they wish to influence.

There are several methods which lobbyists may seek to persuade an MP to use in
favour of their cause. MPs ask over 50,000 Parliamentary Questions (PQs) each year.
Questions are printed on the order paper on the day after they are tabled at the table
office and again on the day they are to be answered. Over 90 per cent of answers are
written, and are a good way to bring a matter to the attention of Ministers and other
MPs. Lobbyists may seek to persuade an MP to ask a question on behalf of a particu-
lar organisation or to support a particular cause. All questions and answers appear in
Hansard.

MPs can also put down an Early Day Motion (EDM) on the order paper to call the
House, government or individual MP to take action. Six sponsoring MPs are needed
to start an EDM, and each time another name is added to the list the EDM is reprinted.

MPs also have the chance to affect policy by working in party committees or depart-
mental groups.

The system

The experienced lobbyist Charles Miller has offered Figure 8.2 as an illustration of the
political system. Whitehall departments and the European Commission draft policy and
implement decisions formally made by Ministers and Commissioners. The latter are
influenced by officials who control the flow of information and access to the politi-
cians. Special Advisers have a significant role in the decision-making process in some
departments, and there are cabinets who act as advisers to Commissioners. Advisory
committees and task forces in the UK and Committees of Experts in the EC, made up
of outside specialists, may also act as consultation bodies.

Quangos are public bodies that are not part of government departments but which
administer policy and may distribute money, for example the Arts Council.

Local government contributes to planning and policy, and may distribute money for
economic development locally. The work is mainly done by officers who service
committees of elected members. Regulators such as OFTEL and the Health & Safety
Executive administer statutory controls.

The parliaments may formally adopt decisions, but as can be seen, there are many
different influences before a subject is debated in parliament.

European political institutions

The main institutions of the European Community are the European Council, the Council
of Ministers, the European Commission and the European Parliament. The European
Council consists of all heads of state and meets twice a year. The Council of Ministers
includes ministerial representatives of the member states, in proportion to their popu-
lations. The Presidency is held by member states in turn. The European Commission
consists of 20 Commissioners, appointed for a five-year term by the member states'
governments. The European Parliament is made up of 626 European MPs who sit in
political groups and are elected every five years. These institutions are supported by
civil servants and other advisers. The legislative process is mainly governed by the
Council, the Commission (which has the right to initiate proposals) and the Parliament.

The System

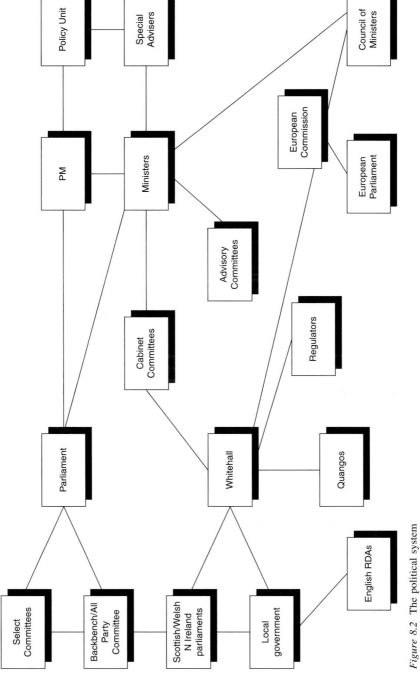

Figure 8.2 The political system

Source: Miller 1998

Knowing where and when to enter this process, and who to approach, is key to achieving a successful outcome for a lobbying campaign.

Key factors

Charles Miller (1998) suggests the following key factors that influence campaigns:

Merit of case	70%
Constituency concerns	15%
Big battalions (organisations, interests)	15%
Media	10%
Pressure groups	5%
Courts	1%

The merit of the case is the most influential factor. The case needs to put forward workable policies, supported by accurate facts and figures researched from credible sources. If governments have committed themselves to take action, a good lobbyist will take account of this and suggest constructive alternatives. Professional lobbyists would be expected to know which element of the system to approach and how that element would wish to be treated. By treating receivers of information as stakeholder publics, lobbyists can increase the likely success of their case. Due thought needs to be given to how the system would receive the information and respond to it. Miller also suggests that the bulk of issues are settled by negotiation, rather than by a simple lobbying process.

Other lobbying arenas

Simon Bryceson believes that lobbying is now taking place outside the parliamentary arena. The World Trade Organization (WTO) has the power to set trading legislative standards. Catalytic converters now have to be fitted as standard in new motor cars, and obviously this measure has benefited the manufacturers. Some of the global organisations have competing priorities. The World Bank places an emphasis on cash crops like tobacco over subsistence farming, yet the World Health Organization discourages tobacco use. The perceived ability of these organisations to affect everyone's lives can be seen in the rise of pressure group activity directed against them, as evidenced by the demonstrations during the WTO talks in Seattle in 2000.

In the UK the 1998 Competition Act replaced the Monopolies and Mergers Commission with the Competition Commission. The remit of the new body was still to investigate and report on proposed mergers, but the emphasis shifted towards considering whether decisions would mean better services for consumers. The chair of the Commission Dr Derek Morris stated that the Commission would prioritise consumer interest over all others, and that its proceedings would be more transparent. Chris Savage, director of competition and regulation at Shandwick Public Affairs, felt that new skills would be needed to 'build coalitions and mobilise support'. Rod Cartwright, head of GCI Political Counsel, did not see a need for new skills: 'Our role has always been to help clients build a groundswell of support for an issue . . . But the importance of support from third parties has grown.' As the number of audiences has widened, Cartwright felt that 'Strategic message delivery needs more work than before' (quoted in Freeman 2000).

The Competition Commission held public hearings of the debate on price-fixing in the motor industry in July 1999. Whilst members of the public were not able to make submissions, they were able to attend hearings which previously would have been held in private (Freeman 2000).

In the remainder of this chapter, two contrasting case studies will be presented. The first is from Railtrack, and examines the activities of a well-resourced in-house public affairs department. Railtrack has a long-term national agenda. The second case study looks at the Voice of the Listener and Viewer (VLV), a small pressure group dependent on member subscriptions for its income. Despite this, VLV has held several conferences with well-respected speakers and has been invited to submit responses to government bodies.

Case study 1: Railtrack

Railtrack is part of the now privatised rail network in the UK and was created by the 1993 Railways Act. The company owns the rail infrastructure, including track, signals, bridges and all 2,500 stations. Whilst privatisation freed Railtrack from the necessity of approaching the Treasury each year to gain funds to keep the trains running for the next twelve months, the rail industry receives a substantial although decreasing level of public subsidy and is therefore accountable to the government. Privatisation has also increased expectations of the industry, not only from politicians but also from the general public. Whilst Railtrack does not run trains, and its customers are the train operating companies rather than passengers, the infrastructure obviously substantially affects the travelling experience.

Railtrack is affected by the decisions of the Rail Regulator, who reviews access charges. The first review is underway for implementation in 2001, and any changes in charges would seriously affect Railtrack's business.

The geographical spread of the rail network means that all but a few parliamentary constituencies contain a railway line, station or both. Therefore MPs are interested in how Railtrack's actions will affect life for their constituents. The Labour government is also pro-public transport and wishes to operate in partnership with business. With the Strategic Rail Authority emerging under the responsibility of the Department of Transport, Environment and the Regions, Railtrack needs to have a coherent and consistent public affairs policy.

Simon Miller, Head of Public Affairs for Railtrack, stated in an interview with the author:

> Decision makers want to deal directly with companies rather than consultants. Whilst the latter have an important role to play in helping you shape strategy and key messages, it is important that the company is seen to lead in contacting politicians and civil servants. We are moving to a situation where we are retaining an agency on an ad hoc, project basis rather than on a retainer, but we are predominately doing the work ourselves, in-house. Whilst the team has increased in strength and moved from being a mere packhorse to being involved in strategic thinking, there are still only four people in my team.
>
> The days of wining and dining to crack an issue, or of the company chairman being able to pick up the phone to a politician because he knew him at Oxford are largely behind us. We have to be more cerebral than that. No lobbying is better than bad lobbying. If you mess it up, it can have a negative effect so that it is harder to make an approach the next time.

As well as having to prepare for and put our case to the regulatory review, and be aware of the implications of the emerging Strategic Rail Authority, we have two major construction projects underway at the moment. One is the Channel Tunnel rail link, which is the first overland railway to be built in Britain this century. This country has an appalling record of getting such projects built on time and to budget. It is taking place in a very overcrowded part of the country, and we have to handle our dealings with the new line's neighbours, local media and councillors, very professionally.

The other project is the upgrading of the west coast mainline. It's the most well used piece of track in Europe with over 1,000 trains per day, but it's been starved of resources for decades and the infrastructure and the rolling stock are clapped out. We are trying to do something about it, whilst keeping the neighbours happy and keeping the trains running at the same time.

There is a place for big numbers, like the fact that Railtrack is spending over £17 billion on the infrastructure over the next ten years, over £4 million every day. But the surest way to the hearts and minds of MPs is to break it down to constituency sized chunks. Also, if you speak to most rail users they won't say that it feels like they are travelling around on a network where investment is at record levels. One reason is that we haven't been very good at communicating what we are doing, and the other is that, like the water industry, you can't actually see our investment. If you don't repair a tunnel, or the track or the signalling system, it may affect the running of the trains if you don't do it, but it is hard to make a high visibility impact.

One area where we can make a visible difference is in the area of station improvements. We are doing up all 2,500 stations over five years. I can then make an individually targeted package of information for each MP which will contain details of what we are doing in their patch. On average, we have at least one MP visit to a station site each week, where they can don a hard hat, see what work we are doing and get local coverage in the media. Improvements to station surfaces, better disabled access, more bike racks, repairing the clock tower, they can see what they are getting for the money.

I am also responsible for a team of six people at Waterloo who deal with customer complaints and manage a complaints helpline. We can analyse where complaints are coming from and what those complaints are, whether it is vibration from trains, noise or vandalism, and match our activities to their agenda. If they get dissatisfied that's when they write to their MP, and an MP's view of the world is shaped by their postbag. We want to stop the 25,000 people who write to us complaining from writing to their MP. Whilst 25,000 might seem a lot, eight billion passenger kilometres are travelled each year, and half a million people live within 50 yards of a railway line, so it's all comparative.

There is an emerging understanding of who is responsible for what but I think it is still incomplete. Now, there are 35 train operating companies, three rolling stock companies, Railtrack, plus freight companies and maintenance contractors, so there are 60 companies operating in a field where there used to be only one. Reputations level down, not up, and it is difficult to be regarded as better than the worst performer. There has been some friction between Railtrack and the operators where we didn't agree on where the balance of responsibility lay, but we do work together with the Association of Train Operating Companies and with PR peers from those companies. We have organised seminars to talk through issues facing the rail industry and how we might deal with them, sharing best practice in the industry. We are all in it together and we can't afford not to work together.

Whilst it is important to work directly with those who make decisions, the media still has an important part to play. You have to be careful not to negotiate through the media, with government ministers feeling like they have been ambushed by reading something in the media which they should have heard directly from you. This can put them in an embarrassing position. The media is important as an influencer, particularly local media.

It's important to network within the company to draw out the raw information needed for political communications. A close relationship with the Chief Executive and senior directors is essential so that public affairs does not become marginalised. It's also important to make contacts lower down the company with middle and lower managers who will know the issues in detail.

Simon Miller operates within a major corporate environment. This is in contrast with VLV, described below.

Case study 2: Voice of the Listener and Viewer (VLV)

VLV came into being at the end of 1983 in response to a proposal by Richard Francis, Managing Director of BBC Radio, to turn Radio 4 into an all-news current affairs channel. Around 200 people wrote in support of a piece in *The Sunday Times* calling for an association of listeners, and a public meeting was organised in November 1983. Even though the Radio 4 plan had been abandoned, it was still felt that there was a need for an independent consumer body for broadcasting. With a small start-up grant from the Rowntree Foundation, Voice of the Listener (VoL) held its first conference in May 1984. It also made its first submission to the government enquiry on value for money given by the BBC World Service. By 1985, in its submission to the Peacock Committee on the financing of the BBC, VoL was speaking for viewers as well, and so changed its name to VLV in 1991.

'There was nowhere in the system for listeners and viewers to make a positive input', says General Secretary Jocelyn Hay. 'Individuals can complain to any number of institutions, but there was no way of making a collective representation.' She discovered this when the Independent Society of Business Advertisers (ISBA) was lobbying in favour of advertising on the BBC, with a direct channel through the Department of Trade and Industry (DTI).

> There was also no formal requirement for the Broadcasting Standards Commission to take account of listeners and viewers, but we have forced them to consult us and other organisations. However, the Consumers Association only deals with the quality of what you buy, like television sets, but it doesn't stretch to encompass citizenship issues. We cover both.

VLV is still the only organisation in the UK speaking for listeners and viewers on a range of broadcasting issues. It aims to safeguard quality and editorial integrity of broadcast programmes, and promote wider choice. Undue influence by advertisers, politicians and commercial interests over broadcasting is resisted, and the association also seeks to raise awareness of the importance of broadcasting in national culture.

Major submissions and responses to government have followed, as well as a series of lectures and a quarterly newsletter (Figure 8.3). In 1992, VLV produced a programme

Spring 2000 - No. 61

BULLETIN

VOICE OF THE LISTENER AND VIEWER The Citizen's Voice in Broadcasting

Minister spells out benefit of digital television

VLV's Sixth European Conference

OVER 100 VLV members and guests gathered to hear the Secretary of State for Culture, Media and Sport speak in the first of VLV's Westminster 2000 seminars on 9th March.

"Digital television will bring real benefits to consumers. It will be especially important for people who are housebound or who need signing or other specialist services," he said.

Mr Smith set two crucial criteria to be met before the final switch over to digital television. Everyone who can currently receive the free-to-air analogue channels (99.4% of the population) must be able to continue to receive them in digital; and the price must be within reach of people on low incomes. 95% of viewers must also have digital signals actually coming into sets within their homes. He believed this could be completed by 2010.

In order to monitor the process the Government will conduct checks every two years against these key criteria of availability and affordability with the help of a Viewers' Panel on which VLV will be represented.

Early in the next Parliament, new legislation will be needed to replace the present Broadcasting and Telecommunications Acts in order to help Britain maintain the lead it currently has in digital television and technology. In a rare first for government, the Department for Culture, Media and Sport has jointly with the Department for Trade and Industry, set up a team to draft a White Paper which will be presented to Parliament this

Secretary of State Chris Smith with VLV chair, Jocelyn Hay, at the seminar

autumn to form the basis for the new legislation. He would welcome VLV's input in formulating it, he said.

Mr Smith replied to a number of questions before leaving early for a division in the House.

He recognised the problem of achieving good reception in some areas, including Wales, Scotland and Eastern England and the Government is exploring a combination of technologies to ensure a better spread of signals. The initial band of digital multiplexes is now in place and he would wait before making any decisions about expanding it.

Digital radio offered a lot but he felt the switch-over to it would be slower than for television. He did not feel that digital radio would be overtaken by the internet for a long time.

A regulatory environment which understands the genuine need for regulation of broadcasting and the need for freedom in personal communications was important; he was aware of the

danger that in both the USA and UK, where competition law has been used to break up public monopolies, there is now a risk that private monopolies might replace them.

The recent licence fee settlement would require the BBC to make real savings and more effective use of its resources. No advertising would be allowed on the BBC's main channels but he had deliberately not mentioned the future of BBC Resources or BBC Worldwide in his speech to Parliament because he had left other choices to the BBC.

He set education as a top priority when he announced the recent BBC licence fee settlement, he said, together with improving its core services and the devolved services for Wales, Scotland and Northern Ireland.

If the BBC wanted to establish a dedicated digital children's channel it should submit a proposal to him for public consultation. This is now a statutory obligation.

'Public Service Broadcasting in the Information Society' is the theme for VLV's 6th international conference at the Royal Society of Arts, London from 17-19 May.

The speakers include: **Michael Wills MP**, UK Under Secretary of State for Learning; **Jean-Bernard Munch**, Secretary General, European Broadcasting Union (EBU); **Robert Madelin**, Director General, Trade Directorate, European Commission (EC); **Jean-Eric de Cockborne**, Head of Unit, Regulatory Framework, Directorate for the Information Society (EC); **Patricia Hodgson**, Head of BBC Policy and Planning; **Mark Byford**, Chief Executive, BBC World Service; **Werner Rumphorst**, Director of Legal Affairs, EBU; **Carolyn Morrison**, Chair, CDMM Committee, Council of Europe and Head of International Policy, UK DCMS; **Andrew Graham**, Balliol College, Oxford. Key issues on the agenda are:

● the role and funding of public service broadcasting in the digital enviroment;

● the new round of WTO negotiations;

● European audio visual policy initiatives;

● the funding and production of indigenous children's programmes;

● media literacy and lifelong learning.

Further details from VLV office.

Figure 8.3 VLV Bulletin

Used with permission

in the BBC2 Open Space series. In 1993, at its first conference, the president of the European Broadcasting Union spoke to a non-industry body for the first time. After his appearance, VLV was invited to submit a response to a consultation on audio-visual material conducted by the European Commission. 'We are dealing with five or six different directorates in Europe', says Jocelyn Hay.

> They include telecommunications in DG13, the internal market in DG15, international relations is dealt with by DG1 and DG24 is consumer affairs. There is an incredible complexity of issues that we are dealing with. As well as MPs and civil servants in Whitehall, we deal with the Home Office on data protection and changes to the Representation of the People Act, the DTI on the convergence of television and telecommunications, although our main channel is through the Department of Media, Culture and Sport.

Her latest concern was to safeguard the interests of individuals in the proposed new European Bill on Copyright, which aimed to prevent viewers recording digital audio material from television for their own use. She was concerned that the legislation could lead to the prevention of video recording of programmes. 'Somebody has to get in at the beginning, when the legislation is being set up, or it will be too late.'

Membership of VLV now numbers around 2,500, including overseas and corporate members. Current objectives include safeguarding Channel 4 as a public corporation. Performance of radio and television stations, including cable and satellite, is monitored. 'We are concerned about the future of parliamentary broadcasting too', says Jocelyn Hay.

> There is commercial pressure for ratings, and people turn off during parliamentary broadcasts, but they are an important part of the democratic process. The BBC wanted to move parliamentary broadcasts on to long wave (LW) radio only, which is much harder to find and involves retuning if you are listening in FM. The original draft of the renewal of the BBC's Charter in 1996 left out the requirement for daily reports on proceedings, which we fought to have reinstated.

The society is run by Jocelyn Hay and five part-time administrators, calling on twelve volunteer committee members on an *ad hoc* basis to spread the load. With this small workforce, VLV runs between seven and ten conferences each year, produces a newsletter and various publications, responds to consultations by national and European bodies, and has given evidence to three Select Committees. The association submitted a response to the panel reviewing the future of BBC funding, recommending the raising of the licence fee.

The VLV conference in Cambridge in April 1999 on the future of broadcasting attracted a high calibre of speakers, including Patricia Hodgson, Director of Policy and Planning for the BBC, and Paul Smee of the ITC. Despite this, prices for attendance are kept to a minimum to ensure accessibility for all. Funding comes mainly from subscriptions and donations.

One of the successes of which Jocelyn Hay is most proud is the prevention of money from the privatisation of the BBC transmitter network disappearing from BBC coffers.

> We challenged the government that as the transmitters had been bought with taxpayers' money, the Treasury could not keep the proceeds of the sale. We threatened a judicial review and they backed off. We had a lot of help from Ray Snoddy

at *The Financial Times*, who gave us some good media coverage. In the end the BBC got to keep 80 per cent of the money, which they used to fund development of their digital channels.

Note

1 Interview with the author.

9 Business ethics, public relations and corporate social responsibility

Ian Somerville

Public relations discourse in relation to corporate social responsibility tends to utilise language and concepts derived from ethical doctrines such as utilitarianism, Kantianism and 'rights' theories. This leads to significant claims for corporate social responsibility programmes. For example, businesses maintain that such activity is a recognition of the duties and responsibilities that companies have to the wider community, or that they contribute to the common good by benefiting both the company and society. This chapter will explore the nature of the ethical doctrines which business appeals to, the debate concerning corporate social responsibility in particular, and how corporate social responsibility is justified in practice.

Business is a social phenomenon. Societies have developed various kinds of social rules, such as legal rules, or even the rules of etiquette, which act as a framework or guide to behaviour. Moral rules are sometimes regarded as just another set of social rules, but societies are structured around moral rules in a peculiarly fundamental way. In fact moral precepts are frequently used to criticise the other kinds of social rules which guide human conduct. Most notably there can be clashes between moral rules and legal rules. The 'race laws' in the USA, for example, or the 'apartheid laws' in South Africa, were eventually perceived to be so immoral that the only moral course was to disobey them. Clearly one may disagree with particular moral rules or question the possibility that 'definitive' answers to ethical problems are possible. Nevertheless it is the case that, in all societies, a great majority of people accept that they *should* adhere to certain fundamental moral rules. Breaking these rules will meet with sanctions of various kinds, from disapproval and ostracism to, in certain cases, legal penalties. Moral rules help to structure social relations, and many of the decisions that individuals and businesses make must take account of them.

However, behaving ethically in this basic, passive sense is not normally what is meant by corporate social responsibility. Corporate social responsibility involves the idea of business being proactive in its relationship with a range of social actors and doing more than just trying to avoid breaking moral rules. A key example of corporate social responsibility in practice is *corporate community involvement* (see Chapter 12). The term 'social responsibility' implies that business is motivated by more than just self-interest and is, in fact, attempting to promote the collective self-interest of society at large. This can be differentiated from, for example, corporate sponsorship where 'the company's managers will expect a tangible return for their money' (Varey 1997: 118).

Up until this point we have been using the term 'ethical' or 'moral' as if it were an unproblematic concept about which there is widespread agreement. This is certainly not the case. It is important to clarify some of the language and concepts *vis-à-vis* ethical debate because, as we will see, public relations specialists tend to discuss corporate social responsibility using language taken directly from ethical theories. The first section in this chapter will discuss several key ethical doctrines which have emerged historically. The next section will relate these ethical theories to debates surrounding whether or not social responsibility is desirable at all. The final section will discuss how ethical theories inform the language of public relations and impact upon the practice of corporate social responsibility.

Ethical theories

In ethical theory the first and most profound division is between the assumption that it is possible to know moral right from wrong and the denial of that assumption. *Cognitivism*[1] is the term used by philosophers to describe the belief that there are objective moral truths which can be known and consequently that a statement of moral belief can be true or false. *Non-cognitivism* is the term used to describe the belief that morality is subjective or culturally relative, that is, in regard to moral right and wrong there are only beliefs, attitudes and opinions. Cognitivist perspectives such as utilitarianism, Kantianism, and 'rights' theories have had a significant impact on business ethics and the concept of corporate social responsibility in particular, but there have also been attempts to argue that business ethics is best seen from a *cultural relativist* standpoint.[2]

Ethical theories, which argue that it is possible to know right from wrong, can be divided into two groups. There are those, like utilitarianism, which assess moral right and wrong in terms of the consequences of actions – the *consequentionalist* perspective – and those, like Kantianism and 'rights' theories, which do not – the *non-consequentionalist* perspective. From the consequentionalist perspective we look at the results of actions in order to make a moral judgement about those actions. From the non-consequentialist perspective there is no immediate appeal to beneficial or harmful consequences to determine whether actions were morally right or wrong.

Utilitarianism

The classic consequentionalist theory is utilitarianism, which states that actions are not good or bad in themselves, but only in so far as what they are good or bad *for*. Utilitarianism is the notion that an action is right only to the extent that it causes more good than ill to be produced. The classic formulation of this position is that of the English philosopher Jeremy Bentham (1748–1832). Bentham identified utility with happiness. Happiness is the only thing desirable as an end in itself and all other things are only desirable as a means to the end of happiness. For Bentham, therefore, actions are right to the extent that they maximise happiness or, at least, minimise unhappiness.[3] Bentham was not particularly concerned with the happiness or unhappiness of individuals. For him it is the 'common good' that is the arbiter of right and wrong. This is Bentham's greatest happiness principle which suggests that an action or process can be classified as good when it provides 'the greatest happiness for the greatest possible number'.

The standard objection to utilitarianism is that it requires the promotion or maximization of 'goods', such as economic growth, in order to achieve *utility* and permits

the sacrificing of individuals and minorities 'for the greater good'. Donaldson (1992: 129) notes that:

> [Utilitarianism] begins with the impeccable principle of 'beneficence', and ends with the malevolence of the Victorian workhouse and the inability to prevent punishment of the innocent, or discriminatory application of the law, so that favoured groups are virtually immune, while disfavoured groups pay the price, as tends to happen in income policies, and sometimes, in the control of ethnic groups in the labour market.

This ethic of welfare would also allow the telling of lies to protect the reputation of the corporation. So, for example, if a company was saved from bankruptcy because its image and reputation were enhanced by lies told by company representatives to journalists, this may well be seen as a permissible act. From a utilitarian point of view the welfare of those human beings whose jobs had been saved is weighed against the breaking of trust with other human beings.

An ethic of duty

Utilitarianism can be contrasted with the non-consequentionalist ethical position which argues that it is *motivation* rather than *consequences* which is the determining factor in deciding whether actions are ethical or not. This perspective is generally referred to as deontological, from the Greek word for duty (*deon*), and is a doctrine that is primarily associated with the German philosopher Immanuel Kant (1724–1804). Kant argues that ethics is grounded in notions of duty and it follows from this that some actions are morally obligatory regardless of their consequences. According to Kant, an act is carried out from a sense of duty when it is performed in accordance with what he calls the 'categorical imperative'. Kant defines the categorical imperative in two separate but mutually supportive formulations.

> I ought never to act except in such a way that I can also will [desire] that my maxim should become a universal law. . . . Act in such a way that you always treat humanity . . . never simply as a means but always at the same time as an end.
>
> (Kant 1964: 70–96)

For Kant 'universalising' a maxim basically involves ensuring that the principle upon which we act should be one which we can recommend everyone else to act upon. The second formulation centres ethics on the relationship between human beings. In the case of lying to protect the reputation of the company in order to secure jobs, Kant would suggest that you shouldn't be prepared to act in this way unless you are willing to let everyone tell lies. Telling lies in order to make someone carry out your will also transgresses Kant's categorical imperative by treating another human being as merely a means to getting what you want.

The chief problem with the deontological doctrine is demonstrated where there is a clash of categorical imperatives. One has a duty never to lie but what if by lying one is fulfilling one's duty to prevent the murder of another human being? Kant actually insisted that if a murderer were to ask you the whereabouts of their intended victim you had a duty to tell them and not break the precept regarding lying. Therefore even when it negatively affects the welfare of other human beings one must fulfil one's duty.

An ethic of rights

Kant's deontological doctrine is closely connected with theories which proclaim that there are 'rights' to which every human being is entitled. In both positions there is a status common to all human beings which affords them protection from abuse by others. To infringe a person's human rights is to fail to treat him or her as an end in themselves. Like Kant's position, this viewpoint is broadly non-consequentialist and rejects utilitarianism. According to these theories we cannot sacrifice individuals and minorities to the common good when to do so would be to abuse their human rights.

Rights theories were developed during the political turmoil of the seventeenth and eighteenth centuries by radical thinkers who sought to change traditional hierarchical social structures which tended to be held together by notions of allegiance to an unelected sovereign. The foundational assumption of 'rights' theories is that over and above mere human law there is an objective moral order, the 'natural law', which sets limits to the power of rulers. In requiring justice of governments, the natural law conferred rights on the governed. The generally agreed list was life, liberty and, sometimes, property. These were proclaimed as 'natural rights' bestowed on people by the natural law. They were rights which governments could neither grant nor take away, people possessed them by virtue of being human. Governments could rule but they were bound 'contractually' to honour these basic rights.

In the writings of the English philosopher John Locke (1632–1704) the 'contract' became 'social'. That is, it was no longer deemed to be a contract between governments and people, but rather between the people themselves to set up and empower a government. This is an immensely influential concept and has tended to be enshrined in various 'declarations', from the American Declaration of Independence to Article 1 of the Universal Declaration of Human Rights which states: 'All human beings are born free and equal in dignity and rights.'

Theories that claim that there are inalienable human rights suffer from a similar problem to the theory that human beings have duties and responsibilities which they must not disregard under any circumstances. What happens when two different 'rights' clash? In the case of lying to protect the reputation of the company and therefore jobs, how does one weigh the 'right' to work against the 'right' of people to be told the truth?

All of the classical ethical theories have inherent problems and it is fair to conclude that none of them seem satisfactory unless they are qualified. As Chryssides and Kaler (1993: 103) note:

> So the aim of serving the common good has to be tempered by the admission of rights and responsibilities. Likewise rights and duties cannot generally be examined separately and neither can they be pursued regardless of any consideration of collective welfare.

Cultural relativism

Before turning our attention to the significance of these debates for corporate social responsibility it is important to note that there are accounts of business ethics which reject the idea – maintained by the classical ethical theories – that there are 'objective' standards of right and wrong. Pearson (1989), in embracing the concept of intersubjectivism, offers an argument which places public relations at the centre of efforts to construct a business ethic. For Pearson, 'post-modern rhetorical theory offers a powerful

and cogent theory with which to conceptualise public relations theory and business ethics' (1989: 121). According to this view all truths, including moral truths, emerge out of a process of negotiation and debate. There are no objective standards of right and wrong only subjective views on what constitutes right and wrong. Moral rules are intersubjective in that they are arrived at through agreement between different subjective viewpoints. Pearson argues that this communication process is the key to business ethics for it is in this process 'that the moral truths shaping corporate conduct are grounded' (p. 122). According to Pearson this approach offers equity, that is, the decision as to what actions are ethical emerges through the communicative interaction of all sides. This depends on accepting that public relations, insofar as it plays 'the central role in corporate communication', also 'plays the major role in managing the moral dimension of corporate conduct' (p. 111). Pearson here seems to be advocating a conception of public relations practice similar to Grunig and Hunt's (1984) two-way symmetrical model.

Whilst a theory of public relations which emphasises the centrality of dialogue seems attractive it should be pointed out that there are several issues here which need to be resolved. First, the issue of 'power' seems to be largely ignored. It might be possible to think of a situation where all relevant groups are represented regarding an issue but it is difficult to imagine a situation where all the participants will be accorded equal status. There is an additional problem in that a process of dialogue has to stop somewhere and a resolution to which everyone agrees might not be possible. A decision might have to made which is only in the interests of the majority and it is hard to see how one could prevent this from collapsing into utilitarianism, where you rely on maximising happiness for the greatest possible number.

Pearson's cultural relativism suffers from the major stumbling block that all parties must agree that all actors involved in an issue are equal. Based on that foundational assumption all parties can then arrive at a mutually satisfactory outcome through dialogue. By insisting on this foundational assumption it seems that Pearson is actually insisting on something similar to the notion that all human beings have 'rights' or that everyone should be treated as an end, not merely as a means. However, it is clear that these assumptions do not emerge out of the process of symmetrical dialogue, they are a prerequisite for it. Pearson then, relies on older established ethical doctrines to guarantee his model. But what have these ethical theories to do with public relations and, more specifically, what have they to do with corporate social responsibility? Even a cursory glance at the literature explaining most corporate social responsibility programmes reveals that the language and concepts we have just discussed, the 'common good', 'contractual rights', 'duties' and 'responsibilities', are all terms which have tended to be used in describing or justifying corporate social responsibility.

Should business be socially responsible?

In this section two contrasting views of corporate social responsibility will be discussed. In some senses they represent the extreme poles of opinion on this issue. In practice the attitude of most companies to corporate social responsibility will occupy a position somewhere between the two. Ethical doctrines play a role in justifying both perspectives. For example, Friedman, who rejects any conception of corporate social responsibility, justifies his 'free market approach' from a utilitarian standpoint. On the other side of the debate corporate social responsibility is viewed as a necessary and integral part of the 'stakeholder approach', an approach which is ultimately justified from a Kantian perspective.

The social responsibility of business is to increase profits

Milton Friedman, the Nobel prize-winning economist and advocate of *laissez-faire* capitalism, argued against the idea that business has a social responsibility. He claimed that 'there is one and only one social responsibility of business – to use its resources and engage in activities designed to increase its profits' (Friedman 1993: 254). Friedman insists that it is wrong to suggest that corporations can have social responsibilities, since, for him, only individuals can have responsibilities. He claims that the actual responsibilities of the corporate executive should be narrowly defined. He writes:

> In a free-enterprise, private-property system, a corporate executive is an employee of the owners of the business. He has direct responsibility to his employers. That responsibility is to conduct the business in accordance with their desires, which generally will be to make as much money as possible while conforming to the basic rules of the society, both those embodied in law and those embodied in ethical custom.
>
> (Friedman 1993: 249)

By claiming that businesses have only one social responsibility, to maximise their profits, Friedman is in effect saying they have no social responsibilities. He does not say that moral rules have no place in relation to business practice, in fact while pursuing profits business must conform to what he refers to as 'ethical custom'. He seems to be making a distinction between first and second order ethical rules, the basic moral rules of society (the first order) and social responsibility precepts (an optional second order). He does not elaborate on what the rules based on ethical custom are, but he does give some indication as to what the second order rules might involve. He castigates businessmen for 'preaching pure and unadulterated socialism' when they speak of 'responsibilities for providing employment, eliminating discrimination, avoiding pollution and whatever else may be the catchwords of the contemporary crop of reformers' (1993: 249).

According to Friedman, the doctrine of social responsibility makes two claims. These are that business must actively seek to do good (that is, not just avoid transgressing 'ethical custom') and this 'good' must not be done for profit, that is, it must not be done with self-interest in mind. If it was, Friedman would have no objection to it. But is actively seeking to do good easily distinguishable from the mere avoidance of doing evil? Friedman seems to believe it is but it is difficult to see how the examples that he points to demonstrate this. It could be argued that some of the examples he lists, 'eliminating discrimination' or 'avoiding pollution', are doing 'good', but at the same time they are actions which are engaged in getting rid of or avoiding social evils. What Friedman's own examples illustrate is that on many occasions the moral choice is between doing good or, by default, doing evil. Chryssides and Kaler (1993: 232) note:

> Friedman's assumption of a neat division between 'ethical custom' and business social responsibility takes too narrow a view of both. The first cannot be confined to simply the passive avoidance of evil or the second to just the active pursuit of good because very often good and evil are simply two sides of the same moral coin. Friedman is therefore wrong to assume that acceptance of 'ethical custom' has no implication for the adoption of socially responsible policies by business. Clearly it has; if only because such is the power of business over people's lives that its failure to do good will very often result in great evils being permitted to flourish.

It is not only Friedman's definition of corporate social responsibility which is flawed, there are also problems with the arguments he presents against corporate social responsibility. One of his key arguments, sometimes referred to as 'the agency argument', is that managers of corporations are merely *agents* of the shareholders in the companies they work for. The owners of businesses, the shareholders, are the only people to whom managers are accountable and the only responsibility managers have is to act in their interests. This means maximising profits so that the shareholders will make as much money as possible from their shares. Friedman presents his premise about a manager's role *vis-à-vis* the shareholders as a 'statement of legal fact' (Chryssides and Kaler 1993: 234). While other interests may be taken into account,[4] Friedman is largely correct in stating that the managers of a corporation must ultimately serve the interests of the shareholders. However, in British and US law the corporation is a separate legal entity and is not identified solely with any particular group – employees, shareholders or directors. It is precisely this issue of 'legal identification' which *incorporation* is meant to resolve. This means that whilst employees, shareholders and directors may, and do, change, the corporation carries on as the identifiable possessor of legal rights and duties. Chryssides and Kaler (1993: 229) note that:

> [B]ecause they are employed by the company rather than its shareholders, changes in shareholding do not, of themselves, affect the legal position of employees, be they managers or workers, they continue to be employed by the same company. In an important respect, changes in shareholding do not even affect ownership. It is the company as a corporate entity which owns the assets of the business. What the shareholders own is a right to a share of any distributable financial surplus. They in effect own the company rather than its assets. Consequently, the right of the company, acting through its employees, to utilize those assets is legally unaffected by changes in shareholding.

Managers therefore are not directly the agents of the shareholders in the way that Friedman wishes to imply, although shareholders are, in roundabout way, the owners of the business. Friedman's assertion that the interests of the corporation ought to be exclusively identified with its shareholders' must be seen in the context of his advocacy of the values of free enterprise. These values involve a combination of egoism and utilitarianism, a view that claims that if everyone pursues their own self-interest within a free market, the result is the greatest happiness, or economic well-being, for the greatest number of actors within that market. This argument, that only the interests of shareholders are important, is not universally accepted. There is, in fact, an argument that the managers should act as the agents of all groups associated with the corporation and not just the shareholders. Those who support this view reject Friedman's 'stockholder model' in favour of what is usually referred to as the 'stakeholder model'.

Kantian capitalism and the stakeholder approach

The 'stakeholder model' is so named because those who propose it argue that the task of the corporate manager is to balance the interests of all the different groups who have a 'stake' in the company. These groups might include shareholders, employees, customers, suppliers, the local community and even broader society. The interests of the shareholders in increasing their profits is only one interest amongst many that the management must consider. This model requires the corporation to take account of its social responsibilities. Evan and Freeman (1993) argue from a Kantian perspective for

adoption of the stakeholder model. They utilise Kant's categorical imperative to argue that all human beings have a right not to be treated as merely a means but as an end in themselves. Corporate policy must consider all of its stakeholders. They go on to argue that all affected groups should actually have a role in determining company policy. Evan and Freeman (1993: 255) state their belief in a Kantian ethical doctrine explicitly:

> We can revitalize the concept of managerial capitalism by replacing the notion that managers have a duty to stockholders with the concept that managers bear a fiduciary relationship to stakeholders. Stakeholders are those groups who have a stake in or claim on the firm. Specifically we include suppliers, customers, employees, stockholders and the local community, as well as management in its role as agent for these groups. We argue that the legal, economic, political, and moral challenges to the currently received theory of the firm, as a nexus of contracts among the owners of the factors of production and customers, require us to revise this concept along essentially Kantian lines. That is, each of these stakeholder groups has a right not to be treated as a means to some end, and therefore must participate in determining the future direction of the firm in which they have a stake.

They argue that, in the USA, changes in the legal system have been progressively circumscribing the idea that the corporation is only run in the interests of the 'stockholders'. They point to a number of legal cases in the USA which show that although stockholders' interests are still paramount, other interests, customers', suppliers', local communities' and employees', have increasingly secured protection under the law (Evan and Freeman 1993: 255–7). Friedman's viewpoint, they would argue, is slowly being overtaken by changes more in line with a stakeholder approach.

In the stakeholder model the corporation coordinates stakeholder interests. It is through the corporation that each stakeholder group makes itself better off through voluntary exchanges. They argue that the 'corporation serves at the pleasure of its stakeholders, and none may be used as a means to the ends of another without full rights of participation in that decision' (p. 262). From the stakeholder perspective corporate social responsibility is not an optional extra. It is integral to the responsibilities of the company and the company must pay as much attention to its social duties as it does to maximising profits.

The practice of corporate social responsibility

This section will analyse the language public relations specialists use to explain corporate social responsibility programmes and will suggest that they tend to rely upon the language of the classical ethical theories to do so. First, however, it is important to locate the role of public relations within the practice of social responsibility. When business organisations decide to involve themselves in local communities they usually attempt to explain why they are doing what they are doing. This task of explanation is usually allocated to the company's public relations department. This is hardly surprising since public relations specialists tend to play a key role in setting up corporate social responsibility programmes in the first place.

Public relations and corporate social responsibility

'Come & See' is very much a PR initiative – the question is, does PR stand for Public Relations here, or Propaganda Really? The message is that nuclear power . . . is clean and green . . . that radiation has always been around and is natural . . . also that nuclear power is safe . . . I'd heard that word 'safe' used a lot, and it was beginning to acquire a kind of Orwellian charm.

<div align="right">

(*Scotland on Sunday Magazine*,
quoted in Tilson 1993: 432)

</div>

The practice of corporate social responsibility is usually regarded as a public relations function because this is where a company meets the public outside of the usual roles of producers and customers. There is, however, another key reason why public relations specialists have tended to be associated with corporate social responsibility, namely, the claim that public relations can be a mechanism within liberal, pluralist society which has as its *raison d'être* the realisation of 'laudable social goals' (Gandy 1992: 133).

For J.A. Pimlot (1951), the historian of public relations in the USA, public relations is intricately connected with what he views as democratic ideals. He writes: 'They [the public relations specialists] are experts in popularizing information . . . the better the job of popularization, the more smoothly will society function' (quoted in Pearson 1992: 257). Heath (1992: 20) argues that 'professional communicators have a major voice in the marketplace of ideas' but that ultimately these voices 'compete to achieve cooperation – the collective and coordinated actions of people in society'. Cutlip *et al.* (1995: 134) go further and argue that public relations practitioners 'must operate as moral agents in society' and they must be prepared to place 'public service and social responsibility over personal gains and special private interests'.

These claims that public relations is concerned with the public interest are in part a reaction to the kinds of remarks noted above – that PR stands for 'propaganda really' – about the visitor centre at Scottish Nuclear plc. However, it is also clear that there is a significant strand within public relations theorising which claims that its practice can have a positive contribution within society, although this usually comes with the proviso that practice needs to be transformed (Grunig 1989). It almost goes without saying that there is bound to be a tension between this conception of public relations serving the interests of society and the requirement that it serves the interests of the corporation. This tension between responsibility to the needs of the company and responsibility to the needs of society is sometimes exposed by the language used in corporate documents that attempt to explain the practice of corporate social responsibility.

The language of corporate social responsibility

Companies frequently justify corporate social responsibility programmes by referring to the notion of 'enlightened self-interest'. For example, community programmes may be justified with the utilitarian argument that 'everyone benefits'. The company's image is enhanced and a local community materially benefited. Neil Shaw, chairman of Tate & Lyle plc, explains the mutual benefits of community programmes:

Our community activities, both in the UK and abroad, focus particularly on initiatives in the localities of our plants and the provision of direct assistance for individuals seeking further educational attainment. In addition, we also encourage secondment

of employees to particular projects in the belief that, not only can this make a worth-while contribution to community activities, but in doing so, the experience will enable volunteers to develop their own management potential.

(Newman 1995: 99)

L'Etang (1996a) notes that while corporate social responsibility programmes are indeed justified on utilitarian grounds there seems to be little attempt to actually evaluate and quantify the effect of such programmes. She points out that if such evaluation is lacking then companies 'will not be in a position to claim that they have contributed to happi-ness. In short, corporate social responsibility justified on utilitarian grounds needs to demonstrate cost-benefit analysis from the perspectives of donor, recipient and society in general' (p. 92).

It is also the case that information which public relations departments supply frequently alludes, in Kantian language, to the organisation's responsibilities or duties to the community, or society as a whole. Lord Raynor, chairman of Marks & Spencer, states: 'There rests on all companies, particularly large organisations like ours, a respon-sibility to assist through donations and help, the charities and agencies which exist in the community' (L'Etang 1996a: 91). L'Etang (1996a) notes that claims are seldom matched by the practice of corporations. She argues that a Kantian approach to corpor-ate social responsibility would focus on the motivation behind the programme, because seeking benefit from carrying out your responsibilities would not be ethical. From this perspective a corporate social responsibility programme needs to demonstrate that it is motivated by duty, and not self-interest (enlightened or any other kind). If a company were attempting to improve its image via community involvement then it would be treating beneficiaries as a means and not as ends in themselves and thus breaking Kant's categorical imperative. L'Etang (1996a) points out that if corporations took on board Kantian principles then their corporate social responsibility programmes might be managed rather differently. If the beneficiaries of corporate social responsibility are to be treated as ends in themselves then they should be accorded equal status in defining the relationship between the corporation and themselves. Whilst the language of the classical ethical theories is adopted to explain and justify corporate social responsi-bility, companies tend not to fulfil the full implications of these ethical doctrines and can leave themselves open to the charge of cynicism.

A further problem is that companies do not restrict themselves to justifying corpor-ate social responsibility solely from a utilitarian or a Kantian perspective. Robert Clarke, chairman of United Biscuits, states: 'Our commitment to community involvement stems from our strong sense of social responsibility combined with the realization of the commercial benefits that it brings . . . a generous and far-reaching sense of community responsibility – are essential to effective long-term business performance' (Newman 1995: 99). L'Etang notes that in 'many cases corporate literature is confusing because it appears to appeal to both utilitarian and Kantian principles yet apparently delivers on neither' (1996a: 93). This point, while accurate, can perhaps be explained to some extent by the fact that the classical ethical doctrines need to be qualified by each other in order to arrive at an ethic which balances rights and obligations with the 'greater good'. There is another reason for the appeal to different ethical doctrines and this involves the recognition that corporate discourse has many different audiences. The next section will discuss the case of Telewest Communications plc which is an example of a corporate donor justifying its social responsibility in different ways, to different audiences.

The 'discourses' of corporate social responsibility: Telewest Communications plc

The Public Relations Department of Telewest Communications plc, in its 'community information pack'[5] (available 1996–7), states that 'Telewest's most significant contribution to local communities is through its educational initiative – Cable in the Classroom.' In the pack Telewest points out that it is working with local authorities to provide multi-channel cable television services and interactive internet access to all schools within the Telewest franchise areas. The community information pack does not discuss corporate social responsibility explicitly, but implicitly there is a message throughout the pack to the effect that Telewest is fulfilling its duty or responsibility to local communities by helping out in this way.

Obviously this kind of project requires a significant level of expenditure and the company's 1997 Annual Report had to explain 'Cable in the Classroom' to the shareholders. The project is discussed in the section entitled 'Building stronger relationships with customers' and here more utilitarian language is used to explain the benefits of the project for the community and the company. The Annual Report states: 'Our activity in local communities extends beyond the construction and marketing phase and is best evidenced by our involvement with schools and colleges.' Regarding the decision to offer these services to local communities the report notes: 'The offer has helped us to develop a positive role in the community, and to enhance awareness of our product with future customers.' It later adds: 'The decision has received strong endorsement within educational, political and regulatory circles and will further strengthen our position in the communities we serve.' The key point here is that the same corporate social responsibility programme can be explained or justified in different ways, using different language, depending upon the expectations of the audience. If the 'utilitarian' explanation used in the Annual Report had been used in the community information pack the media may well have focused on the phrase 'enhance awareness of our product with future customers' and the programme might well have been portrayed as a cynical exercise in product placement. If the Annual Report had merely contained an explanation of the project and the expected benefits for the community, shareholders may well have asked what the benefit of all this expenditure was to Telewest and ultimately to them.

Conclusion

With regard to the role of public relations in corporate social responsibility, there would appear to be two choices. Public relations practitioners can use corporate social responsibility as just another element in 'the creation, or "engineering" of consent' in order to foster 'a favourable and positive climate of opinion toward the ... institution' (Steinberg 1975, quoted in Gandy 1992: 133). Or they could try to realise the idea that public relations can act in the public interest (Grunig 1989, Cutlip et al. 1995) by making genuine attempts to discover the requirements of community stakeholders and help companies be more responsive to social needs. To achieve the latter a stakeholder model is a prerequisite. This model argues that a corporation should be run in the interests of all the groups which have a stake in it. All stakeholder groups including the potential beneficiaries of the corporate social responsibility should contribute to the decision-making process. This would demonstrate that companies are treating the beneficiaries of corporate social responsibility with 'good will' and as ends in themselves.

Portway (1995) makes the point that there is a requirement to track the company's performance in a way that can be reported to its community stakeholders. This kind of measurement and evaluation can then take its place 'in managing stakeholder relationships alongside customer satisfaction programmes and employee opinion surveys' (p. 229). Evan and Freeman (1993: 265) admit that this may seem 'utopian', but it would appear that until all business audiences are convinced that corporate social responsibility is more than just self-interest, public relations departments will continue to use different explanations, based on different ethical doctrines, to justify corporate social responsibility to their different audiences.

Notes

1 For a comprehensive explanation of this terminology and a discussion of perspectives and issues relating to business ethics see Chryssides and Kaler (1993).
2 This discussion does not assess the impact of religious morality which obviously has a profound influence upon business ethics in many cultures. The theory that certain actions are right because God commands them – for example, in the Bible, the Qur'an or the Torah – is sometimes known as the Divine Command theory (Chryssides and Kaler 1993: 84). Occasionally in discussions surrounding issues of corporate social responsibility it is asserted that certain groups such as the Quakers displayed an altruistic approach in their business dealings and gave help to local communities. L'Etang (1996a: 84) notes that there is a confusion here between 'philanthropy' and 'social responsibility'. I would agree but would add that there also seems to be a fundamental misunderstanding of what motivates such religious groups who act in the way they do because certain kinds of behaviour, toward employees and society, are prescribed in the Bible.
3 To suggest that we can measure happiness seems rather unrealistic but it could be argued that the discipline of economics 'has attempted, indirectly, to introduce an element of quantification in that consumption of goods and services is said to satisfy wants' (Chryssides and Kaler 1993: 92). It is certainly the case that economics and utilitarian ethical theory have a long historical connection and there is a degree of conceptual and terminological overlap. For example Chryssides and Kaler (1993: 93) note that 'in economics the capacity in goods and services to provide satisfaction is spoken of as their utility'.
4 Interestingly the 1980 Companies Act permits British company directors to have regard to the interest of employees, but this is an option they are legally free to exercise rather than a duty which has to be fulfilled (see Chryssides and Kaler 1993: 234).
5 The 'community information pack' was sent to anyone in the franchise area who requested it, individuals, schools and local press and community groups. There was very little explanation of the kinds of cable services which Telewest would be supplying, but there was a great deal of information about the impact on the environment of installing cable and the general possibilities of the cable technology for business, education and so on.

Part III

Stakeholder
public relations

10 Media relations

Public relations has its origins in the field of media relations. This is one of the reasons why the two are repeatedly used as interchangeable terms, especially by journalists. It may also go some way to explain the knee-jerk antagonistic reaction of some journalists to public relations – one journalist has even been heard to remark, 'Without PR people, journalists would be the lowest organism in the food chain.' It is true that early practitioners were publicists and press agents whose main aim was to gain 'free' press coverage at any cost, and the truth was not allowed to get in the way of a good story. Modern day publicists still behave in this way (Max Clifford, often erroneously referred to by the media as a 'PR guru', is dealt with in Chapter 3).

However, with the growth in the maturity of the PR profession, not only has it come to concern itself with the wider issues of strategic and corporate management which were discussed in Part II, but a more ethical mode of interaction with the media has evolved. According to Grunig and Hunt (1984) over 50 per cent of practitioners operate the public information model of PR, where the dissemination of information is the main purpose. Whilst this model emphasises honesty, it still does not really address the opinions of stakeholder groups. Practitioners have taken on board the need for openness and accessibility to companies' affairs.

The basics of media relations

The first exponent of this method was Ivy Leadbetter Lee (see also Chapter 1), who in the early 1900s worked for coal operators in Philadelphia threatened with strike action by the United Mine Workers Union. He issued a Declaration of Principles, which stated, 'We aim to supply news ... Our matter is accurate.' The Declaration went on,

> Our plan is, frankly and openly, on behalf of the business concerns and public institutions, to supply to the press and public of the United States prompt and accurate information concerning subjects which it is of value and interest to the public to know about.
>
> (quoted in Grunig and Hunt 1984: 33)

Media relations is still the activity on which the majority of PR practitioners spend most of their time. Wragg argues (in Bland *et al.* 1996: 66–7) that

The purpose of press relations is not to issue press releases, or handle enquiries from journalists, or even to generate a massive pile of press cuttings. The true purpose of press relations is to enhance the reputation of an organisation and its products, and to influence and inform the target audience.

Whilst it is largely of a tactical nature in practice, good media relations can contribute to longer-term strategic objectives, such as:

- improving company or brand image
- higher and better media profile
- changing the attitudes of target audiences (such as customers)
- improving relationships with the community
- increasing market share
- influencing government policy at local, national or international level
- improving communications with investors and their advisers
- improving industrial relations.

As such, media relations forms part of most strategies in the following chapters in Part III.

What exactly do media relations consist of? There are a multitude of books which deal with the mechanics of contacting the media, how to write press releases in a specific format that conforms to the needs of journalists, and the best ways to target and distribute this information. Most stress the five Ws (who, what, where, when and why), and the need to make the release appropriate to the style and content of the targeted publication or broadcast, although not too closely in case journalists feel threatened. There is even a whole book devoted simply to how to write a press release (Bartrum 1995). A variety of methods of contact are put forward. Media releases can be supplemented by press conferences, media briefings, exclusive interviews, feature articles and photo opportunities. Haywood (1990: 193–217) provides a useful set of checklists. Advice is also offered on selectivity in targeting. 'Far too many news releases are sent to far too many publications', says Jefkins (1994: 154), urging the use of one of the many companies which supply up-to-date media listings.

A study of these texts serves to indicate that despite the expansion in the number of media titles and the development of satellite, cable and electronic broadcast media, media relations is carried out in the same way that Ivy Lee did it. The proliferation of media has led to 'a perpetual, global slow news day' (Gulker, quoted in Theaker 1997), so that PR practitioners may find it easier to get their material used by the media. On the other hand, the greater number of titles has led to the development of smaller, niche outlets, so practitioners have to be more aware of the exact nature of the audience they are trying to reach.

Whilst there are pages of advice on how to write media releases, how to target regional and specialist media and build up personal relationships with journalists, little account is taken of new technology or its impact. Haywood (1995) stresses that it is important to understand how the media work, yet much of his advice concerns the print and broadcast media. Indeed, standard advice on writing media releases (double spaced lines, wide margins) is a descendant of the days when journalists received hard copy through the post, marked it up and sent it off to typesetters for it to be made up to be printed. Stone (1995: 177) refers to the expansion of cable and satellite leading to the

practice of producing 'infomercials', or advertisements that resemble television pro-grammes. White and Mazur (1995) suggest that media relations may give way to 'links based on a larger number of possible communication channels and more responsive forms of communication'.

The impact of new technology

It is true that expansion of the electronic media is happening at such a rate that any book, with its lengthy production schedule, could never hope to keep up. But is the revolution in media relations as far reaching as that in information technology? The unsurprising fact is that the impact of new technology varies according to individual journalists, the media they work in and the industry sector.

Martin Wainwright, northern editor of the *Guardian*, said, when interviewed in 1997, 'New technology has not changed the way I work. It's easier to have a press release to hand while typing on screen.' On the other hand, Maggie Walshe, a freelance PR practitioner with clients in the information technology and digital television area, said 'Media relations has completely changed' (Theaker 1997).

In order to gain an impression of the impact of new technology, a survey was carried out by the author in March 1999. Three hundred questionnaires were sent out to jour-nalists working in national and regional press, both daily and Sunday titles, national and regional radio and specialist IT publications. A response rate of 26 per cent was achieved, although this was overwhelmingly from the regional media. Only 8 per cent of journalists from national media replied, 18 per cent from IT publications, and 28 per cent from regional media. However, the information received provides an inter-esting snapshot of journalists' attitudes.

Questionnaires were sent out by email, fax and mail, randomly selected from the sample. Only 12 per cent of questionnaires sent by email were responded to, as against 29 per cent sent by fax and 35 per cent sent by mail.

Journalists were asked how many releases they received each day, and which method of contact was most frequently used by PR practitioners, whether they received infor-mation by mail, phone, fax, email, courier or other methods, and which methods they preferred. Tables 10.1–10.3 show the responses received.

Journalists receive a great deal of information each day, of which media releases are only one source. Nearly a quarter receive over 100 releases, so the amount of time available to read this information is strictly limited. 'There is nothing a busy journalist hates more than receiving reams of unsolicited press releases, and the situation is even worse when the information is delivered in a format the recipient does not like dealing with', says Mary Cowlett (1999c).

It would seem from the responses to the survey that the majority of PR practitioners are continuing to use the traditional method of hard copy in the post, with the second most popular method being the fax, presumably because of its speed. But the majority of journalists (apart from one wag who replied that he would prefer not to be contacted by any of these methods at all) seem to prefer it that way. It has to be said that although more journalists would prefer to receive information by email than do at present, 75 per cent of those who expressed this preference work for IT publications, where the level of familiarity and expertise with new technology would be expected to be higher. This is confirmed by Jo Chipchase's survey of IT journalists, which is reported in Chapter 18. Commercial distribution houses have introduced rolling programmes to verify which journalists like to receive information on which subjects, and how they

Table 10.1 Number of press releases received daily (%)

Less than 20	11
20–50	39
50–100	28
Over 100	21

Table 10.2 Methods of delivery most commonly used (%)

Mail	61
Fax	39
Email	9
Phone	3
Courier	0

Table 10.3 Method of contact preferred (%)

Mail	48
Fax	46
Email	15
Phone	8
Other (face-to-face)	1

want it delivered. PR Newswire Europe has over 100,000 entries, which are updated weekly for the most important titles, less frequently for more specialist contacts. There is also a split, where the UK, Germany, France, Italy and Spain are higher priority than the Vatican and the Faroe Islands. Media Information has set up Prnet, which has 5,000 registered journalists who specify what subjects they are interested in. 'Because people are emailed with information on topics they have requested, this means they can pull down the news stories which interest them the most', says sales and marketing manager Paul Mitchinson. PiMs can create customised lists of contacts, incorporating fax and email numbers as preferred (Cowlett 1999c).

Also, other problems are associated with the use of email, such as being unable to connect to the server, errors caused by use of an incorrect address and inability of the recipient to download large files and read attachments. Those who send releases in this way should type the release directly into the email, or save it as a text document in Word and attach it. Use of the subject line for a headline and provision of contact information should be considered in the same way as conventional releases. Freelance journalists also have the added cost of having to pay for the length of time they are online, and do not wish to receive unsolicited material.

Journalists have perennially complained about media releases being addressed to the wrong people and poorly targeted. The author's survey also asked what the main problems were with releases. Table 10.4 shows the results.

Whilst it would seem that PR practitioners have improved by correctly addressing their releases, the majority of journalists still feel, as Jefkins above, that too many

Table 10.4 Problems experienced with media releases (%)

Irrelevant	66
Not newsworthy	65
Over branded	32
Badly written	25
Boring	25
Wrongly addressed	4

releases are being sent to them which are not relevant to their publication or programme. More efficient targeting can have significant effects on costs. 'Four years ago, our postage bill was about £10–15,000 per month: now it's down to around £3–5,000', says Katie Kemp of Text 100. She also feels that the advent of the internet has increased journalists' expectations of a more personal service: 'Five years ago we'd speak to maybe 50 journalists each day, while now we speak to around 200' (Cowlett 1999c).

Despite the fact that a few journalists commented that they could not recall any examples of good PR, there were signs that antagonism between journalists and PR people is not as widespread as commonly held. Several quoted local councils, police and health authorities, housing associations and utilities as providing good service. One journalist mentioned a leisure company which were 'masters at forcing us to do stories'. Others gave general hints, such as 'Don't try to oversell the product. Look for a human angle. Think about people.'

Follow up calls were particularly disliked.

> The most irritating practice is following up phone calls to the editor asking if we have received a release which had no bearing on us at all and was probably binned. We certainly won't remember a release unless someone local was involved.

Some felt that 'the jazzier the packaging, the brighter the release, the better the story', whilst others commented, 'I've never found any PR stunt to be of any great help in selling a story to me. If the story is good it will sell itself, but bad PR can kill a good story.' Several referred to well-written releases, which were backed up by available contacts: 'Simply and interestingly written, relevant to our target audience and area'; 'Focused and relevant, good visuals worked out and interviewees lined up'; 'An embargoed press release which offers interviews in advance'.

Whilst PR practitioners are often encouraged to be persistent, knowing when to stop is also valuable: ' I like PR people who know that "no" means "no", particularly when they are trying to flog a dead horse.'

Although there are more media titles, staffing in the newsrooms has been reduced, with the result that journalists can rarely take time away from their desks and are dependent on news sources to come to them. However, there is more information around and more places to pick it up from, deadlines are tighter, and where new technology has come into its own is with a greater amount of background research being carried out online rather than through personal contact. One journalist responded, 'Good relationships between PR people and journalists are a real bonus.'

PR practitioners have also to keep up with developments in the broadcast media. In the field of radio, 15 years ago there were just 50 commercial stations, now there are more than 225. This has meant that radio can be used in a more targeted way, as

different audiences have stations which deal with different tastes. 'There was a lack of understanding among PR agencies as to how to target radio stations. We used to get the same press releases as magazines and they had nothing to do with what we wanted on our programmes', says Sarah Braben, former marketing director of Capital Radio. As with other media, targeting is the key. Ideas which are most welcome are those with a local slant but national relevance, preferably featuring someone the listeners know, with something entertaining and informative. Using specialist broadcast facilities, enabling an interviewee to give several interviews down the line to several local stations from a central point, can mean reaching millions of listeners. The BBC has five national and 39 local stations, but has a greater sensitivity to news items with commercial connotations (Shelton 1999). This medium is set to increase in importance with the advent of digital radio.

The use of the internet has affected media relations as journalists are able to obtain information straight from a website rather than waiting for press releases. 'The internet can also make an organisation more porous, and information can flood out . . . an employee or anyone else with a grudge can easily make information available to a wide audience', says Shelton (2000). The development of the internet is discussed in detail in Chapter 18, but also affects many of the other areas discussed in Part III. The use of the internet in issues management and lobbying has already been covered in Chapter 8.

The following case study is included to show the workings of a busy media relations specialist working within a well-known retail company, Marks & Spencer.

Case study: Sue Sadler, Manager, Food Press and PR Office, Marks & Spencer

For some years, M&S was the benchmark for quality produce and clothing. Indeed, the company was so confident that for many years it did not spend anything on advertising, relying on the reputation which had been built up over many years. With ructions in the boardroom in late 1998, the company found it could no longer rely on its past successes. Problems at top management level and a severe drop in profits had far-reaching effects on all aspects of the company. Clothes were denounced as dowdy by the fashion press. The corporate affairs director left in 1997, and was not replaced until 2000. The fact that the company decided to look externally to fill this position rather than following its normal practice of promoting from within was also seen positively. However, speculation about possible takeovers still had to be quelled. Financial and corporate help was hired from Brunswick, recognising that M&S had previously neglected this area. Whereas five years ago the product spoke for itself, M&S has had to fight for coverage more recently (Cowlett 2000a). On the fashion side, the introduction of the Autograph designer range is going some way towards improving the fashion ranges.

Sue Sadler has had the job of dealing with the food side of the company's product ranges.

> The overall aim of press relations is to enhance the company's image, and in my area we do that through enhancing the value that they put on our products.
>
> It's a priority to respond to journalists in time for their deadline. They are often given impossible deadlines, and if we don't deliver in time we're of no value to journalists at all.
>
> Targeting is a perennial conflict. The temptation is to send it to everyone, on the basis that the more people that get it the better, but that can be the worst thing.

It can have a negative effect. If you are constantly sending the wrong thing you are going to alienate them, so that by the time you do have something that might interest them, they will probably throw it in the bin. The food area is very clear cut. Some write about recipes, some write about products. It is our job to know what they are interested in and be specific in what we send them.

When we first started using a consultancy, they said, 'Don't be too hidebound, although that person may be writing about that area now, they may write about something different in future.' They advised sending releases out to more people, but we started to get complaints. The advantage of being in-house is that you get to know your sector better.

Although things have been difficult for Marks & Spencer most journalists getting something from us will at least think it is worth reading. We have been careful to create a specific image for the food area.

It's also important to build up credibility on a personal level. Journalists want to be able to get hold of people straight away, so we have to make sure the office is always staffed. Most will ring up to get a quote to supplement any media release – you can't beat the personal touch. Journalists can feel that they are part of a long list if they get a press release, you are more likely to have success with a story through offering exclusives by phone.

The food area has its fair share of issues to deal with.

There are one or two product recalls each year. Some milk chocolate bunnies were found to cause an allergic reaction, and we found that they had been made on a production line next to one where nuts had been used and some dust may have blown over. There are clear guidelines about what we do in those circumstances to inform the media and the public.

Marks & Spencer had sold organic produce in the early 1990s, but had stopped selling it because the consistency of quality and supply was poor. However, consumer interest in organic produce has increased and, after consumer research, the company decided to re-enter the organic market in 1998. 'More of us became questioning consumers and as a result producers were forced to reconsider the way they cultivated their land and raised their animals', says Catey Hillier. The market is growing – Sainsbury's sales of organic food now top £1 million per week (Hillier 2000).

A press release was issued in May 1998 (Figure 10.1), and journalists were also sent samples of the organic produce to encourage them to cover the story. Initially there were two questions to answer: the company was sourcing produce from abroad and was only introducing seven lines in 21 stores. An internal briefing document was produced to help staff answer these questions. The limited product range was offered as an initial market exercise which would be extended if successful. Background was provided on the fact that UK producers were more seasonal and therefore M&S could not source the majority of their range from them. However, the company organised an organic produce supplier conference in July 1998 with its top 20 produce suppliers to inform and encourage them to apply for organic accreditation from the Soil Association. (Soil must be left for two years to break down pesticide residues before produce can be claimed to be organic.) M&S introduced further organic products in January and March 1999.

Genetic modification (GM) of food also caused problems for Marks & Spencer. Initially, M&S welcomed the emerging science, and issued a statement in May 1998

MARKS & SPENCER
food news

May, 1998

MARKS & SPENCER LAUNCHES ORGANIC FRUIT AND VEGETABLES

Marks & Spencer has responded to customer demand by launching a small range of organic fruit and vegetables.

The range of seven products, which is available in 21 stores initially, includes avocado, tomato, baby tomato, red pepper, red apple, golden apple and potato.

This launch follows an increasing demand for foods which have been naturally produced, while protecting and enhancing the environment.

Following the launch, Marks & Spencer is actively looking at extending the selection to include more organic fruit and vegetables.

Like 80 per cent of organic produce sold in the UK, the fruit and vegetables have been sourced from overseas. They have been packed to M&S' rigorous standards in the UK.

More...

St Michael

The M&S Food and Wine Press Office
Michael House Baker Street
London W1A 1DN

Want to know more? Please contact the Press Office
tel: 0171 268 8777 or fax: 0171 268 2777

Figure 10.1 Marks & Spencer press release on the launch of organic food
Used with permission

ISSUED: 15 March 1999

M&S ANNOUNCES BAN ON GM INGREDIENTS

Marks & Spencer has today announced that it will be removing all genetically modified ingredients from St Michael food products. As all food sold in Marks & Spencer stores is 100% own-brand, we will be the only major retailer where customers can purchase any product on the shelves with full confidence that no GM ingredients or their derivatives have been used.

This decision has been made after careful consideration of our customers' views. Although we believe that there is a place for genetic modification, customers are concerned about the speed at which these developments are being pushed through.

"We have to put our customers first and we made this decision as a direct result of listening carefully to their views. These changes to our food products will be made as quickly as possible," said Dr.Tom Clayton, Head of Food Technology for M&S.

Marks & Spencer will continue to monitor developments in GM technology and will consider any opportunities which bring direct benefits to our customers.

A GM helpline is available to answer customer queries on...

For further information, please contact: Maya van Eerde
 Sue Sadler

Figure 10.2 Marks & Spencer press release on the use of GM food

Used with permission

that 'good science, well applied, is an essential principle of our business'. The statement made clear that the only GM ingredients used by the company were soya and maize, which had been declared safe by the appropriate authorities. All products containing GM ingredients were to be clearly labelled, and all data on any new GM products would be analysed to assess their safety and impact on the environment. However, rising consumer disquiet led the company to announce in March 1999 that it would be removing all GM ingredients and derivatives from its products (Figure 10.2). Whilst stressing that they remained confident in the safety of GM ingredients, the company made it clear that customer concerns had led it to take the decision. The announcement was made once the company felt confident that it could source all its ingredients from alternative supplies, and the transition period for the changeover would

be the following three months. By taking the initiative and becoming the only major retailer at the time who would have no products containing GM ingredients on its shelves (it sells 100 per cent own brand), M&S gained a great deal of positive coverage, with such emotive headlines as 'Marks and Spencer bans Frankenstein food'. The company also set up a GM helpline to answer customer queries.

The organic range is promoted in stores with posters and cards, and a customer brochure has been produced which explains some of the more complicated aspects of organic production. The M&S Select Farms traceability scheme enables produce to be traced back to a specific farm and even, in the case of meat products, animal.

Whilst concerns have more recently been raised about safety issues such as the risk of *e. coli* poisoning through the use of manure, a consumer backlash has yet to happen, and supermarkets have continued to work to meet a consumer demand for a perceived healthier lifestyle (Cowlett 2000b).

Media relations forms a major part of public relations in certain areas, but it can be seen that other techniques are also used to supplement and support media activity. It is far better to be pro-active in company policy and provide the media with positive stories to cover. It also allows organisations to set their own agenda and look ahead in a strategic way, rather than simply reacting to journalists' negative queries if they think they can uncover some wrongdoing.

The following chapters will contain references to media relations, set in the context of wider strategies which use a variety of techniques and tactics to communicate with a wide variety of stakeholders.

11 Internal communications

··

Whilst most of the issues discussed so far concern publics external to an organisation, one of the most important groups of stakeholders is a company's employees. Organisational rhetoric often quotes the fact that 'our people are our most important resource', but the reality of whether this resource is cared for is patchy. New initiatives like Investors in People[1] enable companies to focus on their workforce, but even these are sometimes followed in a mechanistic way. Companies can survive and indeed prosper without taking the needs of their workforce into account. However, it is generally agreed that good external relations and policies should have a solid foundation on good internal communications, that an informed workforce is more likely to be motivated to work productively, and that this reinforces the company's licence to operate in its community (see also Chapter 12), where a substantial number of employees are likely to live.

Good internal communications may not just be about differentiating your company in terms of consumer branding. Cowlett (1999b) quotes a survey of 275 analysts and portfolio managers by Ernst & Young in 1998 which found that investors base their decision to buy or sell stock in a company on non-financial as well as financial performance. 'Investors' perceptions of improvements in areas such as corporate strategy, innovation and the ability to attract and retain talented people can have a major impact on the share price.' A study by the *Journal of Marketing* stated that 68 per cent of customers defect from an organisation because of staff attitudes or indifference (Cowlett 1999b). Conversely, another survey found that 41 per cent of customers said they were most likely to buy a company's products or services again if staff treated them well, regardless of advertising, branding or promotional activity (MORI/MCA 1999). These findings emphasise the importance not only of employees' understanding the company and their role within it, but also of their actual commitment to the company objectives.

President of the International Association of Business Communicators (IABC) UK David Hammond is positive that organisations have learnt this lesson. Speaking at the IABC conference in Dublin (21 November 1999) he announced the results of an IABC survey which show that 51 per cent of organisations have well-defined communication strategies and that 52 per cent of senior managers support the importance of a strong communications programme to achieve business goals. In addition, 71 per cent of senior managers actively integrate communication into their business strategy.

> Treating people – not money, machines or minds – as the natural resource may be
> the key to it all . . . No organisational relationships are as important as those with
> employees at all levels.
>
> (Cutlip *et al*. 1985: 311)

Employees are not an homogeneous stakeholder group, but consist of workers, manage-
ment and board, who perform different functions within the organisation, such as produc-
tion, administration, and services. Unions may negotiate on behalf of different groups
of employees.

Communication operates in many ways within an organisation, flowing downwards
from senior directors and management to workers, upwards from the shop floor, and
between groups and individuals. Some routes may work well, others may be blocked.
How they work is normally a product of the culture of the organisation, whether it
involves employees or not. When communication doesn't work, the grapevine steps in
to fill the gap. The grapevine, made up of rumour and gossip, is not controlled or
controllable. It is always in existence, but its effects can be moderated if communica-
tion flows are working well. Problems may arise if the grapevine is the only form of
communication, or is seen as more reliable or important than information sent by
management.

The goals of employee communication
...

Cutlip *et al*. (1985: 315) propose that 'The goals of employee communication are to
identify, establish and maintain mutually beneficial relationships between the organisa-
tion and the employees on whom its success or failure depends.' They identify (p. 317)
four stages of employment where effective communications are vital:

1 The start – attracting and inducting new employees.
2 The work – where instruction, news and job related information should be dissem-
 inated.
3 The rewards and recognition – promotions, special events, awards.
4 The termination – breakdown of equipment, layoffs, dismissals.

Communication should work towards achieving the organisation's objectives. Employee
awareness of operations, problems, goals and developments will increase their effec-
tiveness as ambassadors, both on and off the job. Asking for input to improve how
things are done will encourage them to participate in the organisation.

Management should demonstrate a real interest in the employees' concerns, for
example by organising attitude surveys, suggestion schemes and stimulating the upward
flow of communication. There must be a response to this information, so that employees
feel that their opinions have been taken into account. If this does not happen, they may
be more dissatisfied than before, as their expectations of change will have been raised.
Involving employees in decision-making could lead to fewer stoppages and increased
efficiency. Good internal relations impacts on the bottom line. Top management must
support schemes to involve employees and take their opinions on board, or else such
schemes will be seen as mere gimmicks and will be abandoned. 'The most common
failing in employee communication is that it is too busy selling a management view
downward. It neglects to stimulate an equivalent upward flow' (Cutlip *et al*. 1985: 329).

The four eras of employee communication

Grunig and Hunt link the 'four eras' of employee communication to their four models of public relations (see Chapter 1). In 1964, C.J. Dover described the first three:

1 The era of entertaining employees (likened to press agentry) in the 1940s, to convince them that the organisation was a good place to work. This kind of communication may have given rise to Townsend's view that 'reading an employee communication is like going down in warm maple syrup for the third time' (quoted in Grunig and Hunt 1984: 240–1).

2 The era of informing employees (like the public information model) in the 1950s.

3 The era of persuasion in the 1960s (two-way asymmetric).

To these, Grunig and Hunt (1984) added a fourth:

4 The era of open communication (two-way symmetric).

Like the four models of PR, the four eras are not mutually exclusive, as all four kinds of employee communications are still carried out by companies today.

How management shapes communication

Grunig and Hunt (1984) summarise four kinds of management theory and show how the structure and environment of an organisation affects employee communications. Structured organisations centralise decision-making at the top, have formal roles and rules, and are likely to operate in a static environment. *Machine theory*, set out by Katz and Kahn, describes a group of theories which 'treat the organisation as a machine whose control and co-ordination can be engineered' (Grunig and Hunt 1984: 240–1). Employees have little freedom, tasks are subdivided into simple parts and roles are standardised. Communication in this arena is only necessary to instruct employees how to complete their task, is downwards from management and is mainly in written format, providing information which reinforces management's control. Management in this kind of company emphasises downward communication and discourages horizontal communication between groups of employees.

Studies in the late 1920s and early 1930s suggested that employees were more productive if management paid attention to them. Chester Barnard, president of the New Jersey Bell Telephone Company, published a book stating that 'the first function of the executive is to establish an effective communication system' (Grunig and Hunt 1984: 240–1). Communication was seen as something to make people feel good rather than to help them do their jobs. This gave rise to *human relations theory*, which encouraged the warm maple syrup kind of publication referred to above, where management policies are always presented in a positive, unquestioning fashion, and the emphasis is on social events. Employee news concerns those who are 'hatched, matched, dispatched' – new babies, marriages and retirements.

Barnard believed that informed workers would be more willing to co-operate with management. Instructions were replaced with expressive communication, but the downward flow of information was still emphasised. Suggestion boxes, company social events and visits by management to work areas were merely superficial gimmicks rather than genuine attempts at upward communication.

The next two areas of theory that Grunig and Hunt examined are related to less structured organisations, operating in a dynamic environment. As well as trying to control their environment, they adapt to it. They must be open and flexible to be able to cope, and receptive to innovation. Decision-making is decentralised.

Human resources theory developed from human relations theory, but advocated actual involvement rather than just lip service to it. The starting point was Maslow's hierarchy of needs, which stated that human beings first pay attention to basic needs such as food, shelter and security, but once these needs are met, they look for self-esteem and self-actualisation. Other theorists who built on this include McGregor, Likert, Herzberg and Black and Mouton, where 'open communication with employees about organisational decisions that affect their jobs makes up an essential part of the desirable management theory' (Grunig and Hunt 1984: 240–1). Communication flows upwards and downwards, as well as between groups. These theories state that employees will work best in a less structured environment with an open, symmetric communication system.

Finally, *systems theory* maintains that no one structure will be appropriate for all organisations, in contrast to the previous three theories which were 'all or none' theories. Some organisations within a static environment will be centralised, with a communication system which mixes both instructions and expressive communications, emphasising downward flow from management to workers. Less educated and specialised workers will be most satisfied with this structure, but it would not work for professional employees. They would be more satisfied in an organisation within a dynamic environment with open and complex communication flows. Thus different organisations will choose different models of employee communication, depending on their environments and organisational goals.

Systems theories have further developed, with several thinkers drawing on different fields of research. Gregory (2000) reviewed these developments, beginning with Buckley, who based his adaptive systems model on cybernetic research, emphasising the importance of feedback to initiate change. In this model, organisations change over time, and interact with their environment to do so. Maturana and Varela drew on biology to argue that the environment was part of the organsation. Callon and Latour developed actor–network theory (ANT) which suggested that a person was one actor in a network which included nature and machines, and that each actor had equal importance. Networks were rarely stable, and each actor would have a different degree of influence at different times. Morgan used Bohm's chaos theory to define management's role as shaping and creating contexts 'in which appropriate forms of self-organisation can occur' (Gregory 2000: 272). Whilst order cannot be forcefully imposed on an ever-changing system, equilibrium will always eventually emerge. Gregory suggests that these theories, together with the rapid change in society brought about by the internet (discussed later in this chapter and in Chapters 18 and 19), mean that public relations practitioners will not only have to be technically competent, but will also require analysis and awareness of the environmental context of organisations in order to devise success programmes of communication.

Internal communication and company objectives

'Truly successful internal communications turn organisations from machines into intelligent organisms which learn and grow', according to Dawn James, the director in

charge of Shandwick International's Change Management and Internal Communications practice.[2]

Quirke (1995: 71, 75) believes that 'The flow of ideas, information and knowledge around the organisation [is] crucial to success. The role of communication as the process by which this flow is achieved is central to the management of the organisation.' He continues,

> A business can only achieve its best when everyone's energies are pointed in the same direction and are not at cross purposes. Employees need to have a clear picture of the overall direction and ambitions of the company [and] a clear sense of where he or she fits in and how [they] contribute to the company's goals.

Quirke sees this need for change reflected in the shift from a limited number of internal communications techniques, such as noticeboards, memos and company newsletters, to more interactive media such as meetings, forums, video conferences and email. Like Grunig and Hunt, he warns that different communication strategies are needed for different kinds of organisation. He links the choice of strategy to three categories (see Tracey and Wiersema, quoted in Quirke 1995: 79).

Organisations that concentrate on operational efficiency focus on providing reliable products at competitive prices, and on keeping overheads down. Communication here resembles the machine theory model, creating greater understanding of roles and priorities.

Other companies may place more emphasis on closeness to the customer. Companies segment their markets and then match products more specifically. They want to build long-term customer loyalty. Communication is more flexible, and feeds customer feedback into the organisation. Upward communication is encouraged, and workers make decisions to solve problems, more along the lines of the human resources theory model.

The third kind of organisation focuses on product leadership, and must innovate to compete. Communication flows become yet more complex, both from outside and from within the organisation, involving feedback and brainstorming sessions across departments.

Internal communication and company development

Quirke also suggests that internal communication depends on the stage of development of a company. When first starting up, few people may be involved and communication takes place informally and frequently. As the company grows, employing more people, communication starts to become more functional and formal. This may eventually lead to devolving responsibility to senior division managers and communication will become more fragmented, concentrating on the division or unit rather than the company as a whole. At this point, central management may step in to co-ordinate communication to ensure all employees are aware of corporate messages. The danger here is for bureaucratic overload and a lack of responsiveness, and the grapevine may become more important. Managers start to form networks to cope with the complex organisation, bringing together people from across functions.

Quirke then moves on to the formation of a communication strategy, looking at what is needed from employees at each stage of the development cycle. Beginning with

awareness, he suggests using noticeboards, memos, annual reports for employees and email. Communication will be essentially one way, with little interaction or feedback. Evaluation would be concerned with whether employees received or saw the message.

If understanding is needed, more feedback and information tailored to a specific group must be added. Messages will be complemented with rationales, and feedback will be used to refine communication. Quirke suggests the use of roadshows, video conferencing and presentations to groups, enabling some interaction and participation.

Further interaction will be needed if employees' support is sought. As well as understanding, acceptance is necessary. The focus shifts from education, and methods could include business forums and training events.

The next step on Quirke's communication escalator is involvement, requiring dialogue rather than one-way communication. Team meetings could be used to disseminate management thinking, with cross-functional teams set up to solve issues raised. Feedback forums would be set up to inform managers of difficult issues which they need to resolve. Finally, if commitment to a new strategy is needed, employees must feel a sense of ownership and involvement in developing that strategy. Interaction, team problem-solving sessions, forums and talkback sessions could work here. Management must demonstrate willingness to listen and accept feedback without retribution. Each step on the escalator builds on the one before, and 'the basics [must be] in place before pursuing innovative technologies or radical sharing of views and opinions'.

Communication principles

Stone (1995) sets out several principles for communicating with staff. The primary audience may not necessarily be the entire workforce, but the opinion leaders and formers. Each person in this primary audience should feel that they are being personally addressed. Next, the primary audience should understand what they are being asked to do as a result of the communication. Whilst concentrating on ensuring information gets to the primary audience, Stone points out that employees have family and friends, some of whom are influencers within the local community. He stresses the need for clarity in language, keeping the gap between information and action as short as possible, and measuring and evaluating the effects of communication. Stone concludes by advising that communication needs to be continuous, so that staff do not feel that management only informs them when there is bad news, a crisis, or when unpopular work practices are to be introduced.

Hendrix (1995) starts by advocating research into an organisation's reputation with its employees and whether existing forms of communication are effective. A survey of employee attitudes may reveal issues such as low morale and frustration with policies that could inform the objectives for the programme. He sets out a variety of impact objectives, such as:

• to increase employee knowledge of organisational activities and policies
• to enhance favourable employee attitudes towards the organisation
• to receive more employee feedback.

Output objectives could be:

• to recognise employee accomplishments in employee communications
• to distribute communications on a weekly basis

- to schedule interpersonal communication between management and a specific employee group each month.

Once objectives have been set, appropriate techniques can be selected, from notice boards, displays, telephone hotlines, payslip inserts, internal television, videos, meetings, teleconferences, newsletters, direct mail, leaflets and email. The final part of the programme involves evaluating the success of the programme in order to adjust it and learn for the future.

The importance of understanding culture

The context of internal communications is discussed by Puchan, Pieczka and L'Etang (1997). They set internal communications within a discussion of the nature of organisations, based on the work of Gareth Morgan who developed metaphors for different views of a organisation 'as a machine, as an organism, as a brain, as a prison' (Hart 1995). They go on to look at structure and culture, and how that can affect the role and scope of public relations.

'Research shows that for all the millions spent on internal communications over the past 10 years, employee satisfaction has barely improved.' Quirke (1995) says in order to achieve effective communications companies must understand how their employees listen to the messages they are sending. In a reference to basic communication theory, Quirke states that employees decode the information they receive, and that organisational culture refracts communication, obscuring the message.

Thomson states (in Hart 1995), 'companies need to manage the emotion, feeling and beliefs that motivate people to apply knowledge constructively'. Internal communications specialists MCA commissioned MORI to conduct a survey of 350 staff across companies employing more than 1,000 people, which revealed that only 35 per cent of respondents would strongly agree that they would recommend their company to others. Half said that they understood organisational goals, but only a quarter said they were committed to giving their best to help the company succeed. Harkness feels that 'The reason internal communications campaigns often fail is because at the research stage people don't ask what the emotional hooks are for people within an organisation' (quoted in Cowlett 1999b). Whilst awareness and understanding have been achieved, commitment has not. A survey carried out by MORI at the end of 1998 found that only 11 per cent of all workers in the UK trusted and believed what directors of their company said (Pawinska 1999).

Christine Daymon (2000) feels that disregarding the effects of culture may be why 'communications strategies often lead to misunderstandings and even resistance'. She argues that all communication takes place within a cultural context which acts as a filter. Most of the theories examined above stress control of communication as the answer, whether employees are involved or not. Daymon suggests that a wider perspective is needed. She also suggests that many management theorists ignore the fact that 'culture might emerge from other groups besides management or from an amalgam of influences and experiences'. She advocates the use of different perspectives in devising communications strategies. Using the example of a new commercial television company, she shows how the messages given by management about efficiency and cost minimisation were interpreted by employees as changing the company's focus from making excellent programmes to skimping on expenditure. All communications were then viewed through this cultural filter, with the result that communications led to organisational conflict rather

than harmony. To avoid this problem, attitudes and beliefs of different groups within the organisation must be researched: 'With a better understanding of the complexity of organisational communication . . . managers may be better equipped to deal with it.'

Internal communication in times of change

Internal communication is particularly important in times of change. Research is stressed as the first step by James Harkness of internal communications and change management specialists Banner McBride (Harkness 1999). He shows how communication must be integrated into each stage of the change process, emphasising both giving facts and listening to concerns and reactions to the change (Figure 11.1). The first step is a stock-take of the situation. Interviews with managers ascertain the key messages, which are then used with discussion groups of employees. This also gives employees the chance to air their opinions, complaints and suggestions. Building on issues raised here, a questionnaire might be devised to further encourage employee involvement. Focus groups and one-to-one interviews could be conducted with a range of people. This process can also inform the language which is used for different groups, and indicate how different groups like to receive information. In an exercise for GNER, it was found that older people preferred to receive information in written form, but younger staff preferred to hear news face-to-face.

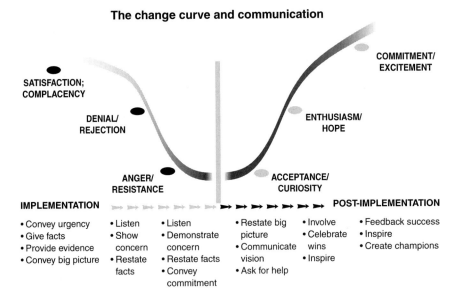

The change curve and communication

Figure 11.1 The change curve and communication

Banner McBride has taken the classic model of the change curve and adapted it to use in an internal communication setting. This diagram demonstrates how internal communication strategy can be shaped to support people as they move through the various stages on the change curve.

Source: James Harkness (1999), Banner McBride. Used with permission

Changing work patterns

Changes in patterns of work have and will continue to impact on how companies communicate with their staff. Working from home is becoming more common on all levels as technology advances. Fax machines, laptop computers, modems and mobile phones increase the flexibility and fragmentation of the workforce. 'Hot-desking' has appeared, where staff use remote electronic media to stay in touch, and use any desk available when they come into the head office.

One of the most important developments in the field of internal communications is the rise of the intranet. This is a system of making information available to all employees or members of an organisation on an internal website, accessible via a PC. It can be a dramatic change to the culture of a multinational company, as not only can all employees communicate internally with each other via email, but they can also receive information simultaneously, from head office. A discussion panel set up by the International Association of Business Communicators (IABC) on their website produced several interesting comments, such as 'It's provided a major cultural revolution in the way we work, think and communicate. It's turned a control culture into an empowered culture. It's turned our doers into thinkers.'[3] Bearing in mind the discussion of management theory earlier in the chapter, it can be seen that organisations introducing such a change in communication need to be aware of the ramifications. Other comments include 'With 70,000 people around the world, our intranet has truly allowed a global community to develop'; 'It fosters collaboration and the carrying out of the organisation's business strategy. It should also do it in a way that's going to save resources.'

Challenges and issues in creating an intranet are many. Information must be co-ordinated and managed so that it can be accessed quickly. For an effective intranet, employee buy-in is also important, so consultation must take place before set up. Training in how to communicate may also be necessary, to avoid long-winded reports tying up the system. Technical ability of employees must be addressed, as must access to PCs. The technology is immediate, so employees expect anything on their screens to be up to date and communication must constantly be updated. Responsibility for updating and entering information must be clear, so that conflicting information is not posted.

The creation of a newsgroup is a controversial and sensitive issue, and several court cases in the USA have used internal emails to prove their cases. However, giving employees the ability to discuss current issues which affect the organisation can also be valuable and engenders a sense of involvement. Information overload must be avoided, so that the key messages get through. Access to the internet and intranet also raises fears that employees may abuse the system, and spend longer 'surfing' than actually doing their job.

The implications for the public relations function within the organisation are clear: 'Instead of running a small department of internal communicators, I suddenly found I had every employee in the company as a communicator. As the intranet has mobilised our workforce, I am now responsible for information flow architecture.' Other companies may find that staff functions change, to manage the site and a network of correspondents who manage their own sites within the intranet. Obviously the amount of printed information will decrease, although those who used to contribute to and produce internal publications may simply input their information in a new way. The PR function will also need to work in partnership with the human resources and information technology departments to ensure that the intranet is effective for all employees.

Future developments will include the refinement of knowledge management so that information can be increasingly personalised. Forms of the intranet may be expanded

to suppliers and customers. One panellist on the IABC website predicted that people would be able to access the intranet from their Palm Pilot, anywhere in the world, to access corporate information to close a sale and communicate an issue, just like mobile phones.

Neil Melvin, of Smythe Dorward Lambert, also points out that 'Intranets need to evolve constantly and even the best systems need to be reviewed to reflect changing business strategies, needs and capabilities. Any intranet is only as good as its content' (Melvin 1999). After identifying business objectives for setting up the intranet, a new structure must be created to support the objectives. An intranet will create new relationships between employer and employee. Using and managing the intranet is a new process in itself, and new tools may also have to be provided, such as different ordering systems. To ensure that people start to use the intranet, change must begin at management level and be communicated effectively to the rest of the company.

Dawn James adds a note of caution:

No-one can deny the internet and company intranets are the single most successful 'pull' information systems ever introduced. However, as a 'push' mechanism, organisations must be careful not to overestimate the potential for improving communication and sharing best practice via the email system. Many people simply don't read many of their emails, others consider corporate communications information on a par with 'spam' e-marketing and ignore them. The key is to make emails actionable.

Case studies have been selected to illustrate different issues within internal communications. The first, from 1995, involves developments in internal communications by a computer software distributor coping with the change from a small business to one with increasing numbers of employees on several sites. The second examines the problems of communicating in a merger situation.

Case study 1: ISA international/BRAHM Public Relations

ISA International, one of the first firms in the computer consumables market, started in a back room in Bradford and has grown into a £140 million European business. The majority of the sales staff work in telesales and are under 30. In the mid-1990s, the company was keen to retain its workforce. A new managing director undertook a review of corporate strategy in 1994. The company's objective was to improve business by ensuring high motivation and loyalty amongst its staff.

The research stage encompassed a staff opinion survey, through a series of face-to-face lunchtime meetings with the managing director. Six issues were pinpointed: communications, recognition and reward, organisation, work environment, training, having fun. From this BRAHM PR developed a mission statement for the company to sum up the objectives of the programme. The statement was:

ISA will be the number one distributor of computer consumables in the UK, measured in terms of size, profitability and by the quality of our people. We will provide a working environment which attracts and retains motivated and qualified people whose individuality is valued and respected. We will provide the necessary resources to develop all our people.

This was summed up in the slogan 'Building a Better Business ... and having fun doing it'. To meet the objectives of the mission statement, a wide-ranging programme of activity was devised, centring on the personality of the new managing director, to demonstrate positive change.

Communication was used as the key to facilitating change throughout the company. Three meetings were staged throughout the year outside working hours, involving the entire workforce. Key issues were outlined and progress on meeting targets reviewed. A Book of People was produced, with a photograph of every employee with their job title and extension number. Copies were distributed to all staff. A regular newsletter called *In Touch* supported the changes, as well as reporting the activities of the new Fun Club. Specially produced birthday cards were sent to all staff, signed by the managing director. The company Christmas party started with a humorous short video reviewing the year, followed by the announcement of the Employee and Sales Person of the Year awards.

Four elements were used to motivate staff. Two awards recognised ten and five years' service, with a special event, gifts and certificates for each. Sales Person and Employee of the Month were assessed by measuring performance against sales targets or ten criteria for non-sales staff. Ten winners received certificates and were featured on posters in the reception areas and had a celebration dinner with the managing director. BRAHM developed an incentive scheme called Passport to Prizes, with all staff being awarded points on the basis of the monthly award assessments. These points could be exchanged for prizes from a catalogue. The two best performers during the year, the Employee and Sales Person of the Year, were awarded a Caribbean holiday.

Staff had raised the issue of organisation, saying that rapid change had made structure and responsibilities unclear. Booklets with organisation charts were distributed to all staff. A new dress code was introduced to make the working environment more informal and relaxed. Better training was recognised as an urgent requirement. A three-person training team was set up with long-term plans for closer working relationships with local training providers. An individual development programme was introduced for each employee.

The average age of the workforce was 23, and initial discussions with staff showed that they felt that fun had ceased to be a part of the company's culture. As well as ensuring that memos and newsletters had a humorous tone, money was allocated to a Fun Club which ran several family and staff events.

Appraisal was built into the programme through several methods, both informal and formal. Increased manager/staff contact through monthly employee appraisals for the awards scheme resulted in regular feedback from staff which was used to adapt the communication programme. The company's trading performance also improved, indicating a more focused and motivated workforce. A communications audit was undertaken of staff response to the new programme. This was used as a benchmark for future analysis. A majority of staff felt that internal communications had improved since the start of the programme, and over 75 per cent felt more motivated as a result.

Published with the kind permission of the Institute of Public Relations and BRAHM PR

Case study 2: Merger of Grand Metropolitan and Guinness to form Diageo

On Saturday, 10 May 1997, John Harben and Lynette Royle, internal communication team leaders of Grand Metropolitan and Guinness, were called to a City of London solicitor's office. They spent the rest of the weekend in other meetings, preparing to tell 100,000 employees worldwide throughout the two organisations on the following Monday morning that the two companies would merge.

The guiding communication principles were:

- to respond to communication needs of staff, measured both informally and formally
- that staff should never hear a story first from the media, necessitating speed of communication with all employees
- that communication should be open and candid, avoiding corporate comment and jargon
- that legal restrictions during the offer period had to be adhered to, necessitating liaison with company lawyers at each step.

'We had to start with the rational issues first', says John Harben. Communication had to reach all employees at more or less the same time, across all time zones and in 18 languages. Rapid staff feedback was a priority, and worldwide telephone polling was carried out by an outside, independent company to ensure confidentiality. Telephone hotlines, fax and email were made available to gauge an early indication of staff's communication needs and reactions to the merger.

A weekly newsletter, *Merger Update*, was distributed to 14,000 people, often as an email attachment that could be cascaded or forwarded to colleagues (Figure 11.2). As well as using adapted media releases and explanations of what was happening, staff feedback and reactions were also included, such as the infamous reaction to the merged company's new name Diageo, as in Don't Imagine Any Great Employment Opportunities.

Communications explained the benefits of the merger while recognising that a long period of uncertainty about individual jobs was inevitable. At the same time, people had to continue working hard to achieve targets. Two of the divisions had to compete with each other in the marketplace – International Distillers and Vintners (IDV) and United Distillers (UD). Only after the merger was complete in December 1997 could they begin to integrate – a process that continued until June 1998.

In addition, all staff had to understand the restrictions of the offer period, such as not sharing customer information and only nominated spokespeople being allowed to discuss the merger with the outside world.

It was clear that there would be at least 2,000 job losses in the two drinks businesses after the merger, so feelings of job insecurity had to be tackled openly. Managers were given advanced warnings of important announcements so that they could answer questions from their people.

Immediate actions included sending a presentation pack with slides, speakers notes and Q&As to 1,000 managers for them to present to their people at the time of the external announcement. Hotlines were set up within 24 hours of the announcement and the first *Merger Update* was distributed a day later. The bulletins were translated into five main languages, with more complex translations taking place locally. A Merger Special audio tape, based on Grand Metropolitan's regular management audio programme, was recorded and throughout the merger period a further three were produced.

GRAND METROPOLITAN
.... adding value 🐾🐾🐾

MERGER UPDATE

Issue 29 – Friday 7 November 1997

Diageo leadership meeting and beyond

The Executive teams of the four companies of Diageo - Burger King, Guinness Brewing Worldwide, Pillsbury and UDV - and key corporate centre staff **are meeting** in Gleneagles, Scotland, next Thursday and Friday (13 and 14 November). Two-thirds of the agenda for the 75 attendees, many of whom will be meeting each other for the first time, will be concerned with the **vision, values and behaviours** of the new company; the remaining third will be on **business strategy**, including attention to '**Managing for Value**'.

Says John McGrath: "The balance of our agenda reflects the fact that, at this early stage in the building of a leadership community for Diageo, the only real corporate glue will be **our shared vision for Diageo** and some common, observably different leadership behaviour in each business.

"I believe that we must leave Scotland on Friday night with **absolute clarity about what Diageo stands for** and I expect every participant to give clear and consistent messages to our 85,000 employees around the world in the following days".

Early recipients of these messages, aided by print and video materials, will include the 200 UDV managers who will meet **Jack Keenan and Finn Johnsson** on the UDV roadshow that starts on 17 November:

18 November	Asia and Pacific teams briefing in Hong Kong
19 November	Latin American teams briefing in Miami
20 November	North American teams briefing in New York
24 November	International Regional teams briefing in London
26 November	European Regional teams briefing in London
1 December	Global Operations and Central Function teams briefing in London

Jack and Finn will describe **UDV's vision and values** and how they see UDV as part of the Diageo family of businesses. The roadshow agenda also includes a status report on in-market integration in 1998 and the emerging Operating Framework for what will be the world's largest drinks company.

FTC decision

In response to questions from staff about the timing of the **Federal Trade Commission's decision**, IDV Legal Director David Scott has told *Merger Update*: "Some people have asked whether there is any significance in the fact that we did not receive the FTC decision on the merger before the 27 October target date. **There is no cause for concern.**

Continued overleaf

Figure 11.2 Grand Metropolitan merger – newsletter update

Listeners heard senior personalities being challenged by John Harben, bringing written communication to life. 'Staff drive around a lot as part of their job, so it's a good way for them to be able to access information. Also, a tape conveys emotion, so it's multi-sensory', says John Harben. Circulation grew from 1,300 to 2,500. A typical piece of feedback noted 'It's great to hear the personalities and how they respond to unexpected questions. It tells you a lot more about them than the printed word.'

The chief executive of IDV, Jack Keenan, and the managing director of UD, Finn Johnsson, talked face-to-face to their senior managers in a series of small meetings. More than 300 managers were reached this way.

From June 1997, more emphasis was placed on informal face-to-face communication in teams, with regular monthly team briefings for managers so that they could then brief their own people immediately. Special guides were produced detailing the agreed process for filling jobs in the new company, with tips for interviewers and interviewees. A commercial communication manual was produced for both sales forces so that they could answer customer queries. Communication planning guidelines were issued to new senior managers to ensure consistency and high standards.

Evaluation was carried out by telephone polling worldwide, and by the end of the process in January 1998, the results showed that 79 per cent of staff believed that the new company would be well managed, and 92 per cent that it would be successful. When asked what rumours they had heard recently, 91 per cent replied 'none'. Furthermore, 61 per cent felt that since hearing about the merger their morale was good. The survey was carried out by Smythe Dorward Lambert, who commented,

> The psychological health of the organisation seems to be due, in no small part, to the regular, trustworthy and concise communication from the centre, reinforced by growing numbers of managers having the confidence to conduct local briefings where people can discuss and challenge what's going on.

The process showed John Harben the importance of storytelling in communication.

> Good communication needs emotion. Leadership must be compelling, with big characters. Over 100 weekly meetings were held where staff met the chief executives, who were candid about what was happening. The speed at which we had to work reduced corporate lying, and so staff felt that they could trust their leaders and the information they gave. Including irreverent comment led to a lack of fear, so staff also felt that they could express their views and concerns. The tone overall was that the companies were choosing to merge, not being a victim to the process.

The declared scope of the internal communications team at Grand Met was that 'Our basic technology is the conversations that we all have every day. Conversations carry stories and one challenge is to help make management's stories as rich, coherent and engaging as those on the grapevine.' A distinction was made between formal communication such as publications and electronic media, and informal communication which is more powerful and about face-to-face conversations. This was illustrated with the rainbow diagram (Figure 11.3). It can be seen that this approach clearly links back to the initial discussion of management theory.

As John Harben points out:

> One impact of the merger was to reinforce the superior power of informal communication. More than being simply aware, people wanted to understand what was

Internal Communication Planning

Figure 11.3 The rainbow diagram

Source: John Harben. Used with permission

going on with the merger. The connection between formal and informal communication was brought home as, week after week, the team found and gave responses to questions from managers and staff at all levels about 'what's happening on the merger' which they could bring into their own meetings and conversations.

John Harben also sets out three domains of communication:

- *Production* – many people spend a lot of work time in this rational domain. A task is described, people use their left brains to apply logical and deductive processes to its achievement.
- *Values* – this includes what people feel about their work, their team, the company and so on. People apply their emotions and bring intuition and aesthetic judgements into play.
- *Explanation* – this encompasses how people in a company can share a broadly similar and involving story about 'what's going on round here'.

It is important, Harben feels, to address the latter two domains just as much as the actual production:

Until one knows something emotionally, one does not know it completely. The team could write and broadcast the rationale for the merger for months and yet it would take minutes to get people to understand the rational stuff if it came from their manager in a well-planned face-to-face meeting.

Reproduced by kind permission of the Institute of Public Relations and John Harben

Notes

1 Investors in People (IP) is a government initiative which relates to human resources practices within companies, who can apply for IP status.
2 Interview with the author.
3 The address of the website is <www.IABC.com>.
4 Interview with the author.

12 Corporate community involvement

...

> An institution's relationships with its neighbours in its community are crucial
> because these neighbours supply the organisation's workforce, provide an
> environment that attracts or fails to attract talented personnel, set taxes,
> provide essential services and can, if angered, impose restraints on the
> institution or industry.
>
> (Cutlip *et al*. 1985: 393)

In Chapter 9, corporate social responsibility was examined. The question was raised whether the rise in the number of companies taking responsibility for their actions and their effects on their environment was a genuine contribution or an empty gesture. Corporate community involvement (CCI) is the face of corporate social responsibility in practice. Cutlip *et al*. (1985) seem to be clear that any such involvement is down to basic self-interest, to enable the company to have an easy life. 'A corporation can gain competitive advantage by having the goodwill of local communities', agree Werbel and Wortman (2000: 124). However, Peter Smith (1988) used the findings of the *Tomorrow's Company* Inquiry, set up by the RSA in 1993, to point out that 'only through deepened relationships with and between employees, customers, suppliers, investors and the community will companies anticipate, innovate and adapt fast enough, while maintaining public confidence; this is termed "the inclusive approach"'. He concluded, 'the pursuit of business self-interest through wealth creation can lead to community well being . . . but what is meant by wealth creation and business self-interest have to be very enlightened interpretations'. He suggested that unless companies gave value to customers in the form of quality of standards and service, they would suffer in the current competitive marketplace. CCI could therefore be seen as a necessity rather than a luxury. The RSA Inquiry concluded similarly that companies have to earn their 'licence to operate'.

Roger Cowe and Jon Entine (1996), in examining the problems faced by the Body Shop and Ben & Jerry's when their proclaimed environmental projects were found to be less than effective, stated that 'it's no longer acceptable for capitalists to argue that their only responsibility is to maximise returns for shareholders . . . the boards of large, private companies must recognise responsibilities beyond their traditional and legal duties'.

At an accountability conference in January 1999, Chris McKenzie of Friends Provident stated: 'There is still no measure of the relationship between ethics and financial performance. No one can quantify the impact of social and ethical performance on

shareholder value, but damage to reputation can wipe out millions of that value.' Robert Waterman (quoted in Future Foundation 1998) concluded, 'Companies that set profits as their No. 1 goal are actually less profitable in the long run than people-centred companies.'

In this chapter, the role of CCI will be examined and how it may be used to motivate staff. Several case studies will demonstrate the types of activity that may be involved in a successful programme, and the concept of success will be examined by reference to an evaluation model.

Definitions of CCI

A definition of CCI would be a good place to start. 'It can be a number of things', says Graham Savage at the Millenium Commission. 'Providing money or people, or advice, something that may be only indirectly measurable.' 'Planned investment in the society in which you operate', says Ellie Gray, corporate development manager at the Prince's Trust. 'Putting the philosophy of corporate social responsibility into practice and making a real difference in people's lives.'[1]

Portway (1995: 219) states that, contrary to Cutlip's view, the distinguishing feature of the corporate philanthropy model of CCI is that the company does not expect anything in return for its contribution. Harrison refers to the fact that whilst companies are not the state and should not provide services and facilities which should be provided by welfare agencies, they are still part of the society in which they operate and need to consider their corporate behaviour as part of the role they play in society. She goes on to refer to Peach's model of the impact of business on its environment. The initial level of impact simply covers paying taxes, observing the law and dealing fairly. The second level recognises the need to minimise negative effects and act in the spirit as well as the letter of the law. The third level organisation 'sees itself as having a responsibility for a healthy society and accepts the job of helping to remove or alleviate problems' (Kitchen 1997: 129). The third level company is, however, rare.

Mapping the community

Cutlip et al. (1985) discuss the make-up of the community, illustrating it with a power pyramid to show that the community is not homogeneous. The top level consists of major employers and landowners, the next corporate and commercial executives. Underneath that level come PR executives and journalists, together with council officials. The bottom layer of the pyramid contains small-business managers and professionals such as ministers, teachers, personnel directors, social workers, accountants and factory managers.

Cutlip et al. also break down the category of 'prime movers', into the following:

- Employees' or members' families.
- The press, radio, TV and commentators.
- Clergy, teachers, officials, retailers, union officials and industrialists.
- Organisations such as planning commissions, welfare agencies, youth groups, veterans, and cultural, service and political action groups.
- Crusaders such as protest groups, petitioners and the rumour factories.

Other important groups in the community consist of independents who cannot be identified with any prime-mover group, and the dissidents who will resist change of any kind and can rarely be won over or persuaded.

CCI activities

Cutlip *et al.* (1985: 405–5) go on to list seven kinds of activity which can be used in CCI:

- The open house: a tour of the facilities of the organisation, enabling large numbers to come onto the premises. Easily accessible exhibits, guides and the participation of employees can give them renewed pride in their workplace.
- Special events: ground breaking for a new building, the completion of one, special seminars linked to the company's products, such as a safe driving school run by a motor manufacturer.
- Extended internal publication circulation: with the addition of some specific news, the internal publication can be circulated throughout the community to enable a wider knowledge of the company's activities.
- Volunteer activities: encouraging and enabling employees to perform voluntary service for local organisations, including secondment.
- Local advertising: controlling and focusing the message for local media.
- Contribution of funds: sponsoring or donating money to local organisations, whether in cash or kind.
- News services: tailoring information to the needs of local media.

O'Malley (1999: 46) reports that 'SmithKline Beecham decided to celebrate the 10th anniversary of Beecham's takeover by Smith Kline by inviting all its 55,000 employees to spend one day, on full pay, working for local healthcare projects.' She suggests that giving schemes be matched to charities that employees are interested in, to achieve a positive impact on morale.

O'Malley goes on to list some powerful examples of CCI and reasons for its use. Ruth Lewis is senior manager in community relations at British Airways. She feels that payroll giving has been successful there because 'our staff fly regularly and they see that there are a lot of people in the world who are less privileged'. Diageo commits £20 million each year to CCI, and boasts one million hours of volunteer work worldwide. Whitbread sees 'business benefit' as its prime objective in CCI, according to volunteer programme manager Christine de Cruz. 'In communities where we have active employees, the communities have a very high regard for the company.' In 1994, a MORI survey found that 88 per cent of the public agreed with the statement that 'a company that supports society and the community is a good company to work for'. Marks & Spencer uses development assignments to further managers' skills. By using their skills in an external environment, they often learn at an increased pace. Companies benefit from having a presence in the community and when staff return they bring back further skills.

A study by Business in the Community (BITC) and the Corporate Citizenship Company in 1996 and 1997 found that the skills most developed through CCI are communication, collaboration, leadership, teamwork and creative thinking. Anglian Water (AW) set up a 'transformation journey project' scheme after privatisation, to

encourage creativity and personal growth amongst employees, so that entrepreneurial people could fill the gaps left after downsizing. Each Journey Group chose their own project. Most chose a community-related one, including one group which installed a water supply for an Albanian village. More than 3,000 of AW's 5,000 employees participated. Clive Morton of AW lists a variety of benefits that could be tailored to several stakeholder groups:

> The PR function is likely to be turned on by the effect on image; the CEO by the view of the board and the City by 'responsible capitalism'; customer services will enjoy better feedback; procurement should see better supply-chain links; HR people put employee development high on the list.
>
> (quoted in O'Malley 1999: 46)

Setting objectives

As with all aspects of public relations, setting objectives is the prime step when carrying out CCI. This area of corporate activity used to be subject to what was anecdotally referred to as the 'chairman's wife syndrome', or the support of activity according to whim or personal interest of senior management and their spouses. As O'Malley (1999: 49) states 'By developing its own strategy a company can proactively decide what types of activity it wishes to participate in and why: it can then respond much more effectively to requests that are not consistent with its strategic directions.'

Portway (1995) uses the example of IBM's focus on issue management to determine the kinds of activity the company will support. Some issues which affect the company may not be suitable to be addressed through CCI, but an initial review can determine the wider picture. There is also a Community Advisory Panel which has responsibility for the Community Investment Programme, consisting of community leaders and IBM managers. In this way, the concerns of the community are fed into the process. Finally, as one of the key objectives of the CCI programme is 'to promote the morale and motivation of employees', a location manager in each IBM site is used to channel employee input. The result of this can be seen in the areas which IBM has chosen to support. One of the focus areas is education and training, given that the education system needs to equip people with the skills to make the most of IT. Another area is support for people with disabilities, as personal computers can provide them with new opportunities for education and employment.

The need for CCI

CCI is now an accepted part of corporate behaviour. Wheeler and Sillanpaa (1997: 275) report that 'In 1993, more than 90 per cent of large companies in the US had a community involvement programme, more than two thirds allowed time off during work for volunteering and 63 per cent had a community involvement fund.' In the UK, in 1995 a survey found that only a third of large companies had a volunteer programme and only 44 per cent of those allowed time off for volunteer activities. Less than two-thirds offered financial support. In 1996 a MORI poll found that 82 per cent of people in Britain believed that a company's activities in society are important in forming an opinion about the company.

In the USA, high risk industries in particular have been aware of the need to inspire trust in the communities where they operate by adopting policies of openness and communication. Wheeler and Sillanpaa identify several approaches to the issue of CCI. Paternalism in the early industrial era involved distributing wealth locally through wages and through investment in infrastructure such as schools. The size factor meant that some large companies became a component of the local scene where they operated, such as General Motors in Detroit. The community investment approach involved largesse distributed to community organisations where companies had head offices or local operations. The consultation approach sets up channels of information and communication to avert the concerns of the community from becoming hostile. Finally, the mutual development approach sees volunteering in the community in work time as beneficial to both community and organisation. A report on Employees and the Community showed that those who volunteered improved competencies, particularly people skills such as customer focus, communication and collaboration (Wheeler and Sillanpaa 1997).

The CCI process

The process for ensuring local community participation is described by Wheeler and Sillanpaa as beginning with a determination of the scope of an audit of current policy, and deciding on success indicators. The next stage is consultation with the community, then an internal audit, before agreeing objectives. Some external verification of the policy may be asked for, before a statement is published and the policy is adopted. They see this as a cyclical process, constantly reviewing and auditing the CCI agreement.

They stress that CCI has to be real, two way and inclusive. Transparency is also vital, in terms of how engagement happens and how it is measured in cash and other values. If, for some reason, a company has to withdraw from involvement, they suggest that negative consequences will be reduced if these two ground rules have been adopted.

Grunig and Hunt (1984: 270) state that

> Most organisations participate in the community because they realise that a strong community helps them to be a stronger organisation. Employees will be more satisfied if they live in a desirable community and better employees can be attracted to work there. Employees working in highly constrained job situations also become more satisfied with their job if the organisation helps them to use their talents in the community.

Although measurement is also important, Graham Savage remains sceptical. In an interview with the author in June 1999 he stated: 'The nature of British business is no less short term than it has ever been.' This may not be the case in the USA, as Werbel and Wortman (2000) reported: 'Companies appear to use corporate philanthropy as a tool to respond to negative media exposure' suggests that US companies recognise the benefits of investing in such activities to repair damaged reputations as well as build good ones.

Case study 1: Trees of Time and Place
(Ketchum Communications for Esso UK plc)
...

In 1995, the international furore over Shell's plans to sink the Brent Spar in the North
Sea highlighted the importance of building relationships with environmental organisa-
tions. Ketchum was appointed by Esso UK plc to provide strategic PR advice and
support for its environmental and community relations programme. Esso had a wide-
ranging community action programme supporting educational and environmental initia-
tives but research among opinion formers showed that awareness of this was low. The
company's objectives were to:

- focus Esso's CCI on the environment
- build relationships with environmental organisations
- raise awareness of Esso's CCI among opinion formers.

Esso had previously supported on an *ad hoc* basis a number of projects involving trees.
Trees are a good absorber of pollutants, including vehicle exhaust emissions, which
provided a link with Esso's principal product, petrol. For this reason it was decided to
develop a flagship community involvement campaign designed to position Esso as the
company in the UK most concerned about trees. This resulted in Esso working in part-
nership with 12 environmental organisations to launch the Esso Living Tree Campaign.
The success of this campaign prompted Esso and its partners to consider developing
one common initiative which focused on how people might commemorate the millen-
nium by making a positive contribution to their environment.

The resulting initiative was called Trees of Time and Place and invited people to
gather seeds from trees that meant something special to them, grow them and plant the
seedlings back into the local landscape. It helped to engage people rarely touched by
practical conservation in direct community action.

A prerequisite of the campaign was that it had to be sustainable. The PR objectives
were to:

- launch the campaign to opinion formers (environmentalists, politicians and business
 leaders) communicating Esso's involvement
- demonstrate business leadership in corporate citizenship by creating new partner-
 ships for the benefit of the environment
- launch the campaign to the general public
- promote opportunities to involve a broad range of individuals.

Activities

The announcement of Trees of Time and Place was made to opinion formers in the
spring of 1997, at a time of year when trees are at their most beautiful. The date coin-
cided with Chelsea Week, a key date in the UK horticulture diary. Speakers included
Norman Painting (Phil Archer in *The Archers*) who was also vice-president of the Tree
Council; Chris Baines, an independent environmental adviser; and Keith Taylor,
chairman of Esso UK plc. More than 120 key opinion formers attended, including MPs,
civil servants and the media. A personalised tree growing kit was given to all guests,

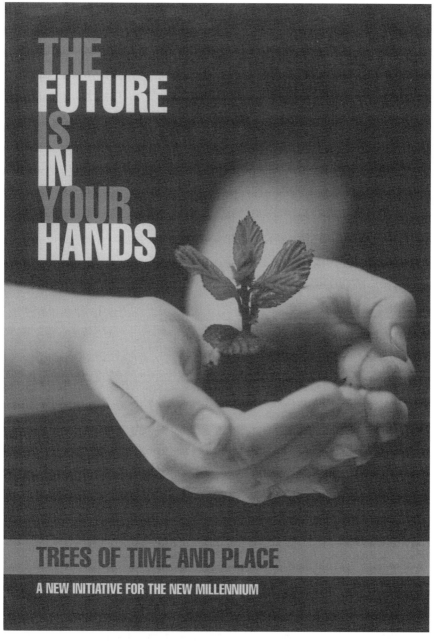

Figure 12.1 Example of material produced for Trees of Time and Place

Reprinted by kind permission of Ketchum Communications

including an embossed Trees of Time and Place terracotta pot and copper tree label. Because the pots were so popular, more were produced to give to figure heads and opinion formers supporting the campaign. These included HRH Prince Charles and David Blunkett, Secretary of State for Education and Employment who was presented with a pot which had the message in braille. To maintain interest, the concept of creating a Parliamentary Forest was devised. More than 30 MPs responded to an invitation to collect acorns from their constituencies so that they could be grown, and the seedlings planted back in the millennium year.

A range of free information sources outlined the campaign's aims and how to take part. These included a leaflet which opened into a poster; a Grow it Yourself card for acorns; a campaign partners list; a pledge card and a seed gathering chart (Figure 12.1). The pack was sent to everyone calling the helpline, which was set up to co-ordinate requests and distribution of literature; record pledges to grow a tree from seed; and give further technical guidance and information on events. A website was created at <www.totap.org.uk>. Tailored materials were developed for schools.

In May 1996, Esso's Walk in the Woods campaign had been launched on the back of the UK's first survey on the public's attitudes to trees. Commissioned from MORI by Ketchum, this highlighted that one-third of people in the UK had never walked in the woods. The campaign was aimed at getting families to enjoy woods when they were at their best.

Building on these activities for opinion formers, the public campaign for Trees of Time and Place was launched in the autumn, on 16 October 1997, the 10th anniversary of the Great Storm. It also coincided with the seed collection season. Regional media, youth and special interest media were the main focus. A video news release (VNR) was produced which starred ex-Dr Who Peter Davison, Chelsea pensioners and children gathering seeds at London's oldest tree in Barnet. This received extensive airplay on ITN, BBC, *Countryfile*, Channel One and Bloomberg TV. Blue Peter ran a feature from the Blue Peter Garden, including practical tips on growing trees from seed. A syndicated tape was produced for regional radio stations and interviews were arranged with specialist gardening programmes. A 'trees' supplement was commissioned by the *Independent* to coincide with the anniversary of the storm, aimed at increasing awareness of the value of trees and the campaign. *Gardeners' World* magazine adopted the campaign and ran a feature launch in September, with monthly follow-ups. By developing different angles, coverage was gained in a wide range of publications, including regional newspapers, parenting and country living magazines.

Results

In a survey of oil industry journalists, Esso's rating as an organisation concerned about its social responsibilities moved from 8 per cent (one of the lowest) in 1996 to 20 per cent in 1997.

Since 1997, more than 80 organisations have become partners in the scheme, including Whitbread, Ordnance Survey, Virgin Trains and Marks & Spencer.

In 1998, over 700 items of coverage were gained, the majority of which were in regional newspapers. Although only 1 per cent of the total coverage was from television, this represented 6 million in viewing figures. Over 12,000 calls were made to the helpline for the information pack.

Research by the Tree Council shows that over 3 million trees were planted as a direct result of Esso's National Tree Week in 1996, and over 700 events were held as part of the Walk in the Woods campaign.

In an interview with the author in May 1999, Sam Fulton, account manager at Ketchum, reported:

> The main benefit of the campaign for Esso is that it has improved the company's standing with opinion formers. They have been able to target them and show that they are supporting something that can make a real difference.
> Esso sees itself as making it possible for the partners to deliver co-operative projects. Some of the organisations involved have never worked together before. The partners drive the campaigns and deliver the projects, and Esso funds that, including literature and PR support. Activities are not usually branded as Esso events, to avoid alienating people. They are aware that their image is not going to change overnight because of their involvement, but the campaign is long running. It will continue past the millennium into 2000. Through working with the 80 partners on Trees of Time and Place, Esso has identified five or six that it could work with in the future on other themes.

Esso has also used involvement with the campaign to motivate staff. Everything is covered in the staff magazine, and staff have worked with organisations close to where they are based. In Leatherhead they are working with Surrey Council. Ketchum has also become involved, almost like a partner, and the chairman took part and gathered seeds.

Evaluation and planning are key to the campaign's success. As Fulton explains:

> Research is fed in to inform what we do in the future. There is a master activity plan which lists the four main objectives of the campaign, which includes details of what partners are doing to support each one. Ketchum is accountable, and there are measures to assess whether we achieved what we said we would.

Is co-operative working the future of community relations? 'This kind of project is fairly unusual at the moment', thinks Fulton.

> It has made the partners look at long-term benefits of their activities and connect them to a strategy rather than just short-term actions. However, some organisations are shy of losing their own corporate identity by joining together with others. It has been an unusual project for Ketchum, it's felt like we have had 80 clients instead of one.
> The key event was Seed Gathering Sunday, making it a day when everyone could go out and get involved. Once they had done that, they could be given more information about the next stages and link them with a partner organisation so that they weren't left on their own. Ordnance Survey has set up a map so people can look and see where their tree is planted, that they grew from seed. People can feel that they are part of a bigger campaign that will have an effect into the next millennium, and they have become more environmentally aware generally. I'm still surprised by how excited people can get about something really simple.

Case study reproduced by kind permission of Ketchum
and the Institute of Public Relations

Case study 2: The Prince's Trust: evaluating CCI – the Excellence Model

Ellie Gray is one of two Corporate Team managers at the Prince's Trust, managing a team of corporate fundraisers and also fundraising directly herself. She advocates the use of a partnership approach to provide a framework for CCI, and employs the European Foundation for Quality Management (EFQM)/Business in the Community (BITC) Excellence Model. The model uses a nine-point plan to ensure effective planning, implementation and measurement of CCI (Figure 12.2).

> Ten years ago, the Prince's Trust had to raise £40 million. Those relationships are now coming to an end and we have to think about the future. We have a strategy now, and we have to find a fit. Philanthropic gestures are almost all completely gone, we have to put a good business case for why an organisation should support us.

The Excellence Model enables charities and companies supporting them to benchmark and evaluate CCI activity.

Using a hypothetical example, based on several real-life partners, Ellie Gray illustrates how the model works. The activities of the Prince's Trust include a Business Start-up Programme for young people aged 18–30. Around 4,000 new businesses are set up every year. The Volunteers Programme provides a personal development and training course for young people aged 16–25, most of whom are unemployed, linked to New Deal, a government programme aimed at providing training for young unemployed. Programmes are delivered through franchises, and the Trust uses a network of volunteers as well as professional staff. There is also a pool of celebrity ambassadors. The profile that the Prince's Trust would communicate to a potential supporter emphasises the fact that it is a high profile charity active in local communities, with a UK-wide network. It is the biggest voluntary sector provider of business start-ups in Europe, and the largest voluntary sector deliverer of New Deal. The Trust also emphasises innovation and influences government policy.

The hypothetical potential supporter is assumed to be a high profile company with a UK-wide network of 8,000 employees. It is a member of Business in the Community

Figure 12.2 The EFQM/BITC Excellence Model

(BITC) and has a history of charitable giving which is rather dispersed. The company is looking for a more focused strategy.

> We would be looking for an equal partnership, we wouldn't want to be seen as a poor relation. We need help in meeting our core costs for our existing programmes. Companies should not always look for something new, with a little creativity an existing activity could be 'packaged' to meet the partner's needs and expectations. If you work with a charity that has built a reputation over ten years, you are likely to get more out of it than by creating something similar.
>
> In order to succeed, a company's CCI strategy needs to be agreed and owned at board level so that those responsible for its execution have the right backing. The commitment must be clearly communicated, and staff at all levels should be encouraged to get involved. CCI should be reflected in the mission and values of the organisation. The potential for a long term partnership is especially important for any charity. The programme should also meet recognised standards and meet a proven community need.

The hypothetical partner might have the following objectives for its CCI programme:

- strengthening the licence to operate
- better brand familiarity
- cost effective development of staff skills and competencies
- enhanced image.

The company also wants to fit in with current government thinking, which seeks voluntary sector expertise to achieve its social and economic aims of social inclusion and UK competitiveness. This might lead to an identification of CCI programme components of employee community involvement with staff training and personal development opportunities built in. These fit with the Trust's objectives of delivering programmes which raise self-esteem, change attitudes, develop skills and support young people into work.

The Excellence Model has nine principles for successful CCI. Each of them has a number of points that can be scored to demonstrate how effective the partnership is. The first five are enablers:

- *leadership* – top level support for CCI, how leaders create a culture where CCI is an integral part of the organisation
- *policy and strategy* – how the organisation implements its CCI mission through a clear focused strategy, supported by policies
- *people* – how CCI is used to manage and develop employees at an individual, team and organisation-wide level
- *partnership and resources* – how the organisation manages and costs its CCI investment, both cash and in kind
- *processes* – how CCI activities are managed and monitored to create value for stakeholders.

All of these can be allocated a numerical value, to total 50 per cent of the relationship. Ellie Gray also suggests that the charity can use the formula to look at its own

performance, and whether the results gained from the partnership make the relationship worthwhile.

The other side of the equation is results, which likewise can be allocated a value, and form the other 50 per cent. The four remaining principles are:

- *community partner results* – what the organisation is achieving in relation to its community partner, and whether the needs of the charity are being met
- *people results* – what the organisation is achieving in relation to its own employees, and whether their expectations are fulfilled
- *society results* – what the organisation is achieving in relation to the communities in which it operates, and whether their needs are being met
- *key performance results* – what the organisation is achieving in relation to its planned business objectives.

Geoffrey Bush, Group Community Relations director, Diageo, has said, 'Corporate community involvement is a two-way street where value flows to the company as well as from it.' The kind of benefits that a charity like the Prince's Trust could offer might include enhancing corporate reputation by association. If the company is reducing staff, affecting the local economy, the partnership can also be used to put something back into the community at the same time. Association with the Trust could also help influence opinion formers, so strengthening the company's licence to operate and building customer loyalty. Product sales could be benefited through cause-related marketing, and the association may also contribute to recruitment, staff development and motivation. 'Employee motivation is increasingly what leads companies into a relationship, because they can see the benefits of developing skills in this way. Some are even building it into their appraisal schemes', says Ellie Gray.

> There are many ways to exploit the PR potential of a CCI programme. The Trust is expert at running events like awards ceremonies, conferences and exhibitions. We offer branding opportunities wherever possible, and can generate local and national media coverage. We can produce publications to support the programme, and articles for inclusion in the company newsletter. We have a freephone and website which can carry credits and acknowledgements. By linking with the Media Trust and its Community Channel, we can also increase the number of broadcast opportunities available.

Once the programme is agreed, roles and responsibilities must be defined in order to deliver it. Ellie Gray suggests the following organisation:

- a steering group, with representation from both company and charity
- a programme team to execute the programme, with access to extra resources when needed
- there should be an account manager to ensure effective communication and continuity
- communications staff to get the message across and feed back outcomes
- a PR consultancy to provide additional support. This could be the consultancy which the company uses for its other areas of operation, or one of the increasing number of specialists in CCI.

The Trust can also use volunteers as outreach workers, and its regional networks and staff to provide co-ordination.

> At its best, such a partnership is a route to better performance. Collaboration between public, private and voluntary sectors can achieve more than just one sector working alone. Each partner will have something vital and fundamental to offer.
> I can use the Excellence Model with potential partners, even if I don't go through it all so graphically, to demonstrate what both sides might get out of the partnership. Although being from the Prince's Trust is more likely to get my foot in the door, we are also perceived as a rich charity which can discourage people from wanting to get involved. We have to deliver our programmes in a professional, business-like manner.

The end of a relationship can be as important as the beginning.

> The exit strategy is important. With the Prince's Trust, the programmes affect people's lives, and if sponsors decide to pull out suddenly that can have a really widespread effect, with people being left as stranded assets. There must be some kind of legacy built in.

Case study material reprinted by kind permission of the Prince's Trust. Excellence Model copyright EFQM/BITC.

Note

1 Interviews with the author, June 1999.

13 An introduction to financial public relations

Keeley Middleton

M any people in PR are unclear about financial PR and investor relations and there is little literature around to help clarify its role and activities or set out clearly its aims and objectives. Financial PR is not PR for financial services companies, such as accountants or banks. This is financial services marketing. Financial PR is the management of communication between a listed company and its financial audiences. A listed company is a company whose shares are traded on the Stock Exchange. These companies have to operate within the rules and regulations of the Stock Exchange and report on their activities and financial performance to their investors. They are assisted by advisors: a corporate financier who helps to develop the business by exploring ways to fund growth; a nominated broker who manages the buying and selling of the shares; an accountant who audits the financial accounts; a lawyer to ensure compliance with the laws governing commercial companies; and a financial PR advisor who helps build awareness and understanding of the business in the City.

Financial PR is frequently referred to synonymously with investor relations (IR). The distinction between the two disciplines, in practice, is a grey area as the two work side by side. IR refers to the management of the relationship with investors and potential investors (the latter may also include past investors) and is usually handled by a company's nominated broker. It is clearly distinguished from financial PR in its management of the investor base, where new investors must be found to replace those who have realised their investment. Financial PR is concerned with raising awareness and building understanding amongst primarily the City's opinion formers who influence investors and potential investors. These are often referred to as 'third party' audiences.

The working environment

The City is a money market comprising people who have money and people who need money. In the UK this exchange takes place on the London Stock Exchange which is made up of two markets: the main market where most stocks are traded, and the alternative investment market (AIM), which was set up in 1995 and is designed for younger and fast-growing companies. There are over 2,900 companies quoted on the Stock Exchange. The list is published daily in *The Financial Times*. The London Stock Exchange is also responsible for providing trading services and regulating the market.

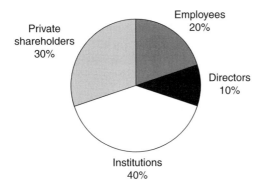

Figure 13.1 Potential share capital of a quoted company

Companies become quoted for a number of reasons: to raise capital so they can invest in growing their company; to enable original investors (such as venture capitalists) to realise their investment; to raise the company's profile; to provide employees with incentives. The aim of the stock market is to act as a catalyst for growth and a company will be expected to raise capital more than once to ensure continued growth. To encourage investment a company therefore needs to communicate its attraction to potential investors and maintain the support of existing investors, which is where financial PR comes in. Figure 13.1 shows how the share capital of a quoted company might be divided.

The City audiences

The City comprises all those people who have an influence over who invests in a particular company. Listed below are the main audiences that concern financial PR.

Institutional investors (existing shareholders, potential shareholders or past shareholders)

The main investors in quoted companies are large institutions such as pension funds. When individuals put money into a pension fund or insurance policy it goes into bigger pots of money known as 'funds' which are then invested in listed companies. Large institutions (such as M&G and Prudential) are influential investors as they will often hold a significant stake in an individual company, anything between 1 per cent and 20 per cent. The company's relationship with its institutional investors is primarily managed by its broker. However, institutions will be influenced by 'third party' or independent comment in the media and from analysts, and are therefore an indirect audience for financial PR.

Analysts

Investment analysts research and comment on selected companies listed on the two markets. It is their role to provide investors and potential investors with detailed research about companies and the sectors in which they operate. They also make

recommendations about whether shares in a particular company should be bought, sold, held on to or avoided. Analysts are the key opinion formers in the City. It is the unique responsibility of financial PR to encourage and manage the relationship between a company and the analysts who follow it. Analysts tend to cover a sector and/or specialise in a particular kind of company (for example smaller companies). More and more cover not only UK stocks but also European stocks.

Private client brokers

Stockbrokers act for private individuals who have money to invest, buying and selling shares on their behalf. They will offer advice to clients, if asked, about which companies to invest in. A stockbroker's opinion about a company will be influenced by what information is available, either through what is written in the press, or if he or she has access to analysts' research. Financial PR is used, where appropriate, to manage this relationship.

Private individuals

With internet trading the importance of the private individual has increased and this has many implications for financial PR and investor relations, which are discussed at the end of this chapter.

The financial press

This refers in the main to the City press, that is, *The Financial Times*, the business pages in the national and regional papers, financial journals such as *Investors Chronicle*, and investment journals like the *AIM* (Alternative Investment Market) *Newsletter* or the *Growth Company Investor*.

The Financial Times (FT) is the newspaper most widely read by the City. It sets out to be a paper of record, but will also make independent comment about companies that can influence investors. The City or business pages in the national and regional papers are also important. Columns such as Tempus (*The Times*) and Questor (*Daily Telegraph*) provide influential and analytical comment, especially to private investors. Regional papers are read by regional analysts and investors – not all of the City influencers operate from London. The City or business pages in the Sunday papers are read by all audiences and take a more analytical view of companies, often speculating on company results due to be announced in the week ahead. Tipster columns such as 'Diary of a private investor' (*Sunday Telegraph*) often stimulate share dealing on Monday mornings. Financial journals, such as *Investors Chronicle*, offer a more in-depth analytic digest of company results and news and provide investors with accurate market information. Their comments about a company can prove very powerful as they also offer buy and sell recommendations to their readers (mostly the private investor). The comments and tips made in the press can and do encourage trading in shares, causing a share price to move. One of the jobs of financial PR is to encourage favourable comment about a client company.

A recent example of how influential newspaper tips can be was highlighted by the *Daily Mirror*'s 'City Slickers' column, when journalists were sacked after they reportedly bought shares which they subsequently tipped. Many of the shares rose in price after the tip and some were sold the following day by the journalists.

The trade press

Trade publications are not generally the target of financial PR, although they are read by analysts who follow a specific sector and may also be read by investors.

Other media

The written press is the main target for financial PR as it reaches the key audiences, and provides them with analytical comment. Financial PR does not always make good TV or radio news, and the time constraints of both make in-depth analysis more difficult. Programmes such as Radio 4's *Today* can help set the day's agenda. Financial PR does make good broadcast news when the company's product or activity directly affects the consumer. For example, the hostile bid for Forte by Granada was given a lot of coverage and was used to communicate with investors in both companies. Broadcast media must be used in relation to who is being communicated with.

Wire services

The wire services such as Reuters, PA News and AFX are the fastest disseminators of information. Their headlines reach journalists almost as fast as news breaks. For financial PR stories such as company results, the speed of getting the news out is crucial to ensuring it reaches the agenda of the financial press.

Internet news services

Citywire, Hemscott.net, FT.com, to name but a few, are now an increasing influence. They are read by private investors, fund mangers, analysts and companies. They receive their news directly from RNS (see p. 164) and the wire services. They provide these audiences with up to the minute market information.

Figure 13.2 shows the flow of information between the financial PR audiences.

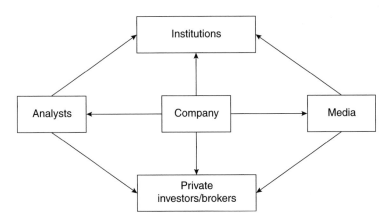

Figure 13.2 Flow of information

The rules and regulations[1]

The rules of the Stock Exchange that concern financial PR are those relating to the disclosure of information, especially price sensitive information. These rules are listed in the *Yellow Book* for companies listed on the main market. For companies trading on AIM the rules are contained within *The Rules of the London Stock Exchange*. There is also a series of AIM publications including guides for companies, guides for investors and rules for companies. The Stock Exchange also has a team dedicated to the AIM market. There are two overriding principles behind the rules: the timely disclosure of information, and the equal treatment of all shareholders. A company has an obligation to notify the market without delay of any major new developments and any change in the company's financial condition or in the expectation of its performance.

Within the Stock Exchange is the Company Announcements Office, which operates a wire service, RNS (Regulatory News Service). Once information is displayed here it is deemed to be in the public domain and can be disseminated further. There are many arguments over the true fairness of this system. The City audiences all have access to RNS but smaller private individuals do not. However, the internet is now giving the private investor access to the same information as the City, including RNS announcements.

There is no strict definition of what price sensitive information is, other than any information that the market does not know about, which if known would cause the share price of a company to move. The Stock Exchange produces two publications on this topic: *Guidance on the Dissemination of Price Sensitive Information* and *The Continuing Obligations Guide*. Large deals, such as mergers, acquisitions or takeovers, must be disclosed to the market. However, the fact that a new marketing assistant has been appointed within the company is unlikely to move the share price. All information for release should be checked by the company's broker as it is their responsibility to ensure the company complies with the market regulations. In some cases the decision will be left to the Stock Exchange. It also worth noting that the rules and guidance on them are subject to continual review.

The aims of financial PR

The main purpose of financial PR is to ensure that the share price of a company adequately reflects its value and to help liquidity in its shares. It does this through creating and maintaining awareness and understanding about a company in the City and achieves its aim by encouraging favourable 'third party' interest and comment.

Financial PR exists only for companies listed on the stock market. According to Jonathan Clare, managing director of Citigate Dewe Rogerson:

> Good financial PR will reduce the cost of raising capital for a company. If a company wishes to raise money through the market and its share rating is low then it may not be able to raise the required capital on acceptable terms. Its share rating may be low because it has not projected itself sufficiently so the City understands and approves of its business strategy.[2]

A company also needs to have 'liquidity' in its shares, that is, sufficient shares are traded to create a market. Investors can be discouraged from investing in stocks that are 'illiquid' as it may be difficult for them to realise their investment at a later stage. Companies with little liquidity are more likely to have a lower share rating.

Communicating what exactly?

The City judges a company by its financial performance and its growth potential. Financial PR can help to communicate this through raising awareness of a company's activities and business strategy.

The communication also involves managing the City's expectations of a company. For example, if the City expects a 20 per cent growth in profits and a company reports only 5 per cent growth, the result is disappointment. Disappointment may lead to investors selling their shares and discourage other investors from buying, which would bring the share price down.

Case study 1: Richmond Foods plc

Richmond Foods plc is a frozen confectionery company. Its sales are made up of private label ice cream and ice lollies for supermarkets (80 per cent) and ice lollies for the impulse market (20 per cent). The company makes its profit during the summer period. Its financial year historically ended 31 December, but following a merger and change of name it was decided to change the year end to 27 September to coincide with the end of its main trading season. The implications were that the company would report a loss for its first six months to 27 March (interim results) as it covered the winter period, where previously the company reported a small profit for the first six months to 31 June which had included some summer trading. It was crucial for the company to inform its investors and the City that the change of year end would mean reporting a loss at the interims. This was done, first, by including in the annual statement the following paragraph (note the formal tone of the language, which is very particular to financial PR):

> The change of year end from 31 December to 27 September coincides with our change of name, from Treats Group plc to Richmond Foods plc. This shortened reporting period defers the fourth quarter of the calendar year, which is traditionally a period of operating loss (expected to be less than £1.5 million), into the current financial year. This means prior to the exceptional items referred to above that the result for the calendar year would be a small profit.

It was then restated at the time of the AGM when the company issued a trading update which incorporated another reference:

> In our Annual Report, I indicated the likely results of the fourth quarter of the 1998 Calendar Year, which now constitutes the first quarter of our new financial year. It was expected that this quarter would report a loss of less than £1.5million. I am pleased to advise you that the loss was £1.35 million, which means that prior to the exceptional items referred to in the Annual Report, the results for the 1998 calendar year would be a profit of £0.3 million.

The financial PR made it transparent to investors and the City what the calendar profits would have been and this also exposed the results of the first quarter of the new financial year. Therefore, when the interim results were announced, the City had already anticipated the loss for the first half.

	JAN	FEB	MAR	APR	MAY	JUN	JUL	AUG	SEP	OCT	NOV	DEC
Financial calendar	Year end			Preliminary announcement	Report & Accounts produced	AGM	Half year end		Interim results			
Analysts/ regional brokers				Distribution of results Meetings held	Report & Accounts distributed	AGM statement distributed			Distribution of results Meetings held			
Institutions				Distribution of results	Meetings & visits	AGM statement distributed			Distribution of results	Meeting & visits		
Financial Press				Distribution of results		AGM statement distributed			Distribution of results			
Other press					Capitalise on corporate activity throughout the year							
Meetings	PR Meeting		PR Meeting		PR Meeting		PR Meeting		PR Meeting		PR Meeting	

Figure 13.3 Carbo plc, financial timetable 1999

Note: Some institutions like to have the Report & Accounts before any meetings are held.

When to communicate

All listed companies have what is known as the financial calendar (Figure 13.3), consisting of preliminary results, interim results and an annual general meeting (AGM). These are the times the listed company is legally obliged to disclose its financial performance. These announcements also provide a platform on which to build strong relationships with the financial audiences.

Preliminary and interim results

When a company reports full year figures these are referred to as its preliminary results. Once the full year figures have been audited and the company's board of directors has approved them they must be announced to the market without delay. The annual report is produced subsequently, but must reach shareholders not more than six months following the year end. A company is also required to report its half year figures in the same way and these are referred to as its interim results. A smaller report is produced for shareholders at this time and must reach them within four months of the half year end.

The first announcement of the figures (either preliminary or interim) is made to the Stock Exchange using its news service RNS. On that day meetings are held with major investors, usually institutions, and also with analysts and the media. A typical day is timetabled below, but this varies depending on the size of the company.

7.00 a.m.	Announcement of results – preliminary statement made via RNS
7.45 a.m.	Company directors available to speak to the *Evening Standard*
	Available to speak to regional evening papers
	Available to speak to wire agencies
	Available to speak with the broadcast media (where appropriate)
8.00 a.m.	Meeting with the sales team of nominated broker
9.30 a.m.	Meeting with City analysts/private client brokers
10.30 a.m.	Meeting with journalists/press conference
Lunch	With institutional investors
P.M.	Meetings with institutional investors (arranged by company's nominated broker)

Financial PR is responsible for advising on and managing the timetable for the day including organising meetings with the media and presentations to analysts. The broker will arrange meetings with the institutions. As smaller shareholders do not always receive the annual report the same day as the company announces, it is vital that the results are reported appropriately in the media.

The presentation of the results is key to creating understanding. Little notice will be taken of a badly written, uninformative chairman's statement or presentation. The chairman's statement must contain everything the company wishes to convey to its City audiences, as all information for subsequent press releases and presentations must come from this. One of the main roles of financial PR is to assist in the writing of the chairman's statement and presentation, ensuring that the key messages are communicated effectively. Ahead of the announcement questions should be anticipated and answers prepared to ensure the consistency of information given.

Following the results valuable feedback is obtained from the analysts. This provides information on how a company is being perceived.

The annual report

All listed companies are legally required to produce an annual report for their share-
holders within six months of their financial year end and 21 days before the annual
general meeting. The *Yellow Book* contains a list of items that must be included which
refer in the main to the disclosure of the financial accounts and significant corporate
or business activity for the year just ended. The annual report also provides the company
with an important communication tool. Shareholders, the media and analysts will refer
to it throughout the year. It is a marketing tool and can be used to introduce the busi-
ness not only to potential investors, but also to potential customers. Its appearance will
create an immediate image of the company. A fund manager was once reported to have
said: 'You can always tell how well a company is doing by how much gloss it uses
in its annual report.'

The AGM

The annual general meeting (AGM) is a legally required meeting held after the finan-
cial year end for shareholders. At the AGM a company has the opportunity to release
a trading update to the market via RNS. The Richmond Foods case study showed how
this can be used to good effect in managing City expectations.

The event varies from company to company. Not all capitalise on the advantages of
meeting their main audiences face-to-face. The *Investors Chronicle* (Hore 1999)
commented:

> AGMs are an opportunity for companies to give more information to shareholders.
> Not just price sensitive trading news but information about the products and services
> it provides so that investors have a deeper knowledge of what they have put their
> money into.

It went on to say: 'AGMs are the only point in the year when institutions and small
shareholders can be treated on a truly equal footing.' The article criticised companies
that do not make the most of their AGM.

Any price sensitive information given out at the AGM must either already be in the
public domain or be simultaneously announced over the RNS.

The location also varies and is dependent upon the location of the company's
head office and the number of shareholders expected to attend. A company that produces
an interesting or clever product could hold its meeting close to the factory and give
shareholders the opportunity to visit the site, to bring about a better understanding of
its activities.

Communicating outside the financial calendar

There are long periods when a company is not obliged to communicate with its investors.
Activities outside of the calendar might include analysts' site visits to see the opera-
tions of the company. This provides a platform for creating greater understanding about
a company and allows analysts to get a better feel for how the company works and
also an opportunity to meet management below board level. There may also be meet-
ings with private client brokers if a company has a large number of private investors
on its register, or if it would like to have more. A company always has to exercise

extreme care when hosting visits and meetings not to disclose any information other than that which is already in the public domain.

In the Carbo plc case study at the end of the chapter a full financial PR and IR programme is undertaken, utilising the opportunities to communicate in the financial calendar as well as hosting meetings and visits outside of it.

Communicating during transactions

Flotations

An initial placing offer (IPO) or flotation is when a private company goes public and becomes listed. The process involves finding investors to buy the shares when they are first traded on a named day. In this situation financial PR and IR work very closely together. The private company will appoint a nominated broker and a corporate financier who are responsible for the technicalities of the float and also for marketing the company to large institutional investors. It is the role of financial PR practitioners to support the IR role by raising awareness and creating understanding in the City about the company. This is achieved through gaining appropriate media exposure and analyst briefings.

Mergers and acquisitions

Globalisation is one of the key drivers behind the recent spate of mergers and acquisitions as sectors continue to consolidate. The City expects that most listed companies will at some point complete a merger or acquisition and expects to see it as part of the company's growth strategy. Financial PR helps manage the City's expectations about the nature and timing of a likely deal. A company may do this by making reference to its strategy at the time of its results. However, confidentiality and Stock Exchange rules on shareholder information restricts what can be said outside of a formal announcement.

Many large mergers or acquisitions may require money to be raised on the market through the issue of new shares and may also need the permission of shareholders. The company's broker and other advisors will prepare a legal offer document for shareholders setting out all details of the deal. This will be sent directly to shareholders who are asked to vote either by proxy or by attending the extraordinary general meeting (EGM). In most cases shareholders must have the 'offer document' not less than 21 days before the EGM so that they have adequate time to analyse and assess the deal.

The role of financial PR in these transactions is twofold: to encourage shareholders to vote in favour of the proposed deal, and to encourage new and existing investors to buy the new shares issued. Ahead of the document being posted a Stock Exchange announcement (a summary of the legal offer document) is prepared for issue via RNS. On this, the City will base its first opinions. Press and analyst briefings will be arranged on the day of the announcement. Briefing meetings help to create a deeper understanding of the deal, ensuring accurate comment in the financial press and a positive reaction from analysts.

Hostile takeovers

When one listed company tries to take over another without its agreement this is a hostile bid. One of the most famous was when Granada took over Forte in 1997. The

aim of financial PR and investor relations in this situation is to persuade shareholders that the management of one company is more capable than that of the other company. This battle is most often fought out in the media.

The PR programme ahead of Granada's announcement ran for two years, with financial PR and investor relations working hand in hand. Granada ensured it had good communications with its shareholders and third party audiences and made clear its strategy for growth. Forte, however, had a record of poor communication with its investors. Granada successfully took over Forte and demonstrated the importance of good communication.

A more recent example of a publicly fought bid is the three way hostile bid by Bank of Scotland and Royal Bank of Scotland for NatWest, which was won by Royal Bank of Scotland after the main shareholders agreed its offer over NatWest's desire to remain independent and Bank of Scotland's offer.

Each hostile bid is unique with its own issues to complicate the process. Financial PR and investor relations programmes are tailored accordingly, but with the same aim of winning the confidence of the other company's shareholders, as well as many other critical audiences, ranging from employees to regulators, customers to suppliers. The activities of all parties involved are closely governed by the Take-over Code, as well as the Stock Exchange's rule book (*Yellow Book*) and the Companies Acts.

Evaluation

The main measure of financial PR is share price. The share price of a company should reflect its full potential. A company that has financially performed well should have a share price equal to, or better than, its peers' and reflect the performance of the sector as a whole.

Current issues facing financial PR

Europe

The London Stock Exchange is now working to ensure closer links with Europe and is looking at ways of making pan European trading easier. *The Financial Times* currently lists the top 300 European stocks in the same way that the FTSE 100 stocks are listed, making it easier for investors to monitor the best and worst performers.

Greater links with Europe's stock markets is likely to increase the investor base and so there will be a greater need for communication. The challenge for financial PR and investor relations will be to find ways of communicating with an enlarged and multi-cultural audience. International IR and financial PR is not new, it is a niche that could become mainstream practice.

The internet

In the US dealing in shares over the internet (E*Trade) is not new, but the UK is only just waking up to its potential. Increasingly stockbroking firms are offering internet dealing services and according to *The Sunday Times* (Hamilton 1999) retail stockbroking in Britain faces a revolution.

A survey in *Investors Chronicle* (Temple 1999) commented:

> One of the most compelling reasons for becoming an online investor is the vast amount of free information on offer. It is now possible, for example, to research companies online entirely from free sources of information and to use a web based broker to deal in the shares you want to buy.

It is estimated that nearly all the FTSE 100 and around two-thirds of the Mid 250 companies now have websites as well as many small companies. The internet not only provides companies with an opportunity to supply information to their financial audience, but also gives them more control over the information disseminated, therefore not just relying on third party interpretation. Most private investors do not have access to RNS so rely upon their stockbroker to provide them with news about the companies they invest in, or find out information through the media. But the news that a small company has made an acquisition may not always be reported in the media due to the small size of the deal and therefore the private investor will have no knowledge of it. The internet provides companies with a channel through which they can get that information out to investors almost immediately. For further information on PR and the internet see Chapter 18.

Case study 2: Carbo plc

Background

Today Carbo plc is a European-based manufacturer and distributor of industrial abrasives, with production facilities in the UK, Italy and Germany, selling globally via a network of wholly-owned and independent distributors.

In 1993 Carbo was a mini conglomerate tight for cash. It was made up of five divisions including a successful abrasives business. This was at a time when the City was averse to conglomerates and the company consequently suffered from a steadily falling share rating and an overhang of shares (this is where shares are sold but there are no buyers for them). The management had developed a long-term strategy to take the business forward by becoming a focused abrasives business. To fulfil the strategy it was necessary to dispose of the non-core divisions.

Between 1993 and 1999 the group disposed of nine properties, made six acquisitions of small abrasives businesses and made seven non-core business divestments. This change necessitated a strong financial PR and IR programme to ensure its investor community was kept informed of, and supported, the changes.

The programme

Carbo defined its target audience as investors and influencers:

- investors – institutional fund mangers and private investors
- influencers – the financial media, analysts and private client brokers.

Before embarking on the programme Carbo established its key messages. It was important to clearly define the new strategy and the rationale behind it so that subsequent actions undertaken would be expected.

The directors of Carbo initiated regular contact with institutional fund mangers, analysts and the financial media through meetings and presentations at the time of its preliminary and interim results. In addition to this they aimed to create a better understanding of the business by analysts, private client brokers and the financial press through hosting visits to Carbo production sites across Europe. On one occasion Carbo successfully took some of its institutional investors to one of its overseas sites in Milan. The visit ensured a greater understanding by the investors of the overseas operations and therefore increased their confidence in the business.

The outcome of the programme was that the falling share rating stabilised and then increased as investors were found and liquidity was restored to the share market. Carbo's share rating is now in line with its sector rating as well as that of its peers. The programme is ongoing.

Notes

1 Control over the listing rules moved from the London Stock Exchange to the Financial Services Authority in April 2000. The *Yellow Book* is now purple.
2 Personal interview, 1999.

Acknowledgements

I am grateful for contributions from David Nolder, Shirley Whiting and Jonanthan Clare at Citigate Dewe Rogerson; Ken Jackson, chief executive, Carbo plc; Andy Finneran, finance director, Richmond Foods plc; and John Holland, Richard Williams and Mark Compton, London Stock Exchange.

14 Public sector public relations

..

W orking in the public sector is a challenging area of PR. As well as all the normal legal, ethical and technical considerations, public sector PR involves a greater range of stakeholders than in the private sector. These stakeholders are more likely to have overlapping characteristics. A local council is often the largest employer in its community, so residents may be employees, council tax payers and recipients of a vast range of services from education for their children to refuse collection. With public services such as the fire brigade, ambulance and police, the highly emotive level of their work is also complicated by questions of funding and national governmental policy over which they may have limited control.

Complications
..

Added complications for local government include the fact that policy is set by elected representatives, who operate on a party political basis, whilst council officers who carry out those policies are forbidden by law to engage in any political activity. Councillors who once may have felt that they were elected to act as their conscience directed are now required by central government legislation to be more responsive to their stakeholders. Local government has had to shift from a service delivery mentality, saying in effect to recipients of services that what was on offer was the only alternative, to a more marketing orientation, seeking the views of service users on what services should be delivered and in what way. During the 1990s, councils have also been subjected to compulsory competitive tendering (CCT), which has seen many services previously provided by council staff outsourced to private companies, and indeed the delivery of the public relations function is one service which has been affected. Many local government PR officers have had to operate more like internal consultants, working with the different council divisions, and some have left to start up their own consultancies, specialising in working with local government on a private basis.

Councils have also changed their mode of delivery and have reorganised, some deciding to provide services locally to improve access, rather than forcing service users to come to a central office. Changes in provision have necessitated changes in staff skills, from specialist to generalist, working in an office dealing with many issues rather than in a specific service.

Recent changes in devolution of power to the Scottish Parliament and Welsh Assembly have brought other layers of decision-makers into the arena. The decision of the Scottish Parliament not to charge university students the £1,000 annual tuition fee now paid by students in England and Wales has caused problems for local authorities who administer student grants, and will have far-reaching consequences in terms of student numbers and budgets for the future.

There are also different levels and tiers of local government, and getting the relevant stakeholders to recognise which services are provided by district, county or town councils is a tough job. In 1994, the Local Government Group of the IPR estimated that nearly 1,000 PR professionals were working in local government. Often the local council's press office is the mainstay of news for the local press. As part of the Citizen's Charter, councils were required to publish their performance on a set of 60 to 80 indicators in the local newspaper (not a freesheet) by the end of 1994. These covered everything from speed of answering the telephone to refuse collection (Harrison 1995).

Beginnings of PR in the public sector

The Crombie Committee was set up in 1947 to establish terms of reference and to advise on the creation of a professional group of civil servants to provide the necessary links between government and the media. The Crombie Report set out the role of the Information Officer. There were four objectives:

- to create and maintain an informed opinion about the subjects with which each department deals
- to use all methods of publicity where suitable to help the department achieve its purpose
- to assist and advise in all matters bearing on relations between the department and its public
- to advise the department on the public's reaction to the policies or actions of the department.

In a later reference Crombie insisted that the Chief Information Officer must have direct access to the Minister, that his work and that of his subordinates would bring them into direct relationship with all branches of the department at all levels. Most importantly, the CIO should be made aware of developments in the policy of the department at the earliest practicable moment and should be consulted at the earliest stage on matters relating either to the informing of the public or to the response of the public.

The Information Officer was not regarded as anything other than a Press Officer and there was no hint of the enormous range of disciplines contained in the Government Information Service (GIS). In 1975 there were 1,250 Information Officers, but only 18 per cent were engaged in press work. The range of skills covered included dealing with producing articles, books, speeches, briefing materials, films, tours for overseas journalists, art and design, translation, and researchers. Objectives were stressed: 'The sponsoring department takes the lead and calls on the advice and common services of the Central Office of Information (COI) to provide the raw material.' Harold Wilson, quoted in the *IPR Journal*, said 'The Information Officer's duty is to give facts . . . It is no part of his duties to engage in political propaganda. We are not engaged in an exact science' (James 1975: 11, 13).

Keeping politics and PR apart

Public relations practitioners working for local or central government work for the council or the government of the day, not any particular political party, and as mentioned above they are legally bound not to act in a political way. The Government Information Service is the overall authority for PR within central government, together with the Central Office of Information. PR practitioners within the GIS may work for any of the broader government departments, such as the Department for Education and Employment (DFEE) or the Department of Trade and Industry (DTI). This will involve working to provide PR and information campaigns supporting government initiatives. Regional offices provide staff to look after foreign journalists and dignitaries, and for ministerial and royal visits to their region.

The role of the COI

The role of the COI encompasses three areas:

* to tell the public what government is doing on their behalf and with their money
* to make the public aware of their rights and obligations
* to persuade the public to do something, for example to use condoms as a protection against AIDS.

(Cole-Morgan 1995: 64)

Most information divisions have three sections: press, publicity (advertising, books, films) and briefing. The COI is a common service department that produces publicity material on a repayment basis at the request of ministerial departments in the UK and overseas. The Director General oversees four groups within the service, dealing with production of material for use in the UK and overseas, and client services, who oversee day-to-day relations with customers.

In 1975, about half of the COI staff were employed in overseas services. Their priorities were to provide the following:

1 Information about positive political, social, environmental and particularly economic developments.

2 Publicity for British exporters participating in BOTB supported joint ventures, trade missions and other events overseas; and publicity for major UK trade fairs.

3 Publicity for new and improved products, processes and services, showing in specific case history terms that British industry is producing the goods buyers want overseas.

4 Extended publicity for products and services whose excellence is such that they reflect credit on British industry as a whole.

5 Publicity designed to show the achievement and reliability of sectors of British industry and commerce.

6 Publicity for research and development that shows that British exporters are backed by scientific and technological initiative and follow through of a high order.

(Cole-Morgan 1995: 70)

PR in local government

According to Brian Harvey (1995: 73) 'Local authorities vary considerably in the importance they place on professional public relations practice.' He lists the following objectives of the public relations function (1995: 75):

- to establish, maintain and project the authority's corporate character and identity
- to create understanding of the policies, procedures and activities of an authority, by keeping customers as fully informed as possible
- to respond, where appropriate, to criticism of the authority
- to establish and maintain effective channels of public communication available to the authority, and to develop a full range of appropriate techniques
- to create and maintain within the authority an awareness of the need to communicate with its various customer groups, and to ensure a sustained level of responsiveness to customer needs and opinions
- generally to manage the authority's public relations function and to advise on the public relations implications of the policies and activities of the authority and on the formulation of public relations policies.

More and more local authorities are using market research to obtain an understanding of their customers. Derbyshire and the Wrekin Councils employed this approach to good effect in 1986 and 1988, and started the trend. Market research provides a clear basis for undertaking activities and shaping future policies, as well as measuring levels of satisfaction with existing services (Harvey 1995).

The Local Government Acts of 1986 and 1988 form the basis of the legal constraints placed on public relations for local authorities. These and the subsequent legislation mentioned below were introduced by the Thatcher government, which sought to limit the powers of local government. The 1986 Act prohibits local authorities from issuing political publicity. A separate account of expenditure on publicity must be kept, and publicity is defined as 'any communication, in whatever form, addressed to the public at large or to a section of the public'. The 1988 Act sets out the factors to be taken into account in deciding whether any publicity material is considered to affect public support for a political party. In December 1987, the Local Authorities (Publicity Account) (Exemption) Order was passed, setting out what items could be excluded from the account. The original definition of publicity was so broad it could have been taken to cover any correspondence or message, so making the account meaningless. In 1988 the Code of Recommended Practice on Local Authority Publicity was published, covering content, style, subject matter, costs, dissemination, advertising, recruitment, publicity about individual members of an authority, timing and assisting others in providing publicity. The code urges a responsible approach, that content must be relevant to the functions of the local authority. Cost-effectiveness is emphasised. The need for local authorities to publicise and explain their policies and decisions is recognised, but a warning is given about the use of public funds to persuade the public to hold a particular view on a question of policy. 'Objective, balanced, informative and accurate' are the keywords. The careful targeting of information is recommended, but at the same time information should be made available to all those who want or need it.

There are no restrictions on publicising comments made by council officers, but publicity about individual members of the authority is limited to those who represent

the council as a whole, such as the mayor or the leader of the council or a particular committee. Publicity that deals with controversial issues cannot be issued between the notice of an election and polling day.

The Local Government Officers (Political Restrictions) Regulations 1990 set out a salary level above which staff become politically restricted. Officers would have to resign from their jobs before announcing an intention to stand for election as an MP, MEP or local councillor. There is no other sector of public relations which finds itself with such a range of rules within which it must operate. Any local resident can challenge local authorities and their public relations officers in the courts or through the district auditor (Fedorcio et al. 1991).

A changing future

The elections for London's mayor, though focused on the personalities of those standing, gave an indication of the Labour government's plans to change the structure of how councils operate. With increasingly poor turnout at local elections, councils are barely representative of those whose lives they affect. Devolution of power to the Scottish and Welsh assemblies, and continuing efforts to create a successful Northern Ireland parliament, reflect the government's agenda on encouraging regionalisation and so to address the democratic deficit. The establishment of the Greater London Authority on 3 July 2000 recreated a pan-London council, which oversees the individual borough councils and provides a unified strategy for the capital. The Local Government Bill 2000 requires councils to consult communities on how they wish to be governed. The choice will be between three structures:

- a directly elected mayor working with a cabinet of 10 members or 15 per cent of the council, whichever is smaller
- a directly elected mayor with a council manager
- a cabinet formed by the ruling party or coalition, with a leader selected from its members.

A referendum will be held if requested by 5 per cent of the electorate, to decide which of the options to employ. Councils will also be required to set up Scrutiny Committees which would be able to examine the mayor, cabinet or officers of the council about their decisions, advise them on issues and make recommendations on budgets. A Standards Committee will oversee ethical issues and ensure councillors act in accordance with a Code of Conduct.

'The idea that local authorities would treat the residents they serve as consumers might have appeared laughable a decade ago, but now quality and relevance are the watchwords', says Adam Hill (2000: 18). Reviewing the effects of the introduction of Best Value in April 2000, which requires councils to prove that they have proper public consultations over services and who provides them, he quotes Adrian Roxon, MD of Citigate Westminster, as advocating that the four C's of the programme – challenge, compare, consult, compete – should be complemented by the addition of communication. Several councils had started to address the fact that individual departments were ploughing their own furrow in terms of public relations, setting up their own media liaison functions and issuing conflicting messages. Lewisham decided to strengthen its central communications department to provide a unified approach, while Liverpool and Birmingham reorganised the PR function to make it part of customer relations to create

consistency. However, Mark Fletcher at Reputation, a consultancy which has worked for several local authorities, stressed that the main challenge for PR professionals is in internal communications, to enable council workers to understand the changes and sign up to them.

Two case studies have been chosen to illustrate the nature of PR in the public sector. One is from a local authority and the other from the Metropolitan Police. Common ground includes the need for transparency and public accountability across a wide range of initiatives. Both are subject to external conditions beyond their control, with an agenda set by national government according to political considerations. The local authority has the added complication of working to elected representatives.

Case study 1: Milton Keynes Council

Milton Keynes became a unitary authority with its own council in April 1997. As part of submitting a proposal for the formation of the council, extensive public consultation had taken place. Businesses, churches, and the general public helped form the shape of the council from the start. All services for children were placed in one directorate, rather than separating them into their constituent parts. Three years on, consultation is now embedded in the operation of the council. Citizens Panels have been used to inform many different policies and practices, from examining how to deal with travellers to the content of council tax leaflets. Each year a MK 2020 conference takes place where representatives of groups across the authority are invited to share their vision of the city in the future. The process is also two way, in that Milton Keynes Council put in a bid for formal city status, and asked all those groups to support that bid with their own activities.

Peter Heaton was appointed Marketing and Communications Manager at the end of 1998, and one of his first tasks was to produce a communications strategy for the council. This covered why the council should communicate, what it should communicate and to whom. It also looked at how that communication took place at the time, and what changes should be made, as well as a plan to assess and improve performance in the future. A series of audits of all areas of communications was proposed. Recommendations on how media contact should be managed were included, with details of how that could conform to the Local Government Act 1988 and the 1990 Code of Practice for Local Authority Publicity.

In February 1999 the council was the first local authority to hold a referendum on setting its budget. The process had started the previous June, driven by the Labour Council Leader, Kevin Wilson. After being flagged up through the local media, the traditional consultation process started with local groups in December. Some 900 letters were sent out, asking for their views on which services should receive priority, so that the offer put to the local residents could be refined. Posters were also sent out later in the campaign to be displayed in the organisations' offices.

The council's free publication, the *Messenger*, was used to good effect, with supporting editorial covering the various issues in detail. The January/February 1999 *Messenger* carried an article which encouraged residents to vote, indicating the council's preferred option. Whilst this could be publicised, it could not be advocated, as this would have contravened the Local Government Act 1988 (see p. 176). Three options were given, and all involved rises in council tax allied to cuts in services – there was no good news. However, the council was able to set out comparisons with surrounding authorities which showed that its council tax was lower than all but one of them.

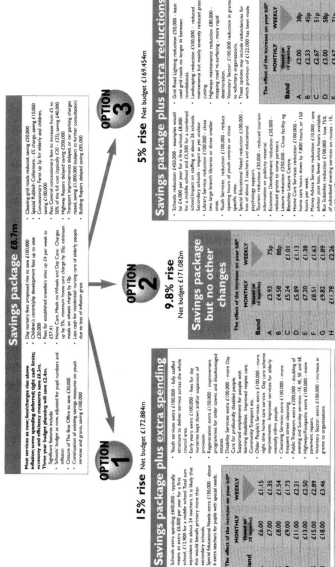

Figure 14.1 Milton Keynes Council referendum leaflet

Used with permission

All tax payers in the city were sent voting papers, with information about the three options on offer and voting instructions (Figure 14.1). Voting took place from 1–19 February 1999. Having a referendum on the budget issue was felt to be important because of the very poor turnout in the local authority elections. Only 26 per cent had voted, so the councillors who had been elected represented the choice of only a quarter of the population. To make it as easy as possible, voting was allowed by post and telephone. The target was to achieve a 30 per cent turnout, and this was surpassed by the fact that 45 per cent of residents voted. 'In terms of democracy, the referendum was more cost effective than the election', said Peter Heaton.

'Whilst the consultation process was going on, we had constant committee meetings where we had to justify our budget for PR activities', he continued. 'Everything has to be cost effective in local government.' The PR department also had to ensure that all copy sent out from the council was accessible and written in plain English. Local radio advertising was used to encourage voting, and felt to be very good value. Media interest was encouraged and managed by carrying out an initial informal media briefing before the consultation process, followed up with one-to-one meetings to explain council policies.

A press conference was held to announce the results of the ballot. 'It was the best turnout for a press conference that wasn't for a disaster', said Heaton. 'As well as local press, local radio and local television, *The Times*, *Guardian*, Radio 4 and 5 also came. We were able to put them in touch with ordinary people to add to their coverage.' A clear majority came down in favour of the council's preferred option, a 9.8 per cent rise in council tax. This was heartening for the council's campaign, as only 30 per cent had voted for the cheapest option, a 5 per cent rise in tax. Furthermore, 24 per cent had voted for a higher rise in tax of 15 per cent.

> We were all trying to predict through the process what the turnout would be. Most of us also felt that there would be a majority in favour of the cheapest option. I think we were lulled into a feeling that people begrudge paying their council tax, despite the fact that when we did informal vox pops in the town centre, there were an awful lot of people saying that they weren't going to vote for the cheapest option because they had children at school, and so on. People were making the connection between the amount of tax they paid and the services that could be provided. One of the good things to come out of the referendum was that people were not focusing on how much tax they were paying, but on what services they wanted to pay for.

The referendum was used as a foundation for similar exercises. In September 1999, an article in the *Messenger* set out the council's plans for setting the budget in the next financial year, with an objective of setting it by October. Whilst not holding another full referendum, residents were encouraged to have their say and contribute to the budget setting process again. A questionnaire was published, and three public meetings were held in different parts of the city.

During the voting process, all PR staff took it in turns to answer the general queries helpline to hear what questions people had. 'I think the nature of the questions revealed that in terms of the council's PR, we were starting from a lot further back than we'd like to think. Some of the questions showed that we needed to inform people about the democratic process as well.'

Peter Heaton sums up the challenges facing public relations practitioners in local government:

A lot of council services are not branded, although we think we're quite good at it in Milton Keynes. Some services become obsessed with marketing themselves, like leisure centres, so that popular services break away and don't appear to belong to the council at all. What councils can then appear to get left with is public toilets, dead rats, graffiti and gypsies.

Another problem is that what we do isn't essentially exciting, or tangible, like shovelling rubbish off the streets or educating thousands of children each day. It's not news.

Starting to use market research to find out what people actually wanted was an important step in local authority PR. Now that we have the Best Value system of performance measurement we can also see improvements. There is a Scrutiny Commission in Milton Keynes, which is a cross-party group of councillors which can call things in and tear them apart. There is much more openness than ten years ago.

In local government there is always the extra dimension of accountability. All our business is conducted in public. If you wanted to find out how much I earn, you can, you can stand up in council meetings and ask questions about what the council is doing. If only commercial businesses had to conduct their affairs in the same way!

We have to be accountable about what we spend, as it is public money. There is always something else that could be done with the money, and often PR is seen as a luxury item. The referendum cost £70,000, which is the same as two teachers. It is always an emotive pay off.

Historically we have not been too good at telling people what we do. There are many different jargons in local government. For instance, planners refer to modal shift – that means getting people to change their mode of transport, in other words trying to get them to stop using their cars so much. The PR department sets up the communications framework, but then it is the job of every manager to communicate effectively. There is also a difference in that whereas the private sector companies may have a board of a dozen, we effectively have a board of 51 elected councillors, some of whose views are diametrically opposed to the views of others, who regard it as a legitimate activity to ring up the local press, send out controversial letters and press releases disagreeing with council policy and decisions. In fact, they are institutionally allowed to state their opinion, that's part of the deal with local democracy. But those councillors also have a role to represent the council.

It's also important for councils to have a wider outlook than their own patch. We have to lobby MPs and the key civil servants, as more of our money comes from central government than from council tax. We don't believe that we get enough money, and of course, like us, every local authority thinks that it is a special case.

We also have to influence the voluntary sector so that they know we are doing a good job, and the business community. We have an extremely complex set of audiences: council tax payers; residents (who may not all pay tax); library users; those with no children or grown up children who may resent paying council tax when 70 per cent goes towards education; those who live here but commute to work so may not use local services. A lot of the services we provide are very personal in education and social services, and there are always crises to deal with. In the council, the buck stops here.

With thanks to Milton Keynes Council

Case study 2: The Metropolitan Police and Neighbourhood Watch

For the past six years, the Metropolitan Police (Met) has had to cope with the after-math of the murder of black teenager Stephen Lawrence in a racially motivated attack. The Lawrence family's misgivings about the conduct of the investigation into their son's death in April 1993 led to an initial internal inquiry, then an inquiry ordered by the Police Complaints Commission and finally a public inquiry which resulted in the Macpherson Report in February 1999. That report contained the conclusion that the Met was 'institutionally racist'. In response, the Met launched its Diversity Strategy, admitting that there had been 'issues of confidence and trust' between the Met and ethnic communities for some time. Working with the Commission for Racial Equality (CRE), the Met has continued to hold public forums and police briefings to promote its strategy. However, with a workforce of 27,000 police officers and 14,000 civilians, there are doubts about whether the strategy has really changed things. 'The commit-ment of John Grieve [Deputy Assistant Commissioner and Head of the Racial and Violent Crime Task Force] and his officers has not yet reached the fingers and toes of the Met in relation to all of their dealings with black people on the street, all of the time', according to Barbara Cohen, Principal Legal Officer for the CRE (quoted in Gray 1999: 10–12). Internal communications is a vital part of the work of the PR depart-ment within the Met, ensuring that all staff understand the 'corporate' policies.

The effect of the Lawrence case is still being felt. Even when the Met launched its Diversity Strategy it was criticised for doing too little, too late. 'One of the added diffi-culties for us with the Lawrence Inquiry was that we were no longer dealing with our regular media contacts', said Charles Dodsworth, Deputy Director of Public Affairs and Internal Communications.

> We deal with the crime reporters daily. They know us and know they can trust us. That's not to say that they won't be critical, but they do understand the problems we face. The correspondents assigned to the Lawrence Inquiry were new to us. We didn't know them and they didn't know us. Much of the criticism was justified but for a while we were on the back foot until we got to grips with the situation.

He echoed Peter Heaton's sentiment, 'In the Met, we make all our mistakes in public.'

Another aspect of the work of the Met is that it is not dealing with an homogeneous area. 'We have just reorganised from five areas within the Met to three. Every one of the previous outer London areas was bigger than any other in the country, and on top of that we have Central London, with the royal family and vast number of public events to police', says Dodsworth. In 1998, the Met policed 2,885 demonstrations, pickets and other public order events; 32 ceremonial events; 354 football matches (there are 13 football league clubs within the Met's boundaries, more than any other police area in England and Wales); and 334 other sporting events. Within the areas are 32 boroughs, each with their own problems and priorities.

Each of the three areas is headed by an assistant commissioner, who also has respon-sibility for particular issues London-wide. 'We act almost like an internal PR consul-tancy', says Dodsworth.

> We discuss with each assistant commissioner what budget they have available for campaigns, and try to plan ahead throughout the year. We could do more planning, after all we know approximately what our budgets are likely to be and even the

number of incidents. The police tend to be better at reacting to crises – when the nail bomb went off in Brixton in 1999 it was amazing to se the whole place spring into action.

Like local government, the Met is governed by legislation. This tends to be more about its priorities for action than how its PR is carried out. The Crime and Disorder Act 1998 contained the Labour government's commitment to reform the youth justice system, build safer communities and improve the performance and efficiency of the criminal justice system. With regard to the last point, all agencies were required to speed up procedures, increase co-operation and work towards long-term problem-solving.

The Met published a comprehensive list of performance indicators in the Report of the Commissioner of Police of the Metropolis for 1998/9. The Met will also be affected by the introduction of an elected Mayor for London. The Mayor's budget is likely to be around £3 billion. The cost of the Met is currently £1.7 billion. The commitment to performance indicators is also entrenched within the PR operation. 'All our budgets have built in pre and post research', says Dodsworth.

Other legislative constraints include the information that can be given out. 'We have to be careful in our day-to-day dealings and careful of the language we use, because of the rules about *sub judice* information. If we arrest someone, we cannot give out their name, but only a description', says Dodsworth. Other areas where the police have to be careful about the release of information is when it may cause widespread panic. When the IRA staged a water contamination scare, the PR department worked closely with the media not to release detailed information until after an arrest had been made.

The Neighbourhood Watch scheme is an example of the police working with local communities to tackle crime. When the original schemes were launched in 1983, even the advertising showed little old ladies looking through their net curtains. The schemes were most successful in white, middle-class, suburban areas. Numbers peaked at 12,500, but many of the schemes became organisations merely on paper. By 1998, there were only 5,800 schemes covering 800,000 Londoners. The Met relaunched its scheme with a poster featuring a group of meerkats to symbolise the fact that people in a Neighbourhood Watch scheme are responsible for watching and caring rather than snooping (Figure 14.2). Meerkats were chosen after research showed how positively people viewed the animals. People also identified with the natural instinct of the meerkats to work as teams, looking out for each other and their young and building strength through unity. Inner city areas where there was a more pressing need were targeted.

A year later in June 1999, the Met negotiated a £1 million sponsorship deal with *Yellow Pages*. Forces can raise up to 1 per cent of their budget through sponsorship but it must be spent on non-essential police work. The three-year partnership aimed to support several projects in the community including providing street signs about the Neighbourhood Watch scheme, a London-wide training programme for Neighbourhood Watch co-ordinators, and the translation of publicity material into key non-English languages.

As well as a launch event at the House of Commons, with Home Office Minister Paul Boateng, Chief Executive of the National Neighbourhood Watch Scheme Sue Yoxall, the then Met Commissioner Sir Paul Condon and Head of External Relations from *Yellow Pages*, Richard Duggleby, the Met PR department used its publication, the *Link*, to publicise the scheme. The *Link* contains stories about the Met's involvement with the community and is distributed London-wide. New information packs and

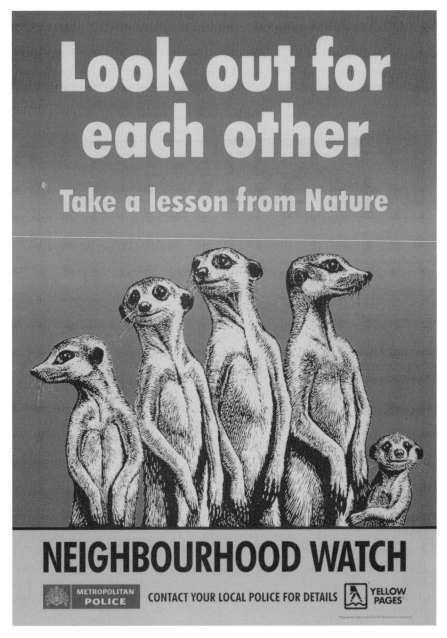

Figure 14.2 Metropolitan Police–Neighbourhood Watch campaign poster
Used with permission

leaflets were also produced. The scheme and the sponsorship also received media coverage. The new partnership was timed to coincide with the National Neighbourhood Watch Community Safety Week, and events were staged throughout the week to encourage people to mark their property to make it less attractive to burglars.

The Met's Community Safety and Partnership Unit concentrates on building effective partnerships with the community, and Neighbourhood Watch is part of that brief. Community and crime prevention officers also work with Neighbourhood Watch schemes, attending the initial start-up meetings to offer advice on security and provide a local link for the scheme members. As well as tackling one of the force's aims to reduce the level of burglary, vandalism and other street crime, the CSPU and the involvement with Neighbourhood Watch also show the increasing commitment of the Met to work with all sections of the community.

With thanks to the Metropolitan Police

15 Consumer public relations

..

Public relations in the field of consumer relations is often regarded as marketing communications. Marketing, as we have seen, is the identification of the needs of consumers, and how to satisfy those needs profitably. Organisations who class consumers as one of their main publics or stakeholder groups are likely to be relating to them as buyers of their products. Within the field of consumer PR, several further specialisms exist. Each has to deal with the particular media within its area, and the specifics of the market. Fashion PR has to gear itself to the timetable of the seasons and the catwalk shows in the main cities of Milan, London and New York and lead times on influential magazines, whilst also looking ahead to the next best thing. Those who deal with clients who produce fast-moving consumer goods (fmcg) have to have different approaches to those who deal with clients who produce white goods (fridges, household appliances) and cars, where the buyer is making a decision which will involve a substantial sum of money.

Grunig and Hunt see President Kennedy's message to Congress in the early 1960s as the main impetus for the rise in consumer relations programmes: Kennedy 'declared four basic consumer rights: the right to safety; the right to be heard; the right to choose; the right to be informed' (1984: 316). Consumer specialists were appointed to the office of Special Assistant to the President for Consumer Affairs to respond to the needs of consumers. Companies gave added value to their products by producing general educational literature such as an insurance company which produced booklets on managing stress and other health topics.

PR v. marketing?

..

Public relations and marketing are often seen as adversarial. Marketeers tend to see PR as a subordinate part of their armoury of tools, and indeed businesses reinforce this by the organisation of their communication function. Public relations practitioners would see marketing as part of their remit, for it is primarily concerned with selling products to consumers. All organisations have a need for public relations, but not all are involved in marketing. The Fire Service carries out community and media relations, but does not try to convince people to start more fires and so use their services more.

What is clear is that public relations and marketing should be corporate allies, working together for common goals. Kitchen (1997: 227–34) gives details of a survey carried

out amongst the marketing and PR personnel in seven UK firms to explore the relationship between the functions. Areas of overlap were found. Whilst the growing importance of PR was generally agreed, it appeared that marketing budgets were still substantially higher. PR was viewed as important for marketing support by the marketeers, whilst PR executives saw this as a minor area and viewed issues management, employee communications and corporate communications as their priorities. However there was general agreement that PR was part of integrated marketing communications.

Cutlip, Center and Broom (1985: 495–6) list seven forms of assistance to the marketing function which PR can perform:

1 Publicising news and events related to the launching of new or improved products or services.

2 Promoting established products or services, to the extent that they are newsworthy.

3 Creating a favourable image of 'the company behind the product'.

4 Arranging for public appearances of marketing spokespersons.

5 Probing public opinion in market areas.

6 Focusing news media attention on sales conferences and other marketing events.

7 Assisting in programmes concerning consumerism.

The last refers to the increasing activism of consumers in their expectation that the goods and services they buy should fulfil the promises of related publicity material. One aspect of this can be seen in the rise of consumer watchdog programmes, which publicise where companies have failed to deliver a good response to complaints. In the early 1990s, Hoover was the subject of a hostile campaign by the BBC consumer affairs programme *Watchdog* with regard to a promotion which offered free flights with the purchase of certain products. The company underestimated the potential demand for their offer, with the result that it had underbooked the number of flights. In order to satisfy everyone who claimed their flights, a profitable promotion turned into a massive loss maker. *Watchdog* sent an undercover researcher into one of the travel companies dealing with the claims, where they managed to secretly record one of the managers briefing staff on how to discourage claimants from taking up their free flights. The company did not put up a spokesperson until *Watchdog* had featured the problem several times. The marketing manager in charge of the promotion was sacked, and the company lost a considerable amount of consumer goodwill.

Marketing communications

Norman Hart (1995: 25) defines marketing communications as 'across the board communications to help move a potential customer from a state of ignorance towards a position of decision and action'. He goes on to describe the adoption process:

1 Awareness. The individual becomes cognisant of the innovation but lacks information about it.

2 Interest. The individual is stimulated to seek information about the innovation.

3 Evaluation. The individual considers whether it would make sense to try the innovation.

4 Trial. The individual tries the innovation on a small scale to improve their estima-
tion of its utility.

5 Adoption. The individual decides to make full and regular use of the innovation.

'Marketing communications encompasses any form of communication that contributes
to the conversion of a non-customer to a customer, and subsequently to the retention
of such custom', says Hart (1995: 25).

Hart suggests that customers do not buy a product but rather satisfaction, so that
they buy holes rather than drills. Customers base decisions on the benefits they perceive
from the product. Packaging and presentation will affect this perception. Size, weight,
colour and smell all appeal, often on an unconscious level. Brand name is also part of
the total 'product offering'.

How does PR fit into marketing communications? The traditional elements of the
marketing mix are the four Ps – product, price, place and promotion. Price can indi-
cate good or bad value for money; in some cases a high price signals quality or pres-
tige. Place means the kind of outlet where the product can be obtained – a product will
be viewed differently if it is sold on a market stall rather than in a high street depart-
ment store. Promotion refers to the media and messages used to influence buyer deci-
sions. It is here that PR contributes most, bringing a range of activities which can
support and supplement advertising and marketing. The selection of which medium to
use to convey the messages will depend on the target market, and the most effective
communication is often referred to as the 'media mix'.

The size of the market is the first consideration when deciding which tactics to use
when communicating with various publics. A group of people who are involved in any
decision are often called the buying decision unit, or BDU. If only ten BDUs are to
be approached, personal contact would be the most appropriate medium. If there are
1,000, direct mail editorial publicity, demonstrations or telephone selling could be used.
With 100,000, mass media advertising would be best. Different media have different
kinds of impact – a press advert can make an impression only by means of text and
photography, but if it is in a magazine it will have a longer life than a TV advert. The
TV advert, however, has the advantage of movement, colour and sound. This is further
exaggerated when shown in a cinema.

Stone (1995) quotes research from the 1970s which identified six main zones of
influence within families when making decisions about buying various products. These
were:

- man's influence
- woman's influence
- children's influence
- man and woman
- man and children
- woman and children.

This was followed by research in 1991 which found that children were the main influ-
ence on the purchase of video games (61 per cent) and women were dominant in the
purchase of dishwashers and food processors (69 per cent and 67 per cent). Only one
area was male dominated – satellite television aerials (72 per cent) (Stone 1995).
Information on buying decisions can inform the public relations practitioner when

devising campaigns, selecting the appropriate tactics to carry messages about particular products to specific publics.

The kind of message is the next consideration. A simple message could be conveyed by a poster, but a complex or technical one would need to be presented in the specialist press. In selecting media, cost must be considered in two ways. First, the actual price of using the medium selected and whether this fits the budget available. Second, a cost per contact should be evaluated to see if the medium delivers cost-effectiveness. Personal contact by a salesperson will obviously cost more per contact than using the national press.

Timing also affects what medium is to be used. Television, radio and the press can deliver a message quickly, within 24 hours. Trade and specialist media have longer lead times, trade fairs and exhibitions are infrequent. Which medium is to be used will depend on when the message needs to be delivered.

Branding

Consumer PR and marketing communications are most often concerned with brands, the value of a name of a product or company, and how this affects people's buying behaviour. In some cases, the company name is the brand, like Virgin, Sony or Kodak. Association with a corporate brand like this may affect consumer decisions. In others, the brand names are well known, like Fairy Liquid, but the parent company less so, like Unilever or Procter & Gamble. In some cases, like soap powder, companies produce different brands which then compete with each other in the marketplace.

Two different approaches can be taken to branding. HSBC Holdings chose to rebrand its Midland Bank operation in the UK. Richard Beck, head of group external relations, stated 'By unifying the group, we will have better global recognition.' In contrast, when Axa Equity and Law merged with Sun Life in July 1997, it chose not to rebrand Sun Life financial products as the name was more well known in the UK than the parent company (France 1999).

Naomi Klein feels that 'the role of branding has been changing, particularly in the last 15 years . . . the brand itself has increasingly become the product'. Thus 'Nike was about "sport" not shoes; Microsoft about "communications", not software' (Klein 2000). Companies are now projecting their brand onto many different products. Klein links

Figure 15.1 Enduring brands

Source: David Bright, Barclays Bank

this increase in branding activity with the tendency of multinationals to shift actual production away from where the goods are bought, and points to the dangers of corporate employment practices in developing countries. She quotes the protests in Paris and Seattle, where rioters attacked McDonald's and Starbucks, as evidence of a backlash against global brands.

David Bright, Barclay's head of market research, also concludes that branding means everything that surrounds a company's offerings, 'from external communication to staff behaviour and physical surroundings'. He believes that both rational and emotional elements underpin the most enduring brands (Echo Research 1998) (Figure 15.1).

Consumer buying behaviour

The PR practitioner also needs to consider the attributes of consumers, and what contributes to their buying decisions. Various writers have put forward suggestions about publics and their motivation.

Grunig and Hunt (1984: 160) define four kinds of public:

- publics active on all issues
- publics apathetic on all issues
- publics active only on an issue or small number of issues that involve nearly everyone in the population
- publics active only on a single issue.

These kinds of publics relate to environmental, minority and consumer issues. Grunig and Hunt also discuss the behavioural molecule developed by Richard Carter, which is related to consumer behaviour, and was further developed by Michael Ray, who suggests four stages in consumer behaviour:

- developing a need (detect)
- searching for and comparing alternatives (construct, define)
- purchasing (behave)
- postpurchase (detect).

Publics who recognise a problem and do not feel constrained are likely to be the most active users of consumer information. Grunig and Hunt's research found three different kinds of consumer publics when they looked at how people decided which supermarket to use. The first, working-class public, thought about comparing stores but was constrained by lack of transport from making changes. The second, professional public, where both partners were likely to be working, was constrained by time and simply shopped at the nearest supermarket. Finally, a middle-class public felt least constrained and was able to make a considered choice between supermarkets. This group were most likely to be aware of consumer programmes and advertisements.

Kotler suggests that buying is the result of inputs and outputs (Williams 1989: 156). Stimuli for buying include price, quality, availability, service, style, options and image. These can be delivered to the consumer by a variety of channels, such as advertising, salespeople, friends, family and personal observation. After processing this information, the consumer makes a choice of product, brand, dealer, quantity and frequency.

This is one of several 'black box' models, which concentrate on the external factors that can influence behaviour. The consumer's thoughts are hidden in a black box, and the marketeer evaluates the relative importance of the external stimuli in order to form a marketing strategy.

Other models of behaviour include personal variable models, which take account of values, beliefs and attitudes. Fishbein developed a model which stated that an attitude was built from beliefs about attributes of an object, weighted by the importance of each of these attributes. Comprehensive models attempt to take both external factors and personal variables into account. A useful summary of the main theoretical models can be found in Williams (1989).

Keller and Aaker (1998) conducted an experiment to find out what aspects of a marketing campaign affected consumers' evaluations of corporate credibility. They suggested that there were three elements to this credibility: corporate expertise, where the company was thought to be able to competently make and sell its products and services; corporate trustworthiness, the extent to which a company is thought to be honest, dependable and sensitive to consumer needs; and corporate likeability, or how likeable, prestigious and interesting the company is.

They investigated three kinds of corporate marketing activity, emphasising product innovation, environmental concerns and community involvement. Corporate expertise was found to be the most important factor in the evaluation of any new product, rather than environmental or community concerns. This suggests that a new product offered under an existing strong brand name will benefit from that association, even if it is beyond the company's normal product range. Examples of this in the UK have been seen particularly in relation to Virgin, which has expanded from record shops into other areas of leisure such as cinemas and air travel, as well as into financial products.

France (1999) has stated that 'The reputation of a company depends as much on the strength of its corporate brand as it does on the quality of the products it sells.' In a competitive market, where products can easily be matched on price, the corporate brand may be the difference in building consumer loyalty. Giles Fraser, MD of information industries at Hill & Knowlton, agrees with Keller and Aaker and thinks that strong brand names give companies an advantage in the market place. However, contrary to their findings, he believes that

> People are increasingly interested in not only the product and service they buy but the company behind the product. They want to know it is ethical in its business practices, that it pays a good wage to its people, that it puts something back into the community.
>
> (quoted in France 1999)

He suggests that people buy from successful companies because it says something about them as consumers.

Keeping customers

Marketing communications is not only concerned with obtaining customers, but with keeping them.

> It is generally accepted that only about 10 per cent of dissatisfied customers ever complain. These are the ones you and your firm have the best chance of satisfying and retaining, because they have identified themselves and defined a problem for

you. Of the other, silent 90 per cent, you can be pretty certain that only 10 per cent will ever buy from you again. The rest . . . are lost, possibly for ever. Even if you could get them back it would cost five times as much as keeping them happy in the first place.

(Stone 1995: 141)

Stone states that customer satisfaction is based on quality and meeting expectations. He suggests that it is easier to build relationships with customers if enhancements are offered, such as rewards or bonus points for regular shoppers (like the plethora of super-market loyalty cards). Other enhancements could include add-on services, like free kitchen design from suppliers of kitchen units.

Companies are now starting to look at lifetime customer value (LCV). This takes into account the costs of acquiring a customer – direct mail, research, capital invest-ment – as well as the likely profits to be made once the customer is won. In competi-tive businesses, the churn rate, or how many switch to a rival supplier in any one year and therefore how long an average customer is retained, must also be factored in. Market valuations for many e-commerce businesses make assumptions based on LCV. Amazon, with 6 million customers, is valued at over $3,000 per customer (Wileman 1999). Companies need to define whether some customers are unprofitable, in that they cost much more to obtain and retain than they spend in return.

In fashion PR, emphasis lies squarely on media relations. Richard Edwards (1999) quotes a number of sources. Debenhams fashion PR head Catherine Sturgess reports that the company sees a noticeable increase in sales whenever one of their products appears in a magazine or newspaper: 'People come in and ask for the products they have seen. Some of them come in clutching their copy of Marie Clare.' Anne Rafter, MD of Stephanie Churchill PR, says 'If you pick the right publication for the brand you are working on, well-targeted editorial can generate huge sales.' However, this means a move away from the blanket coverage press release to a more focused and strategic approach. Regional as well as national press is important in targeting potential customers. Because of their dialogue with fashion editors, and having to have an aware-ness of consumer interest, fashion PR practitioners are developing two-way channels of information between the boardroom and the fashion media, which in turn influences consumer trends.

This awareness of consumer needs must extend to staff relations, particularly in the retail sector. Work on brand and corporate reputation can be undermined by a customer's poor experience in a store. Peter Hutton of MORI says 'The first major study to reveal that happy and committed employees lead to happy and loyal customers was done in the early 1990s by Sears Roebuck in the States. It has had a major impact.' Linda Barber of the Institute of Employment Studies found that stores where staff were more satisfied (because they were better managed and looked after) generated a £200,000 increase of sales per month (F. Murphy 1999). So consumer PR needs to link into human resources and internal communications so that their work is not wasted.

Types of campaign

It is useful at this point to revisit the types of PR campaign that are available, so that PR activity in the consumer area can be viewed as part of a broader whole. According to Patrick Jackson of Jackson, Jackson and Wagner in New Hampshire (Newsom *et al.* 1993), there are six types:

- public awareness
- information with awareness
- public education
- reinforcing attitudes and behaviour
- changing attitudes
- modifying behaviour.

Hendrix (1995) sets out impact and output objectives for consumer relations programmes. The former might include increasing knowledge about the company's products, promoting more favourable opinion towards the company, stimulating greater participation in consumer relations programmes, and encouraging more positive feedback from consumer groups. The last could involve distributing more consumer publications, developing employee consumer seminars, and meeting with important consumer groups. All of these objectives should be underpinned with prior research into consumer attitudes, and expressed in precise terms of percentages and timescales. Some tactical activities to meet these objectives include advising management and staff about consumer issues, developing an efficient consumer response system, handling customer complaints through a customer relations office, and liaising with external activist consumer groups.

The case studies presented below have been selected to illustrate different approaches to consumer PR. The first concerns work undertaken for a small family food business in Yorkshire by Harrogate-based consultancy Cicada PR. The other examines how an in-house department and consultancy worked together in the motor industry.

Case study 1: Shepherds Purse Cheeses Ltd and Cicada PR

Shepherds Purse Cheeses Ltd is the UK's biggest producer of sheep milk cheese, based in Thirsk. It is a small family business, employing eight people. It produces ten cheeses, including Yorkshire Feta, which won a gold medal at the British Cheese Awards (Figure 15.2). In October 1997, managing director Judy Bell discovered that feta had been registered as a Protected Designation of Origin (PDO) in 1996, so that only feta produced in Greece could be labelled as such. The company had five years before the name of its cheese had to be changed.

Shepherds Purse Cheeses worked with Cicada PR to develop a strategy to increase sales of the cheese, but also to make consumers aware of the need for a name change. It was also decided to lobby government to change the PDO on feta. A campaign was devised to fight this European legislation, stressing that the name change could harm sales of Yorkshire Feta and seriously affect this small business – a David and Goliath angle.

The campaign mixed media relations with lobbying. Initially, the Yorkshire Feta campaign was targeted at local papers and regional business publications. The story was picked up by national media. Judy Bell and her son Justin undertook a media relations course, and appeared on regional and national radio and television. This sparked considerable support from the public, who wrote to the company suggesting new names for the cheese.

Alongside this, every Yorkshire MP was approached for their support. More than 34 per cent replied positively. The Refreshments Department of the House of Commons

Figure 15.2 Shepherds Purse Cheeses

Used by permission of Shepherds Purse and Cicada PR

was asked to serve Yorkshire Feta, and it was added to the Regional Menu of the Members and Strangers Dining Room.

On 16 March 1999, the Court of Justice annulled the registration of the name feta as a PDO. In addition, Asda approached Shepherds Purse Cheeses to sell Yorkshire Feta under their regional cheese banner. Sales in 1999 rose by 30 per cent. Judy Bell said, 'We were a small successful company but not well known across the country. We would never have dreamed that PR could have such a positive effect on our bottom line.'

With thanks to Shepherds Purse Cheeses and Cicada PR

Case study 2: Daewoo Cars and Jackie Cooper PR

Daewoo was launched on 1 April 1995 to the public in the UK, with a goal set by the Korean parent company of achieving 1 per cent of the market in its first year. Although that may sound like a small target, Hyundai, Daewoo's main competitor in its home Korean market, has not achieved that ten years after its entry into the UK. In April 1995 Daewoo was simply another Asian car marque in an already overcrowded market.

The task set by the parent company meant that the Daewoo management team had to do something very different from other manufacturers. The approach they took was a classic customer-centred marketing campaign. First, surveys were commissioned to find out what the public liked about buying cars and what they didn't. An opening offer of 200 cars, free for one year, in return for customer feedback, was set up. The response crashed the BT lines. Such attention grabbing tactics meant that in the first year, public awareness of the Daewoo name rose from 4 per cent to 98 per cent.

Results of the survey showed that customers didn't like the negotiation process of buying a new car, and that the actual price was often £1,500–£2,000 above the list price with delivery, road tax and extras. Women also felt that car salesmen tried to pull the wool over their eyes. The findings were used to put together a complete package, with free servicing, including parts and labour, for three years, a fully inclusive price with no extras, and AA breakdown cover. 'Initially we never presumed to say that we had a cutting edge product,' says Alison Moran, marketing manager of Daewoo Cars UK. 'We always focused on the package, and the benefits to customers. We wanted to reach beyond the motoring pages and enthusiast magazines, because a majority of the car buying public never went near them.' Daewoo outlets were designed with children's play areas and cafés. This approach led Daewoo to take on Jackie Cooper PR (JCPR), a consultancy which was more well known for its consumer clients, six months after the launch.

'We have a stubborn refusal to niche brands, and for years that was what the car industry had been doing', says Robert Phillips, managing director of JCPR. 'With Daewoo we had a brief to go for a wider consumer environment.' JCPR looked at how women drivers were treated in showrooms, sending a woman in different clothes, short skirts or business suits, into car retail outlets. A man sent into the same outlets was able to obtain a far better price. They then staged an event for women's press editors, many of whom had never been along to any event staged by the car industry. Penny Mallory, who presented the Channel 4 motoring programme, was invited, along with women rally drivers and mechanics who gave instructions to the journalists about manoeuvring and maintenance. This approach continued, with work being done

in association with the Suzy Lamplugh Trust on safe driving tips, and producing a one-off redesign of the Matiz car by the clothes designer Wayne Hemingway of Red or Dead. 'We didn't get traditional motor show coverage with the Matiz', says Phillips. 'It was a picture story and was covered in the women's press, shopping and fashion pages. It outstripped the launch of the new Ibiza, the new Jaguar and the new Rover in the UK.'

'Now we do have a big story to tell as well', says Moran.

> The Technical Centre at Worthing represents a huge investment in the UK. We have a young enthusiastic team designing and styling Daewoo products worldwide from a European taste perspective to make them more appealing. It brings in about £15 million per year to the town, and has completely transformed what used to be a retirement town into one of the most prosperous places in the country.

Whilst coverage of Daewoo cars has rarely been flattering, Moran feels that the detail of the products and the dialogue with customers provides strength (Figure 15.3).

> When we launched the Nubira we set up consumer panels, and fed back comments from customers. When we launched the new version in summer 1999, those comments were taken into account, including better back support in the seats, three point seatbelts in the back and even down to moving the cup holder.

This is built on the customer focus of the Korean parent company. 'The Chairman has announced that customers who have been with Daewoo for some time should be taken to Korea to see how the cars are made, to make them feel part of the Daewoo family, which is a very Korean perspective', she says.

Another of the new practices that Daewoo introduced was selling its cars through its own outlets, with staff paid a salary rather than dependent on commission. 'It costs so much in advertising, marketing and PR to get a customer, and if you lose them you have to spend it all over again', says Moran.

> For years, car manufacturers had been spending huge amounts on advertising, then handing their customer facing dealings over to a third party. They never had any control over training or the point of sale approach. We have direct control over the image that the customer sees, and that is a big advantage in the market.

In-house and consultancy work closely together, and that includes marketing and advertising personnel too. 'We enjoy working on the account because there has been no ownership of ideas by any one agency', says Phillips. 'The original creatives at Duckworth & Finn gave all of us permission to use their catch line, "That'll be the Daewoo". The sales promotion on the 4×4 was originally a PR idea, we've just sparked off each other.' This is reflected in-house, says Moran.

> Advertising doesn't start until the cars are on sale, but PR activities start about a year in advance to flag up the developments. We have regular regional and national meetings, where creative concepts are presented so that we are all aware of what is in the pipeline. The staff base is quite young and co-operative. We can then take the themes of each other's campaigns and carry it across to our own area.

'It's allowed PR to come into its own', says Phillips. 'PR has been the glue that bound it all together. The team here is committed to the brand, and has a passion and energy that has enthused the media as well.'

Daewoo Cars Ltd
Daewoo House **News Release**
Homestead Road
Rickmansworth
Hertfordshire
WD3 2LW
England

FOR IMMEDIATE RELEASE
22 July 1999

THE NEW DAEWOO NUBIRA

Daewoo Cars today lays claim to an unofficial crown: the fastest mover in the automotive business. The arrival of a new-look Nubira barely 24 months after its initial launch underlines Daewoo's ability to spot changing market trends and to adapt to them as quickly as possible.

Changes to the Nubira – it means 'go anywhere' in Korean – also emphasise Daewoo's customer commitment: some of the improvements made to the car follow suggestions from Nubira owners proving that not only does Daewoo listen to its customers, it acts on their comments.

The new-look Nubira arrives after a period of intense activity from the Korean car maker. Just two years ago, automotive observers were stunned by the arrival of not one, not two, but three brand new ranges from Daewoo, a company then emerging from a 20-year joint venture with General Motors

The new Lanos, Nubira and Leganza models progressed from concept to reality in less than 36 months. Such a short lead time would have been remarkable enough if it involved just one new model, but all three ranges had been developed simultaneously – an extraordinary achievement.

But Daewoo is not a company to rest on its laurels. Less than 12 months later, the company unveiled the critically acclaimed Matiz city car – another totally new car – to bring its range to four.

Following Daewoo's take over of SsangYong, comprehensively improved versions of the Korando and Musso off road vehicles were launched earlier this year. And now, comes a extensively improved Nubira, incorporating a total of 90 significant changes.

Principal changes to the Nubira include revised front and rear styling bringing it in line with the Daewoo 'family' look and adding a total of 25 mm to the length of the car; a totally new interior with improved ergonomics and more space; and re-engineered power plants and drivetrains offering greater performance and economy with lower emissions.

Other improvements include enhanced safety, greater refinement and higher levels of standard equipment.

Despite all the changes, however, the prices for the new Nubira are exactly the same as they were for the outgoing model. The full line-up is:

Nubira SE 1.6 saloon £12,225
Nubira SE 1.6 estate £13,225
Nubira CDX 2.0 saloon £13,225
Nubira CDX 2.0 estate £14,225

ends ...

for further information please contact:

Alison Moran **Neil Reeve**
Public Relations Manager **Press Officer**

Figure 15.3 Press release for the launch of the new Nubira by Daewoo and Jackie Cooper PR

Used with permission

JCPR has used its experience in other consumer fields to introduce a new media relations approach in the car industry. 'In the first Motor Show that we did, everyone else had dolly birds on their stands', says JCPR divisional director Ian Withington.

We had Marguerita Pracatan singing her ode to the Daewoo concept car – it brought the whole show to a halt. The following year, when we were issuing new models and saying goodbye to the old ones, we hired a French performance artist, Monsieur Mangetout, who eats metal, to eat his way through an old Nexia. Mangetout complained that he didn't like the indicator lamps.

Withington also illustrates how PR can amplify the media opportunities of the company's practices.

With the 1,000 test drivers of the Nubira, we found that one of them was a grandmother, so we had a crash test granny. We also had an ex-James Bond stunt double. All of the test drivers had some local media which we could approach with photo opportunities and stories.

JCPR's commitment to the brand is a prerequisite, believes Phillips.

We would not do anything to damage the equity of the brand, nor anything to conflict with the advertising or marketing. There is trust between us and the client. You must have either that passion for the brand or the passion for the challenge to do good PR for a product.

That passion extends to their other clients, like Procter & Gamble and Baileys.

Evaluation is built into everything JCPR does. 'We can't provide guarantees, but we can evaluate', says Phillips. 'We always try to use both quantitative and qualitative methods.' This sometimes involves trying to measure the ripple effect of customer recommendation:

Recently, we were briefed to get people talking about a particular brand. We organised a focus group, asked them who they had told about the product, then got those people in, and so on. We wanted to measure what we had been trying to do – media coverage doesn't do that.

Phillips and his team's passion for their clients is matched by his own for his profession. 'PR is the corporate banking of the new millennium', he says.

With thanks to Jackie Cooper PR and Daewoo Cars
(All quotes from interviews with the author, June 1999)

Good PR cannot guard against all eventualities. Problems in the Korean economy led to Daewoo's bankruptcy in 2000.

16 Business-to-business public relations

'**N**o public has grown in importance as much as the retail trade', said David Bernstein, and then discussed the inadequacy of putting an 'exhortatory ad in *The Grocer* telling the retailer to stock up now' (Bernstein 1989: 102). Manufacturers have to talk to the retailers and tailor their offer to get them to stock their goods. They also have to be careful that in dealing with their distributors, they do not contradict messages that they are giving to their other stakeholders.

Consistent tailoring

In non-grocery products it is just as important to ensure consistency, whilst tailoring that message to the particular concerns of the stakeholder. Businesses that other businesses may want to communicate with are not homogeneous either. They may be suppliers of raw materials, and so have to understand the company's systems, needs and market opportunities. Deadlines must be met, and invoices submitted for payment to fit in with any cheque-run timetable to avoid financial disputes. They may distribute a company's products – few manufacturers sell direct to the consumer, but operate through retailers and agents. The rise of internet shopping has affected this area, with direct sales of airline tickets and books to the fore. Thus retailers in certain areas need support from manufacturers to encourage consumers into their outlets. For some manufacturing companies, other businesses are their customers, because of the products that they produce, such as heavy machinery.

One historical example of how business-to-business PR is important in getting products to market is that of Birds Eye. When the company introduced frozen foods, few retailers actually possessed the freezer cabinets which would enable them to stock and sell the products. Direct advertising and PR activity to consumers would have been wasted if there was little possibility of them being able to buy the products. Consequently, Birds Eye had to conduct a PR programme with retailers, showing them the benefits of buying the cabinets and stocking products, before consumer activity began.

Management Today classes PR consultancies as operating in the business-to-business area, and indeed Countrywide Porter Novelli won the Business-to-Business category in its 1999 Unisys Service Excellence Awards. The company's winning qualities were described as 'strong leadership, clear vision and unifying values', and the consultancy's

approach to accountability and servicing its clients' accounts was praised. Managing director Paul Miller was quoted as saying, 'Proving that PR pays measurable dividends is a vital ingredient of customer satisfaction.'

Cinderella?

Paul Vousden, managing partner of VLP, a PR consultancy which specialises in business-to-business (BTB) PR, feels that it is often regarded as the Cinderella of the PR world. In a letter published in *PR Week* (14 May 1999) he wrote

> Our clients and their industries may not be as sexy and headline hitting as those within the consumer sector [but] they are still immensely important ... the BTB marketing industry is worth £8.1 billion and PR is an important part of this sector.

BTB is not significantly different in the techniques used, but mainly in their application. The publics targeted are likely to be much smaller. In some instances, each separate individual approached within that public can be targeted separately. If a company is selling large items of printing equipment, the audience will be known. PR here creates the atmosphere in which items can be sold. The reasons for the buying decisions are also professional, rather than personal. Buyers are looking for equipment to help them do their job, or to ease the process for others. PR must reach all members of the company who contribute to a buying decision, sometimes referred to as a Buying Decision Unit (BDU). 'A lot of people fall into writing for the professional in all that they do', says Vousden. 'People are still consumers, and many of them are not very technically minded, apart from their own field.'

Getting the language right

Victoria Tomlinson, managing director of Harrogate-based Northern Lights, believes that few companies really understand about getting their product across to buyers through the media.

> I spent a day with a regional newspaper's business desk and could not believe the large numbers of press releases that failed to make any point. They were written in heavy technical jargon, had no story and did not highlight the 'so what' aspect to readers. An example was the launch of a new valve with a long description about its technical features but absolutely no mention as to why it was better than a competitor's or how it would change a manufacturer's product. The most complicated process can be written in plain English and understood by a non-technical person.[1]

Another example of this is in the construction sector. 'We do a lot of work where we are approaching architects', says Vousden.

> They are buying a solution to a problem rather than something with hyperthermic values. There has to be a balance between giving a technical description of the product and showing those technical aspects to be the benefits of buying it. The buyer is still interested in what's in it for them, just like any other product.

Precise targeting

One of the traditional methods used in BTB PR is media relations using the trade press. The range of trade titles means that publics can be precisely targeted. Some specialist publications work across an industry, such as *Caterer and Hotelkeeper*, others reach people in particular job functions in several industries, such as the *Accountant*. 'Sixty per cent of the media relations we do is with the trade press', says Vousden.

> We are trying to move away from sending press releases into getting longer pieces and features in particular trade magazines. We are also increasingly looking at the national press, as people who read the trade press also read the nationals. If people are buying grommits and they have been featured in the *Daily Telegraph*, it helps to build the brand.

Whilst media relations may be the core of BTB, other techniques are also used extensively. For particular clients, a series of presentations to key decision-makers may be used. Exhibitions are useful for demonstrating products, although they are becoming increasingly expensive. Newsletters may also be sent to clients and potential clients informing them of company developments. BTB is an area which is seeing increasing use of new technology in communications too. Facility visits also help to demonstrate the product to potential buyers and journalists, but should have a proper structure. 'Journalists have less time, they are under pressure. However, they are still willing to come on a visit if it features a trip abroad, which is a very good way of getting their undivided attention for the length of the trip', says Vousden.

> We had an Italian client that made safety barriers, so we took a party of journalists to see them in situ in Italy where there is a higher level of crime. There was also time to see the factory where they were manufactured, as well as some sightseeing in Venice.

Lobbying is used by some clients. Thames Gateway, a partnership of twelve London boroughs, asked VLP to raise their profile prior to the 1997 general election. Thames Gateway promotes a mixture of manufacturing, housing and social facilities in any development in their area. It was feared that under a new Labour government, their role might be subsumed under a cross-London body. VLP came up with the idea of turning the tables on politicians and doorstepping them. Using a prop doorstep, existing and prospective MPs were stopped by the Director of the partnership, and given information about why it was so important for the partnership to continue and emphasising the concerns of being on London's doorstep. Of course, media were briefed in advance that there would be good photo opportunities available. Candidates for the area were also invited to an event at Canary Wharf, which Nick Raynsford, who subsequently became Minister for London in the new government, attended. This benefited Thames Gateway, as Raynsford continues to be supportive of the partnership.

Sometimes products have to be re-packaged to show customers the unique features of a particular supplier. Selling energy to businesses is fairly difficult, as buyers tend to concentrate purely on price. Eastern Electricity found that it was too expensive to pursue domestic consumers, and that business clients were more profitable. On talking to the sales team, they found that most businesses wanted to feel that Eastern understood their particular needs. Whilst Eastern is not the cheapest in the market, savings can be made by some manufacturers. Those who can manufacture their product at any

time and stockpile until needed can take advantage of cheap tariffs overnight. One such business was cement, so a package was put together for cement manufacturers, showing how they could run their machinery and make substantial savings. Eastern also found that by analysing electricity demand, other information about a business could be deduced. A holiday camp owner could tell which nights were the most popular because of changes in demand.

Measuring success

'One of our difficulties is in getting clients to give us the evidence of outcomes of PR activity so that we can measure effectiveness and evaluate', says Vousden.

> We do have our own system for measuring and analysing media coverage and attendance at seminars. The hardest thing is to get feedback from clients about enquiries, sales leads and actual sales. We do use informal feedback from influential people in the field, which whilst it is not statistically valid can be very useful. We also look at what we have done and what we have achieved for clients every three months. This process alone can help clients to focus on what they are spending, what their objectives are and what the outputs are.

Tomlinson is a champion for measuring success of PR activities against business goals: 'It is a sad fact that 30 per cent of PR professionals say that their work cannot be evaluated and more than half are content to evaluate purely on the basis of media coverage.' She advocates setting clear business objectives for each PR campaign, such as numbers of enquiries, increased sales, improved recruitment, better share price or reduced staff turnover:

> It is hard relating PR to these sorts of results but it is worth doing. Just the process of setting measurable goals is a good discipline. It concentrates the mind on what you want to happen as a result of the PR, ensures you have evaluation processes in place, and makes sure that success or failure can be measured. This gives a good base to improve on for the future.

Four case studies have been selected to show the variety of BTB PR, two from VLP and two from Northern Lights.

Case study 1: Moving the mountain to Muhammad – Symonds by VLP

Symonds is a multi-disciplinary consultancy in the construction sector, although its interests lie across property, transport, IT, acoustics, health and safety, and infrastructure. Each discipline was to receive two months' PR consultancy every 18 months, on a cyclical basis. In the interim, PR activity would be carried out by the discipline director.

This caused problems as the particular trade media's interest did not coincide with the timing of the PR activity. Also, VLP found that problems of over-servicing the client were exacerbated with this system. To increase the efficacy of the relationship for both consultancy and client, VLP proposed a Virtual Press Office. The account team

SYMONDS' £450 MILLION WORLD RECORD TUNNEL

Symonds and Øresund Tunnel Contractors (ØTC) are delighted to announce the successful completion of the largest immersed tube tunnel in the world. The last of the 20 giant tunnel elements was successfully placed on Wednesday, 6th January 1999.

The 4km immersed tube tunnel, designed for ØTC by Symonds, forms part of the link between Copenhagen in Denmark and Malmo in Sweden and will carry a four-lane highway plus a twin track high-speed railway.

Work started on the tunnel just under two years ago when the first of the 20 segments left the dock in August 1997. Each of the 20 reinforced concrete tunnel elements is 175m long, 40m wide and weights 55,000 tons. Despite an accident in August 1998 when the ill-fated element 13 lost a bulkhead panel and sank, the contractor has managed to maintain the programme and the whole link is on schedule to open on time in July 2000.

Colin Gray, Symonds' project director said: "We are delighted with the results so far, which are a tribute to the commitment, team work, planning and ingenuity shown by all involved in the project."

The tunnel is not quite finished. The last metre of tunnel has to be built between the final two elements placed. This is a complex underwater operation that will be undertaken over the next two months. It will then be possible to walk the 4km from the Danish mainland to the artificial offshore island of Peberholm.

The installation of the road, railway and tunnel lighting, ventilation, control and communication systems means that the tunnel will take a further year to complete before it is handed over to the owner, Øresundskonsortiet. All parties are confident that the link will open on schedule.

Ends.

Editor's note
Photograph available upon request.

About Symonds
Symonds is an industry leader in providing strategic consultancy and management services. We provide expertise in Facilities Management, Project Management, Cost Management, Civil Engineering, Building Engineering, Transport and Environmental services. The company employs over 1100 people world-wide and has an annual turnover in excess of £72 million. Vivendi, the major multinational company, now owns Symonds. More information about Symonds can be found by accessing its web site: www.symonds-group.com

Figure 16.1 Material produced by VLP Ltd for Symonds

Used with permission

spent a day at the client's offices each week, and phone calls were diverted at other times to give a fully staffed point of contact for media enquiries about all aspects of Symonds' activities. Instead of sticking to a rigid timetable, VLP dealt with media enquiries when they arose, and responded to development in each discipline. Minor matters were dealt with internally. The VLP team also benefited from higher visibility and new contacts with key personal within the organisation and were able to turn material around more quickly.

VLP also worked on a new Symonds product. The traditional method of making a tunnel is to bore under the sea or river bed. Symonds developed a method of constructing concrete tubes which could be floated into position and then submerged. Once in position, water was pumped out and the tunnel was filled with compressed air. The technique was perfected on a link between Denmark and Sweden, the longest submerged tunnel in the world (Figure 16.1). In order to maximise media coverage, VLP and Symonds came up with the idea of producing a computer model showing how such a tunnel could link Ireland and mainland Britain. The presentation was turned into a news story, with resulting coverage in the *Observer*, the *Mirror*, the *Sun* and Irish papers and on Radio 4. 'This was a technical company, who few people had heard of, and suddenly they were in the national media', says Vousden. The company achieved a lot of coverage and associated goodwill, which led to good contacts with the British and Irish governments.

With thanks to VLP and Symonds

Case study 2: Constructive communications – Building Performance Group (BPG) and VLP

BPG is a firm of consultants specialising in whole life performance (WLP), a system that forecasts the maintenance costs of buildings over their life span from design to demolition. This is especially useful to property owners with tight budgets such as local authorities and housing associations. BPG was relatively unknown outside its client circle. Resources for promotional activity were limited, but as a growing business the company was able to qualify for part funding of the work of VLP under a Business Link scheme, Going for Growth.

The key communication objectives were to position the company as an industry-leading expert in the field of WLP, and to increase BPG's profile in the trade press.

VLP identified existing and potential buyers of BPG's services, and set out to place feature articles and case studies in the relevant trade media (Figure 16.2). Editors were invited to register the areas of interest to their publication, and a series of introductory meetings was set up with journalists. Each sector of the media identified was targeted in turn, starting with construction, then social housing and facilities management.

VLP also worked with BPG to co-ordinate its marketing communications, and monthly progress meetings were held to update the client and ensure that activity reflected the communication objectives. Additional support was provided at exhibitions and advice given on advertising schedules.

Between June 1998 and June 1999, 11 in-depth feature articles about the issues facing the industry and the solutions BPG could provide were published across the key target sectors. In addition, 35 news articles concerning contract wins and appointments helped to raise BPG's media profile. Substantial coverage was gained in *Building*, the leading construction industry magazine, and over 30 enquiries were received which directly

PRESS INFORMATION

Your Ref:

Our Ref:

**Building
Performance
Group**

*architects
engineers
project managers
surveyors*

11th May 1998

BPG EMPLOYS INNOVATIVE TECHNIQUES TO RESTORE MODERN MOVEMENT HOUSE

Leading building consultancy Building Performance Group has been appointed to restore the external fabric of St. Ann's Court, the Raymond McGrath Grade II* listed house in Surrey.

St. Ann's Court, completed in 1937, was probably the finest work of influential Australian designer Raymond McGrath with its bold plan layout based on a circle. The use of early reinforced concrete techniques and the new arguably pioneering use of shuttering to achieve a heavily boardmarked finish, make it an architectural landmark.

The work, which is due for completion by July 1998, will involve the use of Ferrogard, a relatively new product that protects steel reinforcement in concrete from corrosion. Ferrogard is applied directly to the concrete without destroying its fabric, making it ideal for renovation of Modern Movement concrete.

/...more

Directors
A. D. Mackay
*BArch RIBA
(Managing)*
M. A. Fordham
DipArch RIBA
R. G. Hellyer
FRICS MCIOB
K. Robson
CEng MICE MIStructE
R. G. Sadgrove
BSc CEng MIStructE
P. Wornell
MCIOB MMS

Associate Directors
J. Bonner
BSc(Hons) ARICS
K. P. Bourke
BA(Hons) ARICS MPhil
R. J. Madders
DipArch RIBA
B. M. Major
*DipSurv DipBldgCons
ABEng ARICS*
T. T. Phan
BA(Hons) AFA
R. J. Sully
BSc ARICS
A. C. Swabey
ARICS
C. J. B. Watson
BArch RIBA FBSH
A. G. Wilkins
DipSurv ARICS

Associates
B. Herbert
FICW
R. L. Spelman
BSc ARICS
R. C. Tej
BSc CEng MIStructE

Grosvenor House 141-143 Drury Lane London WC2B 5TS
Tel: 0171 240 8070 ■ Fax: 0171 856 4306 ■ Also in Scotland
Building Performance Group Limited. Registered at the above address.
Registered Number 1573939 London.

Certificate No. F S 25722
ISO 9001

Figure 16.2 Material produced by VLP Ltd for BPG

Used with permission

resulted from media coverage. Invitations to speak at industry conferences were received, and there was a significant increase in the number of new business leads.

With thanks to VLP and BPG

Case study 3: national Investors in People week – Yorkshire and Humberside Training & Enterprise Councils and Northern Lights

In July 1994, the nine TECs in Yorkshire and Humberside decided to carry out a joint campaign for the first time, to support the national Investors in People (IIP) week in October. Northern Lights was appointed to work with the marketing and IIP managers from each of the TECs. The consultancy was asked to convince businesses of the benefits of IIP, and a key target was to get businesses to commit to the scheme.

The TECs carried out research into why companies were not committing to IIP, and as a result agreed a brief with Northern Lights. The key elements were to produce company profiles explaining IIP and the key benefits, hold company visits so that managers could see how IIP worked in practice, co-ordinate an advertising campaign in the *Yorkshire Post*, and generate positive media coverage in a range of media including trade press. Northern Lights also found that journalists considered previously produced material to be couched in 'official government speak'.

Ten case studies were selected, ensuring regional spread and a variety of industries. Northern Lights managed the media campaign, which consisted of company visits, interviews with senior and junior staff, obtaining suitable photographs, writing feature articles for use by the regional media and a press launch in Sheffield. The Hambleden Group was also appointed to produce data comparing company results of IIP companies against non-IIP companies in the region, which was turned into a report by Northern Lights showing improved company results for IIP companies. Inside Investors visits were also set up with each of the ten companies, which were publicised to each TEC's company contacts.

Northern Lights worked with Teesside TEC to convert an existing advertising campaign for use in the *Yorkshire Post*.

The campaign was devised and launched within three months. Media coverage was five times more than agreed targets, and 95 companies in the region committed to IIP. The Inside Investors programme was fully booked. In the two weeks around the campaign, 70 calls were received, and seven regional radio interviews covered the survey results. Major features appeared in the main regional daily business press, as well as in the main business magazines. Trade press coverage was also successful.

Other benefits included the successful co-ordination between the nine TECs, which countered criticisms of wastage of public funds when operating separately. Case study material produced by Northern Lights was then used by the TECs in their own publicity materials. Journalists also commented on the quality of the materials produced. The TECs plan another co-ordinated IIP week in the future.

With thanks to Northern Lights and Yorkshire and Humberside TECs

Case study 4: Turning business around – Peatey's Coatings and Northern Lights

In December 1995, Peatey's Coatings, a 50-year-old family business, appointed Northern Lights to help with a survival strategy. A firm which had installed £0.5 million worth of new plant at Peatey's had gone bankrupt, and commissioning of the new equipment was delayed by six months. Interest on the loan and delayed production income against a turnover of only £1.25 million meant that the company was facing a severe cash crisis.

Previously, the company had not had a salesforce, marketing or PR function, relying on the quality of its work to bring in new business. Production difficulties meant that clients had put work out to other metal coaters. Peatey's needed to regain this business, plus additional work to fill its increased capacity. When Northern Lights was appointed, the company was facing a possible closure within two months. The following targets were agreed for the PR campaign: to gain £10,000–15,000 additional work from existing customers each month and to gain £8,000–10,000 new business from five new customers each month. The consultancy budget was very small.

Northern Lights worked with the client to analyse the most profitable type of work and the most profitable type of customer. Peatey's carried out research with existing customers to ascertain their perceived strengths, what percentage of their work was placed with Peatey's and what percentage with their competitors. Results showed that some customers were putting 25–50 per cent of their work with competitors, and it was decided to target these customers first. The main strength of Peatey's was felt to be the quality of its work.

The key messages were agreed to be that the company was back to full production and Peatey's work was of better quality than its competitors'. Northern Lights also wanted to make the company stand out from others. An initial publicity route, using the fact that the managing director was a woman in a man's world, was rejected as it focused on an individual, Ruth Chapman, rather than the company. Northern Lights suggested that Peatey's should become the first company in the country to give a guarantee for metal coating work, and to use Ruth Chapman's appointment as a director of Leeds TEC to emphasise the company's commitment to training and quality.

A marketing, sales and PR strategy was devised, covering target customers, how to approach them, customer service and dealing with phone enquiries. Three of Peatey's customers were interviewed and quotes on their reactions to the guarantee were used in media releases. A press launch and photo shoot were arranged, and Ruth Chapman was given media training. Media releases and photos were also sent to the key regional business and trade press.

Articles appeared in all the key local business and trade press. This included five major local business press articles, four in local business magazines and six in the metal finishing trade press. All referred to the new plant investment, training or quality. The turnaround was dramatic. In December 1995, Peatey's made a £6,000 loss. The first article appeared in January 1996, and orders of £10,000–20,000 were placed. By June 1996, Peatey's had made a £40,000 profit in the first six months of the year. Ruth Chapman was invited to speak at six major conferences, which also brought in new business. The company's technical expertise has been recognised and staff have been expert witnesses in legal cases. Another company in a similar situation contacted Peatey's for advice, and a long-term mutual relationship developed.

Ruth Chapman commented,

Before appointing Northern Lights we were facing possible closure. We had never done any PR before and I didn't really have any idea what it could achieve. Everything Northern Lights did was focused on our business, and as a result everyone in the company has more confidence in ourselves, our product and our marketing. As soon as the first article appeared, the phone started ringing and it's never stopped. Seeing us in the media gave customers confidence in us and the orders started rolling in. The bank was happy and now we are going from strength to strength.

With thanks to Northern Lights and Peatey's Coatings, and V. Tomlinson

Note

1 Unless otherwise stated, quotes are taken from interviews with the author.

17 Cause-related marketing

..

The links between PR and marketing have already been examined in Chapter 15, and an indication of the motivation behind consumers' decisions summarised. Cause-related marketing (CRM) has grown into a discrete area of marketing communications, and PR has a major role to play in making such programmes work.

So what exactly is CRM? Business in the Community, which set up a cause-related marketing campaign under Sue Adkins in 1995, has defined it as 'a commercial activity by which businesses and charities or causes form a partnership with each other to market an image, product or service, for mutual benefit.[1] This specification of CRM as a commercial activity moves on from sponsorship, which might include the donation of a one-off amount to a charity, or the provision of equipment to a special needs school, for instance, into a clear statement of a need to fit into the commercial objectives of an organisation.

Why CRM is gaining importance
..

The results of surveys carried out by BITC found that:

- 74 per cent of consumers think that it is acceptable for companies to involve a charity or good cause in their marketing

- 86 per cent of consumers agree that when price and quality are equal, they are more likely to buy a product associated with a 'cause'

- 61 per cent agreed that they would change retail outlet for the same reason

- 86 per cent of consumers agree that they have a more positive image of a company if they see it is doing something to make the world a better place

- 67 per cent of consumers feel that CRM should be a standard part of a company's business practice (The Winning Game, BITC Research 1996)

- 70 per cent of marketing directors, community affairs directors and chief executives believe that CRM will increase in importance, 75 per cent felt that CRM could enhance corporate or brand reputation and 42 per cent said it was important to achieving overall company objectives (Corporate Survey II, BITC CRM Research 1998).

As part of its work the cause-related campaign at BITC aims to generate awareness of CRM amongst businesses, as its surveys indicated that 'acting in a responsible way is no longer seen as an optional extra' and that 'the consumer sees business responsibility in this area as second only to government'. The BITC website reports that 'Cause Related Marketing offers an increasingly legitimate method for businesses to take on their responsibility to address social issues, and positively affects consumer perceptions of companies.'

Company, consumer and charity reactions

Of the 450 companies BITC surveyed in 1998 (Corporate Survey, BITC CRM Research), 73 per cent indicated some level of CRM spend, and the average amount invested was £310,000. Resources were more likely to come from community affairs budgets than from marketing. The benefits that were associated with CRM included enhancing corporate reputation, achieving press coverage, raising brand awareness, increasing customer loyalty and building increasing sales.

The most important causes for consumers were medical/health, schools/education and training, and environmental issues. In order to make a successful CRM partnership, BITC felt that it was essential that both organisations and charities should clearly identify their target audiences, understand the interests and motivation of these groups and develop programmes accordingly. There should be a clear link between the organisation and the charity it supports, like British Gas working with Help the Aged to support elderly people during the winter and providing insulation and energy conservation advice. The company announced an initial two year £5 million deal in January 1999 to run a home insulation programme, and fund the heating of day centres and lunch clubs and a Help the Aged advice line. Direct help with gas bills for elderly people most at risk was also provided (C. Murphy 1999). Case studies at the end of this chapter will discuss some other recent successful CRM partnerships.

BITC also carried out research amongst charity representatives attending a conference in May 1999:

- 65 per cent had been involved in CRM
- 92 per cent felt that it would increase in importance in achieving fundraising objectives
- CRM programmes raised £14.5 million for 1997/8 – a 60 per cent rise on the previous year.

Objectives that the charities felt that CRM could fulfil were raising funds and awareness, enhancing their own profile, shared learning with companies and promoting understanding. Whilst they were clear that CRM was a commercial activity for companies, they also felt that the charity must ensure that the value of the return was enough for their own investment of time and effort. Most of the CRM partnerships resulted from existing contacts, whilst desk research, previous experience and recommendation were also used to find suitable partnerships. One of the concerns was to ensure that the cause was protected.

Enlightened self interest

Jerry Wright, Lever Brothers' marketing director, called Persil's support of the Funfit scheme for 3 to 11 year olds, 'enlightened self interest – a combination of a worthy cause and an opportunity to target heavy detergent users such as the parents of young children'. He also stated, 'These kinds of things will be increasingly important to brand success in the future' (quoted in C. Murphy 1999: 20).

Some companies use CRM as an alternative to reducing price. Daddies Sauce began an on-pack promotion with the NSPCC in September 1995, donating 1p from every bottle sold to the charity. 'It has helped us to compete on a platform that doesn't devalue the ketchup category', said Andy Jones, marketing manager at IIP Foods. The company also chose the charity on the basis that as 40 per cent of ketchup was consumed by children there was an obvious link (C. Murphy 1999).

Other examples of CRM include NatWest's Face to Face with Finance programme in schools. It helps schools teach money management, and is careful not to use heavily branded promotional material, whilst conceding that it is 'loosely part of marketing to the 14 to 18 age group'. New Covent Garden Soup launched a special soup in November 1996 to help promote Crisis, a charity for single homeless people. As well as a donation to the charity, the soup carried information about Crisis and a donations hotline number. Tesco also agreed to donate 10p per pack for the first 50,000 cartons sold in its stores (C. Murphy 1999). The link between soup and the homeless is well established. The NSPCC has developed several successful CRM partnerships, including one with Microsoft on its Full Stop campaign in 1999, aimed at raising £250 million to fund its operations over a number of years (Gofton 1999). Dr Martens linked with Shelter, as the two biggest issues of concern to its target market of 16–25 year olds were unemployment and homelessness. Linking with Shelter was the ideal way for manufacturers R. Griggs to make a positive contribution to these social issues. BT chose to link with Winston's Wish, a charity which helps children cope with the death of a close family member, encouraging them to talk about what has happened. This emphasis on communications led BT to fund the appointment of a national development officer (C. Murphy 1999).

A calculated strategy

CRM is a calculated strategy in which everybody wins. Indeed, NCH Action for Children's research in 1993 was entitled 'The win win situation'. However, at that time, three-quarters of PLCs interviewed had no company marketing policy on CRM. Later research, entitled 'Who Chooses', recognised the importance of pester power, and 71 per cent of those surveyed thought that a child's view was at least equally important to the parents' when it came to purchasing decisions. (This research contradicts that on consumer behaviour discussed in Chapter 15.) However, what was more important was that 67 per cent of children and 60 per cent of parents in this survey felt they would be more interested in buying a company's product if it were associated with a charity. Thus the new generation of consumers is growing up with an expectation of company involvement in CRM. Tony Mainwaring at NCH said 'The economic reality for companies is that the youth market offers huge potential and the opportunity to build customer loyalty and develop relationships from an early age' (Jackson 1997: 22).

The British Gas link with Help the Aged demonstrates a key factor in the success of CRM. 'We are moving away from the "buy our product and we'll donate 10p to

this charity" approach', says Adkins. 'A relationship between a charity and a company has to be more than a fling.' The British Gas project was the result of nine months of customer research. The company believes that credibility must be established before making direct product links. 'If we were obviously trying to sell more products, consumers would be rightly suspicious of us', said Simon Waugh, director of marketing at parent company Centrica. 'It needs time and long-term commitment to create a degree of trust.' Thompson and Pringle (in C. Murphy 1999: 41) say 'The charity promotion is usually looking for a quick fix. The CRM campaign is looking for a fundamental and long term change in brand image and in the approach to the tackling of a cause: it's strategic and not tactical.'

Communication of the programme is an important element and must be handled correctly. 'You have to be up front about the corporate motives for what you are doing. Consumers expect you to gain from anything you do. If you don't admit it, they'll be suspicious', says Adkins. In order to make the process of communication easier, the Media Trust has launched a free-to-air digital channel, the Community Channel, featuring programmes made by the voluntary sector. The ITC has also granted it the right to screen advertiser-funded programmes to enable companies to publicise their CRM partnerships (C. Murphy 1999).

Competition for donations, donor fatigue and the National Lottery have led to charities working together to increase the effectiveness of their activities. 'Jealousies between charities are disappearing', says Adrian Batt at direct marketing agency DMS. 'They are now working together for their shared interest.' Occam is a collective name for 100 charities which pool their donor files to make direct marketing more affordable for all. A campaign to promote legacies as a way of giving to charities in March 1999 was funded jointly by Blue Cross, Imperial Cancer Research, the NSPCC, Oxfam, the RSPB and Shelter (Bird 1999). Total charitable donations fell from £5.3 billion to £4.5 billion from 1993 to 1997, and on average people give just £1.00 per month to charity (Wall 2000). Doubts about evaluation remain, but C. Murphy (1999) states 'All the evidence shows that the companies which are doing well are advocates of CRM.' She also emphasises the need to look for long-term benefits.

Company policies under the ethical microscope

The rise in CRM projects has led to a closer examination of a company's policies and practices by both prospective CRM charity partners and consumers. A US-based children's clothing company launched a scheme supporting Oxfam but had to abandon it when it emerged that some of its products were produced by under-age workers in sweat shops in the developing world. The Red Cross' decision to take £250,000 from Nestlé was reported in January 2000. Under the headline 'Does your charity take dirty money?', the dilemma was discussed of whether to take money from a subsidiary of a company that had been told by the Advertising Standards Authority in 1999 that it should not repeat its claim that it had responsibly followed World Health Organization guidelines in the promotion of its baby milk products in the developing world (Wall 2000).

The Charity Commission advises that charities should not take money from companies that perpetrate the problem the charity is trying to solve. The Red Cross took money from Nescafé after an investigation in which it was assured by the WHO that the organisation was now complying with international law on the marketing of baby

milk powder, and under the condition that should that change, the charity reserves the right to end the relationship. Greenpeace refuses to take corporate money or government funding to ensure that its independence and credibility cannot be compromised. It does not even take donations made by company cheques but only accepts individual ones. The campaigning arm of Greenpeace does not have charitable status because it is deemed to be political. Marketing director Annie Moreton explains, 'We're often in conflict with companies and we need to keep our campaigns completely clear of external influence.'

There are only a few charities that could afford to work without corporate support. Different considerations also apply for different charities. Whilst cancer charities would not work with tobacco companies, Crisis not only accepts money but cigarettes too, which it hands out to homeless people. 'We could stop, but what would the people we help say? They all smoke', said a Crisis spokesperson. Wall (2000) feels that CRM is often just a short cut to the moral high ground for a company, and quotes Stephen Lee, former head of ICFM, the professional body of fundraisers, as saying, 'It's a con. It's a mechanism dreamed up by business to promote business, with very strong rhetoric about partnership which is usually absolute rubbish.' Lee recommends a formal, written policy and advises caution in forming relationships to avoid alienating private donors. Few charities have such a policy, but simply follow the guidelines of the Charity Commission.

In 1996, two students approached Nestlé for an ad in their alternative newspaper. Nestlé chose to use the space to print a rebuttal of accusations concerning its marketing of infant formula in developing countries. Two years later, the Advertising Standards Authority upheld a complaint about the ad from a pressure group called Baby Milk Action. The ad stated that Nestlé 'marketed infant formula ethically and responsibly'. The ASA ruling stated that Nestlé could not support this claim. The Authority found that free formula had been given to hospitals in Bangladesh in 1993 and in China in 1994.

The first boycott against Nestlé was in 1977 in the USA by the Infant Formula Action Coalition. The National Union of Students will still not take ads from the company. In 1994, the Oxford Diocese called on the Church of England to disinvest in Nestlé, and the General Synod endorsed a boycott of Nescafé in 1991. The Liberal Democrats' Youth & Student Group put forward a motion to the March 2000 conference calling for support of the Nestlé boycott. Nestlé has been dogged by the issue for over 20 years. Cause-related marketing could not cure the problem without the company changing its business practice to take account of the activists' suggestions.

McDonald's chose to fight accusations about its practices through bringing a libel action against two activists, who were able to make their case widely known through the internet. Shell had to consult environmentalists and campaigners about the disposal of its Brent Spar platform. 'The problem that these companies are facing is that information about their activities is becoming ever more widely available', says Hamish Pringle, former vice-chair of Saatchi & Saatchi (quoted in Wilkinson 1999: 28).

Consumers feel that companies should have ethical labour policies in developing countries. A 1997 MORI opinion poll on ethical shopping commissioned by CAFOD found that 92 per cent thought that companies should have minimum standards for labour conditions. Christian Aid has produced reports on the poor conditions and pay for workers involved in producing sports goods.

Marjorie Thompson, director of Cause Connection at Saatchi & Saatchi, describes CRM as 'building a surplus account for the times when you have a crisis' (Wilkinson 1999: 28).

Case study 1: Nambarrie thinks pink! – Nambarrie Tea Company and Action Cancer

Nambarrie Tea Company is Northern Ireland's leading tea supplier, with the top tea brand in the province. In April 1998 the company signed a three-year sponsoring deal with a Northern Ireland (NI) charity, Action Cancer. The sponsorship deal expanded into a CRM programme.

NI has the highest incidence of breast cancer in the world, and the charity organises an annual breast cancer awareness campaign each October. Nambarrie's prime target audience is women, housewives aged 16–60, but they also wanted to address a subgroup of women aged 20–35. The company wanted to rationalise charitable giving into a focus on one main project rather than continuing *ad hoc* patronage, and another important consideration was that the benefits of the partnership should be felt locally, amongst its prime audience.

Communications objectives

- To fully integrate a campaign across all of Nambarrie's marketing activities.
- To secure media coverage prior to and during Breast Cancer Awareness Month.
- To communicate the reasons for Nambarrie's support to a potentially cynical audience.
- To ensure that all communications were mutually beneficial to the company and the charity.

Launch event

The main fundraising device for Action Cancer is the sale of pink ribbons. The assembly and packing of 2,000 boxes with 100,000 ribbons had been a huge logistical task for the charity. Nambarrie took on this task, closing its Belfast factory for a day and devoting staff and management time to packing the boxes. The factory 'closure' was used to stimulate media interest, announcing that 'Belfast's oldest tea company will close its factory floor for the first time since 1860'. Media coverage was achieved across daily press, radio and television, and in trade and consumer press. It also provided a benefit to the company in terms of staff morale, with employees enjoying a break from their normal routine and being involved in something they felt very worthwhile.

In addition, 100,000 special packs of tea were released with an on-pack promotion to donate 5p from every pack to the charity. The company secured presence on Action Cancer's promotional materials, including a province-wide poster campaign, the donation boxes and information cards used with the pink ribbons, banners in city centre sites and on the mobile cancer screening and detection unit. Nambarrie paid media costs for a TV advertising campaign to promote Breast Cancer Awareness Month, raising awareness of both the charity and the company. The company was also involved in other activities during the campaign duration, including hosting the launch, providing vehicles for deliveries and collections, serving tea to volunteers on sponsored walks and providing staff for fundraising and collections.

CRM evaluation

Media monitoring was used to assess the amount of coverage, which included photographs and editorial in all three daily titles, *Belfast Telegraph*, *Irish News* and *News Letter*, features in 12 local trade and business magazines, a live broadcast from the factory on BBC Radio Ulster, and coverage of the factory 'closure' on GMTV.

The company carried out regular brand tracking awareness and found that those who were aware of the CRM relationship responded significantly more positively to the brand. They answered 100 per cent above average to the statement – 'a brand that appeals to me'. Action Cancer achieved a 100 per cent increase in donations during the month, increased attendance at its clinics and a 24 per cent increase in awareness of and telephone calls to its headquarters. For a campaign which had cost the company only £25,000, results were above expectations. Brian Davis, Nambarrie's managing director, said

> This is the biggest public relations initiative that the company has ever undertaken. The return on investment has been enormous in terms of corporate, brand and internal communications. Most importantly, it has benefited our community and our customers, the women in Northern Ireland who buy our tea.

The campaign went on to win the 1999 Northern Ireland Council for Voluntary Action Award for commitment, impact and originality, as well as the first all-Ireland PR Award given by the IPR and Public Relations Institute of Ireland (PRII) and the Certificate of Excellence in the Community category of the 1999 IPR Sword of Excellence Awards.

Reproduced by kind permission of Nambarrie Tea Company

Case study 2: NCH Action for Children and Willow Bakeathon

NCH Action for Children runs over 370 projects around the UK to improve the lives of the most vulnerable children and young people. A range of services is provided for them and their families, including respite care, support for young carers, counselling and mediation for children and families, residential homes and schools. Over 70,000 people are helped annually.

To raise funds, the charity works with many high profile companies using CRM techniques. The charity was Tesco Charity of the Year in 1999, which involved several different promotions with different products including Ben & Jerry's ice cream, Select Crisps, Robinson's squash and Ash Valley Water. Together these activities raised £183,000 for the charity.

In 1999, NCH Action for Children was contacted by the brand team for Willow, a dairy spread made by Dairy Crest, which had been raising money for the charity for two years through its household division. The team wanted to promote the brand and increase voucher redemption. A sponsored cake bake was devised. Willow undertook to print all necessary promotional materials, and the charity secured celebrity endorsement from chef Anthony Worrall Thompson. Packs contained recipes, tips for holding a Bakeathon, and money-off vouchers for Willow packs. The vouchers gave the customer 10p off and generated a 5p donation to the charity. The Bakeathon was promoted through the charity's network and a national press campaign. Supporters were

asked to hold a cake sale, coffee morning, or to just bake a cake and sell the slices to raise money for the charity.

Over 800 packs and 50,000 vouchers were requested, and the first Bakeathon raised over £50,000 for the charity.

Reproduced by kind permission of NCH Action for Children

Case study 3: NSPCC Fort James competition

Fort James is a major manufacturer in the UK kitchen towel market. It launched Kitten Soft Thirst Pockets in 1996, and this was acknowledged to be the fastest growing brand in the 1998 Nielsen/*Marketing* magazine survey. In 1999, the company found out that Procter & Gamble was about to enter the market with the brand Bounty, which was to be supported with a £35 million support package. This was more than all the existing brands currently spent, and more than Bounty would generate in sales in its first year. Fort James did not have the resources to match this spending, and needed to develop a means of holding its sales in the face of this new competitor.

The objective was to devise a consumer activity which would be motivational and link to charity to gain both consumer and retailer support. In conjunction with their PR consultancy Grayling, Fort James linked up with the NSPCC to create a competition for 7–11 year olds to 'Design a Kitchen Towel for the Millennium' (Figure 17.1).

Children at 6,000 primary schools were invited to take part. The winning entries were printed in limited edition packs and sold from October 1999. Children also received prizes of WH Smith vouchers, and the first prize winners in two age groups got a

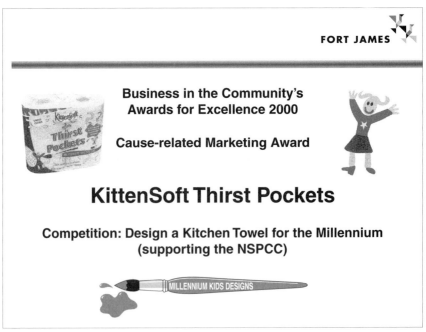

Figure 17.1 NSPCC Fort James
Used with permission

weekend trip to London to be presented with their framed designs. For every pack sold, Fort James donated 10p to the NSPCC. The charity logo was featured on all packs and competition literature.

Despite the heavily supported launch of Bounty, sales of Thirst Pockets continued to grow, with a marketing budget of one tenth the size. The millennium pack promotion saw an all-time high market share for Thirst Pockets in November and December 1999, and demand outstripped estimates and available stock. In addition, the on-pack promotion raised £60,000 for the NSPCC.

Note

1 BITC website at <crm.org.uk>.

Acknowledgements

Much material in this chapter is drawn from BITC statistics, resources and website with their kind permission. BITC, 137 Shepherdess Walk, London N1 7RQ, tel: 0870 600 2482, <info@crm.org.uk>.

18 IT sector public relations

Jo Chipchase

Within the UK PR industry, the IT sector is a growth area, in terms of stature and earnings. According to *PR Week*, during 1998 the UK's top 150 technology sector PR agencies generated a combined fee income of £86 million, accounting for 19 per cent of the PR industry's total fee income that year. Once perhaps considered the unglamorous preserve of specialist business-to-business agencies, the IT sector is now 'where it's at' in terms of attracting clients from the lucrative internet and new media marketplace. With computing and the internet becoming increasingly mainstream, IT companies are asking PR agencies to reach general audiences alongside the 'traditional' public of IT analysts and press, while many consumer campaigns now include an internet/web component. As a spokesperson for *PR Week* pointed out during late 1999: 'There's a lot of "dot com" [website] business around, and the technology agencies are benefiting.'

At present, the distinctions between various forms of PR are blurring, as an element of technology PR – or at least the need to use online media effectively – is creeping into every sector, and practitioners are having to adapt accordingly. Mark Pinsent of technology specialist agency Text 100 suggested during 1998 that the ability for PR practitioners to provide clients with internet-based services would be 'absolutely crucial', and agencies that can diversify into more generalist sectors are 'on to a winner'.[1] (Text 100 has set up various subsidiaries, some of which handle accounts outside the IT sector.) Commenting on the pace of change within the communications environment, Wendy Richardson of the Public Relations Consultants Association (PRCA), predicted during 1999 that 'no PR firm will be in business unless it embraces new technology'.

IT sector skills requirements

When asked to name the concern voiced most frequently by IT sector PR agencies, the spokesperson for *PR Week* answered 'recruitment'. He elaborated that 'getting people who have specialist technical knowledge can be difficult'. Although the 'anorak' image of IT-related roles has diminished, and interest in the internet is no longer considered socially undesirable, industry entrants may consider the technology sector less inviting than 'glamorous' consumer PR. This is despite the fact that career progress within IT agencies can be rapid. A document on Profile Public Relations' website <www.profilepr. co.uk> suggests 'Opportunities are often far greater in specialised areas, such as high-

tech PR. Starting out in one of the growth areas of the industry can be a way of giving yourself the opportunity to move up the ladder quickly.'

However, in a growth sector where technologies advance rapidly and the roles of different communicators are merging (for example 'full service' agencies provide PR, new media and marketing services), are PR skills more important than technical knowledge, or vice versa? Mario Tilney-Bassett of new media agency Sportal has worked within both the IT and the consumer PR sectors. He comments:

> The technology sector needs PR generalists who are capable of grasping technology, or at the very least what the technology means to the end user. For example, you do not need to know how television works to explain the difference between a colour and black and white set.

He adds that technology specialists 'tend to get bogged down in technical issues and can overwhelm the listener with jargon', while claiming that many PR practitioners are 'technophobic'.

Lyle Closs of Ogilvy Public Relations believes there is a need for people who understand and like technology. He comments: 'Clients expect practitioners to understand their business. For technology PR people, a good computer studies degree is preferable to a PR qualification. PR skills can be taught, but a fascination for and love of technology is harder to teach.' Closs emphasises the need for public relations practitioners to adapt their skills: 'Outside the IT sector, considerable ignorance exists . . . consumer and business-to-business PR people will have to learn fast . . . or find themselves out of business in a few years time'.

Taking a similar view, Dave Bennett of Manning Selvage & Lee believes technology sector practitioners need to have a broad skills set, especially as campaigns are becoming more mainstream: 'Some 90 per cent of our accounts are multi-faceted, in that they include some sort of non-IT characteristic. In five years time, there will be no such thing as a wholly IT account, dealing exclusively with trade media and analysts.'

The diversifying IT sector and its audiences

Business-to-business PR

A few years ago, technology sector PR largely involved communicating the benefits of products and services to IT managers, by targeting the publications read by these people. Popular (if unexciting) themes such as cost-efficiency, flexibility, reliability and robustness were used to encourage IT managers to invest in hardware, software and networking products – while making it straightforward to justify their purchases to finance directors and board members. IT messages and audiences were not exactly diverse.

Suzy Frith of IT specialist agency Citigate Technology describes how the situation has changed:

> For many years, vendors of IT services and software found communication easy. Their only audience was the IT department and the only relevant medium was specialist IT magazines. Now the picture is more complex, as IT has come out of the back office and drives virtually all business processes. So, IT vendors still need to sell to the people who make technology work – but they also need to gain the confidence of the board, business managers and users. They are having to think

again about external communications in a highly competitive market in which reputations can be destroyed by ill-chosen words and behaviour.

Frith believes IT companies are immature in their thinking, and need help from PR people to focus on markets, avoiding the previous tunnel vision on technology. In particular, Frith suggests PR people must help IT vendors to:

* realise that the single audience model (targeting just IT managers) is no longer effective
* develop strong brands
* identify and segment target audiences
* create market propositions
* 'develop what they say and how they say it, because communications is not their core business'.

Dave Bennett of Manning Selvage & Lee believes the main industry stakeholders – whether these are small businesses, public sector bodies, finance directors or end users – can be targeted by 'having a sound proposition, focusing on the benefits rather than the technology, and being *creative* about it'. The following case study demonstrates how a campaign for a purely 'techie' product can reach multiple audiences successfully, by using a different message for each type of target press.

Case study: EVUS launches Cambridge Silicon Radio

Cambridge Silicon Radio (CSR) launched in May 1999 – a nine-man team spinning out of Cambridge Consultants Limited (CCL) – with $10m of venture capital funding and some very big ideas. CSR is a 'fabless' silicon chip manufacturer, a very techie business, but with some hot technology. CSR's specialism is building short-range radios onto silicon chips, and the team's expertise had been used in a number of bespoke applications. However, the announcement of the Bluetooth short-range radio technology specification by Ericsson, IBM, Intel, Nokia and Toshiba presented an enormous market opportunity for the team. CSR's ambition was to be the first to market with a single-chip Bluetooth radio – a position that could see it quickly becoming a billion-dollar company.

 As with any start-up, the chief barriers to growth were lack of money and lack of people, and these key objectives needed to be addressed in the company's PR launch, besides CSR making an impact in the electronics industry. A further objective was to position CSR as one of the drivers behind the development and adoption of Bluetooth technology – the success of which would largely be driven by consumer adoption.

 A launch strategy was developed by EVUS, which involved positioning CSR within the key financial media as a well-funded UK start-up, within the electronics press as a technically innovative company, within the local Cambridge media as an excellent employment opportunity for technical professionals and, where possible, within consumer media as a British company bringing an exciting new technology to market.

 The *Cambridge Evening News* was briefed under embargo to run a story on the afternoon of Tuesday, 11 May 1999, the objective being to secure a launch story in the *Financial Times* on the morning of the same day. The launch release would be distrib-

uted to the trade press on the Tuesday. The strategy worked to perfection – although not without the odd drama. The *FT* ran a positive story on page 2 of its 'Companies & Markets' section, the *Cambridge Evening News* ran a large story under the headline 'Spin-off predicted to be world beater' and the key industry title, *Electronics Times*, carried a front-page story with the headline 'Billion-dollar Bluetooth bid'. In addition, a number of national titles, including *The Times* and *Observer*, picked up on the consumer applications of Bluetooth technology, strongly tying CSR to its development.

Although, at the end of the day, CSR's success will be based on selling millions of silicon chips, its ability to do so relies on many different factors. CSR's PR objectives continue to be multi-focused, with campaigns running in the technology, business, national and consumer-orientated media.

Case study provided by Mark Pinsent of EVUS, a division of Text 100

Targeting consumer audiences

Increasingly, technology companies are using mainstream media to reach a wide audience. Techie companies such as Cisco, which manufactures routers (an essential component of data networks), and IBM, which targets the corporate market with 'solutions for a small planet', advertise on prime time TV. After all, countless business managers and end users will be watching and may influence their company's procurement decisions. Similarly, internet ventures now promote themselves through every given medium. Whether consumers are viewing a TV advertisement for the Lycos search engine or a billboard advert for a fashion retail site, they simply can't escape the dot coms.

Caraline Brown of Midnight Communications, a technology sector agency that targets consumer and other audiences with creative campaigns, believes the secret of PR success is to 'keep it simple'. Brown does not believe in focusing just on the technology – rather, she thinks an IT product or service must be seen to have real benefits:

> People want to know how a particular technology will relate to their everyday lives. While technology for technology's sake at one time generated news stories, this is no longer true in a sector where audiences are becoming increasingly savvy. In the old days, the press loved the fact that a product or service had launched on the internet, and that alone would be worthy of coverage. Today, with the high speed of technological change, good PR coverage depends on coming up with an idea that brings the technology alive.

A plethora of new internet magazines emerged during 1999 and early 2000, and Caraline Brown points out that the computing and technical press has undergone a 'radical' facelift:

> Early publications tended to focus on high-end technology users – industry players and computer experts – rather than the person on the street. However, there has been tremendous expansion in the computing and high-tech media, and we are now seeing internet magazines carrying front covers that compete with the likes of *Maxim* and *GQ*.[2]

She adds: 'When you consider that everyone from pensioners to under-5s are embracing the internet with equal enthusiasm, there has never been a better time for IT sector PR practitioners to make an impression.'

The internet as a mass medium

Back in 1995, Warren Newman, an ex-president of the IPR, commented: 'the Internet *is* public relations' – but, at that time, the Net was ranked seventh as an issue of importance by PR practitioners. Today, in view of its audience reach, potential for propagating information and convergence with other media (consider webcasting, Internet Radio, interactive digital TV, etc.) the internet cannot be ignored by anyone operating within the PR industry. According to Nua Internet Surveys <www.nua.ie>, during March 2000, the total worldwide internet population was estimated to be around 304.36 million, with 83.35 million internet users in Europe alone. During May 2000, British internet users numbered around 14 million (source: Continental Research), confidence in e-commerce continues to grow (around 69 per cent of users are said to have visited a retail site) and technologies such as WAP (wireless application protocol), which brings internet content to mobile phones, are provoking considerable consumer interest.

The role of free ISP services, initially taking their lead from Dixon's 'newbie'-orientated Freeserve venture <www.freeserve.co.uk>, has been significant in encouraging widespread internet use, bringing people on to the Net who might not have been interested otherwise. Research by NOP suggests that free service providers are attracting a new type of internet user – generally older and from the C2DE social groups – where previously users were from predominantly younger age groups and ABC1 social rankings. Internet take-up amongst consumers will spiral further when unmetered (flat rate) telephone tariffs for access become commonplace. Market competition and the somewhat problematic unbundling of the local loop (the copper wire between household and exchange) from BT is finally resulting in the introduction of broadband services, such as ADSL, which carry data faster than modems and copper lines, and will make the Net cheaper and more attractive for users. The USA is ahead of the UK in internet take-up because it has benefited from unmetered access for a considerable time.

Even though the UK is still playing catch-up, the Net is increasingly being used as a means of accessing information for a wide range of purposes. For example, in the four weeks preceding the March 1999 NOP survey, a significant number of the respondents had used the web to:

- search for information on a particular company (2.9 million people)
- read newspapers online (1.9 million people)
- locate travel information (1.9 million people)
- search for financial information (1.3 million people)
- shop online (1.3 million people)
- search for employment (1.2 million people).

Redsquare's dynamically updated UK Internet Survey <http://212.95.128.250/redeye/> recently showed that 97 per cent of UK 'Netizens' surf the web, while 94 per cent use email and around 29 per cent use Usenet newsgroups. This is out of a total online population that represented, during early 2000, around 30 per cent of the UK adult population (source: Continental Research). In comparison, approximately 99 per cent of UK adults listen to radio, 98 per cent watch TV and 64 per cent read newspapers daily.

Are PR practitioners using IT effectively?

Paying heed to its phenomenal growth and audience reach, are UK PR practitioners fully embracing the Net? As a requirement for handling IT campaigns, or the online strands of consumer campaigns, surely PR practitioners must be able to find their way round the internet and use email effectively, without appearing luddite? The figures look encouraging: a survey of 180 of the PR Consultants Association (PRCA) members conducted during April 1999, covering all sectors, found that 100 per cent had email and internet access, while 88 per cent had a website and 62 per cent had an online newswire (such as Reuters Business Briefing) (Figure 18.1). These figures would suggest that practitioners are eagerly embracing new technology. However, an agency can have an internet connection without using it for its daily work, just as it can set up an email account without sending any messages. Dormant email addresses and dial-up internet accounts may exist outside the IT sector, where the need to understand and use new technology has not been an essential part of the practitioner's role – although this situation is now changing. A veteran magazine editor commented during 1999: 'You're at the cutting edge within the IT sector. You forget that other people haven't grasped the technology and are still communicating mainly using mail and fax.'

Practitioners who are technologically challenged will feel increasing pressure to update their IT skills at the demand of clients, colleagues and the press. As technology moves ahead, many may take their example from the IT sector. Shel Holtz, a US practitioner and author of *Public Relations on the Net*, believes the IT sector sets a precedent for the PR industry's adoption of new technology:

> Practitioners working in the high-tech sector face a particular challenge – to lead the way by innovating new concepts that apply all the rigorous principles of effective, ethical communication. As representatives of the companies that are developing the technologies that make dynamic, many-to-many communication possible, public relations practitioners have no margin for error. They are expected to embrace all

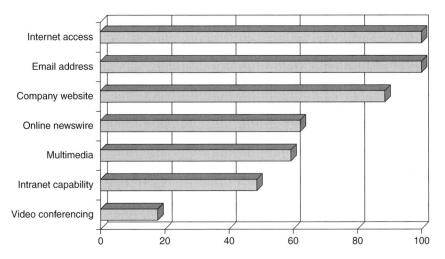

Figure 18.1 Technologies used by UK PR agencies – April 1999

Source: PRCA benchmarking study

capabilities of the technologies they promote, along with all of what is best about traditional communications. Even other communicators expect to follow the leads of the high-tech community.

During 1994, John Pavlik (of Columbia University) had a vision of the PR industry moving towards virtual teams with flat structures, helped by online communications. He predicted that virtual offices would exist, with clients and PR people communicating via email. He also said there would be a shift towards two-way communications, with PR people targeting virtual publics (that is, special interest groups that exist on the internet). Pavlik's visions are coming to fruition, in the IT sector at least. Virtual teams exist at many agencies, as individuals based in different locations can share information easily using email and intranets, as if seated in the same office. For this reason – and because the need for costly facilities provided by the employer is avoided – the use of freelancers is growing. On Pavlik's theme of virtual publics, the internet is being used by PR people to manage corporate reputations, interact with stakeholder groups and create communities of interest (these topics are covered later in the chapter).

Press contact via the Net

As practitioners in the IT sector are fully aware, the internet is highly useful for press contact. Unsurprisingly, the press is a major user of the internet for seeking and disseminating information, and PR people can take advantage of new efficient methods of communicating with journalists. The internet can streamline every stage of the process – from making proactive contact by email to providing timely material for download.

US author and PR consultant Dan Janal (1998) highlights the use of the internet for the following methods of press contact:

- email journalists instead of telephoning them
- communicate with journalists using online discussion forums
- send emails to multiple recipients simultaneously (this saves time compared to putting press releases in envelopes)
- tailor your message to fit individual journalists' needs
- act as a press resource
- look for journalists' queries (for example, on mailing lists and message boards)
- create a library of press releases
- write articles for online magazines
- create online conferences and seminars.

A survey by the California-based Tsantes and Associates shows that between 1996 and 1998, the US technology press increased its use of the web for research from an average of one hour per month to more than 2–3 hours a day. The research suggests that the fundamentals of public relations will change over the next decade, with an increasing focus on online press targeting. It is backed up by the 1998 Media in Cyberspace Study, conducted by Middleberg/Ross (also in the USA), which found that journalists consider the internet important for handling new sources of story ideas. Magazine journalists rank email second in importance after telephone contact (26 per cent claim to prefer it), while newspaper journalists rank it behind personal contact (16 per cent prefer it).

Middleberg/Ross also suggest broadcast journalists are turning to the web for information and that 'as real-time news cycles and online scoops continue to shake the historic operations of print and broadcast media, the PR professional must adjust accordingly'.

In the UK, IT sector journalists are using email discussion forums to seek PR contacts and find information for news stories and features. Popular forums include the new media-focused *uk-netmarketing* <www.chinwag.com/uk-netmarketing> and *UKPress* <www.ukpress.org>, which was set up to cater for journalists and PR people working in IT coverage. The opinions of all people on a particular list can be canvassed at once, which means journalists can save time conducting research.

To help meet the information needs of journalists, many PR agencies, including IT specialists A Plus, Firefly and Profile Public Relations, have set up internet press centres, which provide searchable databases of news releases from their clients (Figure 18.2). Industry-wide press resources also exist, such as *The Source* <www.sourcewire.com> and *PR Newswire* <www.prnewswire.com>. PR agencies can send press releases to these resources, for distribution to journalists who have signed up to receive news on topics of their choice. Journalist Jim Sterne (1998) says of online press resources:

> Reporters need factual information about executives, products and financial conditions. Press sections of websites are useful not only for providing such information to journalists, but they could save PR people from personally handling routine questions. Having a journalist-friendly website won't guarantee good press ... but

Figure 18.2 Firefly's searchable internet press centre

providing information about your company and its products online where journal-ists can find it quickly and easily is a good investment of PR resources.

Although online press resources exist within the IT sector, the survey results presented in Chapter 10, which focuses on media relations, show that the majority of PR practi-tioners are continuing to send press releases to journalists in the post (aka 'snail mail'), followed by fax – and that the majority of journalists prefer this method.

To assess the opinion of the editors of IT publications towards internet-delivered PR material, the author conducted a small survey for this chapter during September 1999. Questionnaires were emailed to 78 editors of national IT and telecoms publications with circulations exceeding 10,000. A response rate of 19 per cent was achieved. It must be noted that a high proportion of emailed questionnaires 'bounced' (failed to deliver), as many of the email addresses given for publication editors were invalid. If the bounced messages are discounted from the sample, the response rate was 29 per cent.

Although limited in sample size, the results provide an insight into IT editors' atti-tudes and can be compared to the results of the survey in Chapter 10, which covered a wider range of journalists – including those working for the national and regional press, daily and Sunday titles, national and regional radio.

In this smaller survey, responses were received from experienced editors – 80 per cent of whom have a minimum of four years' experience in journalism. The selected sample works entirely in the computing/internet/communications fields (with slightly less than half working in the internet field).

A question about the number of press releases received by email showed that only 7 per cent of the respondents receive fewer than five per day, while the majority (36 per cent) receive 6–10 per day (Table 18.1). In comparison, 40 per cent of respondents receive more than 20 'traditional' (hard copy) releases by post per day (Table 18.2). This suggests editors are still receiving more releases by post than email, although the figure is marginal. The fact that 20 per cent of respondents receive fewer than five releases by post per day could be explained – speculatively – by the fact that some editors do not bother to open 'snail mailed' press releases.

Table 18.1 Average number of press releases received daily by email (%)

Fewer than 5	7
6–10	36
11–15	7
16–20	21
More than 20	29

Table 18.2 Average number of press releases received daily by post (%)

Fewer than 5	20
6–10	7
11–15	20
16–20	13
More than 20	40

Respondents were asked to rate their response to various statements about internet-delivered PR material using a scale of 1–5, where 5 is 'strongly agree' and 1 is 'strongly disagree'. The results can be used to indicate the attitude of IT editors towards aspects of online press targeting. Of the various statements requiring a response, the statement that generated the firmest agreement was 'I receive a lot of badly targeted PR material by email', with an average ranking of 4.2. Almost half the respondents gave it the maximum rating of 'strongly agree'.

The next strongest agreement (ranked 3.9) was to the statement 'The internet is a vital tool for PR people to disseminate information', although fewer respondents strongly agreed than with the targeting question. The statement 'I am more receptive to internet-delivered PR material than I was two years ago' was ranked 3.5, while 'I would like to receive more PR material by email' was ranked 3.9, which indicates editors' receptiveness in both cases. The idea that 'hard copy press releases have more credibility than emailed releases' was ranked 2.3, showing disagreement. The statement 'PR people outside the IT sector make efficient use of internet technologies' was ranked 2.1, which suggests there is room for improvement in this area.

The respondents were neutral to the statements 'I often delete emailed press releases from PR people without reading them' (2.9), 'I would rather receive summaries of press releases [by email] linked to web pages containing the full story' (2.8) and 'internet delivered press releases are useful because you can cut and paste material into final copy' (2.9). Slight disagreement was shown towards 'I frequently use industry-wide press resources, such as *Newsdesk* and *The Source*' (2.7) and 'I will not open email attachments from PR people in case they contain viruses' (2.6). The respondents slightly agreed that they 'would rather visit a virtual press conference than travel to a "traditional" press conference' (3.3), and were neutral about the value of using real-time messaging systems for conducting interviews with spokespeople (3.0).

The firmest disagreement from respondents was to the statement 'I monitor what people are saying about companies, products and services in online chat rooms' (1.9), followed by 'I monitor what people are saying about companies, products and services on email discussion lists' (2.0). However, activity in this area may grow.

The following case study demonstrates how the editor of a leading internet title views the role of PR practitioners.

Case study: Paul Douglas, Editor, .net

Within the IT press, contact with PR representatives is vital. Journalists will source newsworthy stories in a number of ways, but the role of the PR agency in setting up interviews, supplying photography and clarifying background information makes an important contribution. Generally, PR/journalist contact is good within the industry, although some PR practitioners lack a deep understanding of their clients. Tactics such as the sending of tacky gifts and glossy press packs may fulfil a role in attracting the attention of a journalist, but are no substitution for a clearly written press release that has been tailored to the readers of the publication to which the material is being submitted. Wrongly targeted press releases tend to annoy and reflect badly on a PR agency, as does calling a publication with a possible news story having never read the publication being approached.

Using meaningless phrases in press releases, such as 'the complete internet solution for the cost-conscious SME' in an attempt to sound au fait with the market is unlikely to get a press release noticed. Getting to the point and saying 'a low-cost piece

of kit that can benefit many small businesses' is likely to receive a more favourable response.

There is no reason that the internet should do away with the PR function as we know it – it is simply a faster, more efficient way to disseminate information. Unfortunately, it is sometimes too easy for a PR agency to mass-mail journalists with irrelevant material simply because it can do so at the touch of a button. With or without the internet, there is still a need for talented staff to write releases, liaise with journalists about possible stories and supply additional information or arrange interviews.

Websites – what works and what doesn't?

PR practitioners, including those outside the IT sector, are being asked to consult clients on setting up websites and running internet-based campaigns. Some agencies have created specific new media divisions to meet clients' needs in this area. Websites are important because they represent a company's image and brand values online, and can be used to communicate cost-effectively with many audiences. Communication through websites may be:

- business to business – reaching third parties, shareholders, potential investors, industry bodies, analysts, trade media, etc.
- business to consumer – reaching customers (existing and potential) or general 'surfers' through information resources, e-commerce systems, entertainment sites, portals, etc.
- internal – providing tailored information to staff and affiliates using intranets, extranets (inter-connected internets) and password-protected areas on corporate sites.

According to a recent study by the *Los Angeles Times*, based on various internet statistics, including those from specialists Media Metrix, the web is shrinking despite continued growth in the number of sites. People are spending less time on general surfing, relying instead on a small selection of trusted sites (in the UK leading sites include the Yahoo.co.uk search engine and the Freeserve.co.uk portal). More than a third of most people's online time is spent at the 50 most popular websites. The study also suggests that word-of-mouth recommendation, known as 'viral marketing', is becoming increasingly important as a means of securing an audience for a website. Conversely, a website's reputation can be destroyed by negative visitor opinion. Boo.com, the internet fashion retail venture that failed spectacularly during May 2000, floundered from the start when UK new media experts voiced their collective lack of faith in its design and functionality.

A successful website should have the following features, according to Kirsner (1998):

- a 'What's New' section – so users can identify the latest content and go directly to it
- a search engine or site map – to ensure all content is straightforward to locate
- a feedback mechanism (an online form or email address), so users can comment about the site and suggest areas for improvement
- consistent navigation (the same navigation system should appear on each page)
- security information (this is particularly important if the site has an e-commerce system where users are asked to enter their credit card details)
- linking instructions – to encourage reciprocal links with other sites

- a privacy policy – if users provide their email address to join a mailing list, they need to be reassured that it will not be passed to third parties without permission
- location and contact details.

A recent survey conducted in the UK by Redsquare revealed that internet users actively dislike:

- *'Data speeds too slow'*. Website visitors will feel frustrated if pages do not load within approximately 30 seconds. This is especially true of people who are using modems at speeds of less than 56k.
- *'Disorganised mess'*. Many sites are inconsistent in their approach to visual identity, navigation, layout and the structuring of information.
- *'Substandard design'*. Poorly designed websites are no more acceptable than sloppy examples of corporate literature.
- *'Slow response times'*. If a website has a feedback mechanism, it is unacceptable to ignore enquiries, or even to take a few days to reply.
- *'Too much information'*. The most effective websites provide succinct, punchy content.

With an increasing number of 'newbies' (new internet users) coming online, it is important for websites to be user friendly and straightforward to navigate – otherwise a proportion of the potential audience will be lost. In new media forums, a debate rages about the use of Macromedia's Flash – which creates animated, multimedia content for websites – on general consumer sites, as users who don't have the latest browser plug-ins (helper applications) are forced to download the software or skip the content. As a general rule of thumb, Flash is considered inappropriate on e-commerce sites, information sites (such as search engines and directories) and anything aimed at a predominantly newbie audience. The use of superfluous Flash content – amongst other unnecessary adornments – was a major contributory factor to the failure of fashion retail site, Boo. However, Flash *is* appropriate for the likes of entertainment sites, music resources and digital art sites. As the roles of new media agencies and PR agencies converge, it will become the role of the PR person to advise clients on such matters.

Website follies on the scale of Boo can be avoided where techies, designers and marketing communications people work together as a team and listen to advice from industry veterans. According to Gusterson (1999), a fusion of technical and communications expertise is necessary to create an effective website. He suggests that PR practitioners who understand the web are well suited to assuming ownership of site content and liaising with technical staff over presentation. He also points out that attention must be paid to writing style, as the web requires something different from the traditional paper-based writing mode. People rarely read web pages word by word, instead scanning the page and picking out individual words and sentences.

PR people should certainly be aware of how to edit material for the web. Suggestions for formatting web page content include:

- keep the word count to around 400 per hypertext page, as information is less easy to read on a screen than on a printed page
- break up body text with sub-headings
- link from a feature or opinion piece to other sites that display relevant information

- include references to other sites as hyperlinks
- include an email address, in case the viewers require further information
- remember that your potential audience is global, even if the site has a local focus
- be sure to remove references to printed material from the copy, such as: 'On page three of our brochure you will find . . .'

Shel Holtz believes PR people need to gain skills in site strategy and editing content appropriately. She commented during 1999:

> The public relations professional is woefully behind marketing and other disciplines in the effective application of the Internet to their trade. Most online public relations is the simple repurposing of existing print material with no measurable objectives assigned to these efforts. If you see a website that is building one-to-one relationships based on data, a website that is applying many-to-many interactivity in pursuit of an organisation's goals, you won't be likely to find a public relations practitioner within ten miles of that project.

Holtz also criticises the measurement process for websites, which has traditionally focused on the number of hits, visits and page impressions attained during a certain timescale. (For example, you could attract 12,000 visitors to your UK-focused women's portal – but is this *really* useful if 90 per cent are young male students living in the States?) Holtz asserts:

> That kind of measurement is akin to asserting that a press release achieved its objectives because it was distributed to a certain number of newspapers. Public relations professionals are employed to influence audiences –- to change or reinforce opinions, levels of commitment, or actions. Measuring the effectiveness of public relations on the web means measuring how well the site influenced its audience. It is incumbent upon practitioners to measure the impact of the site, not the site itself.

The problem may be that many sites do not have a clear purpose from the start. US-based author and PR consultant Dan Janal (1998) believes too many companies go on the web without a set of goals. He suggests: 'Most sites fail because they don't have a strong call to action. There is simply no incentive to move people from being curious to being committed.' In some cases, sites have failed because they were launched before being fully tested – which is usually a recipe for disaster, as companies such as Boo learned at their expense. PR people could help ensure that a site has attainable objectives, that the technical team works with the marketing people, and that live testing isn't conducted on the public.

In many cases, PR agencies need to put their own sites in order. Mark Pinsent of Text 100 identifies various shortcomings:

> [There is] a lack of appreciation of what the visitor wants to see – more commonly, they get what the company wants to tell them. There quite often seems to be a desire to get people off the site as soon as possible, with loads of links to other sites.

He advises against including material that should perhaps be confidential – such as information concerning specific client contacts and PR decision-makers. After all, most

agencies do not wish to inadvertently encourage head hunting of their valued personnel. Nor do they wish to tarnish their reputations as professional communicators by uploading ill thought out content.

Internet reputation management

For communications professionals, a key issue concerning the internet is the interactivity between users and the fact that anyone can voice their opinions without constraint. Unlike other mainstream media, the internet allows two-way and many-to-many communication. Howard Rheingold (1994) described the network and broadcast paradigm. The network paradigm involves multi-directional communications between citizens (for example people holding discussions using email and online forums), while the broadcast paradigm involves the one-way (downwards) provision of information and entertainment (such as NTL providing video on demand). Rheingold accurately predicted that the big players in the internet industry would form alliances and focus on the Net as a means of exploiting the broadcast paradigm, with an emphasis on piping entertainment into homes. However, the influence of virtual communities – the network paradigm – is perhaps more relevant to PR practitioners.

According to David Phillips (1999), a PR consultant specialising in internet reputation management, 'Internet Society' comprises thousands of communities that have their own agendas. Established internet users may be active in numerous online communities, and will frequently carry information (factual or otherwise) from group to group. Online communities use resources such as chat rooms, email lists, newsgroups and bulletin boards to discuss topics of interest. The anonymous nature of online resources, where people can assume any identity they choose, may lead users to articulate things they wouldn't mention in 'real life'. As Phillips points out, the anonymous aspect of the internet changes the nature of 'stakeholder society'. Individuals can participate in many different stakeholder groups and may use interactive resources to influence events as never before, without the need to go through media gatekeepers (that is, editors). In many cases, people will voice their opinions freely about companies and services – and these opinions can spread and prove influential. As a result, PR practitioners need to be proactive in the field of internet reputation management. They need to advise companies about monitoring online forums, setting up information areas on websites and countering negative online comment.

Says Phillips (1999):

> Once companies had control of what was said and believed about their activities. Now every stakeholder has, can and does provide knowledge and opinion freely. Anyone can create a website. Unacceptable practice attracts comment, criticism and active opposition. Companies have to fight for a place in internet stakeholder society.

Virtual forums

One of the main places where comment about companies can propagate is on virtual forums – including Usenet newsgroups, email lists, message boards and chat rooms. According to Phillips (1998), newsgroups attract around 1 million postings every day, and most major companies are mentioned in newsgroups reasonably frequently. He points out that consumers go to virtual forums to find out about products and services

Author: Stuart Pearce	author profile
Email:	email reply
Date: 1998/08/23	view thread
Forums: uk.local.london	post new · post reply
view for bookmarking · text only	subscribe

```
>I was somewhat surprised to find out that the NATWEST does not provide
>PC-Homebanking for individual accounts, only for companies. It is
>otherwise a standard and completely free service in any bank here in
>Denmark.
>
>I will appreciate any response. Thanks in advance.
>
>Leo

If you want free PC banking, try FirstDirect.  They're a telephone banking
service, and a subsidiary of Midland Bank.  I've never had any problems with
them at all, and their service is free even if you go overdrawn. (Within
limits, of course.)

As for NatWest, I wouldn't bank with them if they were the last bank in the
universe.

Stuart
```

View Thread

» Thread Entry Point «

- **Natwest Bank - is it good?** - Leo *1998/08/10*
 - --- Aldnn *1998/08/10*
 - --- Will van Zwanenberg *1998/08/10*
 - ------ Thom Baguley *1998/08/12*
 - --- Adam Cheney *1998/08/11*
 - --- dove98 *1998/08/11*
 - ------ Will van Zwanenberg *1998/08/11*
 - --- » Stuart Pearce *1998/08/23* «
- **Re: Natwest Bank - is it good?**
 - --- Will van Zwanenberg *1998/08/11*
 - ------ Peter Foster *1998/08/11*
 - --------- Will van Zwanenberg *1998/08/11*
 - ------ Matthew M. Huntbach *1998/08/11*
 - --------- Will van Zwanenberg *1998/08/11*
 - ----------- kahunaaccidentale *1998/08/11*
 - --------------- Will van Zwanenberg *1998/08/11*
 - ------------------ Peter Buchwald *1998/08/11*
 - --------------- Penelope Wythes *1998/08/12*
 - ------------------ Will van Zwanenberg *1998/08/13*
 - ---------------------- Terry S *1998/08/13*
 - ------------------------ Jane Ellen *1998/08/14*
 - ------------------ P.D.Stamford *1998/08/15*
 - ----------- David Rees *1998/08/11*
 - --------------- Will van Zwanenberg *1998/08/11*
 - --------- Penelope Wythes *1998/08/12*

Figure 18.3 Newsgroup postings: a potential PR opportunity for NatWest and First Direct but a threat if ignored

from other customers, and often rely on trusted sites: 'The reputation of products and brands is much maligned in newsgroups … damaging and malicious comment can spread like wild fire. Stakeholders need to be aware of the potential difficulties they can meet and the affect they may have' (p. 27).

Phillips believes the PR practitioner can act as an 'internet guardian', protecting corporate reputation in online forums, by monitoring discussions and containing rumours at an early stage. However, PR practitioners must look before they leap. Virtual forums have a strong sense of community and their own sets of rules (or 'netiquette'), and any inappropriate interjections into the ongoing discussions could further damage the corporate reputation the PR person is trying to protect. According to Gusterson (1999), public relations practitioners need to develop skills in this area. He believes monitoring the internet enables companies to:

- formulate defence strategies against online attacks
- act early to contain a crisis
- monitor stakeholder opinion
- gather competitor intelligence.

As part of reputation management in newsgroups, some companies spend time 'seeding' the discussions with favourable comments about their products and services (the online equivalent of a 'whisper campaign'). A number of companies are transparent about their activities in newsgroups, while others use tactics surreptitiously to attack rival brands. Whether or not this is ethical is a point for debate.

In some cases, corporate reputations have been saved by monitoring virtual forums diligently. For example, during March 1999, complaints about Pioneer DVD players began to appear on newsgroups. Pioneer contacted complainants directly by email, and offered to fix their DVDs – an approach that contained the negative publicity, preventing it from reaching a wider audience such as the national press. Conversely, Intel chose to ignore newsgroup discussions about the now infamous floating point error in its Pentium chip. Eventually the story was picked up by the mainstream media and Intel had to spend millions repairing the damage.

The monitoring of virtual forums is especially important to publicly quoted companies. Investors are increasingly using message boards to discuss companies and share stock tips. AgriBioTech saw its stock fall by more than 20 per cent when negative messages were posted on a message board provided by the popular search engine/directory, *Yahoo!*

In some cases, newsgroup postings can provide a proactive PR opportunity. For example, a posting on the <uk.local.london> newsgroup during August 1998 suggested: 'If you want free PC banking, try FirstDirect. As for NatWest, I wouldn't bank with them if they were the last bank in the universe' (Figure 18.3). The discussion soon spread into other groups, taking the NatWest debate to a wider audience. Had NatWest spotted the postings and responded quickly, it could have reversed the adverse coverage and mentioned positive aspects of its service. However, after 24 hours had elapsed and nothing had been done, at best an issues management job could have been implemented. A missed opportunity existed for rivals of NatWest – especially First Direct – to respond and emphasise the benefits of their services. For the PR practitioner, an opportunity existed to act as 'internet guardian' and advise the companies on how to proceed.

Crisis communication

While newsgroups are important to reputation management, websites play a vital role in proactive corporate communications. Websites are particularly useful in crisis situations – but if a company doesn't have a site that acts as an adequate information resource, people will seek (possibly inaccurate) comment from other sources. The Middleberg/Ross Media in Cyberspace Study reveals that journalists are increasingly turning to websites for corporate information, especially during crises. It is advisable for corporate websites to provide online press kits that contain up-to-date background information. If a corporate website is successful in divulging the necessary details during a crisis, it can engender a sense of openness and honesty and help with damage limitation.

During October 1996, an *e. coli* bug contaminated the Odwalla juice company's products, resulting in the death of a child. The company decided to use the web as a third party information resource, which gave the press and public a sense of openness. The site attracted more than 20,000 hits during its first 48 hours. When Swissair lost a flight off Nova Scotia in 1998, it altered the first page of its site within hours to provide information and phone numbers in three languages. In contrast is the case of TWA. When Flight 800 crashed, Boeing failed to provide information in response to the disaster, which resulted in the public turning to alternative internet sources for information about safety records.

Rogue websites

Just as the web gives corporates a voice, it gives consumers a voice too. In particular, disgruntled consumers may air their views about an organisation and its products and services through the creation of 'rogue' websites. Sometimes, a rogue site will use a domain name similar to the company it is attacking, while others take a more generic approach. The following case study demonstrates how an individual can use the web to bypass media gatekeepers and challenge a large corporation over a consumer complaint – in this case, within the aircraft industry.

Case study: Brian Corbett, British Scareways <www.aviation-uk.com>

Brian Corbett set up the British Scareways site during 1996, after he was dissatisfied with the repair work carried out by a BA subsidiary on his small aircraft. Corbett believed illegal documentation had been issued for the repair and refused to take the plane back, believing it could be dangerous. British Airways subsequently took Corbett to court and won the case. However, Corbett says: 'Eventually, through correspondence with BA and the Civil Aviation Authority, I received documentation admitting the original documents were wrong.' He believes this evidence prevents BA from starting legal proceedings against British Scareways. 'BA knows the site is there and leaves it alone, as I could prove my case.'

British Scareways has attracted 45,000 visitors to date and elicits material from disgruntled BA customers and employees around the world (Figure 18.4). 'The site has gone off on a tangent', says Corbett. 'It has become a clearing-house for other people's problems, rather than my own.' Corbett admits he would be willing to turn British Scareways

Figure 18.4 British Scareways site challenges BA over aircraft safety

into a consumer opinion mechanism if BA paid him to do so. 'I'm not trying to black-mail BA – I just want to recoup the money I lost', explains Corbett. 'I don't think BA is a rogue, although its subsidiary was. BA thinks it's big enough to ignore me.'

A spokesperson for BA said:

> We are aware that websites such as British Scareways exist and we take action against them where necessary. However, the airline has no plans to buy out the rights to this or any other site at present. BA has its own legitimate website where customers can make contact with the airline and provide feedback.

Websites and direct action

While other rogue sites target companies such as Wal-Mart <www.walmartsucks.com>, the Ford Motor Company <www.flamingtowncars.com>, and Dunkin' Donuts <www.dunkindonuts.org> (Figure 18.5a), which was bought-out during 1999 by Allied Domecq and turned into a 'consumer opinion site' (Figure 18.5b), the core of anti-corporatism online is the growing number of activism sites. A good example is the McSpotlight site <www.mcspotlight.org>, which was set up to challenge McDonald's during February 1996, after the infamous 'McLibel' trial against two environmentalists from North London (the longest running libel trial in British legal history). The site,

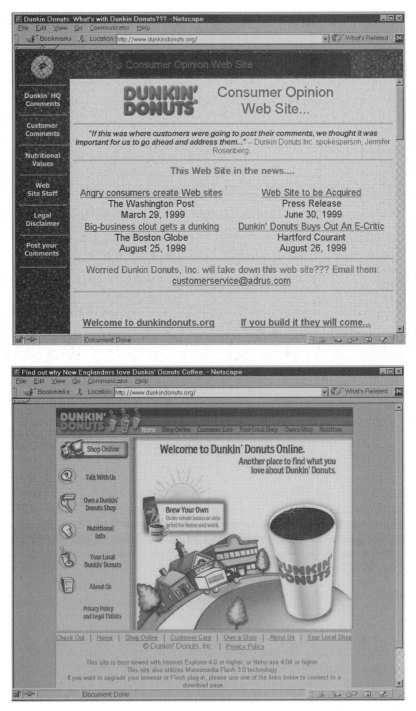

Figure 18.5 Allied Domecq bought out Dunkin' Donuts 'consumer opinion site' (top) and turned it into a customer service resource (bottom)

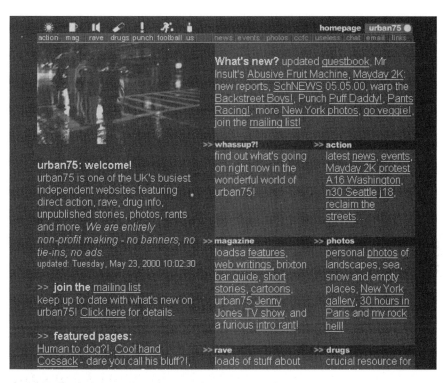

Figure 18.6 urban 75 – a Brixton-run site renowned for direct action

which generated 1.7 million hits in the first twelve weeks of its life alone, now runs a variety of campaigns for activist groups and provides leads to many other organisations. While the 'Wal-Mart Sucks' site thrives as an independent forum for consumer opinion.

During the summer of 1999, the international June18 'Carnival Against Capitalism', which publicised itself via <www.j18.org>, demonstrated how the Net can bring together loose alliances, organise and motivate people and turn words into actions. In the UK, a large-scale demonstration ensued in the City of London. J18 was significant in that it brought together a disparate range of organisations with different agendas and turned them into an activist coalition against capitalism. Sites such as <www.ainfos.ca>, an anarchist site and <www.urban75.com> – a much less intense but quite aggressive site – also look to aid activists.

Mike Slocombe, who runs urban75 (Figure 18.6), comments:

The web allows campaign groups to publicise their actions and forge links in a manner that wasn't possible a few years ago, and attract more people to their cause. After J18, much of the popular press was painting a picture of the protest being almost exclusively attended by thugs, rampaging hooligans and shifty anarchists, with only destruction on their minds. As I was there and had gone for quite different reasons, I wanted to offer an alternative viewpoint, giving the chance for readers to see the other side of the story and make up their own minds. After putting up a photo report on urban75, I was invited to talk on mainstream radio and TV to offer

my version of events, which struck me as evidence of how the web can be a powerful alternative reporting tool.

The future

After considering everything from recruitment issues to the incidence of rogue websites, what does the future hold for technology sector PR? With IT coming out of its box and into the mainstream, and the internet continuing to grow to the extent where it will soon become ubiquitous, PR practitioners will increasingly see their roles expanding to encompass new media. Practitioners in all sectors need to understand online audiences and the nature of two-way communication, and be able to offer consultancy on internet-related matters, such as website planning and development, internet reputation management and online press targeting. Other PR opportunities created by the internet will include lobbying through campaign websites, online sponsorship opportunities and tracking internet coverage for clients (virtual 'clipping' services). Internet press offices and electronic distribution techniques will become important to all PR practitioners, not just technology specialists. As Mario Tinley-Bassett states:

> Whether the internet will change PR for better or worse depends on whether you see it as a threat to established techniques . . . or an opportunity. The PR of the 21st century will grasp technology but not be overwhelmed by it. Ultimately, despite new methods of getting the message across, the human element cannot, and should not, be eliminated.

Note

1 Unless otherwise stated, quotes are from email and telephone interviews conducted by the author during 1998 and 1999.
2 However, the days of lifestyle-focused internet publications may be numbered, as the 'traditional' lifestyle press increasingly covers websites as a matter of course and the hype that has surrounded the internet diminishes.

Part IV

Shaping the future

19 Changing media

This chapter is an attempt to raise questions that will affect the operation of PR in the future with regard to the changing face of the media. That said, the pace of change is likely to render many facts in this chapter obsolete at the time of publication. It is useful to bear in mind the discussions in Chapter 18 about changing methods of contacting these new media.

Attitudes to media reform

It may be helpful to start with a description of recent history, and the debate on control of the media. Curran and Seaton (1991) suggest that debate on media reform is polarised into paternalists and libertarians. Libertarians wish to minimise restraints on freedom of expression, and believe that the public should have a greater right to know how public body decisions are made. Sarah Tisdall was jailed for leaking information to the *Guardian* in 1984, although her crime embarrassed the government about the plans to site Cruise missiles in England rather than endangering the country's defence. Election promises by the Labour Party have not been fulfilled by the Labour government's Freedom of Information Bill, which, it has been argued, restricts information more than under previous Tory law. Debates on privacy law have usually arisen over intrusion by the press into a celebrity's private life, but no government has been willing to dismantle the self-regulation of the press and take on a regulatory function itself.

Paternalists, on the other hand, emphasise the dangers of an unregulated media, and believe that some individual rights such as privacy and fair trial take precedence over freedom of expression. The Broadcasting Standards Council was founded in 1988 in response to concerns about sex, violence and standards of decency in broadcasting. In 1990 it was given the power to force publication of its indictments, although it does not have the power to force compliance with its code. Broadcasting was made subject to the Obscene Publications Act in 1990. Margaret Thatcher favoured both a free market for the media and extensive moral and national security controls (Curran and Seaton 1991).

Opinion is also divided between those who favour public service broadcasting and those in favour of a free market. Furthermore, some want to preserve the traditional system, some to refine public broadcasting, others want no media regulation beyond the law and others feel that some intervention should secure specific public goals. The

free market approach holds that consumers are the best judge of their own interests. However, a free market is dependent on all consumers having equal access to the media to enable them to make a choice. The social market reformers argue that intervention is needed to ensure a spectrum of choice and to keep quality high. Anti-monopoly legislation for the press was introduced in 1965, so that large press groups had to have government permission to buy new titles. From 1965 to 1990, 125 acquisitions came under this legislation, but only five were refused, and none of those involved a major title. Because of this ineffective law, reformers argue that large press groups should have to demonstrate that any takeover would be in the public interest.

High market entry costs mean that many groups and opinions are underrepresented in the press. The public service approach stems from a view that broadcasting should seek to educate public taste, making a wide diversity of programmes available. In addition, information should be given to the electorate to enable voters to make an informed choice in elections, and so increase participation in democracy. The funding of the BBC through the licence fee has long been the subject of controversy, making it susceptible to political outrage if it is seen to be biased by one party or another. Only the government can increase the fee, so the BBC is again subject to political considerations. Whilst the licence fee was confirmed in the latest Broadcasting Act, the BBC was not able to secure the increases it wanted to fund new services.

For commercial media, the Council of Europe and European Commission ruled in 1989 that advertising should be restricted to 15 per cent of daily transmission, and no more than 20 per cent in any hour, and that member states should ensure, 'where practicable', that 51 per cent of fiction and documentaries should originate from the EC. This diluted original proposals after opposition from the US television industry and the British government. Many feared that the increased amount of airtime due to the development of cable and satellite would be filled with poor quality imports from the USA and Australia. Curran and Seaton hope that the media will evolve to have both 'power and responsibility – to the public rather than to proprietors and governments' (1991: 371).

Advocates of public service broadcasting wear many guises. Paul Smee of the Independent Television Commission, speaking at a VLV conference in April 1999 said:

> The evolution of public service television stemmed from Reith's belief that few people know what they want. The ideal of public service broadcasting is geographic universality, universality of appeal to all groups, relating to national identity, distanced from vested interests especially government, competition in good programming and to liberate rather than restrict programming. The strength of public service broadcasting is carried across many channels in the UK. There are regulated requirements for range and diversity of ITV also. Public service quality does not equal highbrow, we need to work with commercial forces, let public service broadcasting evolve, and preserve the regionality of ITV programmes.

Patricia Hodgson, then Head of BBC Policy and Planning, speaking at the same conference, was also in favour of regulation and national support for the BBC.

> Tony Benn said that broadcasting was too important to leave to the broadcasters. Pay TV fragments the audience as they have to compete for audiences to attract advertising. BBC provides cultural glue, for instance 22 million people watched the Christmas edition of *Eastenders*. The licence fee is an investment in the democratic vitality of the nation.

The scene is now set for new regulation of broadcasting, and the government introduced a White Paper in autumn 2000 to form the basis for this. Speculation at the time of writing suggested that this would include allowing a single ITV network and the scrapping of cross-media rules (see also the discussion on mergers and convergence, pp. 243–5). There would also be a single regulator covering media and telecommunications. A report published in June 1999 suggested that the government favours a light regulatory touch (Teather 2000).

Other Bills going through Parliament in 2000 caused more concerns for the future of free speech and access to information:

> The freedom of information bill gives fewer rights to official information than those enjoyed by citizens of the US, Canada, Australia, New Zealand and the Irish Republic. In some respects, the rights are weaker than those under the last Tory government's open government code.
>
> (Dyer 2000: 6)

Blanket exemptions for whole categories of information eroded the right to access many kinds of information that had led to media exposure of major issues such as the threat of BSE to humans and the high death rate of babies with heart defects in Bristol. The Local Government Bill would also take away existing rights to information about local authority decision-making. The Terrorism Bill broadened the definition of terrorism to include religious or ideological causes, so that journalists would run the risk of arrest if they covered the activities of certain campaigning bodies. The Regulation of Investigatory Powers Bill allows the government to monitor email and telephone communications across private networks. These Bills will have serious consequences for the operation of the media.

Mergers and convergence

True to the Thatcher government's belief in the free market, the auction of the new broadcasting licences in 1990 resulted in Big Nine (Anglia, Carlton, Central, Granada, HTV, LWT, Meridian, STV and Yorkshire) and Little Six (Border, Channel, Grampian, Tyne-Tees, Ulster and Westcountry) regional licences. Rules were set that any of the big companies could take over the little ones, but not each other. Yorkshire immediately took over Tyne Tees. When the new licences started in 1993, the rules were relaxed so that big companies could take over each other, but with a limit of two licences per company. Carlton and Central then merged. Meridian took over Anglia and Granada took over LWT in 1994, then new rules came into force in 1996 with a new Broadcasting Act which removed the two-licence limit but retained a cap of 25 per cent of advertising revenue. No one company could control more than 15 per cent of the viewing audience. Carlton took over Westcountry, Meridian (now United News and Media) took over HTV, Granada acquired Yorkshire/Tyne Tees, and STV merged with Grampian. Granada and Carlton collaborated in the launch of the new digital channel ONdigital in 1998 (Horsman 1999).

In November 1999, Carlton Communications and United News and Media planned to merge to become a 'global media enterprise', even though the merger would still have left the resultant company a small player on the world stage. In the UK, however, it would command 40 per cent of TV advertising and cover six major ITV regions.

When the new Broadcasting Bill is tabled in Parliament in 2001, the merged company would be in a strong position. A fragmented ITV cannot hope to compete in the future, and some feel that a single owner for the third channel may be put forward in the new Bill. The merger did not proceed, however. ITV's share of the audience has dropped since new channels were launched, and now accounts for only 20 per cent of viewing in homes where Sky Digital is received (Horsman 1999).

In August 1995, OFTEL (1995) published recommendations relating to the future of telecommunication systems, looking at the future of the interaction between televisions, telephones and PCs, wanting to see the development of broadband switched mass market (BSM) services, promoting competition and regulating dominant systems. This is related to the unbundling of the local loop, also known as the copper circuit between the consumer and the exchange, which will occur in July 2001. Consumers will be able to access the exchange from companies other than BT and benefit from unmetered time. This will increase uptake of internet services by introducing competition in an area formerly monopolised by BT (see also Chapter 18).

What is now clear is that PCs are not the only way to access the internet, email or communication systems. Links through wireless applications protocol (WAP) mobile phones are possible using the phone's screen and keypad. Although services are limited at the moment, this area is set to expand. Cyber cafés are commonplace, even in remote locations, and people can use email forwarding or web-based email accounts to communicate from wherever they can access an internet-connected machine. The accessibility of the internet was especially noticeable in the Kosovo conflict, where information was sent out from inside the war zone, by both sides. This affected reporting on the war, and made consideration of source and bias even more relevant. In addition, Open TV advertises internet access through the television.

Convergence of media, telecommunications and computer industries will give companies the resources to assemble multi-media networks. In January 1994, legislation was outlined in the USA to deregulate the telephone and cable TV industry, allowing cross-ownership and enabling telephone companies to offer cable TV services. In the UK, LWT, Pearson and Kingfisher have formed a consortium with British Telecom to develop video on demand through phone lines. In February 1994, Viacom, which owned a number of cable channels and Blockbuster video rental, took over Paramount, which included control of the film studio and Simon & Schuster books. In 1998 domestic telephone markets in the EU were opened up. Granville Williams (1994: 15) predicts that the possibilities of mega-monopolies across sources of information, education and entertainment will have serious consequences for those without the skills to take advantage of the new media:

> Far from liberalising the flow of communication, and creating new voices, we will see higher levels of concentration of economic power in the media and telecommunication industries, and growing levels of information management by such groups in pursuit of commercial objectives.

Williams states that competing channels financed by advertising tend to aim at the centre ground of taste to maximise audiences, so that choice of programming is reduced. On the other hand, the growing numbers of channels leads to increased demands for programme stock. In order to finance programmes, material which can be marketed internationally is produced, so that national identities become diminished. He suggests that broadcasting control is moving into the hands of major corporations, rather than regulatory bodies with a brief to ensure quality, and that product placement is not

only becoming a multi-million dollar business, but can also affect programme content.

The provision of services will also depend on their profitabilty, so some people may not be able to access them. Larger companies will be able to dominate markets and crowd out competitors. Williams quotes the example of Channel One in the USA which provides educational programmes to secondary schools. Channel One provides satellite dish, VCRs, television monitors and cable and wiring. In return, students are required to watch two minutes of advertising per twelve minute broadcast.

Cross-media ownership and its impact on public opinion were examined in a paper from the Broadcasting Research Unit in 1989 (Barnett 1989). At the end of 1989, nine satellite channels were available in the UK, six of which were owned by News International, which also owns five national newspapers. A survey was carried out to compare opinions of those who read the *Sun*, *The Times* and *Today* with those who read other papers. The survey found that two-thirds of viewers were satisfied with programmes on terrestrial television. News International readers were more hostile to the BBC, and they were more in favour of freedom of channels, more sponsorship and fewer current affairs programmes. They also felt there was too much regulation of broadcasting, and were less in favour of regulation of ITV. Whilst the majority of viewers support the licence fee for the BBC, News International readers opposed it. In conclusion, the report found that opinions about broadcasting held by News International readers were out of step with the population as a whole, and that the editorial policy of these papers was having a significant effect on opinions of readers. 'It is patently true that large numbers of News International readers hold views which are to the parent company's financial advantage.' The report recommended that there should be controls on newspaper interests in satellite TV channels, and indeed that steps should be taken to reduce News International's newspaper holdings 'to protect editorial and journalistic diversity'.

The press online

'Newspapers remain important, [but] no one can be in any doubt that they have been subsumed into a much greater whole', said Roy Greenslade (2000: 14). 'Almost all papers are owned by public corporations . . . the resulting conglomerates are either part of global organisations or seeking to become so'. Pressure to grow and expand has resulted from the need to compete internationally. Media owners have invested across political borders. The four main companies involved in Britain's regional press are US-owned Gannett, Trinity Mirror, Johnston Press and Associated Newspapers. After Wapping in 1986, union-imposed limits on pagination were ended and newspapers expanded into multi-sectioned papers. At the same time, the make-up of the target population has changed. Just over 50 per cent of the UK population is now designated as ABC1, and tabloids have had to change their content to appeal to better-educated audiences. Newspapers still remain the main medium to give context and significance to news stories, but are operating within much larger cross-media conglomerates.

The increase in usage of the internet has led to developments in the way readership interacts with the news media through the setting up of chatrooms associated with media websites. The *Los Angeles Times* closed its chat room in March 2000, due to the nature of comments posted by users which broke the guidelines for its use. The *New York Times* launched Abuzz, where readers ask questions and are routed to knowledgeable sources. The idea is to 'humanise the internet' by creating 'new social networks', and

also to increase registered users. Tribune bought Times Mirror, giving the company 60 sites, including the *Chicago Tribune*. Internet, television and radio outlets are installed in its newspaper newsrooms and journalists work across all media (Helmore 2000).

The NUJ in the UK is concerned about how the development of online news services will affect journalists' jobs and working conditions. There are no standards covering pay and conditions, training or career structure of web editors and authors. Some journalists work for printed media with online versions, and the boundaries between the two are not clear (Russell 1999). Some online publications pay more than the traditional press for commissioned wordage.

Newspapers have invested considerable resources into developing online versions, and Reuters is developing its internet strategy. *The Financial Times* has integrated the news teams working on its printed and online versions into a single team. Web page producers sit at the same desks as page editors working on the newspaper. An increase in original journalism written for the web caused the company to hire additional reporters in London, New York and Tokyo. Where two reporters covered the same area, one's priority was writing for the web, the other's writing for the newspaper. All journalists work for the same company with the same pay structure and conditions. Deputy editor Peter Martin (1999: 17) stated the reasoning behind the move: 'it's now clear that the internet is a central part of our future. We are faced with duplicating our journalistic efforts for the new medium, or finding a way to get the best of both worlds.' At the IPR National Conference in October 1999, *FT* editor Richard Lambert expanded, 'FT.com is not just text online, it has a different front page and different content. PR practitioners are going to have to learn to deal with the different deadlines and agendas of a more diverse range of media.'

Magazine publishers have also ventured on to the internet. The Telegraph group's Handbag.com; Associated Newspapers' CharlotteStreet.com and IPC's BeMe.com are the main three. Aimed at the same audience as the traditional women's press, the subjects covered have been similar, for example relationships, careers and family. Research for Handbag.com found that women have responsibility for 75 per cent of the buying decisions in the home, and so a site which has an audience of working women is potentially valuable to advertisers. In common with most internet businesses, there is no guaranteed income for such sites. The future depends on how e-commerce develops (Shelton 2000). With the failures of internet companies such as boo.com, and the fall in share price of Freeserve (the first firm to offer free internet access in 1998, £850 million was wiped off its stock market value in one day), the future is far from certain.

Other internet-based news companies include the news aggregators like Moreover.com and thebullet.com. These companies take headlines from news sites and feed them into subscribers' websites, with details of where the articles can be found. They also charge the original location of the article a fee when people look up their headline from their site. Companies like Yahoo! don't produce any original news content, but charge 1–3 cents to a publisher's site every time a headline is clicked through.

The paper-based press will also have to deal with the invention of ways to make electronic information more readable. Barnes and Noble already provide software to make books more readable over the internet. Stephen King decided to publish his latest novella, *Riding the Bullet*, exclusively on the internet, but with mixed success. Microsoft has produced ClearType, designed to give text a paper-like quality on screen. Bill Hill, one of the co-inventors, believes 'The move towards screen readable information will change society just as much as the invention of the printing press but it will do it in five years rather than 500' (quoted in Kidner 2000). Xerox is developing e-paper based

on a material called Gyricon, which will enable electronic information to be down-
loaded onto a material that looks and feels like paper, has the qualities of a computer
screen and which can be rolled up like a newspaper.

The digital debate

In 1996, 88 per cent of TV hours were watched on terrestrial, in 1999, 87 per cent of
TV hours were watched on free to air. Despite a slow take up of new initiatives, digital
television is the next change to affect the media. Digitilisation means the translating of
information into electronic 0s and 1s so that it is easier to send, store and manipulate.
This information can be compressed, so that more channels can be transmitted using
the same amount of capacity or bandwidth. Fibre optic cables can also carry much more
information than radio frequencies, and two-way communication is possible using this
technology. About 3 million homes in the UK have signed up to digital television, and
research indicates that viewing habits are changing. Using the electronic programme
guide (EPG) viewers can switch between channels more quickly, they are less tolerant
of programmes they are not interested in, and of adverts. The relaunched BBC Choice
put resources into 15-minute programmes to appeal to 25 to 44 year olds. Such
programmes can be recycled because only a limited audience will see them at any one
time. Grazing may be on the increase, although the typical viewer concentrates on a
few favourite networks rather than continuously scrolling through 240 channels.
Children are more likely to be able to operate the EPG adeptly to screen out anything
they regard as boring (Brown 2000).

The main commercial companies offering digital services in the UK are Sky and
ONdigital, launched in 1998, which had 411,000 subscribers by October 1999. Research
showed that awareness had risen and 30 per cent of consumers expected to buy into
digital. Sky provides a free mini satellite disc and digital box, and charges £40 for
installation if subscribing, £100 if not subscribing. Subscription charges vary depending
on how many channels the customer wants access to. ONdigital also offer a free box
to subscribers. Other services, including online shopping, are also available. But the
way to get news on to the Sky news channels remains the same – a fax and follow-
up call, as long as the story is visual, includes case studies and has interviewees avail-
able (France 2000).

Digital satellite television offers 200 channels, including existing Sky channels, plus
a pay-per-view movie service which is like having video on demand. Packages range
from £6.99 per month upwards. Interactive services use the phone line. There are no
ITV channels available on digital via satellite. Digital terrestrial services include BBC1
and BBC2, ITV1 and ITV2, BBC News 24, Channels 4 and 5, which are free, plus
subscription packages, but only 20 to 30 channels are available. Improved quality of
picture and sound will still be experienced, but there will be no interactive services.
Digital cable television will offer around 150 to 200 channels, with a low set-up cost
and a monthly subscription of £10 which will include a basic package of channels.
However, the content of the channels is unlikely to expand the range of programmes
on offer. Programme making funds have not risen, so many channels rely on re-runs
and cheap imports. At some date in the future, the government will switch off the
analogue service, leaving digital as the only method of delivery. This will enable the
analogue frequencies to be sold to mobile phone companies (Brown 1999).

In the opinion of Gerald Kaufman, Chair of the Commons Select Committee for
Culture, Media and Sport, 'Digital is a blind alley and a waste of resources . . . ten

times as many people surf the internet than have subscribed to digital TV'. In the USA, digital is seen as a sideline, with media companies focusing on developing TV access through the internet. While the BBC has spent £30 million on developing News 24, watched by only 0.1 per cent of the viewing public, BBC Online is the most popular internet site in Europe and could be developed as an interactive news site. CNN posts the best of its reports and programmes on its website already. The commercial cable companies, Telewest, Cable & Wireless and NTL, have all developed their digital services through set top boxes which also provide net access through the TV. In Germany, Bertelsmann, the publishing and media giant, has abandoned TV interests in favour of internet development (Smith 1999).

In contrast, Chris Smith, Secretary of State for Culture, Media and Sport, reaffirmed a commitment to digital: 'Digital television will bring real benefits to consumers. It will be especially important for people who are housebound or who need specialist services.' He has set two criteria before the final switch over, that the 99.4 per cent of the population who can currently receive analogue must be able to receive the free to air channels in digital, and that the price must be within the reach of those on low incomes. He believes that these conditions could be met by 2010, along with a pre-condition that 95 per cent of viewers must have digital signals coming into sets within their homes (*VLV Bulletin*, Spring 2000) (see below).

The future of the BBC

Every week 99 per cent of the population watch BBC TV. The BBC is a unique media institution in that it also has the status of a cultural icon, largely due to its first director general, Reith. The discussions above concerning the various approaches to media reform show what a powerful place the BBC occupies in UK society.

It no longer exists in isolation. Another long-standing broadcast institution, *News at 10* on ITV, was axed in March 1999. In response, in May, the BBC revamped its news programmes, with the *Six O'Clock News* changing to an emphasis on consumer, lifestyle and finance stories. The later *News at Nine* then concentrated on global stories and both programmes began to use more live links and regional reports. The BBC's official line was still that it did not use video news releases (VNRs), although it might occasionally do so if it were unable to get footage itself. It is obvious that with BBC News 24 and the online pages, there is more need for news stories to fill them, and once in the system, stories get picked up by other media (Goddard 1999).

The Davies review in 1999 examined the way the BBC should be funded in the future, grappling with the problem of maintaining a public service broadcaster in an increasingly competitive market. Whilst 99.4 per cent of households can currently receive analogue broadcasts, this may not be the case when they are switched off and digital becomes the norm. There is no legal right for viewers to be able to receive broadcasts. The committee recommended either a separate digital licence or the increase of the current analogue licence to fund changes, as well as increasing private investment in BBC Worldwide and BBC Resources. Evidence was taken in the autumn of 1999 after the report. The Culture Secretary Chris Smith announced that future plans for broadcasting would have to meet two criteria of accessibility and affordability. In a document entitled 'Regulating communications: the way ahead', the government also set out its commitment to foster competitive markets, to ensure that the UK built on its competitive strength, and to take necessary measures to protect the interests of consumers. VLV recommended that there was a need for legislation to ensure that copy-

right owners must sub-licence their rights when the exploitation of that copyright is essential to develop a new information market, and a dominant supplier in a related market refuses to licence the copyright to aspiring entrants. These two conditions exist in European competition law (*VLV Bulletin*, Autumn 1999).

In 1998/9 the BBC informed viewers and listeners: 'The BBC aims to give you a good return on your licence fee – that means providing something for everyone.' As it is funded publicly, the BBC must continually justify its expenditure, and has become increasingly aware of its need to show itself as responsive to viewers' and listeners' needs. In 1998/9 the BBC made specific promises under 12 headings, including responding to devolution in Scotland, Wales and Northern Ireland, changing the mainstream music policy on Radio 1 to appeal as strongly to young women as to young men, increasing subtitling, representing all groups in society accurately, and maximising benefits from commercial activities to the licence payer. In 1997/8, the BBC made 66 commitments under five headings. The Governors concluded that 60 had been met in full, three were met but needed continued improvement and that in the other three, the BBC fell short of the commitment. These last were the commitment to spend one-third of the programme budget outside London and the south east, to ensure that eight out of ten hours' programming is made in the UK, and to represent all groups in society accurately and to avoid reinforcing prejudice.

The history of the BBC's presence on the internet has resulted in two competing websites from the same company. Originally, BBC Worldwide, the commercial arm, set up a site with ICL in 1995. The latter provided most of the money and all the technical support, the BBC provided the content. In 1996, the Director General, John Birt, recognised the importance of online services and set up BBC Online in December 1997, to be paid for from licence fee revenue. The commercial site was called beeb.com. Since then, there have been constant problems with what output is to be presented on the public service site and which on the commercial site, and often information is duplicated. Beeb.com, prevented from using the BBC brand, has now made a deal with Microsoft to get promotion through its websites (*Economist*, 8.5.99: 35–6). BBC Online contains 500,000 pages reflecting news, education and entertainment. Over 3 million hits are received each month – the BBC claims this represents a 42 per cent reach of regular UK internet users. It also contains news and issues forums to build communities online.

As mentioned above, the BBC has made a considerable investment in digital TV services, and those available free through the aerial are BBC1, BBC2, BBC Choice, BBC News 24, BBC Knowledge, BBC Parliament and BBC Text – all paid for by the licence fee.

The appointment of Greg Dyke as Director General from October 1999 led to many changes within the BBC, to make it a more dynamic organisation. The initiatives he introduced ended the internal tendering for contracts and bureaucracy that was a legacy of John Birt. The debate continues about the quality of programmes and services offered by the BBC and how these should be funded, including the extension of commercial activities to allow advertising on BBC channels. The BBC has so far lobbied successfully to avoid this, stressing the quality of its drama, news and children's programmes, which would not be made in a purely commercial enterprise, dependent on private finance.

In June 2000, a key aide of Greg Dyke flagged up far-reaching changes to this approach. Director of Television Mark Thompson proposed abandoning the mixed schedules in favour of using BBC1 as a general entertainment channel and transferring more serious programmes to BBC2. A new BBC3 would show comedy, whilst a fourth

channel would carry serious music and the arts. The flagship *News at Nine* would be moved to 10 p.m. Essentially, the BBC would adopt a similar approach to the variety of themed channels available on cable and satellite. 'I don't believe it would be right to move overnight into fully genre-based channels, but I believe that unless we start the journey soon, we risk becoming irrelevant', said Thompson (quoted in Wells 2000: 9).

The BBC also faces competition from ITN's new 24 hour service, launched in August 2000 and available across TV, digital radio, mobile phones and PCs. The service also reinstates a 10 p.m. weekday ITN news bulletin. Sky News Active is a proposed inter-active multi-screen version of Sky News which will also increase competition in the news arena.

Digital radio

The Radio Advertising Bureau report on the future of commercial radio in 1999 stated that radio was a resilient medium, and would survive the onset of the digital age. Commercial radio stations increased from 46 to 170 from 1989–99, as a result of the splitting of frequencies between AM and FM, additional local licences to diversify listener choice from 1989, and the launch of three national commercial stations allowed for by the Broadcasting Act 1990. This increase is set to continue, with up to 250 stations planned by the Radio Authority, mainly regional and community area licences. Radio Advertising Joint Audience Research (RAJAR) figures have shown a growth in the audience for commercial stations from 40 per cent to 60 per cent of the UK population between 1986 and 1999. The Broadcasting Act 1996 set the conditions for the development of digital audio broadcasting (DAB). Advantages include CD quality sound, a wider variety of services through the same amount of band spectrum, easier tuning to one frequency nationwide, and the ability to transmit information to a screen built into DAB receivers. The Act allows national stations automatic access to DAB, and guaranteed slots for BBC local stations. Local commercial stations would have to compete for slots. Research has shown that radio audiences are not declining, and that even though the choice of stations is increasing, that most people only listen to one or two stations each week. As with the proliferation of television stations on cable and satellite, it will be easier for PR practitioners to target publics more precisely by approaching niche radio stations (Radio Advertising Bureau 1996).

The first national commercial digital radio service Digital One was launched in November 1999. At this time, there were still only a few thousand digital sets in the UK, costing upwards of £800, and early take-up of digital receivers was mainly in car audio systems. The principal shareholder of the company was GWR, which also put two of the new services on the internet and on Sky Digital as well. The company allocated £30 million for its development, but presenters were not initially well known or of high quality. GWR does not expect the channel to break even for at least five to eight years, with a planned raft of soft rock, news from ITN, sports from Talk Radio and an arts, books and comedy channel (Higham 1999).

The BBC plans to offer more services with the advent of digital radio, including a part hours service for the Asian community. Currently 60 per cent of the UK can receive digital radio, although reception varies according to location and house structure. Improved sound quality and variety of services were the main reasons offered for the BBC's commitment to digital: 'We believe it's part of our role as a public service company to make sure our listeners get access to the best and most exiting technology.'

Crystal ball gazing

As stated at the beginning of this chapter, the development of technology is moving at such a pace that one speaker at the VLV conference in 1999 likened it to the old Chinese proverb that if one placed one grain of sand on the first square of a chessboard, two on the next, four on the next, by the time you got to the last, 64th square, you would have covered the planet a foot deep. 'We're in the second half of the chessboard,' said David Cleevely, Managing Director of Analysis.

The advent of Playstation 2 in December 2000 provided DVD video, CD and games console in one, and online gaming too. Scientists at the University of Surrey have developed a way of allowing viewers to insert themselves into game or film action (*Hotline*, December 1999: 41–2). BT's Futuretalk puts forward the possibility of broadband – a fat data pipe which will enable consumers to access a library of films, pay to view, download them through the phone and into the TV ready to watch, like having a video library constantly at your disposal. Broadband may also be available through cable, satellite wireless or ASDL (a high speed data line).

David Cleevely also pointed out at the VLV conference that readers could expect to write the news, not just passively absorb it: 'The CNN site has an emphasis on user choice, and users can send immediate feedback on programmes via email. Information and entertainment will be part of e-commerce.' He warned, 'This could be the end of advertising – suppliers can sell products to all via the internet. Users can expect and get more control.' This could have serious consequences for the array of media which is dependent on advertising to survive.

'To reach a 50 million audience, radio took 28 years, television 13 and the internet five. There are now over eight million users of the internet in the UK in 1998, in 1995 there were two million', said Dominic Riley, head of marketing BBC Online, at the same conference. 'Whilst it is generally younger, wealthier people, growth areas are schools, with the government's commitment to IT, families at home, people at work and public access in libraries and community centres.'

To continue to work effectively, public relations practitioners must keep up with the pace of change and understand the needs of the new media for information. In April 2000 the IPR published a report entitled *The Death of Spin?*, which set out the view that the public's increased access to information would mean that companies could no longer get away with corporate lying, due to the porosity of their public faces. Traditional media involve sending information to passive recipients, on the internet, users generally pull information towards them. The web also has the capacity to allow people to take information and use it for their own ends. It is not difficult to lift content and set up a 'knocking' site, so loss of control over content is also a problem (Shelton 2000). A recent case where Demon Internet agreed to pay £15,000 damages to a physicist who claimed he had been defamed by two postings on the net shows that legislation may start to deal with such cases. In the USA, however, libel laws are less powerful than in the UK and the Internet receives protection under the 1996 Communications Decency Act, which gives the internet service provider immunity (Campbell 2000).

As mentioned in Chapter 18, PR practitioners will have to learn new skills such as using search engines and setting up websites, as well as recognising the implications of reputation management. The IPR report also suggested that the development of the internet was a great opportunity for PR to come into its own, as the means of managing all corporate communications. Internet specialist David Phillips believes that PR will take an overseeing, information management role which will differentiate it from other communications disciplines (Campbell 2000).

But maybe it will all turn out to be a storm in a teacup. Douglas MacArthur at the CAM/TASC lecture in November 1998 questioned the view that television and the internet would converge, in his turn quoting Elizabeth Murdoch at the 1998 Edinburgh television festival: 'The whole beauty of television for most viewers is that it is a passive experience.' Thus televisions and PCs may continue to co-exist in homes, serving different functions, and interactive TV may not be as successful as some companies hope.

20 Research and evaluation – PR grows up?

..

I n the early 1990s, something strange happened. As recession began to bite and budgets were slashed, public relations practitioners began to talk about whether or not PR could be measured, and so prove its worth. Up to that point, no one had really been concerned about measurement of results. 'Gut feeling' was felt to be an acceptable gauge of whether a PR campaign had succeeded. People relied on their own experience to tell them what would work in a particular situation. Puchan *et al.* (1999: 166) suggested that an interest in evaluation was stimulated by 'the consumer interest movement, the implementation of measures to improve managerial effectiveness and the tendency to professionalisation'.

Public relations education has lagged behind the USA, but a Masters degree was introduced at Stirling University, and a postgraduate diploma at West Herts College in Watford. In 1989, the first undergraduate degrees in public relations opened their doors to students in Bournemouth and Plymouth. Leeds Metropolitan followed a year later. Public relations had its own academics now. In an academic environment, lecturers are required to do scholarly research. A research culture began to develop both within and outside higher education.

There was a lot of talk about evaluation which felt like the search for the Holy Grail. If only someone could find 'the way' to measure the outcomes from public relations, everything would be solved.

A decade later, some things have changed but others seem remarkably static. The number of public relations courses has grown, along with the number of staff required to produce erudite publications on the subject, yet PR research in the UK is still in its infancy. There are very few academics actually doing research, and little of it connects with the public relations industry.

The negative reactions with which the students of these courses were greeted by those who had graduated from the school of hard knocks ('How on earth can you teach public relations? You can only learn by doing it!' and 'How can you fill a three year degree course?') are still legion. 'Evidence of any sense of delight, is sadly lacking'. wrote Sue Wolstenholme in 1997. Late in 1998 a senior practitioner was heard to exclaim, 'I never employ anyone with a public relations degree in my consultancy.' There is still a lot of fear and misunderstanding about the content of such courses and the abilities of those who complete them. As their graduates make their way up through the industry, this will change, as, despite statements such as the one above, an average of 85 per cent of those who complete one of the courses approved by the IPR gain

employment in the industry. Several companies are now sponsoring student prizes, anxious to get the pick of the crop.

The level of debate on evaluation has developed, so that the Holy Grail is no longer sought. There is a plethora of techniques which are accepted, from media content analysis to market research. How far these have actually been translated from debate into action is still questionable.

Taking research seriously

Some companies are grasping the nettle. In April 1998, a Forum on Communication Research was held at the London School of Economics. Representatives from academia and industry heard presentations from practitioners who were using research techniques to inform their management decisions. Academics and a market research expert talked about some projects with which they were involved. The main objectives of the forum were to 'bring together practitioners who are grappling with questions of measurement and evaluation with researchers . . . who might be able to help shed some light on the issues', and 'to identify real world problems which could be worked on . . . where companies have a lot of available data but little time to do a usefully thorough analysis'. The latter work would be carried out by graduate students to facilitate the industry–academia interface.

Despite Wolstenhome's (1997) opinion that

If we want to be called professional then we have a duty to be connected to the growing body of knowledge in our discipline and have planned and regular exchanges developing it to add to our experience of the practical outcomes and gain their views on new theoretical approaches

there have been no further meetings of the forum.

Part of this impasse could be due to the academic institutions themselves. Even though many public relations academics have some experience in practice, links with industry are not always maintained. 'Academics are po-faced and supercilious', says David Phillips of Cyberalert.

Commercial researchers and academics could get closer together, and academics could get closer to the industry. You have to be robust in putting your views to industry, you can't live in an ivory tower. They are doing the work, but they are not telling the world about it.[1]

Others in the industry feel that there is a role for purely academic research which could feed into and inform practice. Sandra Macleod of Echo Research was involved in the Communications Forum:

One aim of the Forum was to bring together potential sponsors, to see if we could identify if there was some major research that we all felt was needed. Then we could all put something in the pot to fund it. There is also a need for greater involvement of industry and academia so that both can benefit. There is an interesting trend where more people from a research background are becoming involved in PR, especially in-house, people who have an understanding about how behaviours are influenced, what various audiences feel about organisations. They are turning that into communications messages, turning the PR plan into a dialogue.[2]

Most of the industry outlook on research seems to concentrate on purely practical aspects. Research is often linked to clients, and how information could help consultancies win a pitch for an account (Medhurst 1999). The PR Toolkit (see case study, p. 259–61) includes research and audit as the first step in the PR planning process. Here research is used as a diagnostic tool to develop PR strategy, as well as monitoring the success of that strategy as it unfolds. The checklist to assemble the PR brief encourages the practitioner to work with the client to set out their commercial background and objectives, and audit the existing PR activity. Gathering information is seen as essential in order to set realistic measurable objectives. Unless a definite starting point is defined, it is not possible to effectively measure and evaluate the success of the PR strategy.

There are some encouraging signs that the worlds of academia and practice are coming together. The European professional association, CERP, has set up a European Body of Knowledge (EBOK) project, which seeks to provide gateways into a collection of current research papers in several languages. The IPR has been approached to sponsor the English language portal. The recent agreement on co-operation between the IPR and PRSA has enabled a link into a similar US project. Leaders of the IPR's approved courses have been invited to submit papers for presentation at the national conference and meetings of IPR regional groups. As discussed in Chapter 5, a body of knowledge and research is one of the prerequisites for the development of PR into a profession. Hopefully these initiatives will lead to more co-operative ventures.

Using evaluation in PR

'The public relations industry is worth $24.5 billion worldwide. Public relations evaluation has grown by 30–40 per cent a year over the past five years', stated Sandra Macleod at the IPRA conference in 1997.

The evaluation debate has thankfully moved on from the Holy Grail stage mentioned above. Jon White (1999) recently said 'It's time for us to move on from the search for evaluation methods, which already exist, to applying these in terms of improvements to the quality of management in public relations.' This is a development of his statement in 1994, that the need to evaluate activities in PR is 'partly a measure of professional insecurity' (quoted in Houlder 1994: 20). It is true that many areas of management experience difficulty in measuring effectiveness. Evaluation did not emerge as a distinctive field of professional scientific practice until the late 1960s, and it began to emerge as an issue in PR at about the same time (Noble 1999).

In terms of gaining the budgets to carry out evaluation, Peter Hehir has suggested, 'We get the budgets we deserve. If you can't prove the importance of what you do, you'll stay in a backwater PR department or struggle to keep your consultancy's head above water' (quoted in Purdie 1997: 8). As President of the International Committee of Public Relations Consultancies Associations (ICO), he advised the education of clients to appreciate the issues they faced and to allocate realistic budgets to allow for research and evaluation.

Lip service

The take-up of evaluation in the industry has not been overwhelming, despite a majority view that it is necessary. IPRA published the results of a survey in 1994, which found

that 90 per cent of its members thought evaluation was necessary, but that only 18 per cent frequently undertook evaluative research. Furthermore, 31 per cent felt that 'trying to measure precisely is next to impossible' (IPRA 1994).

'I don't understand why so few communication departments use measurement ... why ever not?' asked John Drummond (1997). Part of his approach was to separate his department at United Utilities into four audience driven units, creating a balance across stakeholders. Internal customers were especially important. He could also show that United Utilities had 'one of the best customer communication ratings of any utility, with overall customer satisfaction up 30% in two years'.

A year after beginning its PR%F campaign in 1998 to encourage client companies to allocate 10 per cent of their budgets to research and evaluation, *PR Week* undertook a major survey to show the uptake of evaluation methods by the PR industry. The results were disappointing. Whilst the majority of practitioners believed that their work could be measured across a variety of disciplines, including crisis management, internal communications and business to business, those working in government relations over-whelmingly disagreed. A total of 20 per cent of respondents still felt their success could not be measured. There was widespread agreement that the PR industry needed to improve its efforts at evaluation, and the vast majority stated that 'I am personally committed to evaluating PR efforts'. However, when it came to the methods which could be used, 'the most commonly used method was media content analysis and press cuttings, closely followed by media reach'. This was despite the fact that only a third regarded the latter as an effective tool to convince budget holders to part with resources to fund it. A worryingly high proportion of 33 per cent said they relied on 'gut feel' to judge their success. The main obstacle to planning and evaluating PR activity was cited as difficulty in obtaining budgets, followed by lack of time. In addition, 43 per cent of respondents gave no answer when asked to state their investment in evaluation (Cowlett and Nicholas 1999). Whilst the debate has moved on, most practitioners still remain in the Dark Ages as far as practising what is preached is concerned.

The value of evaluation

The idea that evaluation is worthwhile and necessary is not new. In his address to the IRR congress in October 1998, MORI Director Peter Hutton stated,

> Evaluation is a sensible part of any PR programme ... There must come a point when you have to ask 'What effect has my PR spend had?' and 'How do I know?' In MORI we have developed a model based on the idea that business success comes from moving people up a hierarchy from awareness, through trust, transaction, satisfaction, commitment and advocacy. There are many different ways of evaluating the success of a PR event or campaign. The most useful, however, will be part of a well executed PR initiative with clearly defined measures of success which relate back to equally clearly defined corporate and communications objectives.

Alison Clarke, of Shandwick Asia Pacific, agrees.

> Evaluation is part of the planning process. It enables one to quantify the lessons learned and develop benchmarks for future measurement. There are a variety of measurement tools now available for all kinds of evaluation, from input (analysis of existing data, focus group, pilot questionnaire), output (statistics on distribution,

media monitoring, media content analysis, communication audit) and outcome (focus group discussion, surveys, pre and post tests). PR can influence beliefs, attitudes, opinions and behaviour.

If the communications function is to be considered as a managerial one, it must refine its instruments of measure . . . to prove it is both useful and beneficial.

The media coverage debate

One of the first and easiest ways of evaluating success in PR was to count the amount of media coverage gained. As the evaluation debate developed, the question of whether press cuttings were enough exercised many column inches itself. The Association of Media Evaluation Companies (AMEC) in conjunction with ICO produced an explanatory booklet in 1997 (AMEC 1997): 'Media evaluation is the systematic appraisal of a company's reputation, products or services, or those of its competitors, as measured by the presence in the media.' AMEC put forward media evaluation as an ongoing management tool which should be part of the business planning process. It stated that analysis involved the weighting of significant elements, the combination of measurement and judgement. This could also give information about trends, as media analysis would be ineffective in a vacuum. To those who argued that media analysis was a mere part of the picture, and not a very useful part at that, AMEC replied that output generated as a result of a PR programme could be measured in articles, papers, speaking engagements; outcomes could be measured by changes in attitudes and behaviours; and 'out-take' by the degree to which the audience retained the message. By using information gained from media coverage in different ways, several aspects could be measured. Share of voice would indicate the total amount of coverage for the industry or topic, and the percentage of that from the client. By examining message content analysis the extent to which coverage communicated the desired messages could be assessed. Trend analysis could track performance over time and look forward from historical information.

AMEC produced a checklist of ten points – starting with setting objectives, defining audiences and key messages, to sharing the results with colleagues and using the results to inform strategy and planning.

> The purpose of media evaluation is to identify patterns and trends and to measure strengths and weaknesses in coverage. It provides communicators with the specialised tools and IT support which professionals in other fields have come to regard as second nature.

According to Krippendorf (1980: 9), 'The pursuit of content analysis is fundamentally empirical in orientation, exploratory, concerned with real phenomenon and predictive in intent.' 'Content analysis can use the past to show what will happen in the future. You have to understand the methodology and trust it', says David Phillips. He also feels strongly that adding up the amount of coverage and equating it to the cost of the same space if bought for advertising is crude and inaccurate:

> The relationship between reader and publication and between editor and reader is symbiotic, and invaded with permission by advertisers – advertising value equivalent (AVE) and editorial are not the same and you can't use same tools to measure effectiveness. There is no advertising equivalent to editorial nor is there a measure

of advertising avoided because of editorial coverage. There is no common measure
for advertising and editorial. Measurable factors include whether it is timely, com-
pelling, relevant, useful, authoritative.

By using media content analysis, Phillips suggests, PR practitioners can see what words
to use in a press release, which journals to go to, which journalists, the optimum times
to send in information, and how long it will take to get into print. Some messages are
not part of the media agenda and some words always have negative connotations.
Content analysis can identify the media agenda which the PR practitioner must work
within.

Phillips questions the value of opinion polls:

> Andrew Cooper wrote a response to general election opinion polls, stating that in
> 1992 they were pilloried as inaccurate by 10 per cent. There were apparently vindi-
> cated in 1997 as they predicted a Labour victory, but they were still 9 per cent inac-
> curate.

Sandra Macleod, speaking at the IPRA conference in 1994, felt that the increasing
sophistication of media content analysis techniques had led to unrealistic demands from
clients.

> Companies need to tailor measurement needs to their campaigns or requirements,
> but I don't think anyone does it properly right now. It's good to integrate commu-
> nications, but then you need to break them down into their specific parts to target
> as precisely as possible. It's rather like being an archaeologist, putting the pieces
> together and then focusing on the details. There is increasing professionalism in
> communications and a recognition that PR is an important part of organisations'
> armouries. In terms of what you are going to get for your bucks, there's more bang
> out of PR than advertising. There is a greater profusion of media titles with tinier
> circulation figures. PR is ideal for getting through to those specific targets.
>
> On the communications research side, where clients used to be happy with half
> yearly or monthly reports, now they want all the coverage about themselves and
> their competitors online the same day. But few companies have management that
> could absorb it daily. We can do that, if it is genuinely part of the decision support
> system, but I don't see that yet in companies. It is a tremendous opportunity to
> respond quickly, and technology has shown that things have got faster.
>
> A hidden agenda of our work is management intelligence. Properly managed,
> corporate reputation grows in value. Nowhere is it more true that perception equals
> reality than in the media. Research in the US has shown that when negative press
> exceeds 20–25% of all media coverage, a corporation's reputation begins to suffer.
> Media content analysis provides a regular measurement of how reputation is shifting,
> why and what can be done about it. Media coverage can anticipate events.

Puchan *et al.* (1999: 172) point out that 'in many cases media evaluation is not
significant in terms of attitudinal or behavioural change' and suggest that more use
could be made of other survey-based research techniques.

Variety of methods

There is certainly no shortage of methods available. Most of these have grown from the various methods of media measurement carried out by commercial companies such as Media Measurement and Echo, but content analysis, though great claims are made for its impact on areas of PR activity other than media relations, is no longer the whole story.

Paul Noble (1999: 15) states, 'There is no one simple, single solution to the problem of public relations evaluation . . . different evaluation methodologies are appropriate at different stages of the process.' Furthermore, evaluation is not undertaken for its own sake, but for a purpose. The large number of variables with which PR is concerned complicate matters. He quotes Patton,

> The practice of evaluation involves the systematic collection of information about the activities, characteristics and outcomes of programmes, personnel and products for use by specific people to reduce uncertainties, improve effectiveness, and make decisions with regard to what those programmes are doing and affecting.
>
> (Noble 1999: 15)

Some practitioners use evaluation in summative form, assessing final outcomes, to offer accountability to clients and themselves. There is room for both formative and summative evaluation and different methodologies are required for different steps (Noble 1999: 18).

Curtis (1999) suggests that techniques used in other areas of marketing communications can be utilised by PR practitioners. 'It's more complex, but it's entirely possible', says Jennie Kettlewell of Bulletin International (quoted in Curtis 1999).

Puchan *et al.* (1999) suggest that whilst evaluation methods are fairly well established, more could be done to assess the impact of public relations at a broader, social level.

Both approaches are recognised in the case studies that follow. The first describes the development and content of the IPR/PRCA/*PR Week* Toolkit. Other studies show how two companies, Media Measurement and Echo Research, have used media analysis to illuminate and refine different aspects of PR activity.

Case study 1: The IPR/PRCA/*PR Week* Research and Evaluation Toolkit

The IPR Taskforce was established in June 1998. *PR Week* identified a similar initiative with the PRCA, and joint funding was agreed in September 1998. *PR Week* then leant support to the initiative by headlining the PR%F campaign in October. Working with Mike Fairchild, as author, and AMEC, the group set themselves a goal of publication by June 1999. Alison Clarke, Vice-President of the IPR, took a presentation to several local group meetings in advance of the main launch of the finished Toolkit to emphasise the importance of measuring public relations. The Toolkit was designed for practitioners, whether in-house or consultancy, clients, PR training and education bodies and journalists. Case studies on best practice were also included. In keeping with the aims of the campaign, evaluation was built in from the start. Content was tested with a client panel, and feedback from users was encouraged. An online version was then developed.

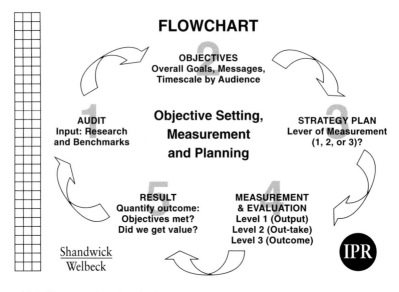

Figure 20.1 The research and evaluation process

Source: IPR Toolkit. Used with permission

The Toolkit built on research commissioned by *PR Week* which showed that one-fifth of practitioners did not believe their results could be evaluated; less than a third mentioned surveys as a research tool; only 16 per cent of public sector respondents felt focus groups were useful; only 3 per cent had ever used pre-testing; and one of the biggest obstacles to evaluation was cost (Echo Research 1999).

The main thrust of the Toolkit rested on the five-step objective setting, measurement and planning model (Figure 20.1). The process was broken down into five stages.

- **Step 1 Audit** Gathering of existing data, such as current communications and leaflets, identifying benchmarks, analysing the current situation in order to set a good brief.
- **Step 2 Objectives** This is the key to well thought out and executed evaluation. Using the organisation's aims, communication objectives can be set, specific to each audience. They must be measurable and with a definite timescale.
- **Step 3 Strategy and plan** This is the part of the campaign where the overall strategy is drawn up, based on the objectives, together with the tactics to be used. Pre-testing of proposed techniques should be employed here.
- **Step 4 Measurement and evaluation** The main question to be asked at this stage is, Are we getting there? Measurement can be carried out at regular intervals. Analysis at this stage might lead to some of the tactics being adjusted.
- **Step 5 Result** At the conclusion of the PR programme or campaign, there is a thorough appraisal of whether the objectives were achieved. Cost–benefit analysis would determine whether value was given, and might also point out things which could be done differently next time.

Each step of the process was then examined in detail, relating to a case study. Information about research techniques was provided, together with a set of worksheets that could be photocopied and used as basic frameworks by practitioners in their own programmes. Finally, a fax-back sheet was provided for feedback. To date, over 1,500 Toolkits have been purchased. An updated version is to be published in 2001

Essentially, the Toolkit emphasised that there was no single industry-wide measure, but that there is a range of tools available. Some were simple and could be carried out by practitioners themselves, others could be bought from specialists. The most effective way of evaluating is to use a combination of tools, and over time it is hoped that PR practitioners can persuade clients and employers to use more sophisticated methods.

Case study 2: Media Measurement Ltd – Listening to People

Changes had occurred in a client organisation, brought about by three major developments in the electricity supply industry. The organisation had been privatised, and taken over by a US-based organisation. All power markets had been opened to outside suppliers. The company needed to improve business performance to increase stockholder worth, as well as react to business pressures in another country and cope with competition in a once closed market. Changes which had taken place within the organisation included reductions in staffing, new systems and procedures, reduction in management levels and the disbanding of a traditional headquarters structure. The organisation had also had to alter its culture to become more customer focused.

The client company was concerned to find out staff reaction to the changes and how changes had been communicated to them.

MML used the techniques developed in media content analysis to examine the product of focus group conversations. Marketed under the title 'Listening to People', the technique was used to examine conversations between employees. A contributing group of 2,500 was identified across the client organisation, of which a response rate of 72 per cent was achieved. A management group of 506 was included in the main group, of which 471 were recorded, or 93 per cent. Two divisions were sampled, Supply and Distribution. The divisions were analysed together, and for some criteria separately. The response group was also split into more specific areas, such as Customer Services and Business Sales.

Staff saw the biggest positive reasons behind the change as reduced network downtime. Productivity and privatisation were seen as dominant positive forces, as was the takeover. However, MML was able to isolate the fact that engineers saw issues related to downtime as a direct criticism of their work. Problems were thought to be due to cost-cutting and further cuts could only make things worse. External reasons for change were much better understood and accepted, and some departments were not aware of any internal reasons for change.

Only a minority of comment relating to the method of change was positive. The top positive message was that it would reduce bureaucracy, but only one-fifth of respondents stated this. A new form of seeking input, Z groups, were mentioned extremely positively by the Business Sales division, but response indicated that these had been implemented unevenly across the organisation. Whilst response in business sales included 'For the first time the company seems to be interested in my ideas', amongst administrative staff the reaction was 'Why ask me, what are the managers paid for?' There was general criticism of the way job reductions had been announced, with comments like 'The managers were too frightened to tell us themselves'.

Staff reactions to the change in terms of the flatter management structure which resulted from the job cuts was mainly positive. The new structure of smaller teams meant that 'We can discuss our problems in the team', and another reaction was 'I feel better about my job'. What was useful to note was that the area affected most by the job reductions, the highly skilled engineering department, perhaps not surprisingly produced the most negative comments. Many talked of colleagues intending to resign. The human resources, on the front line of the change, also found the period stressful. The company was then able to address their concerns in particular.

The final set of comments related to company objectives that the new organisation would be more efficient, and that it would be more customer oriented. Customer Services, Administration and Business Sales were very positive about these messages, and reacted to the new grading system with 'About time we looked after the people that look after our customers' and also 'About time the company started looking after the customers'. Again, the largest amount of negative reaction was in the Engineering department, where it was felt that 'This new structure has got no chance'. This dissatisfaction was significant, as the Engineering department made up 33 per cent of the workforce.

Whilst across the company the majority of the changes had been accepted, inconsistencies in perceptions in specific departments enabled the company to identify problems in their implementation. The main conclusion of the report was to ensure that essential communication took place so that the new customer-focused structure became built into the fabric of the company rather than bolted on to the outside as yet another management campaign.

'Listening to People' reprinted by kind permission of Media Measurement Ltd

Case study 3: Journalist profile

Media content analysis also enables the production of journalist profiles. In one example, Media Measurement analysed the work of James Hopegood for the Bristol & West Building Society. It was able to identify that he had written 17 items, of which nine were relevant to Bristol & West. Articles had appeared in nine journals over a one month period, reaching a cumulative circulation of 2,998,000. The tone of the articles was also analysed, finding that there had been no beneficial treatments; although there had been some factual comments, most were adverse.

The total number of articles mentioning Bristol & West in the nine journals for which James Hopegood had written were also analysed. In contrast, a substantial number of these were positive in nature.

The journalist's most commonly covered subjects were found to be bonus payments from building society conversion, BIM Home Mortgages and the standard variable rate. By comparing his output with other bylined journalists' in the financial area, he was shown to be fourth in terms of the circulation reached by his opinions. Obviously Hopegood was a fairly influential journalist, who was mainly negative about the company.

Bristol & West then had the information it needed to be able to approach this journalist in a more focused way in the future, by relating its products to his most covered subjects.

Reprinted by kind permission of Media Measurement Ltd

Case study 4: British Airways global identity launch, June 1997

The former team at CARMA International* carried out a review of international press coverage generated during the launch and re-branding of British Airways plc's logo and livery as part of its global repositioning. Television and radio broadcasts were not compared as they were not considered consistent enough across the various markets. The study evaluated the international media reaction to the new identity and tracked key issues and messages across each region. Sources for and against the launch were monitored.

The new global identity was unveiled on 10 June 1997, using 50 different images from all continents (Figure 20.2). Launched globally through a business satellite television broadcast, it was seen by 30,000 guests, employees and journalists. The news was featured in the news of 50 countries. The majority (78 per cent) of the coverage was positive. However, domestic coverage focused on the removal of the flag and the simultaneous reporting of stories about the cost of the launch alongside reports of staff disputes.

Internationally, 444 articles were analysed, as well as 165 from the UK. British Airways appeared in the headlines in 79 per cent of the international media, compared with 32 per cent in the UK. Visuals were used in 48 per cent of international articles, and 30 per cent of those in the UK. Pictures of the livery appeared in the majority of these. Most coverage was secured in Europe and the near East. Echo was also able to decipher that within this sector, the most favourable reports were in Cyprus, Denmark and Finland. There was no unfavourable coverage in the Americas.

Apart from the change itself, the most discussed issues were British Airways' global corporate strategy and the cost and scope of the exercise. The use of local artists gave

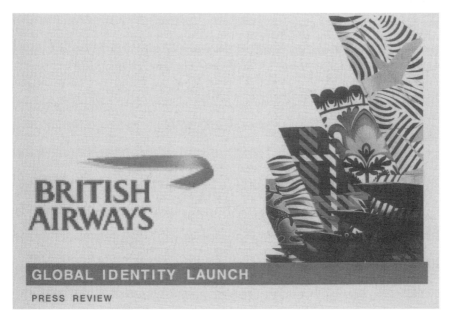

Figure 20.2 British Airways–Echo Research

Used by permission of Sandra Macleod, Echo Research and Carma International

a regional angle to the coverage, and they appeared in 37 per cent of all coverage, often with examples of their work. Echo then broke down the coverage into the leading positive and negative messages in each region. Chief Executive Robert Ayling was the most often quoted source, and local BA personnel and local artists were well cited in their local media.

Echo concluded that the international media had welcomed the global identity change with enthusiasm and support, so that British Airways' global nature came through. The main criticisms about the seemingly unpatriotic rejection of the British flag was strongest in ex-colonies such as Australia, India and South Africa. The fact that some articles addressed the cost of the programme alongside industrial relations problems showed that the rationale of the identity change had to be more fully explained. British Airways has now changed the tail fins back to their original colours, so this would indicate that criticisms of the change proved too difficult to surmount.

* Sandra Macleod and Peter Christopherson now run Echo Communications Research Group. CARMA International is a separate company.

Reproduced by kind permission of Sandra Macleod, Echo Research

Progress?

From the diverse case studies, it can be seen that evaluation has developed in the past few years. Although it is generally more acceptable, the battle is far from won. A slow process of client and practitioner education has to continue. The industry must also resolve its uneasy relationship with academic research if it is to progress beyond an empirical response to organisation and client issues, however much that may encompass a more strategic approach.

If that particular nettle is not grasped it could have more serious consequences for the industry. 'It is about time for PR to stand up and show itself for its true value', says Sandra Macleod. 'Reputation is an asset to your balance sheet, and you have to manage it and measure it. The danger is that unless practitioners are up to the job, more will be lost to the management consultants.'

Notes

1 All quotes from David Phillips are from interviews with the author.
2 Interview with the author.

21 Future challenges for PR

··

T he final exercise in looking into the future concerns the development of the public
relations industry itself. This future cannot be divorced from the debates in the
previous two chapters about the development of the media and the increased use
of evaluation. As well as a review of various articles written on the subject, a straw
poll was taken of influential figures from the PR industry and academia, and young PR
graduates and practitioners, asking them whether the industry's own image was so poor
as to necessitate a name change, and to state their vision of the future.

A growth industry

··

In 1990, Peter Gummer, Chairman of Shandwick plc, gave the annual CAM Foundation
lecture at Trinity and All Saints College in Leeds. He took as his theme 'PR in the
Year 2000'. He stated that whilst at that time the number of people working in consult-
ancies outnumbered those working in-house by four to one, by the turn of the century
companies would 'have an in house function represented at a very senior level, prob-
ably at board or very near board level, able to buy in external assistance, both inter-
nationally and in particular specialisations'. He also estimated that consultancy fees
would rise by 300 per cent to £15 billion worldwide, and that this growth would be
driven by the development of PR in underdeveloped markets outside the UK and the
USA. Important areas for growth were mainly environmental and government PR. 'I
believe that PR will increasingly be seen for what it really is – an indispensable tool
of management' (Gummer 1990).

In 1994, IBDO published the results of a survey on the PR industry which had been
commissioned by the Department of Trade and Industry. The report recognised that the
sector had 'grown spectacularly over the past ten years' and that 'PR is increasingly
regarded as a serious discipline' (IBDO 1994).

Like IBDO, White and Mazur (1995: 251) concentrated on the consultancy sector in
their own look at the future of public relations: 'In future, public relations, involving
skilful management of important relationships and communication with groups of people
on whose support any organisation depends, will come to be regarded as a key task
for senior management.' In order to take advantage of this, 'public relations practi-
tioners will need to develop their qualifications and skills, or will find that their role
will be usurped by others, possibly management consultants, or advisers from other

areas such as marketing or law'. Offering a more strategic service was seen as the main aspiration of consultants. Looking at developments in the USA as a precursor to developments in the UK, two trends were viewed. Whilst more work was being put out on a project basis than on retainer, consultancies were also being used for top level strategic advice. The fact that consultancies elsewhere in Europe were smaller had led to public relations having a better reputation and attracting entrants from economics, law and languages, so that they were able to offer advice on environmental issues and corporate positioning. The key to a number of these issues was the drive to raise standards in the quality of entrants and practitioners, which will be discussed later in this chapter. The two possible futures for PR that White and Mazur envisaged were that it would become more technical, using communications techniques to support marketing activities, or that it would become a social practice, helping organisations to fit in with their social environments.

Does PR need a name change?

Opinions on whether the poor reputation of the public relations industry could be partly solved by changing its name were, not surprisingly, divided. Those who felt that this was a solution offered the following arguments.

> I think we do need a name change – not because the current one is tarnished, but because it is misleading. It pigeon-holes the truly creative PR practitioners and does not reflect the genuine depth and importance of our work.
>
> (Robert Philips, MD, JCPR)

> It would be tempting to do so to reduce the number of times I hear 'It's a PR exercise'.
>
> (Karen Heenan Davies, Dowcorning)

> It does need a name change both to overcome some of the negative associations and to position our discipline more centrally and effectively. Emerging disciplines of relationship marketing, marketing communications and internal communications are not necessarily seen as the province of public relations. I changed my department's title to Communications. The widening of the brief to be a full stakeholder relationship management unit has been very helpful.
>
> (Derek Prior, Director of Communications, Open University)

> Yes, PR is primarily about communication in all its aspects and therefore the industry's name should reflect this. My favoured option would be strategic communications.
>
> (Alison Radovanovic, freelance consultant, Croatia)

> If there was a consensus and everyone stopped using 'public relations' at the same time then I could live with 'reputation management'.
>
> (David Heal, MD, Harrison Cowley)

> PR has got an image problem that, ironically, has been fuelled by the very audience our industry claims to influence – the media. PR fluff or spin doctoring conjures up images of insincere attempts to manipulate the media and to distort or hide the

truth. Organisational communications is probably the best description of what we do. Communication should be at the heart of any organisation, as a means of helping define and crystallise the mission, and helping it reach its goals

(Paul Vousden, MD, VLP)

PR elicits bad perceptions amongst certain people – largely because they are unclear about its function. Max Clifford has done 'true' PR people no favours. A new name could be targeted audience communications or awareness raising and issues management.

(Jo Chipchase, freelance IT PR consultant and author)

Yes, because I wish that practitioners could define what they were about. It's usually corporate communications or marketing communications, which are more descriptive terms.

(Richard Bailey, freelance consultant and trainer)

There would be better understanding of public relations if practitioners were called professional communicators, simply because that is what we do, using the appropriate tool to complete the task in hand.

(Catherine Arrow, Arrow Public Relations)

The many disciplines now covered by this catch-all name should be properly used, promoted and hopefully understood. Professionals know there is a world of difference between consumer PR/marketing communications, investor relations, media relations, public affairs, and the work of Max Clifford, but clients, employers and the general public don't see these specialist activities as anything other than PR.

(Christian Judge, Senior Media Relations Advisor,
TXU Europe)

PR people have been suffering from an identity crisis for as long as I can remember. In a sense it doesn't matter what we call our industry, what matters is that we keep improving the quality of the experience that others have of it. There's no denying that standards vary and that sections of the media have eagerly promoted misconceptions of both 'public' and 'relations'. We have always described ourselves as communications experts, but personally I prefer reputation management because I think it more accurately describes the multi-faceted expertise which most of us offer today.

(Jon Aarons, Director, Financial Dynamics)

Those who felt that the profession should not change its name felt that it would be counter-productive and going against established PR counsel.

Public relations is a beautifully apt and appropriate descriptor of what we do. Whatever your business, we are always looking to forge relationships with the public in order to achieve a given objective. Unfortunately, PR still sees itself as a service rather than a crucial contributor and determinant of strategy.

(Rob Cohen, Glaxo Wellcome)

To abandon PR and replace it with some other term would lay us open to the accusation of attempting to pass it off as some other less openly criticised activity. We would be guilty of not standing up for the profession that we practice and teach.

(Danny Moss, Manchester Metropolitan University)

The difficulty with any name change is finding an acceptable alternative, and I have yet to see one.

(John McMahon, Murray Consulting)

The name PR has only just begun to receive recognition. A name change would cause confusion.

(Kerry Hopkins, PR graduate)

We all get frustrated at various phrases, some complimentary, some fluffy and some downright rude, but if we try and reinvent a name that has embraced this industry for fifty years and more we run the risk of being thought to be concerned about our reputation and that something as fickle as a name change will sort it out. This seems to be fundamentally at odds with what we preach on reputation management.

(Alison Clarke, Shandwick Asia Pacific)

Public Relations is not something you do, nor something you use, it is something you hope to achieve. Ever improving relationships with the publics that are of importance for your organisation is the goal. Public Relations is the umbrella that can embrace many churches, and no other words can more accurately and succinctly describe what it is all about and what public relations people should be doing.

(Francis Carty, Dublin Institute of Technology)

I think the industry has to be thick-skinned and play a long game. Whatever image problems the industry may have won't be solved by changing the name. A number of factors, including the arrival of a government which places unprecedented emphasis on presentation, focus groups and media coverage, have made the industry intriguing to the media and public alike. When I left university in 1986 PR hardly registered on the graduate radar as a possible career – now it is one of the most popular. This should push up the quality of those coming into the industry.

(Simon Miller, Railtrack)

PR has always been about communications between an organisation or individual and their different audiences.

(Ian Wright, Diageo)

We have reached the point where most people who are in a position to hire a PR consultancy know more or less what PR comprises. It is up to us to complete the process of explaining it.

(Adrian Wheeler, MD, GCI)

Even if the body of practitioners decided collectively one day to change the name of the sector, the resistance from marketeers, clients, the public and the media to acknowledge any alternative name would reduce the reputation of our fragile sector to farce. We'd be laughed at. As if a name change would make any difference to the quality of our work. Other planned name changes usually plummet to earth. You can't PR the impossible. Who would be convinced if we 'renamed' British beef?

(Clive Booth, Lewis PR)

The reputation of PR

In November 1999, the US edition of *PR Week* published the results of a survey of 269 chief executives from a range of businesses. This found that 85 per cent of respondents believed that effective management communication affected stock performance. Nearly 80 per cent felt that PR was more important to their company than five years previously. Around 90 per cent of those of the largest companies believed that reputation related directly to profits, and all agreed that PR would become increasingly important. More of those from smaller companies felt that the internet was important in reputation management.

This shift in attitude was linked to the dot com start-ups, where companies which had an intangible product were being valued highly based on a mixture of 'buzz and potential'. Also, the Fortune Yankelovich survey in 1999 showed that companies with a high corporate equity had a higher ratio of spend on PR and investor relations. As more Americans became interested in business because of various stock ownership schemes, the media also subjected business to more intense scrutiny. As Adam Leyland reported in *PR Week US* (1999), Harold Burson, Chairman of Burson-Marstellar, felt that

> Public relations will become more important because the media will become more complex as they proliferate. This will make it more difficult to disseminate messages that can differentiate one entity from another. As this happens, PR will become less an art and more a science.

Howard Rubenstein, Chairman and CEO of Rubenstein Associates, said

> The trends that are increasing the importance of PR will only accelerate in the next five years. The globalisation of business, the intensity of competition, the proliferation of media outlets, the impact of instantaneous communications and the ubiquity of the internet will all continue.

Increasingly, CEOs were becoming involved in the choice of heads of corporate communication. Additionally, if companies had a reputation problem, 56 per cent said the first person they would turn to would be a public relations professional. This importance increased with the size of the company, with 73 per cent of CEOs of companies with revenues of $5 billion or more valuing PR counsel (Leyland 1999).

The PRCA commissioned Echo Research to determine the perceived image of PR in the media during 1999. Whilst there was an increasingly positive link of PR with commercial success, and a recognition that PR had a credible and professional image, in contrast to the US findings, politics and spin doctoring were generally covered adversely. This and the focusing on certain personalities such as Matthew Freud, Max Clifford, Alastair Campbell and Sophie Wessex contributed to the leading negative message, that the PR industry had problems with its own image. The report concluded that creating case studies to show the importance of PR and extending their use in the media would help to inform the general public about the creative strength of the profession. It was also considered critical to find an authoritative representative to comment on PR issues (Echo Research 1999).

Improving quality of entrants and training

Salim Kadebegil (1999) suggested that the future of PR depends both on increased investment in education and training by the PR industry, and on a shift in emphasis in business to recognise the importance of reputation and its management.

Improving professional competence, based on greater investment in training, was one of the issues to emerge from a PRCA Council discussion dinner in March 1999.

PR Week established a Best Practice campaign in June 1999 (Nicholas 1999a), linking to the CBI's Fit for the Future campaign. The objective of Fit for the Future was 'to create major sustainable improvements in the UK's productivity through a massive increase in the number of companies engaged in best practice'. The Best Practice campaign set up a panel of industry leaders, including representation from the IPR and PRCA, Marketing Council and CBI, to discuss a range of issues, beginning with budget transparency and costing of programmes, and encompassing ethics, training, valuing reputation and managing agency/client relationships. Management of multinational campaigns and evaluation were also included. Guidelines resulting from debates on these topics were published in *PR Week*, with the intention of encouraging widescale involvement and feedback from the industry. The emphasis placed on education and training evidenced by the IPR's initiatives in this field have already been discussed in Chapter 5, and will contribute both to improving the calibre of practitioners and to improving the reputation of the industry.

In interviews conducted for this chapter, participants of the informal survey endorsed the emphasis on the quality of entrants and greater investment in training. Rob Cohen saw quality of entrants as linked to the image of the industry:

> As long as tactical PR takes the limelight in terms of attracting new talent into the industry, nothing will change. Only positioning and promoting PR as a cerebral discipline where brain power and strategic thinking are paramount will give PR a place on the board.

'Professionalisation of the industry is key to the future, and this is inextricably linked to education and CPD', said Ralph Tench of Leeds Metropolitan University. 'This involves strong relationships between relevant professional bodies, educational institutions and practitioners. Old models and theories will need reflection and change which will best be transferred to the practitioner community through linking training and education with innovation in practice.' Adrian Wheeler of GCI concurred, seeing the employment of higher calibre candidates as a good sign: 'PR people in general are not good enough at what they do. This is changing fast and needs to change faster.'

Clive Booth felt it could be the solution to eliminating poor practitioners:

> I should like it to evolve so that clients would only want to use professionally qualified PR practitioners, who could only retain their professional status by completing continuous professional development (CPD). In 50 years, when image will be a daily boardroom concern for all businesses, the cowboys might be squeezed out.

John McMahon saw a need to take training seriously: 'The future is bright, but the major constraint is trained young people to take the strain. The tenuous nature of client contracts has placed emphasis on the immediate at the expense of longer term planning.'

Measuring results

The IBDO (1994) report concluded that 'Evaluating the effectiveness of PR remains a hotly debated issue' and that 'the public relations industry may never be fully respected unless it can provide measurement of its value' (Executive Summary, p. 1)

The development of the IPR/PRCA/*PR Week* Toolkit on evaluation (see case study, pp. 259–61) was quoted as an example of improving the image of PR itself, by countering the argument that the effect of PR is hard to measure. 'Evaluation is the rocky but sunlit pathway for PR practitioners to climb, once and for all, out of the quicksand where our work is judged by instinct, gut-feel and intuition', said Adrian Wheeler (quoted in Gray 1998). He also warned that 'There is a pain factor in submitting work to the acid test of evaluation, and it's one that both clients and consultancies are frequently inclined to dodge.' He felt that evaluation of objectives will become normal practice, and 'a sign that PR is at last wearing long trousers' (see IPRA 1997: 49–72).

Alongside the Proof Campaign which resulted in the Toolkit, developments in the USA included work by the PRSA to introduce a new tool to measure and evaluate the impact of PR. A commission on research and evaluation was set up by the Institute for Public Relations at the University of Florida. This led to discussions of whether a global kite mark standard could be developed. As Cowlett (1999a) reports 'There is no way you can have a set global standard when there are so many different needs within a single company from just one campaign', said Mark Adams, Director of Text 100. Mark Westaby, MD of Metrica, warned of the need to pay attention to terminology: 'Even between the UK and the US you have to be careful you are talking about the same thing.' Differences in the importance of various media also complicate the issue, according to Jackie Walford, Senior Vice-President International of CARMA: 'In the UK, the national press is important, whereas in India, Italy and the US, regional press plays a significant role.' Most international campaigns have varying local applications, meaning that a framework of objectives must be established. The major challenge was felt to be persuading clients that measuring outcome was an investment and resulted in bottom line benefits for their organisation. Again, as we have seen in the previous chapter, evaluation is something which the industry is tackling head on.

A note of caution was sounded by Francis Carty:

> At first glance public relations seems to be flourishing, but how much of it is really public relations and how much marketing is not clear. The profession will have to educate its clients and learn to take evaluation seriously and spend more money on it.

Globalisation

In 1996, Kate Nicholas discussed cultural shifts and how they would affect the PR industry in Europe. Several developments were causing difficulties. One was the aim of some larger consultancies to have a unified brand across Europe whilst needing to take account of local regulatory frameworks and cultural values. Clients from the USA and Asia did not have an understanding of the regional differences within Europe. European clients were using US consultancies when they wanted to break into the US market. Growth in the PR industry in France and the Netherlands had driven increased professionalism. Some clients continued to use UK firms as a central buying point for work in Europe, whereas others preferred a more bespoke approach (Nicholas 1999b).

IPRA published a survey of eight countries (comprising the UK, the USA, South Africa, Brazil, Japan, Singapore, Switzerland and Australia) in 1997 which looked at the effects of globalisation on corporate communications. The most important task for PR in the future was thought to be the maintenance and improvement of corporate social evaluation, along with corporate communication based on company strategy. In order to communicate globally, companies would have to use PR professionals native to the different areas of operation. Shareholders, investors and customers were thought to be the most important audiences, with employees ranking fourth. The fact that media were now reaching across national borders also had to be taken into account. There was unanimous agreement that companies would need improved communications in the global field (IPRA 1997).

The question of a European consensus as to what the PR industry represents was identified as a problem in moving forward. Reviewing a plethora of definitions, a common theme was found to be that PR 'helps organisations to establish and maintain good relationships with all kinds of publics which are important for reaching the organisation's goals'. However, the practice of PR was felt to be diverging from this, in that many practitioners were operating in circumstances where they were not allowed to consider strategic activities. Other practitioners were working in integrated marketing communications. The invasion of the PR professional domain by management consultants, lawyers and accountants was also confusing the picture. Setting up a European standard for PR that allowed for different regional and national cultures, as well as recognising the different stages of development of practice, was proposed (van der Laan 2000). As part of the attempt to find an agreed definition of PR, CERP commissioned research in April 1999 amongst organisations and experts across Europe to ascertain the components of PR practice.

Countrywide Porter Novelli also commissioned research on the impact of globalisation and new media on communications in the new millennium. Respondents felt that global organisations would be moving from a decentralised mode to a centralised model. Activities would include investor relations, crisis management, corporate image, public affairs, corporate themes and PR for global business. There would still be local activities such as local stakeholder relations with media, advocacy groups and government. Protecting a company's reputation would continue to be the top priority. Brand building and protection would be seen as part of company reputation. International experience would be provided to company management, and new incentive programmes would reward co-operative global efforts. Successful media stories in one country could be transferred into other markets, as could adverse ones, so international sensitivity must increase. Consultancies could provide leadership in managing global accounts, and in acting as brokers to bring together the best people from different disciplines. There would be a need for a good understanding of strategy globally, but also those working in different countries would have to have the flexibility to tailor programmes and messages to their own local needs (Druckenmiller 1999).

Karen Heenan Davies felt that 'Companies will become more global, so practitioners will need to demonstrate global capabilities, with cultural sensitivity and knowledge to adapt programmes to suit local needs.' Chris Genasi at Shandwick agreed:

> PR will continue to grow in importance as the media and other pressure groups continue to scrutinise companies. Global media coverage means that consistency will be essential. PR will mature to become part of the business decision-making process, rather than something which is done after all the decisions have been made. Managing PR globally will become the norm.

The effect of new technology

At the IPR International Symposium in May 1999, Larry Weber, CEO and Chairman of Weber Public Relations Worldwide, suggested that the evolution of the PR industry was being driven by the availability of new technologies and the shift from text-based to visual communications. Implications of new technology included the redefinition of creative needs, distribution of news and relationship building. The characteristics of the new communications economy were interactivity, immediacy, information richness, individualisation and integration. As well as increasing expectations amongst stakeholders, for instance that emails would be answered within eight hours, it also allowed PR practitioners to develop a dialogue with their constituency, evolving towards Grunig's original model of two-way symmetric communications. Information was becoming more educative rather than attempting to sell products, and this could be customised to suit individuals and specific journalists. He felt that this led to the expansion of PR into corporate reputation management and brand leadership.

The development of the internet as a communications channel was also seen as one of the most challenging areas for PR, and one of its greatest opportunities. 'The internet has given us a direct pathway to the consumer, enabling us to circumvent the media as a filter and to build relationships directly with consumers, while still allowing us to act as intermediaries with the media', said Richard Edelman, CEO of Edelman PR. The increased speed of communications also makes corporate reputations harder to manage, and because of increased access to information, transparency and immediacy of response are needed. 'The internet puts word of mouth on steroids', said Harris Diamond, CEO of BSMG Worldwide. 'If service stinks, if performance lags, if your employees hate you, not only will you hear about it, so will everyone else' (quoted in Leyland 1999).

The author's research revealed the following opinions. Ian Wright saw that:

> The key issue is the development of the media, leading to the fusion of the net and broadcasting. This will affect the way we do what we do and the structure and expectations of our clients and organisations. The need to communicate will remain, but the opportunity to narrowcast by whatever means to specific audiences will advance beyond all recognition. That will increase our work and the demands put upon us.

Alison Clarke agreed: 'The future of the industry will be remote virtual working enabled by technology. Reputation management will be critical to success and all companies will be looking to reflect this.'

Karen Heenan Davies saw the need to acquire expertise as critical:

> Practitioners in the future will have to have a wider range of skills and at a far higher level. Technological change will have a significant impact on communication and those of us in the profession will have to adapt accordingly. Clients will require expert advice on all forms of electronic communication and how to utilise them.

PR will become more scientific and technology will play a huge part. Increased competition will lead to an increased role for PR consultants', felt Kerry Hopkins. 'PR practitioners need to be flexible and expect some convergence with other related disciplines. They need to grasp new technology and understand the potential of new media. There will be a need for "thinking outside the box"', said Jo Chipchase.

Increased demands would be made, thought Catherine Arrow:

The fast-food fix of information demanded by the techno-savvy, 24 hours a day, 365 days a year, could create an ever hungry monster, supplied with poor ineffectual material. The practitioner of the future must ensure that whatever the speed of delivery, quality is maintained and communication is meaningful.

Regulation and the future of practice

Despite concerns about the poor image of PR being related to the fact that anyone can claim to be a PR practitioner (as indicated by respondents to the previous part of the author's survey), the PRCA Council discussion dinner concluded that self-regulation was preferable to statutory controls.

Adrian Wheeler felt that regulation was necessary and desirable in at least two areas of PR work – government lobbying and financial communications, but agreed that self-regulation by the professional associations was the way forward. As to the way that PR is practised in the consultancy field, he felt that medium-sized firms will become squeezed out by a move towards the large firms at the top, with a large number of small specialised companies at the bottom: 'International capability will be the watchword. Those firms which have invested in well-run networks will make hay.' He also forecast a rise in income for PRCA member consultancies from £350 million in 2000 to £1 billion by 2010.

'There will be more mergers and the large multinational agencies will get bigger', says freelance consultant Robert Minton Taylor.

They will broaden their scope to become full service management consultancies and will be more global. Unless the medium-size firms are strong regional players, I see no long-term future for them. The niche players and sole traders will survive because they offer a personal service at a price which the majors are unwilling or unable to provide.

This view was supported by Mark Button of Le Fevre: 'Established consultancies will continue to set up specialist offshoots, and many successful smaller agencies will be bought up by larger multinationals. PR will increasingly be found in the boardroom.'

Simon Miller felt that the perception of PR is changing:

Managers are increasingly valuing the contribution which PR and communications can make to a brand's reputation. PR departments are being seen more as being able to truly support business objectives by effectively promoting the organisation across the full range of stakeholders.

Danny Moss agreed:

There is a greater recognition of the importance of communications and that reputation cannot be taken for granted. In a mature economy it is increasingly difficult to find tangible sources of differentiation and it is the reputation and relationships which organisations establish with their stakeholders which are the drivers of corporate success. The mechanisms of communication are changing and this has forced a rethink of traditional media strategies. A new generation of better-educated

practitioners are assuming positions of authority and bringing a greater understanding of the potential of PR into the boardroom. However, the fundamental tools of the profession are unlikely to change dramatically. The principles of effective PR have not changed, it is the mechanisms through which the practice is conducted that have and will continue to evolve.

Mike Smith of Cardiff University also saw changes in attitude: 'As society matures an increasing number of those whose views matter are beginning to appreciate the importance of managing reputation and that this is a world away from publicity and spinning.'

Robert Phillips forecast a new role for PR practitioners:

Successful companies will be those with real stories to tell, and consumer PR companies will be the storytellers, forging a genuine emotional connection with consumers. More specialists will emerge. Cause-related and community activities will be big. Corporations will finally wake up to the fact that their equity is built on their brands and their interface with consumers. I would like to see more emotion injected into the industry.

Derek Prior felt that technology provided both a challenge and an opportunity: 'The widespread availability of simpler tools via technology will mean more communications tasks can be carried out by non-PR specialists, giving us the challenge of really consolidating the core skills and knowledge that give us a clearly perceptible edge.' In contrast, Alison Radovanovic thought that convergence would occur: 'The future is bright, but not in its traditional format. As the fragmentation of the media leads to the demise of mass audiences, this will in turn lead to an amalgamation of advertising, marketing and public relations, with PR to the fore.'

Others felt that changing practices would impact on the development of the profession. David Heal saw 'more planning, a more integral role within business, more measured and controlled programmes and better targeting of media'. Paul Vousden felt that 'Research will play a much larger role. Consumers and the community will become increasingly important and this will impact on communications. We will be more of a profession in how we go about our business.'

In conclusion, Richard Bailey believed that 'There will be a powerful new role of corporate counsel. PR practitioners will have to understand the whole marketing mix and contribute to integrated campaigns.'

A view from academia

In July 2000, the 7th International Research Symposium took the theme of the future of PR. Several academics presented their views on the future. Judy Motion, from the University of Waikato, New Zealand, suggested that new social movements would lead to an increase in importance for the discipline, and that the relationship side of PR would need development, borrowing from relationship and social marketing. Susanne Holmstrom from the University of Roskilde, Denmark, presented a view of the evolution of PR from an economic necessity to a normal part of the management process. Gunter Bentele of Leipzig University, Germany, also felt that PR would become more important, would become integrated into communications, and would develop into a 'new style' profession, aligned with international standards.

Key issues

As we have seen, the main issues for the future are the calibre of entrants to the profession and the quality of the training they receive after they enter it. This must involve both greater investment in staff and greater willingness to adopt new and more professional practices.

The structure of consultancies may change, with a move towards larger, international companies and small, niche specialists. Practitioners must take up the challenge and opportunities offered by developments in new technology, both in the tactical area of media relations and direct communication with stakeholders through websites and in the strategic area of true company counsel. Awareness of the changing nature of business for clients and employers must lead to a global outlook.

The continuing improvement in the reputation of the industry and the activities of professional bodies in strengthening their codes of practice and contributing to government debates on standards will lead to a better understanding of the nature of public relations. Whilst it is unlikely that legislation will be imposed on entry to the profession, it is to be hoped that this will lead to a recognition of the differences between PR, marketing and publicity. Employers and clients will know what they are buying from practitioners who are not members of the professional bodies and who do not conform to their codes. The phrase 'it's only a PR exercise' may even disappear from common usage as there will be a general understanding of the difference between PR and lying.

With the maturity of the industry it is to be hoped that there will be an adoption of more progressive human resources practices. An industry survey by *PR Week* in 2000 showed that more practitioners were complaining of stress and overwork. With more emphasis on the importance of work–life balance for both men and women, PR may move away from the long hours culture. Against this, the explosion in global communications which has increased expectations of speedy responses will have to be skilfully managed.

Notes

All opinions expressed in this chapter are from interviews or e-mail responses to the survey mentioned in the first paragraph.

Bibliography

Abratt, R. (1989) 'A new approach to the corporate image management process', *Journal of Marketing Management*, 5 (1), pp. 63–76

Adkins, S. (1999) *Cause-Related Marketing – Who Cares Wins*, Butterworth Heinemann

AMEC (1997) *The Power of the Media*, AMEC/GPRA/IPRRE

Baker, M.J. and Balmer, J.M.T. (1997) 'Visual identity: trappings or substance?', *European Journal of Marketing*, 31 (5/5), pp. 366–82

Barnett, S. (1989) *Cross Media Ownership and its Impact on Public Opinion*, Broadcasting Research Unit/VLV, May

Bartrum, P. (1995) *How to Write a Press Release*, How to Books

Berger, A.A. (1995) *Essentials of Mass Communication Theory*, Sage

Berlo, D. (1960) *The Process of Communication*, Holt, Rinehart and Winston

Bernstein, D. (1984) *Company Image and Reality*, Cassell

Bernstein, D. (1989) *Company Image and Reality*, 2nd edition, Cassell

Bines, H. and Watson, D. (1992) *Developing Professional Education*, Open University Press

Bird, J. (1999) 'Harder times mean smarter marketing', *Marketing*, 25 March, p. 45

Black, S. (ed.) (1995) *The Practice of Public Relations*, 4th edition, Butterworth Heinemann

Blamphin, J. and White, J. (1994) 'Priorities through research into public relations practice in the United Kingdom, a report for the Delphi study carried out among UK practitioners and public relations academics in May, June and July 1994', Blamphin and White

Bland, M., Theaker, A. and Wragg, D. (1996) *Effective Media Relations*, Kogan Page/IPR

Blythman, J. (2000) 'Food', *Guardian*, 1 April, Weekend, p. 41

Bowman, P. and Bing, R. (1993) *Financial PR*, 2nd edition, Butterworth Heinemann

Boston, R. (1996) 'Spinning for a living', *History Today*, 46 (9)

Brown, M. (1999) 'Are we getting the television we deserve?', *Woman and Home*, July, pp. 124–5

Brown, M. (2000) 'Kid's stuff', *Guardian*, 20 March, Media, p. 8

Budd, J.F. (1994) *A Pragmatic Examination of Ethical Dilemmas in Public Relations*, IPRA Gold Paper No. 8

Budge, I., Crewe, I., McKay, D. and Newton, K. (1998) *The New British Politics*, Addison Wesley Longman

Burgoon, M, Hunsaker, F. and Dawson, E.J. (1994) *Human Communication*, Sage

Burkitt, B. and Ashton, F. (1996) 'The birth of the stakeholder society', *Critical Social Policy*, 16, pp. 3–16

Campbell, D. (2000) 'Gay teacher takes on evil website', *Guardian*, May

Carter, M. (1999) 'Cause and effect', *Director*, April, p. 29

Cheney (1992) 'The corporate person (re)presents itself', in E.L. Toth and R.L. Heath (eds) *Rhetorical and Critical Approaches to Public Relations*, Lawrence Erlbaum

Chipchase, J. (1995) 'The impact of the internet on PR communications', unpublished dissertation, Leeds Metropolitan University

Chryssides, G.D. and Kaler, J.H. (1993) *An Introduction to Business Ethics*, Chapman and Hall

Clarke, T. (1997) 'Measuring and managing stakeholder relations', *Journal of Communication Management*, 2 (3), pp. 211–21

Cockerell, M., Hennessy, P. and Walker, D. (1984) *Sources Close to the Prime Minister*, Macmillan

Cole-Morgan, U. (1995) 'Public relations in central government', in S. Black (ed.) *The Practice of Public Relations*, 4th edition, Butterworth Heinemann, pp. 60–72

Commission of PR Education (1999) *A Port of Entry*, PRSA

Common Purpose (1999) *Common Purpose Handbook*

Cowe, R. and Entine, J. (1996) 'Fair enough?', *Guardian*, 14 December, Weekend, pp. 30–9

Cowlett, M. (1999a) 'A worldly wise view of PR in the future', *PR Week*, 5 February

Cowlett, M. (1999b) 'Creating a breed of company converts', *PR Week*, 9 April, p. 13–14

Cowlett, M. (1999c) 'Directing attention to your releases', *PR Week*, 16 July, p. 11–12

Cowlett, M. (2000a) 'M&S', *PR Week*, 14 January, p. 8

Cowlett, M. (2000b) 'Organic growth', *PR Week*, 3 March, pp. 10–11

Cowlett, M. and Nicholas, K. (1999) 'The Proof Survey', *PR Week*, 12 March

Curran, J. and Seaton, J. (1991) *Power Without Responsibility*, 4th edition, Routledge

Curtis, J. (1999) 'Stealing a march on R&E solutions', *PR Week*, 24 September

Cutlip, S.M., Center, A.H. and Broom, G.M. (1985) *Effective Public Relations*, 6th edition, Prentice-Hall

Cutlip, S.M., Center, A.H. and Broom, G.M. (1995) *Effective Public Relations*, 7th edition, Prentice-Hall

Cutlip, S.M., Center, A.H. and Broom, G.M. (2000) *Effective Public Relations*, 8th edition, Prentice-Hall

Daymon, C. (2000) 'On considering the meaning of managed communication: or why employees resist excellent communication', *Journal of Communication Management*, 4 (3), February, pp. 240–51

Deacon, D. and Golding, P. (1994) *Taxation and Representation*, John Libbey

Donaldson, J. (1992) *Business Ethics: A European Casebook*, Academic Press

Dowling, G.R. (1994) *Corporate Reputations*, Kogan Page

Dozier, D.M., Grunig, L.A. and Grunig, J.E. (1995) *Manager's Guide to Excellence in Public Relations and Communication Management*, Lawrence Erlbaum

Druckenmiller, B. (1999) 'Global PR in transition', *Insight*, 4, Autumn, p. 1–2

Dyer, C. (2000) 'Four threats to the public's right to know,' *Guardian,* 22 May, p. 6

Echo Research (1998) 'Leading Edge in Communications Research', LSE Forum, 29 April

Echo Research (1999) *The Image of PR*, PRCA Survey, July–December

Edwards, R. (1999) 'Ensuring brands stay in fashion', *PR Week,* 24 September, pp. 13–14

Elton, L. (1993) 'University teaching: a professional model for quality', in R. Ellis (ed.) *Quality Assurance for University Teaching*, Open University Press

Esman, M.J. (1972) 'The elements of institution building', in J.W. Eaton (ed.) *Institutional Building and Development*, Sage

Evan, W.M. and Freeman, R.E. (1993) 'A stakeholder theory of the modern corporation: Kantian capitalism', in G.D. Chryssides and J.H. Kaler, *An Introduction to Business Ethics*, Chapman and Hall

Fairclough, N. (2000) *New Labour, New Language?*, Routledge

Fedorcio, D., Heaton, P. and Madden, K. (1991) *Public Relations for Local Government*, Longman

Femers, S., Klewes, J. and Lintemeir, K. (2000) 'The life of an issue and approaches to its control', *Journal of Communication Management*, 4 (3), February, pp. 253–66

Fill, C. (1999) *Marketing Communications*, Prentice-Hall

Fiske, J. (1990) *Introduction to Communication Studies*, Routledge

Fombrun, C.J. (1996) *Reputation: Realizing Value from Corporate Image*, Harvard Business School Press

France, S. (1999) 'Forging the bond of brand devotion', *PR Week*, 21 May, pp. 13–14

France, S. (2000) 'Opening eyes to a digital future', *PR Week*, 29 January, pp. 15–16

Franklin, B. (1994) *Packaging Politics*, Edward Arnold

Freeman, G. (2000) 'Playing the game', *PR Week*, 28 January

Future Foundation (1998) *The Responsible Organisation*, BT

Friedman, M. (1993) 'The social responsibility of business is to increase its profits', in G.D. Chryssides and J.H. Kaler, *An Introduction to Business Ethics*, Chapman and Hall

Gandy, O. (1992) 'Public relations and public policy: the structuration of dominance in the information age', in E. Toth and R. Heath (eds) *Rhetorical and Critical Approaches to Public Relations*, Lawrence Erlbaum

Goddard, L. (1999) 'Working with the Beeb's new look', *PR Week*, 23 July, pp. 11–12

Gofton, K. (1999) 'CRM', *Marketing*, 25 March, pp. 37–8

Gray, R. (1997) 'Cause for thought', *Marketing Week*, 2 January, pp. 20–1

Gray, R. (1998) 'Does PR measure up?', *Marketing*, 17 December, pp. 27–31

Gray, R. (1999) *PR Week*, 9 April, pp. 10–12

Greenslade, R. (2000) 'A final toast . . . the press', *Press Gazette*, 7 January, pp. 14–15

Gregory, A. (1996) *Planning and Managing a Public Relations Campaign*, Kogan Page/IPR

Gregory, A. (1999) 'A new approach to corporate identity management', unpublished paper

Gregory, A. (2000) 'Systems theories and public relations practice', *Journal of Communication Management*, 4 (3), February, pp. 266–77

Grey, B. (1993) *Investors Chronicle – Beginners' Guide to Investment*, 2nd edition, Century Business

Grunig, J. (1989) 'Symmetrical presuppositions as a framework for public relations theory', in C. Botan and V. Hazleton (eds) *Public Relations Theory*, Lawrence Erlbaum

Grunig, J. (ed.) (1992) *Excellence in Public Relations and Communications Management*, Lawrence Erlbaum

Grunig, J. and Grunig, L. (eds) (1989) *Public Relations Research Annual*, vol. 1, Lawrence Erlbaum

Grunig, J. and Grunig, L. (1992) 'Models of public relations and communication' in J. Grunig (ed.) *Excellence in Public Relations and Communication Management*, Lawrence Erlbaum

Grunig, J. and Hunt, T. (1984) *Managing Public Relations*, Holt, Rinehart & Winston

Grunig, J.E. and Jaatinen, M. (1999) 'Strategic, symmetrical public relations in government: from pluralism to societal corporatism', *Journal of Communication Management*, 3 (3), pp. 218ff.

Grunig, J. and Repper, F. (1992) 'Strategic management, publics and issues', in J. Grunig (ed.) *Excellence in Public Relations and Communications Management*, Lawrence Erlbaum

Grundy, T. (1993) *Implementing Strategic Change*, Kogan Page

Gummer, P. (1990) 'PR in the year 2000', CAM/TASC lecture, 21 November

Gusterson, P. (1999) Various documents on <www.gusterson.co.uk>

Hall, S. (1980) 'Encoding, decoding in the television discourse', in S. Hall, D. Hobson and P. Lowe (eds) *Culture, Media, Language*, Macmillan

Hamilton, K. (1999) 'Stockbrokers wake up to net opportunities', *Sunday Times*, 10 October

Hamilton, P. (1997) *Putting the Pressure On*, The Communication Group

Harben, J. (1998) 'The power of storytelling when cultures merge', *Journal of Communication Management*, 3 (1), Winter, pp. 80–7

Hargie, O. and Tourish, D. (2000) *Handbook of Communication Audits for Organisations*, Routledge

Harkness, J. (1999) 'Living and breathing the brand: the role of internal communication', *Journal of Communication Management*, 4 (1), October

Harrison, S. (1995) *Public Relations – An Introduction*, International Thomson Business Press

Harrison, S. (1997) 'Corporate social responsibility: linking behaviour with reputation', in P.J. Kitchen (ed.) *Public Relations: Principles and Practice*, International Thomson Business Press

Hart, N. (ed.) (1995) *Strategic Public Relations*, Macmillan Business Press

Harvey, B. (1995) 'Public relations in local government', in S Black (ed.) *The Practice of Public Relations*, 4th edition, Butterworth Heinemann, pp. 73–86

Hatch, M.J. and Schultz, M. (1997) 'Relations between organizational culture, identity and image', *European Journal of Marketing*, 31 (5/6), pp. 356–65

Haywood, R. (1990) *All About Public Relations*, 2nd edition, McGraw Hill

Haywood, R. (1995) 'Media relations', in N. Hart (ed.) *Strategic Public Relations*, Macmillan Business Press, pp. 175–94

Heath, R.L. (1992) 'The wrangle in the marketplace: a rhetorical perspective of public relations', in E. Toth and R. Heath (eds) *Rhetorical and Critical Approaches to Public Relations*, Lawrence Erlbaum

Hehir, P. (1997) 'Measure or be damned', *IPR Journal*, October, pp. 20–1

Helmore, E. (2000) 'A city too rude for the web', *Guardian*, 20 March

Hendrix, J.A. (1995) *Public Relations Cases*, 3rd edition, Wadsworth

Higham, N. (1999) 'Digital radio faces long haul to become tomorrow's wireless', *Marketing Week*, 28 October, p. 17

Hill, A. (2000) 'PR takes on challenge of council rebranding', *PR Week*, 3 March, p. 8

Hillier, C. (2000) 'Growing concerns', *Hotline*, Spring, pp. 38–41

Holtz, S. (1998) *Public Relations on the Net*, Amacom

Hore, A. (1999) 'Why small companies don't make the most of their AGMs', *Investors Chronicle*, 19 February

Horsman, M. (1999) 'Tomorrow's world', *Guardian*, 29 November, Media, pp. 2–3

Houlder, V. (1994) 'Getting the measure of PR', *Financial Times*, 8 September, p. 20

Hutton, W. (1996) *The State We're In*, Vintage

IBDO (1994) *The Public Relations Sector*, DTI, October

ICO (1997) *How to get Real Value from Public Relations*, ICO

Ind, N. (1997) *The Corporate Brand*, Macmillan

IPR (1999) *Developing Excellence*, IPR

IPRA (1990) *Public Relations Education – Recommendations and Standards*, IPRA Gold Paper No. 7, September

IPRA (1994) *Public Relations Evaluation: Professional Accountability*, IPRA Gold Paper No. 11, November

IPRA (1997) *The Influence of Globalisation: An Analysis of the Survey Results*, IPRA Gold Paper No. 12, pp. 49–72

Jackson, P. (1997) 'Cause for concern', *IPR Journal*, February, pp. 22–3

James, H.L. (1975) *The Role of the Communication Officer*, COI

Janal, D. (1995) 'Internet ushers in a golden age for public relations' on <www.janal.com>

Janal, D. (1997a) 'Why web sites fail' on <www.janal.com>

Janal, D. (1997b) 'Corporate policies and practices on the internet' on <www.janal.com>

Janal, D. (1998) *Online Marketing Handbook*, John Wiley and Sons

Jefkins, F. (1994) *Public Relations Techniques*, 2nd edition, Butterworth Heinemann

Johnson, G. and Scholes, K. (1999) *Exploring Corporate Strategy*, Prentice-Hall

Jones, N. (1995) *Soundbites and Spin Doctors*, Cassell

Jones, N. (1999) *Sultans of Spin: The Media and the New Labour Government*, Victor Gollancz

Kadebegil, S. (1999) 'Reputation comes with DNA', unpublished paper, October

Kant, I. (1964) *Groundwork of the Metaphysics of Morals*, trans. H.J. Paton, Harper and Row

Keller, K.L. and Aacker, D. (1998) 'Corporate level marketing: the impact of credibility on a company's brand extension', *Corporate Reputation Review*, 1 (4), Summer, pp. 356–80

Kidner, S. (2000) 'Will paper be forced to fold?', *Guardian*, 20 April, Online, pp. 6–7

*Kirsner, S. (1998) 'Must haves' on CIO Web Business Magazine <www.cio.com> August

Kitchen, P. (ed.) (1997) *Public Relations, Principles and Practice*, International Thomson Business Press

Klein, N. (2000) 'Tyranny of the brands', *New Statesman*, 24 January, pp. 25–8

Knight, G. and Curtis, B. (1987) 'The publicity of state subjects', in D. Paletz (ed.) *Political Communication Research*, Ablex

Krippendorf, K. (1980) *Content Analysis*, Sage

Leitch, S. and Motion, J. (1999) 'Multiplicity in corporate identity strategy', *Corporate Communications: An International Journal*, 4 (4), pp. 193–9

L'Etang, J. (1996a) 'Corporate responsibility and public relations ethics', in J. L'Etang and M. Pieczka (eds) *Critical Perspectives in Public Relations*, International Thomson Business Press

L'Etang, J. (1996b) 'Public relations as diplomacy', in J. L'Etang and M. Pieczka (eds) *Critical Perspectives in Public Relations*, International Thomson Business Press

L'Etang, J. (1996c) 'Public relations and rhetoric', in J. L'Etang and M. Pieczka (eds) *Critical Perspectives in Public Relations*, International Thomson Business Press

L'Etang, J. (1998) 'Public relations education in Britain, 1948–73', presented to Public Relations Educators' Forum

Lewin, K. (1935) *A Dynamic Theory of Personality*, McGraw Book Co.

Leyland, A. (1999) 'PR takes center stage with CEOs', *PR Week US*, 15 November

Lloyd, H.M. (1973) *First Report on Standards and Ethics of Public Relations Practice*, IPRA Gold Paper No. 1

McNair, B. (1994) *Political Communication: An Introduction*, Routledge

McQuail, D. and Windahl, S. (1993) *Communication Models for the Study of Mass Communication*, Longman

*McQuail, D., Blumler, J.G. and Brown, J. (1972) 'The television audience: a revised perspective' in D. McQuail (ed.) *Sociology of Mass Communication*, Penguin

*Markwick, N. and Fill, C. (1997) 'Towards a framework for managing corporate identity', *European Journal of Marketing*, 31 (5), pp. 396–409

Martin, P. (1999) 'Into the fold', *Press Gazette*, p. 17

Medhurst, V. (1999) 'Ready made research at your fingertips', *PR Week*, 23 April, pp. 13–14

Melvin, N. (1999) 'Caught in the net', *Preview*, Smythe Dorward Lambert No. 3, Spring

Miller, C. (1998) Hawksmere Lobbying Workshop, London, 11 June

Miller, D. (1998) 'Public relations and journalism', in A. Briggs and P. Cobley (eds) *The Media: An Introduction*, Longman

Miller, G. (1989) 'Persuasion and public relations: two "ps" in a pod', in C. Botan and V. Hazleton (eds) *Public Relations Theory*, Lawrence Erlbaum

Moingeon, B. and Ramanantsoa, B.R. (1997) 'Understanding corporate identity: the French school of thought', *European Journal of Marketing*, 31 (5), pp. 383–95

Moloney, K. (1996) *Lobbyists For Hire*, Dartmouth

Moloney, K. (1997) 'Government and lobbying activities', in P. Kitchen (ed.) *Public Relations, Principles and Practice*, International Thomson Business Press, pp. 168–87

MORI/MCA (1999) Brand Ambassador Benchmark study

Morkes, J. and Nielson, J. (1997) 'Concise, SCANNABLE, and objective: how to write for the web' on <www.useit.com/papers/webwriting/writing.html>

Murphy, C. (1999) 'Brand values can build on charity ties', *Marketing Week*, 25 March, pp. 41–2

Murphy, F. (1999) 'Service with a smile', *Guardian*, 28 October, pp. 14–15

Murphy, M. (1999) CEO Shandwick Europe, speech at the IPR International Symposium 10 May, London

Negrine, R. (1994) *Politics and the Mass Media in Britain*, 2nd edition, Routledge

Negrine, R. (1996) *The Communication of Politics*, Sage

Newman, W. (1995) 'Community relations', in N.A. Hart (ed.) *Strategic Public Relations*, Macmillan

Newsom, D., Scott, A. and Turk, J.V. (1993) *This is PR*, 5th edition, Wadsworth

Nicholas, K. (1999a) 'Setting business guidelines for PR', *PR Week*, 18 June, pp. 10–11

Nicholas, K. (1999b) 'Cultural shifts', *PR Week*, 26 July

Noble, P. (1999) 'Towards an inclusive evaluation methodology', *Corporate Communication*, 15 (1), pp. 14–23

NUA internet surveys (1999) at< www.nua.ie>

OFTEL (1995) *Beyond the Telephone, the Television and the PC*

Olins, W. (1978) *The Corporate Personality*, The Design Council

Olins, W. (1999) *Corporate Identity*, Thames and Hudson

O'Malley, H. (1999) 'Charity begins at work', *Human Resources*, April, pp. 46–9

Pavlik, J.V. (1994) 'Travels on the information highway: new media technology and public relations', paper given to the Public Relations Research Symposium, Ljubljana, Slovenia, 10 July

Pawinska, M. (1999) 'Employers practice what they preach', *PR Week*, 9 April, p. 14

Pearson, R. (1989) 'Business ethics as communication ethics: public relations practice and the idea of dialogue', in C.H. Botan and V. Hazleton (eds) *Public Relations Theory*, Lawrence Erlbaum

Pearson, R. (1992) 'Perspectives on public relations history', in E. Toth and R. Heath (eds) *Rhetorical and Critical Approaches to Public Relations*, Lawrence Erlbaum

Phillips, D. (1995) 'New PR', paper given to the IPR Millennium Force Symposium, Stratford on Avon, 19 November

Phillips, D. (1998) 'Managing your reputation in cyberspace', paper presented at Hawksmere New Media Conference, September

Phillips, D. (1999) *Managing Your Reputation in Cyberspace*, Thorogood

Portway, S. (1995) 'Corporate social responsibility: the case for active stakeholder management', in N.A. Hart (ed.) *Strategic Public Relations*, Macmillan

Puchan, H., Pieczka, M. and L'Etang, J. (1997) 'The internal communication', in P. Kitchen (ed.) *Public Relations, Principles and Practice*, International Thomson Business Press

Puchan, H., Pieczka, M. and L'Etang, J. (1999) 'Rethinking PR Evaluation', *Journal of Communication Management*, 4 (2), November, pp. 164–75

Purdie, M. (1997) 'A measured approach', *IPR Journal*, October, pp. 8–9

Quirke, W. (1995) 'Internal communication', in N. Hart (ed.) *Strategic Public Relations*, Macmillan Business Press, pp. 71–94

Ralphs, S. (1999) 'IT firms send wrong message' from Computing Canada on <www/cips.ca/communications/mediawatch/CompCan/19970707b.htm>

Rheingold, H. (1994) *The Virtual Community: Finding Connection in a Computerized World*. Secker & Warburg

Regester, M. and Larkin, J. (1997) 'Issue and crisis management: fail-safe procedures', in P. Kitchen (ed.) *Public Relations, Principles and Practice*, International Thomson Business Press

Roche, K. (1998) 'Lobbying', unpublished dissertation, Leeds Metropolitan University

Ross, S. and Middleberg, S. (1998) 'Media in Cyberspace Study – 1998 Fifth Annual National Survey' on <www.middleberg.com/toolsforsuccess/cyberstudy98.pdf>

RSA Inquiry (1995) *Tomorrow's Company*

Russell, B. (1999) 'The online message', *Journalist*, May, p. 19

Schlesinger, P. (1990) 'Rethinking the sociology of journalism: source strategies and the limits of media-centrism', in M. Ferguson (ed.) *Public Communication: The New Imperatives – Future Directions for Media Research*, Sage

Schlesinger, P. (1998) 'Scottish devolution and the media', in J. Seaton (ed.) *Politics and the Media: Harlots and Prerogatives at the Turn of the Millennium*, Blackwell

Schmidt, K. (1997) 'Corporate identity: an evolving discipline', *Corporate Communications: An International Journal*, 2 (1), pp. 40–5

Shelton, E. (1999) 'Tune in to the sound of radio', *PR Week*, 7 May, pp. 13–15

Shelton, E. (2000) 'Netting new skills', *PR Week*, 4 February, p. 15

Skolnik, R. (1994) 'Portraits of the "most admired" companies: how public relations helps build corporate reputations', *Public Relations Journal*, 50 (5), pp. 14–18

Smith, I. (1999) 'Television's tangled web', *Scotsman*, 6 August, p. 29

Smith, P. (1998) 'Ethics and tomorrow's company', *Journal of Communication Management*, 2 (3), March, pp. 286–93

Sterne, J. (1998) 'Virtual press box' on CIO Web Business Magazine on <www.cio.com/archive/webbusiness/090198_toc.html>

Stone, N. (1995) *The Management and Practice of Public Relations*, Macmillan Business

Teather, D. (2000) 'Summer of spin', *Guardian*, 29 May, Media, p. 10

Temple, P. (1999) 'Survey: online investing – turning on', *Investors Chronicle*, 8 October

Theaker, A. (1997) 'Has anything really changed?', *Marketing*, November, pp. 12–14

Thompson, J.L. (1995) *Strategy in Action*, Chapman and Hall

Thompson and Pringle (1999) *Brand Spirit*, John Wiley

Tilson, D.J. (1993) 'The shaping of "eco-nuclear" publicity: the use of visitors' centres in public relations', *Media, Culture and Society*, 15 pp. 419–35

van der Laan, D. (2000) 'EU standards for PR', *CERP Newsletter*, January, pp. 11–16

van Riel, C.B.M. (1995) *Principles of Corporate Communication*, Prentice-Hall

van Riel, C.B.M. and Balmer, J.M.T. (1997) 'Corporate identity: the concept, its measurement and management', *European Journal of Marketing*, 31 (5/6), pp. 340–55

Varey, R. (1997) 'Public relations: the external publics context', in P.J. Kitchen (ed.) *Public Relations, Principles and Practice*, International Thomson Business Press

Varey R.J. and White J. (2000) 'The corporate communication system of managing', *Corporate Communications: An International Journal*, 5 (1), pp. 5–11

Vernelle, B. (1994) *Understanding and Using Groups*, Whiting and Birch

Vidal, J. (2000) 'This time it's personal', *Guardian*, 12 April, G2, pp. 2–3

VLV (1999) 'Broadcasting in Britain – what is its future?', Conference, Cambridge, 15 April

Wall, I. (2000) 'Does your charity take dirty money?', *Big Issue*, 24 January, pp. 19–20

Wells, M. (2000) 'BBC must reinvent itself', *Guardian*, 13 June, p. 9

Werbel, J.D. and Wortman, M.S. (2000) 'Strategic philanthropy: responding to negative portrayals of corporate social responsibility', *Corporate Reputation Review*, 3 (2), Spring, pp. 124–36

Wheeler, D. and Sillanpaa, M. (1997) *The Stakeholder Corporation*, Pitman Publishing

White, J. (1991) *How to Understand and Manage Public Relations*, Business Books

White, J. (1999) 'Evaluation must show it can make an impact', *PR Week*

White, J. and Dozier, D.M. (1992) 'Public relations and management decision making', in J.E. Grunig (ed.), *Excellence in Public Relations and Communication Management*, Lawrence Erlbaum

White, J. and Mazur, L. (1995) *Strategic Communications Management*, Addison Wesley

Wilson, D.C. (1992) *A Strategy of Change*, Routledge

Windahl, S. and Signitzer, B. with Olsen, J.T. (1992) *Using Communication Theory*, Sage

Wilcox, D.L., Ault, P.H. and Agee, W.K. (1992) *Public Relations Strategies and Tactics*, HarperCollins

Wileman, A. (1999) 'What's a customer worth?', *Management Today*, June, p. 95

Wilkinson, A. (1999) 'Cause for concern', *Marketing Week*, 11 February, pp. 28–31

Williams, G. (1994) *Britain's Media – How They Are Related*, CPBF

Williams, K.C. (1981) *Behavioural Aspects of Marketing*, Heinemann Professional

Winner, K. (1993) *Effective PR Management*, 2nd edition, Kogan Page

Wolstenholme, S. (1997) 'Raising the standard', *IPR Journal*, October, pp. 12–14

Index